Panic Disorder: Theory, Research and Therapy

THE WILEY SERIES IN CLINICAL PSYCHOLOGY

Series Editor:

Fraser N. Watts
MRC Applied Psychology Unit
Cambridge

Severe Learning Disability
and Psychological Handicap
John Clements

Cognitive Psychology
and Emotional Disorders
J. Mark, G. Williams, Fraser N. Watts,
Colin MacLeod and Andrew Mathews

Community Care in Practice
Services for the Continuing Care Client
Edited by Anthony Lavender and Frank Holloway

Attribution Theory in
Clinical Psychology
Freidrich Försterling

Panic Disorder:
Theory, Research and Therapy
Edited by Roger Baker

Further titles in preparation

Psychology and Criminal Conduct:
Theory, Research and Practice
R. Blackburn

Measuring Human Problems
A Practical Guide
Edited by David Peck and C.M. Shapiro

Panic Disorder: Theory, Research and Therapy

Edited by

ROGER BAKER
Grampian Area Clinical Psychology Services

JOHN WILEY & SONS
Chichester · New York · Brisbane · Toronto · Singapore

Baffins Lane, Chichester,
West Sussex PO19 1UD, England

National 01243 779777
International (+44) 1243 779777

Reprinted August 1992, April 1995

Other Wiley Editorial Offices

John Wiley and Sons, Inc., 605 Third Avenue, New York, NY 10158–0012, USA

Jacaranda Wiley Ltd, 33 Park Road, Milton, Queensland 4064, Australia

John Wiley and Sons (Canada) Ltd, 22 Worcester Road, Rexdale, Ontario M9W 1L1, Canada

John Wiley & Sons (SEA) Pte Ltd, 37 Jalan Pemimpin 05-04, Block B, Union Industrial Building, Singapore 2057

British Library Cataloguing in Publication Data:

Panic disorder.
1. Man. Panic Attacks
I. Baker, Roger
616.85′223

ISBN 0 471 92319 2 (ppc)
ISBN 0 471 93317 1 (pbk)

Typeset by Woodfield Graphics, Fontwell, Sussex, England
Printed and bound in Great Britain by
Antony Rowe Ltd, Chippenham, Wiltshire

Contents

List of Contributors

George W. Ashcroft, MD — Professor of Psychiatry, Department of Mental Health, University of Aberdeen, University Medical Buildings, Foresterhill, Aberdeen AB9 2ZD, UK

Roger Baker, PhD — Clinical Research Psychologist, Grampian Area Clinical Psychology Services, Elmhill House, Royal Cornhill Hospital, Aberdeen AB9 2ZY, UK and Honorary Clinical Lecturer, University of Aberdeen

David H. Barlow, PhD — Director, Center for Stress and Anxiety Disorders, The University at Albany, State University of New York, 1535 Western Avenue, Albany, New York 12203, USA

Robert C. Durham, PhD — Principal Clinical Psychologist, Tayside Area Clinical Psychology Department, Royal Dundee Liff Hospital, Dundee DD2 5NF, UK

William W. Eaton, PhD — Department of Mental Hygiene, John Hopkins School of Hygiene and Public Health, Baltimore, MD 21205, USA

Anke Ehlers, PhD — Department of Psychology, Philipps-University, Gutenbergstr. 18, D-3550 Marburg, West Germany

Robert R. Freedman, PhD — Director, Behavioural Medicine Laboratory, Lafayette Clinic, Detroit, Michigan 48207, USA and Associate Professor,

Departments of Psychology and Psychiatry, Wayne State University

RICHARD S. HALLAM, PhD — Senior Lecturer, Department of Psychology, University College, Gower Street, London WC1E 6BT, UK

MALCOLM MCFADYEN, MSc — Head of Community Services, Clinical Psychology Department, Grampian Area Clinical Psychology Services, 36 Cornhill Road, Aberdeen AB9 2ZY, UK

JÜRGEN MARGRAF, PhD — Department of Psychology, Philipps-University, Gutenbergstr. 18, D-3550 Marburg, West Germany

ISAAC MARKS, MD — Professor of Experimental Psychopathology, Institute of Psychiatry, De Crespigny Park, Denmark Hill, London SE5 8AF, UK

RONALD M. RAPEE, PhD — Department of Psychology, University of Queensland, St. Lucia, Queensland 4067, Australia. Formerly Assistant Director, Center for Stress and Anxiety Disorders, The University at Albany, New York.

MICHAEL R. VON KORFF, ScD — Associate Investigator, Center for Health Studies, Group Health Cooperative of Puget Sound, Seattle, Washington 98112, USA

LESLIE G. WALKER, PhD — Lecturer in Mental Health, Department of Mental Health, University of Aberdeen, University Medical Buildings, Foresterhill, Aberdeen AB9 2ZD, UK

HOWARD L. WARING, MD — Consultant Psychiatrist, Park Side Hospital, Macclesfield, Cheshire, SK10 3JF, UK

CLAIRE WEEKES, DSc — Consultant Physician (retired), Rachel Forster Hospital, Sydney, Australia

MANUEL D. ZANE, MD — Director, Phobia Clinic, White Plains Hospital Medical Center, Davis Avenue at East Post Road, White Plains, New York 10601, USA

Series Editor's Preface

The Wiley Series in Clinical Psychology will present authoritative contributions on topics in clinical psychology where exciting advances are currently being made. The psychological understanding and treatment of panic is one of the topics on which major advances have been made during the 1980s, and this book represents an important addition to the literature on the subject.

The first two sections deal systematically with the description, conceptualisation and classification of panic. A welcome feature of these sections is the emphasis given to the subjective experience of panic and to the heterogeneity of panic episodes. Next, there is a comprehensive review of the various aspects of the etiology of panic, including both biological and psychological ones. There is a growing consensus that the explanation of panic requires a broadly-based, integrative theory; it is therefore welcome that in this section the same authors consider the full range of etiological factors.

Finally, there is a thorough presentation of the available psychological treatments for panic. The currently 'dominant' cognitive-behavioural approach is presented from the points of view of both scientific analysis and clinical practice. However, other innovative psychological approaches, currently less well developed, are also described. Throughout, the spirit of this book is to avoid premature closure in our developing understanding of panic. A clear presentation of recent advances is balanced by a recognition of the fundamental issues that remain to be explored.

Clinical psychology is a field with close links with many other professions and scientific disciplines. I hope, therefore, that the Series in Clinical Psychology will have a broad appeal to all those concerned with the application of psychological knowledge to clinical problems. This particular book will be a valuable resource for psychiatrists, psychologists, and all other professions engaged in providing psychological treatment for patients presenting with anxiety and panic disorders. It will also be of interest to psychologists with a basic interest in emotion who recognize the contribution that the study of abnormal emotion can make to the understanding of basic processes.

FRASER WATTS
Series Editor

Preface

The study of panic disorder is fascinating and important for a number of reasons. It challenges our previous understanding of the anxiety disorders. For many years clinicians spoke of 'free floating anxiety' and in a metaphorical sense the concept of anxiety had become rather 'free floating'—vague, lacking any agreed theory or adequate bedrock from which to construct meaningful research and therapy. The description and delineation of panic and other varieties of anxiety disorder in the *Diagnostic and Statistical Manual* of the American Psychiatric Association in 1980 gave the sort of diagnostic precision necessary to support future growth of research and therapy. And that is exactly what happened. In the short space of nine years new research had emerged, significantly affecting thinking about anxiety amongst the clinical professions.

Panic disorder is interesting too in the sense that no accepted and established position has emerged about its basic nature and causality. It lies somewhere at the crossroads between biology and emotional life, between the psychiatrist and the psychologist. On the one hand it is regarded as a biological disorder responsive to medication; on the other, a psychological phenomenon amenable to psychological intervention. The overlap is considerable, the interrelationships unclear and the boundaries undefined.

Panic, too, sits rather uneasily within the established traditions of behavioural psychology. Panic attacks are by definition subjectively perceived events but with enormous repercussions on a person's behaviour and lifestyle. In this respect they are similar to auditory hallucinations; not directly observable, but capable of generating extreme patterns of reaction in the sufferer. It is perhaps significant that as phobic behaviour somehow became identified as the standard or prototype of the emerging behaviour therapy movement of the 60s, the more subjective 'panic attacks' are becoming one of the acceptable foci for the emerging cognitive therapy movement of the

80s. The study of panic will no doubt force new developments in cognitive therapy and cognitive psychology and will possibly increase the sophistication with which psychology in general approaches subjective phenomena.

Most importantly, the study of panic has had implications for the not insignificant numbers of those who suffer and struggle with panic attacks. The increase in knowledge about panic now means that therapists can demonstrate a depth of understanding about the phenomena described by patients. This can be crucial. Patients may arrive for therapy afraid and ashamed of these 'strange' panic experiences which they assume are unique to them. Does it mean they are going mad, or that there is some serious flaw in their personality? A therapist who communicates his or her knowledge to them can often bring immediate hope and relief; indeed several authors regard the provision of correct information about panic as a type of therapy in its own right. By giving phenomenology and case description a significant role in this book it is hoped that it will assist therapists in developing the sort of in-depth knowledge appropriate to the therapy of panic disorder.

Though *Panic Disorder: Theory Research and Therapy* is comprised of chapters by different leading authorities on panic, it has been organized more like an integrated textbook than a loose collection of readings. An attempt has been made to comprehensively cover the topic of panic disorder. Authors have aimed both for the depth of content expected of a serious text on the topic but with something of the expressiveness of popular texts; interwoven with this is an awareness of the complex conceptual and scientific issues surrounding the whole notion of 'panic disorder'. The attention devoted to describing different treatment programmes in practical detail in Section 4 of this book should make it a valuable sourcebook for clinicians; the emphasis on descriptions of panic should also broadly appeal to students interested in the topic of anxiety.

An attempt has also been made to balance authors between clinicians and researchers, and between psychologists and psychiatrists, while as far as possible having authors from different countries participate so that varying philosophical currents might run through the book. My hope is that this volume will contribute to a greater understanding of panic disorder amongst the clinical and research community and to further development in both theory and practice.

ROGER BAKER

March 1989

Aberdeen, Scotland.

Acknowledgements

I would like to thank and acknowledge the support of Malcolm McFadyen, Head of the Clinical Psychology Department, Community Services Unit, Grampian Health Board, for his helpful support in seeing this book towards publication; also Hazel Naughton whose secretarial help and goodwill greatly assisted me in preparing this book; Leslie Walker and Siegfried Breuning for reading and advising on chapters; Ann Baker for help in typing; and Stephen Bell, Head of the Clinical Psychology Department, Mental Health Services Unit, Grampian Health Board, for the facilities made available to me.

Chapter 1

Introduction: Where Does 'Panic Disorder' Come From?

ROGER BAKER

THE WORD 'PANIC'

> An American battalion holds a reserve position in a shell-torn wood. Enemy artillery has been intermittently strafing the position since dusk. The Americans in their foxholes are getting what sleep they can. At 11.00 p.m. the battalion commander, accompanied by his adjutant, starts an inspection of his lines. A runner dashes up and hands him a message. The major reads it. He calls to his adjutant who is a short distance away: 'Come on! Let's beat it!' The two start to the rear at a dead run. Before they have covered 200 yards the entire battalion is in wild flight behind them. It races more than 10 kilometres before it can be stopped. The message to the major had directed him to report to the regimental command post (at the rear of the battalion) as fast as he could get there. He was merely complying with his orders. (Lanham, 1943)

The phenomenon of an army fleeing in a wild, unco-ordinated panic goes back to the dawn of history. Strangely this panic phenomenon is very closely linked to noise and is described quite clearly before a special word for panic existed; the Israelite army under Gideon, *c*. 1150 BC

> reached the edge of the camp at the beginning of the middle watch (midnight), just after they had changed the guard. They blew their trumpets and broke the jars that were in their hands. . .. Grasping the torches in their left hands and holding in their right hand the trumpets they were to blow, they shouted, 'A sword for the Lord and for Gideon!' While each man held his position around the camp, all the Midianites ran, crying out as they fled. (International Bible Society, 1973)

Many armies have been aware of the disorientating effects of sudden noise on their opponents, particularly at night, and exploit this to the full. Although this phenomenon is clearly reported from ancient times in accounts such as this, Ancient Hebrew or Latin, for example, do not have a separate word for panic as apart from fear or terror. The word derives

Panic Disorder: Theory, Research and Therapy. Edited by Roger Baker

from the Greek *to panikon deima*, that is, fear caused by the action of the god Pan. Pan, the Greek god of flocks, hills, pastures and wild life, was a lover of noise and riot, and was said to have a raucous voice. At the battle of Marathon (490 BC) the Greeks believed it was his raucous voice which put the Persians to flight, and thereafter they worshipped him at the Acropolis.

Not only was panic a battle phenomenon, but Pan was also said to be able to strike groundless fear into unwary travellers who passed through woodlands or valleys by the use of his loud voice. Sounds heard by night in mountains and valleys which gave rise to sudden fear were also attributed to him. One of the earliest uses of the word is from the first-century Greek biographer Plutarch who, referring to the eve of the battle between the armies of Caesar and Pompey says, 'and during the morning watch it was noticed that there was actually a panic confusion among the enemy' (Perrin, 1919).

Thus from early times panic referred both to a group occurrence of a disoriented army, and to the state of fear induced in an individual. Nearly all Western European languages have a similar word deriving from the Greek, close to fear, alarm, and terror, but distinct from it—*panique* (French), *Panik* (German), *panico* (Italian), *pánico* (Spanish), *panik* (Swedish), *panikk* (Norwegian), *paniek* (Dutch).

What are the distinctive elements of panic? First, it implies sudden or groundless onset, in the same sense as a sudden noise might startle us. Secondly, it implies a state of being; of terror or fear. It differs, however, from terror, fear or alarm by implying action. We can say 'He panicked' whereas we have to use the passive—'He was afraid', 'He was terrified'—for these other feeling states. The action is either overt—the obvious one being to flee or escape from danger, as the more recent words 'panic bars' in theatres or 'panic buttons' in aircraft suggest, or it is covert—being mentally disorganised or confused and unable to consider effective actions.

Over the years many new shades of meaning for panic have emerged in the English language, a major one arising from the financial disaster in Britain known as the 'South Sea Bubble' (1720). The British public rushed to buy shares in the South Sea Company and many bogus companies, which soon catastrophically collapsed. The word 'panic' began to be used to describe the reactions of shareholders; 'panic buying' and 'panic selling' are still with us today. The German language has its own word—*Börsenpanik* (panic on the Stock Exchange) for this. Over the following centuries the word was more broadly applied so that, for instance, a text on *Patterns of Panic* (Meerloo, 1950) included instances of panic as diverse as animal stampedes, military retreats, suicidal epidemics, plundering troops, mass hysteria, psychotic behaviour, and lynching mobs. In modern usage the word has been debased to include less catastrophic reactions. We panic when we remember we were supposed to deliver a lecture 10 minutes ago, when we look incredulously at the maths exam paper, or when the letter from our bank manager arrives inviting us to come to discuss our overdraft.

CAN PANIC BE A DISORDER?

The concept of a 'panic attack' is consistent with the earliest uses of the word panic, such as '*Terreur panique*' (sixteenth-century French), '*une panique*, 'Sudden Foolish Frights, without any certeine cause, which they call Panique Terrores' (England, 1603), or in German *eine panische Angst* (a panic type fear). However the concept of 'panic disorder'—the subject of this book—as outlined in the American Psychiatric Association's *Diagnostic and Statistical Manual* (DSM III) is a new and unusual meaning for the word. For a person to have an illness or disorder which periodically generates panic states represents the insertion of a medical metaphor into what was previously only described in an emotional or social context. Certainly 'panic proneness' was said to exist in people, as in sheep; but the idea of a 'panic disorder' might not find instant recognition in the layman used to panicking when he or she gets on the wrong aircraft, or locks the keys inside the car.

THE PSYCHIATRIC ORIGINS OF PANIC DISORDER

The heritage of Freud

How did the concept of a 'panic disorder' arise? What are the psychiatric roots for this apparently unusual application of the word? S. Freud, in his seminal paper, 'On the Grounds for Detaching a particular syndrome from Neurasthenia under the description "Anxiety Neurosis"' (1894) postulated a diagnostic category (anxiety neurosis) which 'has been a stable component in psychiatric classifications throughout the first eighty years of this century' (Tyrer, 1984). 'Anxiety Neurosis' referred to a state of accumulated excitation ('anxiousness') with symptoms of irritability, auditory hypersensitivity and anxious expectation. Anxious expectation was regarded as 'the nuclear symptom of the neurosis', to which the well-worn phrase 'free-floating anxiety' is applied. This anxiousness 'constantly lurking in the background . . . can suddenly break through into consciousness . . . and thus provoke an anxiety attack.' Anxiety attacks, consisting of disturbances in heart action, of respiration, attacks of sweating, locomotor vertigo, etc., are clearly described by Freud and are not dissimilar to the DSM-III description of panic attacks. Freud postulated that anxiety neurosis was caused by a frustration of sexual arousal; he regarded it as being biochemically based, but not a 'disorder' as such: it could affect normal people. The woman develops anxiety neurosis if her husband breaks off intercourse, without troubling himself about the course of excitation in her. If, on the other hand, the husband waits for his wife's satisfaction, the coitus amounts to a normal one for *her*; but *he* will fall ill of 'anxiety neurosis.' In this paper phobias were said to develop from anxiousness, though as Strachey (1962) points out, Freud expressed varying opinions about this and later developed a separate theoretical model for phobias.

The concept of anxiety neurosis became established in psychiatry, although Freud and other theorists pursued an understanding of the unconscious mechanisms underlying psychoneurosis rather than giving much further attention to the 'peripheral' manifestation of the anxiety attack itself (Freud, 1926). The term anxiety attack (from the German *Angstanfall*) was used consistently in the literature up to 1960 to refer to what is now more generally called a panic attack. Even those few writers who did emphasise panic (e.g. Brosin, 1943; Diethelm, 1932, 1934, 1936; Fenichel, 1945; Kempf, 1920) retained Freud's notion of a volcanic sea of anxiousness occasionally erupting in the form of anxiety attacks: for instance Diethelm defined panic in 1934 as 'a maximal fear state which results from prolonged tension and insecurity'. This was to be entirely upturned by the writings of D. Klein.

Anxiety neurosis dissected

D. Klein's 1964 article 'Delineation of two drug responsive anxiety syndromes' not only resembles Freud's 1894 article as a title but was likewise an important turning point in our understanding of anxiety. Starting in 1962 in a study with Fink and continuing throughout the next three decades (Klein, 1969; Klein *et al.*, 1978; Klein, 1981), Klein argued that the tricyclic antidepressant drug imipramine suppressed the anxiety attacks of agoraphobic patients but did not act directly on anticipatory anxiety or avoidance behaviour. On the other hand, benzodiazepines, other minor tranquillisers and supportive therapy were effective in reducing anticipatory anxiety but not panic attacks.

Klein reversed the logic of Freud by proposing that 'panic' attacks appear spontaneously, out of the blue, 'often erupting in a completely calm person in an unthreatening setting'. It is only after a series of such extremely unpleasant experiences that the person develops a 'secondary anticipatory anxiety between panic attacks, often referred to as free floating anxiety'. Thus anticipatory anxiety followed, not preceded, panic attacks.

Klein also proposed a much closer and clearer link than Freud had between panic attacks and phobias. Klein considered phobic avoidance to be a 'tertiary development'. As the person anxiously anticipates further panic attacks he or she avoids situations where the attacks are likely to occur and so the well-known avoidances of agoraphobia are generated. Klein also hypothesised that panic attacks are qualitatively distinct from anticipatory anxiety and have a unique and separate psychobiology. This biological mechanism was thought to be derived from the 'innate biological control mechanism' involved in child–mother contact and separation. He noted that 50 per cent of the agoraphobic patients in his original study showed distinct evidence of separation anxiety in childhood, and that the initial panic attacks had often been preceded by significant object loss.

In the 1962 paper Klein and Fink described anxiety attacks as '"panic" attacks', pointing out that the common term 'anxiety' as used in 'anxiety attack' and 'expectant anxiety' obscures an important underlying difference; the use of the term 'panic attack' reinforces the difference. In all his writings over the next three decades Klein consistently uses the phrase 'panic attacks'.

At the same time as Klein's original study, C. Weekes published her first book *Self Help for Your Nerves* (see Chapter 15), in which she described 'panic spasms' and 'intense waves of panic', providing important insights from the sufferer's viewpoint into why they come to dread panic. In all her subsequent writings (1972, 1973, 1977, 1978, 1984) she emphasised the important role of panic in agoraphobia and anxiety, referring to 'panic', 'the panic', 'a panic', 'flash of panic' or even 'super-panic' rather than 'panic attack'. She did not however hypothesise a separate mechanism for panic attacks and other sorts of anxiety as Klein had done.

Also, in 1959, Roth suggested 'a new form of neurotic illness' which he called the 'phobic anxiety-depersonalisation syndrome'. He related syncopal attacks to phobic symptoms, though he did not use the word 'panic', and particularly implicated depersonalisation experiences in the syndrome. Like Klein he considered the illness to be due to a biological disturbance: Roth considered the underlying dysfunction to be in the temporal lobes or limbic system.

The emphasis on panic attacks was made more prominent by the work of Pitts and McClure (1967). They demonstrated that 'anxiety attacks' could be generated by intravenous administration of sodium lactate, further strengthening the idea of a biological substrate for panic attacks. They operationally defined an anxiety attack by the presence of extreme anxiety, cognitive symptoms such as a fear of having a heart attack, and the occurrence of five somatic symptoms from two different symptom groupings. Feighner *et al.* (1972) refined the set of operational criteria, laying the foundation for future research to be constructed within a consistent framework.

Thus in the early 1960s the word 'panic attack' was used to describe phenomena previously referred to as an 'anxiety attack'. Its separate nomenclature, separation from general anxiety, anticipatory anxiety and phobic avoidance, successful treatment by antidepressant medication, and postulated unique biological substrate, all set the scene for the emergence of the concept of 'panic disorder'.

Actually the use of the term 'panic attack' is a very appropriate application of the word 'panic'. Many of the original meanings of the word 'panic' seem relevant to the phenomenon—its sudden and groundless appearance, 'out of the clear blue sky', its mentally disorganising nature and the desire to escape or flee during an attack. It would also appear that the selfsame phenomenon is referred to in the earliest uses of the word panic in English or French in the sixteenth and seventeenth century, the so-called '*panique terrores*' or '*terreur panique*'.

THE BIRTH OF 'PANIC DISORDER'

In 1975 Spitzer and colleagues proposed 'panic disorder' and 'generalized anxiety disorder' as distinct diagnoses. However it was the publication by the American Psychiatric Association of the *Diagnostic and Statistical Manual III* (DSM-III) in 1980 which enshrined the diagnosis of 'panic disorder' as a distinct condition among the anxiety disorders. In panic disorder the essential features were recurrent panic attacks which occurred unpredictably;

> the panic attacks are manifested by the sudden onset of intense apprehension, fear, or terror, often associated with feelings of impending doom. The most common symptoms experienced during an attack are dyspnea; palpitations; chest pain or discomfort; choking or smothering sensations; dizziness, vertigo or unsteady feelings; feelings of unreality (depersonalization or derealization); parasthesias; hot and cold flushes; sweating; faintness; trembling or shaking; and fear of dying, going crazy, or doing something uncontrolled during the attack. Attacks usually last minutes; more rarely, hours.

If, as a result of panic attacks, the person avoided many situations, the alternative diagnosis of 'agoraphobia with panic attacks' was to be employed. However, it was recognised that panic attacks very commonly produce some avoidance, and so a modicum of avoidance was still permitted for a person to qualify for a diagnosis of panic disorder. Identifying the point at which this avoidance would become large enough for a person to move out of the panic disorder category into the category of agoraphobia with panic attacks was predictably going to present the clinician with a diagnostic dilemma. DSM-III also pointed out that if the same clinical phenomena occurred during marked physical exertion or in a life-threatening situation the term 'panic attack' should not be used.

Table 1.1 Diagnostic Criteria for panic disorder (DSM-III). Reprinted with permission from the *Diagnostic and Statistical Manual of Mental Disorders*, third edition. Copyright 1980 *American Psychiatric Association*.

A. At least three panic attacks within a three-week period in circumstances other than during marked physical exertion or in a life-threatening situation. The attacks are not precipitated only by exposure to a circumscribed phobic stimulus.

B. Panic attacks are manifested by discrete periods of apprehension or fear, and at least four of the following symptoms appear during each attack:

(1) dyspnea
(2) palpitations
(3) chest pain or discomfort
(4) choking or smothering sensations
(5) dizziness, vertigo, or unsteady feelings
(6) feelings of unreality
(7) paraesthesias (tingling in hands or feet)
(8) hot and cold flushes
(9) sweating
(10) faintness
(11) trembling or shaking
(12) fear of dying, going crazy, or doing something uncontrolled during an attack

C. Not due to a physical disorder or another mental disorder, such as major depression, somatisation disorder, or schizophrenia.

D. The disorder is not associated with agoraphobia.

Table 1.1 shows the specific DSM-III diagnostic criteria given for panic disorder. Apart from agoraphobia with panic attacks the other categories under the general heading 'anxiety disorder' were agoraphobia without panic attacks, social phobia, simple phobia (i.e. of dogs, insects, heights), generalised anxiety disorder ('generalised persistent anxiety without panic attacks'), obsessive compulsive disorder, and post-traumatic stress disorder, whether acute or chronic/delayed.

The concept of 'panic disorder' was, however, not without its critics. Apart from the obvious connection with agoraphobia (Klein, 1981; Turner *et al.*, 1986), panic attacks occur in a number of different conditions, such as obsessive-compulsive disorder, simple phobia, social phobia, hypochondriasis, alcoholism, schizophrenia (Arieti, 1959; Barlow *et al.*, 1985; Goodwin and Guze, 1979; Hallam, 1985) but particularly in depression (Uhde *et al.*, 1985; Leckman *et al.*, 1983a). Some argued that panic disorder and depression shared a common biological pathway (Leckman *et al.*, 1983b), others that antidepressant medication was only effective in phobic/panic patients with depressed mood (Marks, 1983), or that panic was a cross-syndromal condition (Grunhaus and Birmaher, 1985). Various clinicians, including Gelder (1986), thought that the classification of a new disorder was premature, that panic attacks were 'merely an index of the severity of an anxiety disorder', and that the diagnosis of 'anxiety neurosis' was still preferable (Tyrer, 1984). This was essentially the position encapsulated in the *Ninth Revision of the International Classification of Diseases* (World Health Organisation, 1978).

In 1987 DSM was revised (DSM-IIIR). Changes were made to the agoraphobia and panic disorder categories, partly to accommodate new research findings and partly to iron out problems that clinicians had found using DSM-III. Table 1.2 shows the new criteria for a diagnosis of panic disorder. In DSM-IIIR the concepts of panic disorder and agoraphobia are fused together more intimately than in DSM-III. Instead of 'agoraphobia with panic attacks', 'agoraphobia without panic attacks', and 'panic disorder', we now have 'panic disorder with agoraphobia', 'panic disorder without agoraphobia', and 'agoraphobia without a history of panic disorder'. By using the term panic disorder instead of panic attack and placing it before agoraphobia this stresses the primacy of panic disorder and also reinforces the notion of agoraphobia developing out of panic disorder. The other categories of social phobia, simple phobia, generalised anxiety disorder, etc., remained relatively similar to DSM-III.

THE OUTLINE OF THIS BOOK

'Panic disorder' is an unusual topic from a research point of view; its specification in the influential *Diagnostic and Statistical Manual* in 1980 virtually represented the introduction of a new creature to the clinical community. Soon the academic journals began to report research on this apparently 'new' disorder, and so rapid was the accumulation of knowledge that panic now occupies an important position in psychiatry and clinical psychology. Keeping pace with the rapidly expanding knowledge base is hard enough, but it is more difficult still to follow the various changes, twists and turns in the developing conceptualisation of panic. An attempt to compile a book on the topic is rather like trying to describe a moving train as it roars past.

Table 1.2 Diagnostic criteria for panic disorder (DSM-IIIR). Reprinted with permission from the *Diagnostic and Statistical Manual of Mental Disorders*, third edition, revised. Copyright 1987 *American Psychiatric Association*.

A. At some time during the disturbance, one or more panic attacks (discrete periods of intense fear or discomfort) have occurred that were (1) unexpected, i.e., did not occur immediately before or on exposure to a situation that almost always caused anxiety, and (2) not triggered by situations in which the person was the focus of others' attention.

B. Either four attacks, as defined in criterion A, have occurred within a four-week period, or one or more attacks have been followed by a period of at least a month of persistent fear of having another attack.

C. At least four of the following symptoms developed during at least one of the attacks:

(1) shortness of breath (dyspnea) or smothering sensations
(2) dizziness, unsteady feelings, or faintness
(3) palpitations or accelerated heart rate (tachycardia)
(4) trembling or shaking
(5) sweating
(6) choking
(7) nausea or abdominal distress
(8) depersonalisation or derealisation
(9) numbness or tingling sensations (paraesthesias)
(10) flushes (hot flashes) or chills
(11) chest pain or discomfort
(12) fear of dying
(13) fear of going crazy or of doing something uncontrolled

Note: Attacks involving four or more symptoms are panic attacks: attacks involving fewer than four symptoms are limited symptom attacks (see Agoraphobia without History of Panic Disorder).

D. During at least some of the attacks, at least four of the C symptoms developed suddenly and increased in intensity within ten minutes of the beginning of the first C symptom noticed in the attack.

E. It cannot be established that an organic factor initiated and maintained the disturbance, e.g., amphetamine or caffeine intoxication, hyperthyroidism.

Note: Mitral valve prolapse may be an associated condition, but does not preclude a diagnosis of panic disorder.

This book has two major, but differing, aims. The first is to provide the reader with an in-depth account of the phenomenology, etiology and treatment of panic. The second is to explore thoroughly the range of models and concepts that are currently applied to panic. The authors are acknowledged authorities in the field, innovative in their approach or have conducted in-depth work in the area. Contributors to the section on phenomenology and treatment were asked to provide practical information and to illustrate their data with case studies, verbatim reports, etc., to make the reading as vivid, practical and interesting as possible. Also, rather than allowing constructs to be implicit, authors were encouraged to make their models of panic and its treatment explicit. A range of constructs are explored in the book, with much convergence of ideas, but not without important differences too. While every attempt has been made to centre on panic disorder and panic attacks, the overlap with agoraphobia is so great that inevitably this topic is also frequently discussed.

The book is organised in four sections: Section 1 deals with the phenomenology of panic, viewing it from a number of different standpoints including 'The nature of panic attack symptoms', 'Epidemiological findings on panic', 'Ambulatory monitoring findings on panic', and 'Personal Accounts of panic'.

Section 2 presents one of the most complex areas in the field, namely how to classify and conceptualise panic. As Kuhn (1962) would have us appreciate, we necessarily view phenomena through a particular set of spectacles—our current paradigms—and it is so extremely difficult to know whether a better set of spectacles exists, or how we would know they were better anyway in advance of a paradigm shift occurring. The chapters 'Classification and research into panic', 'Agoraphobia and panic disorder', and 'A contextual approach to panic', certainly help to heighten awareness of our prevailing constructs and their inadequacies.

Establishing the etiology of a disorder is an extremely complex task—experimental error and logical fallacy are pitfalls ever awaiting those who try. In 'Etiological models of panic—medical and biological aspects' and 'psychological and cognitive aspects' in Section 3 we have the advantage of two authors with an exceptional grasp of the experimental literature on panic; they ably review the evidence for the adequacy of our prevailing medical and psychological models of panic with clear conclusions.

Section 4, devoted to treatment, is the largest section of the book. An attempt has been made to understand in detail the several different approaches to treatment, including pharmacological, cognitive/behavioural, cognitive therapy, cognitive invalidation, and Weekes's self-help approach. Two chapters from Section 2 of the book are also relevant: in addition to discussing issues of classification, two other treatment approaches—Marks's exposure therapy and Zane's contextual therapy—are presented there.

In the last chapter of the book an attempt is made to draw together the central issues and differing views about the nature of panic. It also seeks to provide a schema for characterising panic attacks and to identify potentially fruitful avenues for future research.

REFERENCES

American Psychiatric Association (1980) *Diagnostic and Statistical Manual of Mental Disorders*; Third Edition, American Psychiatric Association, Washington, DC.

American Psychiatric Association (1987) *Diagnostic and Statistical Manual of Mental Disorders*, Third Edition, Revised, American Psychiatric Association, Washington, DC.

Arieti, S. (1959) Schizophrenia: the manifest symptomatology, the psychodynamic and formal mechanism. In S. Arieti (ed.), *American Handbook of Psychiatry*, Vol. I. Basic Books, New York.

Barlow, D.H., Vermilyea, J., Blanchard, E.B., Vermilyea, B.B., Di Nardo, P.A and Cerny, J.A. (1985) The phenomenon of panic, *Journal of Abnormal Psychology*, **94**, 320–28.

Brosin, H.W. (1943) Panic states and their treatment, *American Journal of Psychiatry*, **100**, 54–61.

Diethelm, O. (1932) Panic, *Archives of Neurology and Psychiatry*, **28**, 1153–68.

Diethelm, O. (1934) The nosological position of panic reactions, *American Journal of Psychiatry*, **13**, 1295–1316.

Diethelm, O. (1936) *Treatment in Psychiatry*, Macmillan, New York.

Feighner, J.P., Robins, E., Guze, S.B., Woodruff, R.A., Jr, Winokur, G. and Munoz, R. (1972) Diagnostic criteria for use in psychiatric research, *Archives of General Psychiatry*, **26**, 57–63.

Fenichel, O. (1945) *The Psychoanalytic Theory of Neurosis*, Norton, New York.

Freud, S. (1894) On the grounds for detaching a particular syndrome from Neurasthenia under the description 'Anxiety Neurosis'. In J. Strachey (ed.), *The Standard Edition of the Complete Works of Sigmund Freud*, Vol. III, 1962, Hogarth, London.

Freud, S. (1926) Inhibitions, symptoms and anxiety. In J. Strachey (ed.), *The Standard Edition of the Complete Psychological Works of Sigmund Freud*, Vol. XX, Hogarth, London.

Gelder, M.G. (1986) Panic attacks: new approaches to an old problem, *British Journal of Psychiatry*, **149**, 346–52.

Goodwin, D.W. and Guze, S.B. (1979) *Psychiatric Diagnosis*, Oxford University Press, New York.

Grunhaus, L. and Birmaher, B. (1985) The clinical spectrum of panic attacks, *Journal of Clinical Psychopharmacology*, **5**, 93–9.

Hallam, R.S. (1985) *Anxiety: Psychological Perspectives on Panic and Agoraphobia*, Academic Press, London.

International Bible Society (1973) *The Holy Bible, New International Version*. Judges 7:19-21, Hodder & Stoughton, London.

Kempf, E.J. (1920) *Psychopathology*, Mosby, St. Louis.

Klein, D.F. (1981) Anxiety reconceptualised. In D.F. Klein and J. G. Rabkin (eds), *New Research and Changing Concepts*, Raven Press, New York.

Klein, D.F. (1964) Delineation of two drug-responsive anxiety syndromes, *Psychopharmacologia*, **5**, 397–408.

Klein, D.F. and Fink, M. (1962) Psychiatric reaction patterns to imipramine, *American Journal of Psychiatry*, **119**, 432–8.

Klein, D.F. and David, J.M. (1969) *Diagnosis and Drug Treatment of Psychiatric Disorders*, Williams & Wilkins, Baltimore.

Klein, D.F., Zitrin, C.M. and Woerner, M. (1978) Antidepressants, anxiety, panic and phobia. In M.A. Lipton, A. di Mascio and K.F. Killam (eds), *Psychopharmacology: A Generation of Progress*, Raven Press, New York.

Kuhn, T.S. (1962) *The Structure of Scientific Revolution*, Chicago University Press, Chicago.

Lanham, C.T. (1943) Panic. In J.E. Greene (ed.), *The Infantry Journal Reader*, Doubleday & Doran, Garden City.

Leckman, J.F., Merikangas, K.R., Pauls, D.L., Prusoff, B.A. and Weissman, M.M. (1983a) Anxiety disorders and depression: contradictions between family study data and DSM-III conventions, *American Journal of Psychiatry*, **140**, 880–2.

Leckman, J.F., Weissman, M.M., Merikangas, K.R., Pauls, D.L. and Prusoff, B.A. (1983b) Panic disorder and major depression. Increased risk of depression, alcoholism, panic and phobic disorders in families of depressed probands with panic disorder, *Archives of General Psychiatry*, **10**, 1055–60.

Marks, I. (1983) Are there anticompulsive or antiphobic drugs? Review of evidence, *British Journal of Psychiatry*, **143**, 338–47.

Meerloo, J. (1950) *Patterns of Panic*, International Press, New York.

Perrin, B. (1919) *Plutarch's Lives VII*, Heinemann, New York.

Pitts, N. and McClure, J.N. (1967) Lactate metabolism in anxiety neurosis, *New England Journal of Medicine*, **277**, 1329–36.

Roth, M. (1959) The phobic anxiety-depersonalization syndrome. *Proceedings of the Royal Society of Medicine: Section of Psychiatry*, 587–95.

Spitzer, R.L., Endicott, J. and Robins, E. (1975) Research Diagnostic Criteria (RDC) for a selected group of functional disorders. Manual prepared for CRB-NIMH collaborative studies on depression.

Strachey, J. (1962) Freud's view on phobias. In J. Strachey (ed.), *The Standard Edition of the Complete Works of Sigmund Freud*, Vol. III, Hogarth, London.

Turner, S.M., Williams, S.L., Beidel, D.C. and Mezzich, J.E. (1986) Panic disorder and agoraphobia with panic attacks. Covariation along with dimensions of panic and agoraphobic fear, *Journal of Abnormal Psychology*, **95**, 384–8.

Tyrer, P. (1984) Classification of anxiety, *British Journal of Psychiatry*, **144**, 78–83.

Uhde, T.W., Boulender, J-P., Roy-Byrne, P.P., Geraci, M.F., Vittone, B.J. and Post, R.M. (1985) Longitudinal course of panic disorder: clinical and biological considerations, *Progress in Neuro-Psychopharmacology and Biological Psychiatry*, **9**, 39–51.

Weekes, C. (1962) *Self Help for Your Nerves*, Angus & Robertson, London.

Weekes, C. (1972) *Peace from Nervous Suffering*, Angus & Robertson, London.

Weekes, C. (1973) A practical treatment of agoraphobia, *British Medical Journal*, **2**, 469–71.

Weekes, C. (1977) Simple, effective treatment of agoraphobia, Angus and Robertson, London.

Weekes, C. (1978) Simple, effective treatment of agoraphobia, *American Journal of Psychotherapy*, **32**, 357–69.

Weekes, C. (1984) *More Help for Your Nerves*, Angus & Robertson, London.

World Health Organisation (1978) *Mental Disorders: Glossary and guide to their classification in accordance with the Ninth Revision of the International Classification of Diseases*, World Health Organisation, Geneva.

Section 1

The Phenomenology of Panic

Introduction: The Phenomenology of Panic

> Of all the lines of evidence supporting DSM-III's delineation of panic disorder as a distinct diagnostic entity—its phenomenology and natural history, its pharmacodissection with antidepressant medication, its high familial incidence and concordance in monozygotic twins, and provocative studies with lactate and other agents—surprisingly the least well studied has been phenomenology (Aronson and Logue, 1988).

The aim of this section of the book is to provide a detailed account of the phenomenon of panic: to help establish a sense of its dimensions, boundaries and essential characteristics. To do this we will be examining panic from different perspectives. The first, and probably the most direct perspective, is the descriptive one. Howard Waring, now a consultant psychiatrist at Parkside Hospital, Macclesfield, was formerly a member of the team working with Professor Ashcroft at the Department of Mental Health, Aberdeen University, on panic disorder research. He conducted a two-year research project into the nature and response to treatment of panic attack symptoms in general practice attenders (Waring, 1988). In the first chapter he examines the nature of panic attack symptoms using descriptive, symptomatic and demographic data from his recently completed study.

From this primary description of individuals we pan out to a broader view of the phenomenon, that of the epidemiologist. Michael Von Korff and William Eaton, respectively from the Group Health Co-operative of Puget Sound, Seattle, and the Johns Hopkins School of Hygiene and Public Health, Baltimore, participated in the major National Institute of Mental Health Epidemiologic Catchment Area Programme involving the gathering of information from five different research teams in different sites in the USA. In this chapter they present data on a sample of 9000 people from the NIMH Epidemiologic Catchment Area Programme, emphasising the shortcomings of the usual cross-sectional approach to epidemiological research, and illustrating the necessity of adopting a longitudinal approach to epidemiology in panic disorder.

Ambulatory monitoring is a physiological technique which offers much promise in understanding the psychophysiology of panic attacks. Physiological data can be gathered on subjects as they live their normal daily life at home or work without interfering much with their routine. Obviously such a naturalistic method has many advantages over laboratory investigation in studying real life occurrence of panic. Robert Freedman, Director of the Behavioral Medicine Laboratory at the Lafayette Clinic, Detroit, has been an important and innovative investigator in the ambulatory monitoring of panic disorder, reporting one of the key research studies in this area in 1985 (Freedman *et al.*, 1985). In his chapter he presents illuminating new case study data and compares his results with those of other investigators and with laboratory-based researches.

A panic attack is not basically an event which has a major immediate impact on other people, like physical violence or verbal abuse, and can go relatively unnoticed unless the sufferer chooses to inform others. In order to fully appreciate panic attacks and panic disorder it is essential to examine the process by which patients inform us of their experiences. My chapter on personal accounts of panic looks at the validity and value of patients' reports of panic.

The chapters by Howard Waring, Robert Freedman and myself could be seen as corresponding to Lang's popular conception of the three response systems involved in fear—the behavioural, the physiological/somatic and the subjective. It is hoped that with the additional chapter by Michael Von Korff and William Eaton this section provides a well-rounded picture of the phenomenon of panic.

REFERENCES

Aronson, A. and Logue, C.M. (1988) Phenomenology of panic attacks: a descriptive study of panic disorder patients' self reports, *Journal of Clinical Psychiatry*, **49**, 8–13.

Freedman, R.R., Ianni, P., Ettedgui, E. and Puthezhath, N. (1985) Ambulatory monitoring of panic disorder, *Archives of General Psychiatry*, **42**, 244–8.

Waring, H. (1988) An investigation into the nature and response to treatment of panic attack symptoms in general practice attenders, MD Thesis, University of Aberdeen.

Chapter 2

The Nature of Panic Attack Symptoms

HOWARD WARING AND ELAINE ILJON FOREMAN

A STUDY OF THE PHENOMENOLOGY OF PANIC

Introduction

The experience of panic is of profound personal significance to the individual sufferer. The symptoms of a panic attack are intensely distressing, the person often convinced that they are about to die or suffer some extreme calamity. The intense fear may determine much of the associated behaviour of sufferers such as their presentation to general practitioners in a fearful state, apprehensive that they may be suffering from a serious physical disorder, or avoidance of situations they believe will precipitate further attacks. Invariably their self-esteem is damaged.

This chapter is concerned with providing a detailed picture of the experience of panic. It is based on a two-year study of panic attacks conducted at the Department of Mental Health, Aberdeen University, in collaboration with Professor George Ashcroft and colleagues. The details of this study will be reported elsewhere. The outline of this chapter is firstly to present general information about the phenomenology of panic, and secondly to present several case histories illustrating the different types of onset and forms that panic disorder may take.

The sample of panic attack sufferers was drawn from two medical practices in a small rurally-based community to the north of Aberdeen. Two groups of sufferers were identified; in the first group ('screen detected') consecutive attenders at a health centre were asked to fill in a form which described panic attacks and asked if they had ever experienced this. Positive responders were later followed-up by interview,

Panic Disorder: Theory, Research and Therapy. Edited by Roger Baker

and only those clearly describing panic attacks as predefined by a research protocol were included in the study. Many false positives were excluded. The other group ('direct referrals') consisted of referrals by general practitioners to psychiatrists or clinical psychologists of patients who required treatment for panic attacks. The majority of referrals of such patients from the community in question were channelled into the present study. In all 108 sufferers were seen, 53 'screen detected', and 55 'direct referrals'. In effect the group identified by the screening procedure were 'covert' or hidden sufferers; the second group were patients known to their practitioners who felt they required treatment. The use of two groups allowed us to understand more about how sufferers presented panic attack to the health service, as well as ensuring that the total group sampled was more representative of the population of sufferers.

One of the central aims of the study was to record the subjective sensations of patients experiencing panic attacks. Self-rated questionnaires may be considered inadequate for measuring the complexities and subtleties of subjective experience. As an alternative, a semi-structured interview was designed which had been developed during a pilot study on 15 panic attack patients. The interview, conducted by a clinical psychologist, covered a wide range of topics concerned with the experience of panic. Patients were essentially allowed to tell their own tale, but, in addition, the interviewer classified the responses given, according to the choices provided by the interview schedule. This was followed later by a second interview by a psychiatrist in which a detailed case history was elicited. Much of the data concerning previous experience was, of course, retrospective. J. Margraf and A. Ehlers in Chapter 9 (see Figure 9.5) quote their own research as showing that patients retrospectively report panic attacks as similar in form but as significantly more severe than indicated by a diary measure taken immediately after attacks. Although retrospective reporting should be treated with caution it was felt worth recording as it provides a symptomatic history of the sufferers' complaints which complemented their current presentation. In presenting the results figures for both groups of sufferers have only been quoted if there were significant differences between them. Otherwise the figures are combined in each table and any significant differences indicated.

Presentation of problem

The majority of sufferers with panic attacks in this study did seek help from their general practitioner for their symptoms—Table 2.1 shows the

Table 2.1 The primary reason for attendance to general practitioners. Percentage of patients presenting with each problem.

Reason for attendance	All panic sufferers ($n=108$) (%)
Physical complaint	25
Child ill	23
At least one of panic symptoms	20
Depression	6
Antenatal	5
Contraceptive	5
Repeat physical prescription	4
'Feeling anxious'	3
Headaches	3
Repeat physical examination	2
Perimenstrual problems	2
Cervical smear	1

different ways in which panic attack sufferers presented their problem to their doctor.

Our experience was that about 70 per cent of all sufferers did present their problem in one form or another, but their panic symptoms may not be identified as such by their doctor, and inappropriate treatment prescribed, e.g. minor tranquillisers. In 10 per cent of patients a physical diagnosis may be made because patients acutely distressed by their symptoms may present the physical autonomic symptoms occurring in attacks (e.g. sweating, palpitations) rather than the subjective affect. Also patients may be referred on for extensive physical investigation by specialists such as neurologists or cardiologists. A sizeable number of sufferers ostensibly presented their child's illness as a reason for attendance.

Basic data on the sample

Table 2.2 provides some basic information about the panic attacks presented by the two groups.

The average duration of symptoms was 6–7 years. The range of symptoms (30 and 28 years respectively) indicates just how persistent these symptoms can be. Sufferers described a marked variation in the severity and frequency of attacks over the years. The number of patients experiencing 'spontaneous' or non-situational attacks is considerable. In our study 36 per cent of the screen detected and 53 per cent of the referred patients were having *only* situationally precipitated attacks.

Table 2.2 Basic information about panic attacks.

		'Screen detected' ($n=53$)	'Direct referrals' ($n=55$)	Significant difference between the groups
Number of years since first attack*	$\bar{x}$ x	6.6	7.3	ns
	sd	7.0	6.8	
	Range	30.0	28.0	
		(40 patients)	(48 patients)	
Percentageofpatientswithonset within the 12 months prior to interview		14%	6%	ns
Percentage of patients having situation specific attacks only		36%	53%	ns

*Data only given for those who could remember

The first attack

Expectation of harm

Table 2.3 shows the expectations that patients had concerning their first panic attack as reported in retrospect during interview.

Nearly all patients stated that their first attack caught them unawares (97 per cent). Only 2 per cent of patients made 'nothing' of the attack. Many patients had an expectation of danger; fainting or collapsing was the commonest expectation (56 per cent), with death as the next most common (38 per cent). After the first attack 44 per cent of patients then expected further attacks, but 72 per cent actually had further attacks in the first week. Twenty-nine per cent had one further attack, 33 per cent had 2–5 attacks, and 10 per cent had 6–20 attacks.

Development of avoidance

The diagnosis of panic disorder as described in the *Diagnostic and Statistical Manual* (DSM-III) of the American Psychiatric Association (1980), assumes that there will only be a limited degree of avoidance behaviour associated with panic attacks. A common hypothesis in the literature of panic is that over sufficient time the occurrence of panic attacks will lead to the development of agoraphobic avoidance behaviour. Table 2.4 presents information about avoidance in the week after the first attack.

Table 2.3 Expectations during first attack and current attacks. Percentage of all panic sufferers with each expectation ($n = 108$).

Expectations	First attack (%)	Current attacks (%)
Faint or collapse	56	67
Going to die	38	32**
Lose control	22*	37
Heart attack	18	26
Become insane	16	29
Become physically ill	13	11
Unable to get home	12	33
Make a fool of oneself	12	53
Loss of memory	—	2
Other	—	12
Nothing	2	—
Was first attack expected? — Yes	3	
Expecting further attacks after the first one — Yes	44	

*Significantly more 'screen-detected' patients thought they would lose control in the first attack than 'direct referral patients'. (33 vs. 10 per cent)
**Significantly more 'direct referral patients' thought they would die in current attacks than 'screen detected' (41 vs. 23 per cent).

Table 2.4 Avoidance after the first attack. Percentage of all panic sufferers ($n = 108$).

	(%)
Avoidance started immediately after first attack	66
Strategies taken to reduce anxiety in the week after the first attack	
None admitted	35
Positive self-talk	35*
Stopped leaving house at all	18
Start avoiding situation of first attack	14
Always required accompaniment	14
Requested drugs from practitioner	13
Relaxation exercises	7
Alcohol	7

*Significantly more 'screen detected' patients reported using positive self-talk than directly referred patients (45 vs. 24 per cent).

Sixty-six per cent of sufferers reported that they had begun almost *immediately* to avoid some factor associated with attacks. A number of different avoidance strategies were used in the first week some of which could be termed agoraphobic avoidance (e.g. not leaving the house, requiring accompaniment), others non-agoraphobic (e.g. self-talk, using alcohol). Positive self-talk was the most common type of avoidance occurring in 45 per cent and 24 per cent of the 'screen detected' and 'directly referred' groups of patients respectively. The speed with which avoidance strategies developed in a high proportion of sufferers casts doubt on the widespread incidence of a type of pure panic disorder without any avoidance, and also suggests that the development of avoidance behaviour need not be a prolonged affair.

Current panic attacks

Table 2.5 shows the duration, frequency and severity of current panic attacks for both groups of sufferers.

The patients referred by their general practitioners had significantly more longer-lasting, frequent and severe attacks, but the attacks were disabling in both patient groups. The physical symptoms occurring during attacks are similar to those reported in Chapter 3 by M. Von Korff and W. Eaton, and Chapter 9 by J. Margraf and A. Ehlers, with heart rate increase (71 per cent), tenseness (68 per cent), choking sensations (61 per cent), feeling faint (48 per cent), sweating (40 per cent), and shaking (40 per cent) occurring in the greatest number of sufferers. The psychological

Table 2.5 Duration, frequency, and severity of current attacks. Percentage of each group falling into the categories.

	'Screen detected' ($n=53$) (%)	'Direct referrals' ($n=55$) (%)	
Duration			
Less than 15 minutes	79	49	
Less than 1 hour	13	30	
More than 1 hour	8	21	
			$p<0.01$
Frequency			
1–5 times per day	23	30	
Minimum of once per week	26	53	
Minimum of once per month	51	17	
			$p<0.01$
Severity			
Slight	24	6	
Moderate	42	41	
Severe	31	49	
Very severe	3	4	
			$p<0.01$

symptoms reported during current attacks are shown in Table 2.3. Fears of fainting or collapse were most commonly reported (67 per cent), followed by fears of embarrassment (53 per cent), and loss of control (37 per cent). Comparison of the reported fears of patients during their first attack and during current attacks shows a major increase in the fear of making a fool of oneself (53 per cent vs. 12 per cent). There were also increases in the fear of the inability to get home, as also found by Franklin (1987), of becoming insane, and of losing control.

Panic attack sufferers reported that certain events were associated with their symptoms becoming better or worse. Table 2.6 and 2.7 respectively show these associations.

The significant differences between the 'screen detected' and 'directly referred' patients indicates that the directly referred patients gained more benefit from being accompanied by their spouse or a friend, and talking their problem over with the doctor or a friend. Associating this finding with the fact that 'screen detected' patients reported engaging in significantly more self-talk after their first panic attack, could suggest that the 'screen detected' patients were more self-reliant/benefit less from the help of others. However the significantly greater fear of death in the 'directly referred' group (41 per cent vs. 23 per cent) and the greater duration, frequency and severity of their attacks may simply suggest a more severe symptom profile. The 'directly referred' patients also

Table 2.6 Events that patients associate with making the attacks better. Percentages of each group reporting these events.

Events	Screen detected ($n=53$) (%)	Direct referrals ($n=55$) (%)	Significance of difference between groups
Accompanied by spouse	46	81	$p<0.01$
Focusing mind on something else	57	43	
Quick way home	41	59	
Accompanied by friend	34	59	$p<0.05$
Sitting near door	31	60	$p<0.01$
Talking 'sense' to yourself	39	42	
Talking problem over with doctor	28	51	$p<0.05$
Talking problem over with friend	34	59	$p<0.05$
Object, e.g. dog, umbrella	18	17	
Wearing sun glasses	7	13	
Being close to physical structural support, e.g. walls	7	13	
Other?			
Worry about children's health	21	9	

reported significantly more depersonalisation or derealisation experiences associated with attacks (10 per cent vs. 28 per cent).

'Spontaneous' vs. situationally specific attacks

Patients with 'spontaneously' occurring panic attacks were compared with those describing situationally specific attacks *only*, on a number of dimensions using analysis with both parametric and non-parametric statistics. Patients from the 'screen detected' and 'direct referral' groups were pooled in the analysis, as both types of attack were common to each group. There were no differences between the patients having spontaneous as opposed to situationally specific attacks on Hamilton Anxiety Scale total scores, Hamilton Depression Scale total scores, current frequency, severity, or avoidance, obsessional symptoms, or depersonalisation/derealisation experiences. Patients with situationally specific anxiety reported significantly less diurnal variation in mood than the spontaneous group, and had had the disorder for a significantly greater number of years.

Table 2.7 Events that patients associate with making the attacks worse. Percentage of all panic sufferers reporting these events ($n=108$).

Events	(%)	Significance of difference between groups
Having to queue	53	
Thinking over problems	48	
Feeling depressed	43	
Density of a crowd	43	
Hairdressers	37	
Feeling tired	31	
Physical illness	30	
Having a particular worry	27	
Domestic arguments and stress	24	
Absence of others	22	
Enclosed space	21	
Increasing distance from home	21	
Specific places in the neighbourhood	18	
To have to keep an appointment	17	$p<0.05$*
Presence of particular individual acquaintances	15	
Poor weather	15	
Unfamiliarity of surroundings	14	$p<0.01$*
Worse in winter	11	
Other	7	

*For both events the direct referral group had a higher percentage made worse.

CLINICAL IMPRESSIONS

Introduction

No matter how competent multivariate and other statistical techniques eventually prove to be in their ability to define syndromes, at some point the clinician will fall back on and use both previous experience and the subjective ability to recognise patterns of behaviour and distress. Such a dimension of personal impressionism is not invalid in itself but is, however, incomplete without more objective attempts to examine psychological experiences.

This section, therefore, is primarily concerned with clinical impressions that were gained during the clinical interviews of sufferers during the study. Brief notes were made on each sufferer, in addition to the clinical notes available, and for clarification and confirmation, relatives were interviewed, if possible. The patient sample consisted of 87 of the patients either detected by screening or directly referred. After the study was over an attempt was made to classify the different forms of presentation and types of onset of panic attack. In this section five case studies have been selected which clearly illustrate different types of onset of panic attack. They are examples in which the onset was detected and/or obvious. The main emphasis is on factors relating to the onset of panic attacks rather than to the form of behavioural avoidance which subsequently developed. Some sufferers predominantly showed agoraphobic forms of avoidance, others showed attacks that did not occur in agoraphobic-type situations, and still others had mixed patterns. The particular form of avoidance could occur in any of the types of onset pattern used as illustrations in this section. It should be borne in mind that there were other patients for whom the causes for initial panic attack were not apparent in interview or who had mixed factors operating or who gradually 'slid' into a worsening condition over time without any clear precipitant being detected. These are not represented in the case examples, only clearer cases being used. The initials given to sufferers are fictitious.

Panic attack onset associated with a loss event or actual or perceived threat of separation

Much of the evidence concerning this type of presentation is based upon the patients' own account of their difficulties and it cannot be excluded that the attribution by these patients of the onset or association of disorder with such events is not an attempt to find meaning in the environment for their distress. It should be mentioned, however, that a recurring theme in the histories of sufferers, particularly those detected by screening, was the association by the patient and next of kin of the onset of the disorder some time within the year following a loss event or separation. Although several sufferers reported loss, only eight sufferers (9 per cent) could be grouped exclusively within this type of onset category.

Case Example 1

SSA—a 64-year-old lady was referred by her practitioner with 'agoraphobia'. She described an initial severe panic attack which occurred on an attempt to leave the house to visit a relative two years previously. This, she said, had led to her gradually becoming fearful of leaving her house at all and had reached the point at the time of referral that she was housebound and her husband had to do the shopping for her. She described severe dizzy spells if she attempted to leave the house but sometimes occurring in the house, independently of the motive on her part to leave. She associated the onset of her feelings to the stress associated with her mother's illness at that time. Her mother was aged 84 when she became ill and prior to her initial panic attack the patient was having to leave her work three times a day and would physically run to her mother's house nearby to check that her mother was 'all right'. Eventually her mother, who had a cardiac problem, was taken into hospital and the patient, with her husband, arranged to leave on holiday. She was advised not to do so by the ward sister who told her that her mother 'may not last' until she got back. She spoke to a second nurse who suggested that provided they were contactable it would be reasonable for them to leave on holiday. The patient described a great sense of 'shock' at suddenly being told the seriousness of her mother's condition. She described leaving on holiday, but said that in fact she never enjoyed this and her mother died a few weeks after she returned home. From this time she has been away on two holidays but in fact had not enjoyed either, and since then had lost interest in either holidays or to some extent leaving the house and had also lost some interest in social engagement. She denied feeling depressed although, in the opinion of the author, she appeared to have a degree of depressive mood but without biological symptoms. Her premorbid personality was described both by herself and her husband as always having been anxious, rather shy and relatively unassertive. She had, however, never previously exhibited problems in terms of leaving home or avoiding situations before the onset of her disorder. There was no psychiatric history within the family.

This patient was treated by the author and considered to have agoraphobic type anxieties with severe panic attacks, but in view of the (in the author's opinion) significant depressive component, was treated with antidepressant medication. There appeared to be complete remission of symptoms and at review, 18 months later, there had been no recurrence. In this example, therefore, the presentation appeared to be that of agoraphobic problems with significantly depressed affect, although with a relative absence of biological symptoms.

Five other patients (6 per cent) were diagnosed as having a degree of depressive affect sufficient to merit a diagnosis of depressive disorder. Three of these five attributed the onset of the depression to a separation or loss event. The sampling method used was likely to have resulted in an artificially low proportion of patients with a depressive disorder, as those presenting with primarily depressive symptoms would be dealt with by the regular psychiatric service at the health centre, outside the limits of this study.

Panic attack onset associated with biological disturbance

A number of sufferers had physiological, hormonal or viral disturbances associated with panic attacks. Thirty women described a worsening of panic attacks perimenstrually. One female patient described panic attacks as only occurring during menstruation. Several patients complained that the onset of the disorder had coincided with the period following the birth of one of their children (most frequently the second child) and in a proportion this appeared to have been associated with depressed affect.

Eight patients (9 per cent) presented with 'hot flushes' as their main complaint, alone or in association with another panic attack symptom. Three of these patients were undergoing physical investigations for causes of flushing and one patient had a firm diagnosis of 'brucellosis' made by a private medical practitioner outside the health centre. The females involved were outside the age range normally associated with menopausal symptoms.

The onset of panic attacks in three sufferers (3.5 per cent) appeared to have been associated with an 'acute virus' and what impressed us was the remarkable similarity of the initial symptoms of this presumed virus to acute panic symptoms. In all three cases the general practitioner had made a positive diagnosis of a viral illness, and relatives and the sufferers themselves described a marked change in the sufferers' functioning. Case example 2 gives a clear picture of this 'viral onset' and is used as an example of the broader biologically-based category for the onset of panic attacks. Other investigators have also noted that the panic attacks of successfully treated patients can recur after a viral illness such as a bout of flu.

Case Example 2

Mrs BD, aged 21, was referred by her general practitioner with severe panic attacks. She gave a history confirmed by her husband of feeling well in herself and coping well generally until five months previously when she had had 'acute virus' which had presented with severe stomach pains, nausea, vomiting and diarrhoea, and associated with this had been a shivering feeling with hot and cold flushes. She said that other members of the family had had the upset but that she had had it worst of all. During the illness she said that she began to feel faint and feared that she might vomit. From this point on she found that she rapidly began to fear leaving the house and started to experience panic attacks. There appeared to be no intervening period between the end of the virus and the onset of her agoraphobic anxieties. She also described a sensation of being easily fatigued and a feeling of loss of interest in her housework. At the time of being seen she exhibited marked avoidance behaviour and was being helped by her relatives to go to shops. She described panic attacks in shops during which she felt as if she was going to faint or be sick, and she felt as if she had to leave the shop, and on one occasion did so. She described no other symptomatology and at the time of the initial clinical interview did not appear to exhibit the features suggestive of a depressive illness. She did, in fact, say that she did not feel 'well' but this was a common symptom reported in panic attack patients in general who would often describe periods of feeling unwell during episodes of panic, but with a more persistent feeling of malaise for the day during an episode. It was, therefore, hard to identify this as a symptom associated with a physical disorder. On this occasion, more than one relative was interviewed and all appeared to describe a radical alteration in functioning following this acute onset.

Panic attack onset associated with emotional conflict

Four cases (4.5 per cent) were identified which appeared to be exclusively related to a particular emotional conflict. In two cases the problems appeared to be related to specific types of personality, in one case obsessional, and a second histrionic. In the other two cases there appeared to be no particular degree of abnormality, though in both cases the individual was a young and relatively immature adult. As the types of conflict can vary considerably, two cases have been presented as examples.

Case Example 3

Mr FS, aged 35, was referred with a mixture of anxiety symptoms including a churning feeling in his stomach, diarrhoea, episodes of shaking and periods of depersonalisation and derealisation. In addition, he described short-lasting episodes during which he thought he was going to faint or collapse. These episodes lasted for 20 minutes approximately. When severely anxious he would try to bury himself in mundane household tasks or, alternatively, he would try and lie in bed, tactics which both appeared to give temporary relief. In his estimation he had been married happily for four-and-a-half years and at the time of referral his wife was expecting their first child. He described himself as generally sociable and outgoing. He also described himself as an excessive worrier and being conscientious and fastidious. He tended to find other people not meeting up with his own expectations of them, and also found himself to be meticulous and prone to checking behaviour. He perceived himself as liking things to be well worked out and clearly wished to have everything under his control. He described a second side to himself in which he felt a strong sense of adventure and exploration and had, in fact, expressed this by involving himself in risk-taking hobbies and activities.

The formulation reached in this particular case was that the panic attacks were a manifestation of the conflict which appeared to be rising out of his desires and needs to risk-take and satisfy his needs and his equally powerful desire for control.

This man received six weekly sessions of focused psychotherapy directed at these issues by a member of the Department, with apparent resolution of his symptoms and eventual discharge.

Case Example 4

Miss HT was a 23-year-old student who was referred by her practitioner because of severe panic attacks.

These attacks tended to occur in the evening when she was in her residence. They would come on her suddenly, and she would feel as if she were going to choke or die. She experienced a sensation of wanting to leave the building to get air to breathe and would do so. During the attacks she felt her heart beating and her palms of her hands sweating and experienced paraesthesia in both hands. The problems had started following the separation of her parents and their eventual divorce when she was aged 16 years. She described herself as having a difficult relationship with her father, who she saw as a distant figure and with whom she had never felt close and her mother who she saw as dominating her. She had had heterosexual relationships and was at the time involved in a relationship with a man. She had not in the past appeared to demonstrate any other form of psychiatric disturbance excepting her severe anxiety symptoms. Because of the attacks she had, in fact, been regarded by some of her colleagues as 'hysterical'. She had, however, not exhibited any dissociative or conversion symptoms nor did she appear to demonstrate any other features associated with hysterical personality disorder. She linked the occurrence of the attacks to her mother's telephone calls, and it was usually following her mother calling that she experienced these episodes. There had been a conflict of thought between the girl and her mother regarding her daughter's future, the mother wishing her to return home to stay for a period while she decided upon her future, whereas the girl herself wished to remain independent if possible.

The formulation made in this case was that the panic attacks were a manifestation of the conflict that the girl herself felt about being independent. She had failed to establish a degree of mature separation from her mother, whose influence upon her she was attempting to control. This was interpreted as a maturational problem and she was referred to a group psychotherapeutically oriented day hospital. She appeared to do well with this treatment with resolution of her panic symptoms but a relapse occurred after discharge following her separation from her boyfriend.

Panic attack associated with sudden psychological trauma or threat

Three sufferers (3.5 per cent) were identified in which the onset of the disorder was acute and linked closely with a sudden severe psychological trauma. These cases appeared closest to the traditional conditioning theory model for the acquisition of fears, although this theory would not be the only explanation for the development of subsequent panic attack symptoms and avoidance behaviour.

Case Example 5

Mrs HL, aged 34, gave a four-year history of severe panic attacks and marked avoidance behaviour. During the attacks she had several fears, including the fear that she would become insane, that she would collapse or die and, according to both her and her relatives, the onset of the disorder coincided with the period immediately following a 'near-miss' car accident. The trouble had started when she was driving her family home, her family including her parents and her children, her husband being at home at the time. Living in a rural village on a winding road, she had been travelling along a lane at harvesting time when a tractor with a harvester had appeared as if it were on a collision course with the car. This, in fact, had been an optical illusion because of the particular geography and relationship of the tractor with the road position (similar accidents have been reported in this area, particularly with tractors using headlights at night). She swerved to avoid the tractor and at the last moment realised her mistake and managed to correct the car. She managed to get the car home; in fact from that time on she had not driven since until the time of referral. She described a series of panic attacks also at home during which she felt as if she was unable to breathe and was going to choke and often had to leave to 'get air'. According to information gained her premorbid personality had been that of an anxious, worrying person but who had not demonstrated any avoidance behaviour or experienced panic attacks and who had driven the car quite regularly.

This lady was treated with low dosage clomipramine, increasing to 30 mg and over a period of six months. Her symptoms and avoidance behaviour appeared to gradually remit. On review at 18 months, she had one episode during which she received a second course of low dosage clomipramine for three weeks, but had been off drugs for nine months, driving again and appeared well.

There was another group of sufferers, all female, whom although they had not experienced a sudden psychological trauma, had nevertheless experienced a change in status and occupation associated with the development of symptoms. They described the alteration of role which occurred on being married and changing from a work situation to a domestic one as fairly rapidly leading to low self-esteem, but more particularly lack of self-confidence in terms of independent activity. They could equally well be grouped in the 'emotional conflict' category of onset with conflict being related to issues of dependence and independence.

Other forms of panic attack

A number of sufferers had panic attacks in the context of another disorder. Depressive disorder has already been mentioned. Other types of disorder were three (3.5 per cent) cases of social phobia (there were also a number of patients with panic attacks and who lacked confidence in social situations), two (2 per cent) cases of alcohol-induced panic, two (2 per cent) cases in which panic occurred in patients reporting high levels of prior general tension, and one sufferer with an obsessional disorder.

In the latter case there was considerable difficulty establishing whether agoraphobic symptoms or obsessional symptoms were the predominant presenting symptom. Also two (2 per cent) sufferers experienced panic attacks only at night while lying in bed.

Other investigators have found panic onset to be associated with medical conditions including hypoglycaemia, hyperthyroidism, temporal lobe epilepsy, or administration, abuse, withdrawal or rebound of substances such as benzodiazepines, cocaine, opiates and LSD (see Goldberg, 1988 and Pollack and Rosenbaum, 1988 for reviews). Other psychological factors related to panic onset include experiences during and after wartime combat, natural disasters or delayed recall in adulthood of childhood sexual abuse (Hall and Lloyd, 1989).

COMMENT

The overwhelming impression gained during the study was the variety of clinical settings that panic attacks presented, suggesting more than a single precipitant for the symptoms (Hallam, 1978), although certain clinical patterns were memorable.

Firstly the association made by the patients themselves between a loss event and the onset of disorder appeared to occur with more than expected frequency. The threat of separation, for example, posed by a serious illness in a relative, may be sufficient to precipitate attacks. In such circumstances panic symptoms may appear alone or in combination with depressive symptoms.

Role change may also cause problems, for instance several married women after giving up work developed panic attacks in the setting of low self-esteem and lack of confidence. Several patients seemed to develop the disorder after the birth of their (second) child. Goldstein and Chambless (1978) have previously emphasised the importance of 'entrapment' in such cases, claiming it has a major etiological role in agoraphobia.

Various other types of emotional conflict or psychological or physical stress have been described in this chapter as relating to the onset of the disorder.

Was there any common linking theme to the experiences described by these patients and between the various classes of events? Many experiences involved appeared to be explainable in terms of the concept of loss of control. The panic experience appeared common to all of the various patterns of onset. In this sense it would appear important, therefore, to distinguish between the mechanisms involved in the panic attack and the mechanisms involved in the underlying disorder which may be contributing towards the precipitation of the attack. If the panic attack is considered to be a loss of control experience, perhaps mediated by psychobiological mechanisms, then a variety of underlying changes in biological or cognitive status might precipitate such an event. Thus, in the social phobic the panic attack represents an anxiety associated with a loss of control of their environment, the threat related to their sensitive self-consciousness and performance anxiety. In the agoraphobic the loss of control experience would be essentially the same in terms of its catastrophic subjective implications to the individual, but the threat linked to independent activity rather than social performance.

The difference between the common experience of panic in a variety of conditions and the severe disablement of the chronic agoraphobic may be related to the ease with which avoidance behaviour develops. It seems hard to explain the apparent partial relief of panic symptoms and the enhancement of environmental exploration in the presence of a close family figure without postulating the involvement of some form of social attachment mechanism.

The use of the term 'spontaneous' to describe non-situationally precipitated panic may be a misnomer. Patients experiencing such events did appear to associate them with types of situations, in particular that they occurred when least expected. The difference appeared to be that the precipitant of the spontaneous form was not related to specific visual percepts but was more closely related to general perceptual vigilance. Thus states of relaxation or concentration on non-security oriented cognitions may lead to sudden attacks which catch the victim unawares.

Panic attacks may be the overt manifestation of a final common pathway mediated by psychobiological mechanisms and which imply profound threat to the individual to the point of an appraisal of the failure of security mechanisms. Although considerable clinical variation may occur the behavioural and subjective associations appeared remarkably consistent.

REFERENCES

American Psychiatric Association (1980) *Diagnostic and Statistical Manual of Mental Disorders*, Third edn, American Psychiatric Association, Washington, DC.

Franklin, J.A. (1987) The changing nature of agoraphobic fears, *British Journal of Clinical Psychology*, **26**, 127–33.

Goldberg, R.J. (1988) Clinical presentations of panic related disorders, *Journal of Anxiety Disorders*, **2**, 61–75.

Goldstein, A.J. and Chambless, D.L. (1978) A reanalysis of agoraphobia, *Behavior Therapy*, **9**, 47–59.

Hall, L. and Lloyd, S. (1989) *Surviving Child Sexual Abuse: a Handbook for Helping Women Challenge Their Past*, Falmers Press, Basingstoke.

Hallam, R.S. (1978) Agoraphobia: A critical review of the concept, *British Journal of Psychiatry*, **133**, 314 – 19.

Pollack, M.H. and Rosenbaum, J.F. (1988) Benzodiazepines in panic-related disorders, *Journal of Anxiety Disorders*, **2**, 95 – 107.

**Address for communication:* ELAINE ILJON FOREMAN, Community Psychologist, Avenue House Community Mental Health Resource Centre, 43–47 Avenue Road, London W3 8NJ.

Chapter 3

Epidemiologic Findings on Panic

MICHAEL VON KORFF AND WILLIAM W. EATON

INTRODUCTION

Epidemiology is the study of the distribution and determinants of health states in populations (Lilienfeld and Lilienfeld, 1980). The scope of epidemiology encompasses a wide range of research activities including: establishing the dimensions of morbidity and mortality as a function of person, place and time; quantifying risks of developing disease as a function of host, agent and environmental factors; identifying and defining syndromes; describing the natural history of disease in terms of onset, duration, recurrence, complications, disability, and mortality; identifying factors which influence or predict clinical course; identifying causes of disease, disability and mortality; and evaluating methods of disease prevention and control (Morris, 1975). To date, mental disorder epidemiologists have made modest contributions to the understanding of panic disorder in several of these areas, but the potential of epidemiologic methods for understanding anxiety disorders has not yet been fully realized.

In the last two decades, rich and provocative theoretical bases for epidemiologic research concerning panic and related anxiety disorders has emerged, represented by the work of Marks and Lader (1973), Klein (1980), and others (Brown *et al.*, 1984; Bowlby, 1973; Sheehan *et al.*, 1980; Crowe *et al.*, 1983). During this same period, mental disorder epidemiologists have been preoccupied with the difficult problems of counting cases in community surveys in order to establish the 'true' prevalence and incidence of mental disorders (Regier *et al.*, 1984; Eaton and Kessler, 1985). As the application of epidemiologic methods to the study of mental disorders matures and knowledge about the basic distribution of mental disorders becomes more secure, reasoning about the causes, consequences and control of mental disorders is likely to assume greater importance than estimation of incidence and prevalence *per se*.

Panic Disorder: Theory, Research and Therapy. Edited by Roger Baker

Epidemiologic studies of panic disorder to date (e.g. Weissman *et al.*, 1978; Uhlenhuth *et al.*, 1983; Von Korff *et al.*, 1985), have ascertained the presence or absence of panic disorder during a fixed time period and within the context of cross-sectional surveys. In contrast, clinical reasoning about panic disorder now places increased emphasis on a staged model of development of psychological and behavioural dysfunction following the onset of panic attacks. For example, McFayden (Chapter 13 of this volume) conceptualizes panic disorder as developing in the following stages:

1. The occurrence of panic attacks;
2. Cognitive appraisal of panic symptoms as threatening physical, psychological or social harm;
3. Sensitization to symptoms of panic;
4. Development of strategies to avoid, escape from or minimize the symptoms of panic. Once developed, the patterns of escape or avoidance are considered to be self-maintaining.

This kind of staged model of the development of panic disorder points to the need for longitudinal investigation of the expression of panic disorder. Epidemiologic research needs to shift its focus from classification of cases in cross-section to more complex longitudinal investigation of the natural history of the psychophysiologic, cognitive, emotional and behavioural components of panic disorder. This chapter outlines epidemiologic concepts of the natural history of chronic episodic disease applicable to panic disorder research, and presents findings of the National Institute of Mental Health Epidemiologic Catchment Area Surveys relevant to these concepts.

PANIC DISORDER AS A CHRONIC EPISODIC CONDITION

Panic disorder is defined by a constellation of psychophysiologic, cognitive, emotional and behavioural responses of a human organism that are classified as mental disorder only when they occur together repeatedly over time. As is the case for many chronic diseases, the development of panic disorder can be conceptualized in terms of sequenced stages of illness. Epidemiologic concepts used to describe the staged development of chronic disease include: initiation and promotion (Hopkins and Williams, 1986), onset of disorder, remission, and relapse. The interval between initiation and onset can be referred to as the 'incubation period' of the disorder (e.g. Cobb *et al.*, 1959).

These epidemiologic concepts can be readily applied to a staged model of the development of panic disorder. The onset of panic attacks would correspond to initiation, while cognitive appraisal, sensitization and development of avoidance are processes involved in the promotion of panic disorder. The interval between the first panic attack and meeting full criteria for panic disorder might be considered the incubation period of panic disorder. Remission and relapse refer to the offset and recurrence of episodes of panic attacks and associated dysfunctional cognitions and behaviours.

Within the context of a staged model of the development of panic disorder, the goals of epidemiologic study would include:

1. characterization of each of the stages in the development of panic disorder;
2. estimation of the probabilities of transition from one stage to the next;
3. describing the duration in each stage;
4. identifying factors which control or predict these transition probabilities and durations.

In the case of a chronic episodic condition, like panic disorder, it has been shown that (under steady state conditions) prevalence is a function of incidence, average episode duration and the probability of recurrence (Von Korff and Parker, 1980). This implies that differences in panic disorder prevalence rates by risk factor status might result from differences in incidence rates, differences in episode duration, or differences in the probability of recurrence. Incidence rate differentials could result from differences in factors affecting initiation of panic attacks or factors affecting promotion of panic disorder (including cognitive appraisal, sensitization to panic symptoms or development of avoidance behaviours). Episode duration and recurrence may be influenced, in turn, by rates of remission, rates of relapse, rates of mortality among cases, or any of the factors influencing these rates.

Because of the complexity of the factors which may influence prevalence rates, differences in prevalence rates by risk factor status can be difficult to interpret. Hence, epidemiologic analyses of prevalence data alone provide a limited perspective on how host, agent or environmental factors may be implicated in the development of panic disorder through its various stages. For example, a particular risk factor may be associated with increased likelihood of the initiation of panic attacks, with increased promotion of panic disorder once panic attacks have occurred, or with increased duration or recurrence of panic disorder once a full panic disorder syndrome has evolved. Cross-sectional analysis of prevalence data provides only a limited basis for differentiation of these potentially distinct roles of specific risk factors. Since prevalence data cannot shed much light on the specific role of a risk factor in the staged development of panic disorder, it provides only limited information relevant to the etiology, prevention or control of panic disorder.

While the shortcomings of prevalence data as a basis for understanding the natural history of panic disorder are readily apparent, how to develop epidemiologic data that can shed light on the staged development of panic disorder is not an easy problem. In this chapter, we will consider this question by reviewing selected cross-sectional and longitudinal findings of the National Institute of Mental Health Epidemiologic Catchment Area (ECA) surveys pertaining to panic disorder. In order to elucidate the natural history of panic disorder, we will focus on the influence of age on the expression of panic attacks and panic disorder.

THE EPIDEMIOLOGIC CATCHMENT AREA SURVEYS

The National Institute of Mental Health Epidemiologic Catchment Area (ECA) Program consists of community surveys carried out by five independent university-based research teams. The survey sites included New Haven, Connecticut (Yale University); Eastern Baltimore, Maryland (Johns Hopkins University); the greater St Louis, Missouri area (Washington University); Raleigh-Durham, North Carolina (Duke University); and Los Angeles (UCLA). The surveys included co-ordinated sample surveys of the household and institutional populations of defined geographic areas. At each site there was a one-year follow-up interview. The data presented here are derived from the initial household surveys and the one-year follow-up of the household survey subjects. The objectives and rationale of the ECA surveys are described in greater detail by Regier *et al.* (1984).

The methods of the ECA surveys are presented in detail by Eaton *et al.* (1984) and in a methods monograph (Eaton and Kessler, 1985). In brief, area probability samples of about 3000 persons residing in households were drawn at each site. Household members were selected at random for interview from among those persons 18 years of age or older. Supplemental samples of persons over the age of 65 were interviewed at several of the sites. Persons agreeing to be interviewed participated in a 90-minute interview which included the Diagnostic Interview Schedule, or DIS (Robins *et al.*, 1981). Response rates of 75 to 80 per cent were achieved at each of the survey sites.

The DIS portion of the interview consisted of pre-specified questions directly pertinent to the Third Edition of the *Diagnostic and Statistical Manual of the American Psychiatric Association*, or DSM-III (American Psychiatric Association, 1980). Diagnoses were made from the DIS symptom data by means of computer algorithms which simulated the application of these criteria.

In the case of panic disorder, the interviewer asked a screening question: 'Have you ever had a spell or attack when all of a sudden you felt frightened, anxious or very uneasy in a situation when most people wouldn't be afraid?' If the answer to the screening question was negative, no further probing was done to elicit a report of panic attacks. If the answer to the question was affirmative, the interviewer asked whether or not a series of 12 autonomic symptoms were present in one of the worst such attacks, how frequently these attacks occurred, the age at which the first attack occurred, whether the attacks occurred only in the presence of phobic stimuli, and three questions to assess severity (whether the attack prompted seeking treatment; or use of medicines; or whether the attacks interfered a lot with life activities).

The prevalence analyses reported here employ three levels of case definition. All three levels are restricted to persons reporting at least one attack in the six months prior to interview. The highest level included only persons meeting diagnostic criteria for panic disorder as operationalized by the DIS (that is, an affirmative answer to one of the severity questions; a history of at least three panic attacks in a three-week period; four or more autonomic symptoms in a worst attack; and attacks not related only to exposure to fear-provoking stimuli). The next level included persons with severe and recurrent panic attacks: persons with a positive response to any of the severity questions; and who had experienced either three attacks within a three-week period or attacks in at least six different weeks in their lifetime. The lowest level, simple panic attacks, included the remaining persons who reported a panic attack in the prior six months who did not give an affirmative response either to the severity questions or to the recurrence questions. In the prevalence and incidence rate analyses reported here we included only persons with four or more autonomic symptoms in their attacks at each of the three levels. In the age of onset and symptom profile analyses, we included persons regardless of the number of autonomic symptoms reported. Before applying the symptom count criterion, the median number of autonomic symptoms was four for persons with simple panic attacks, six for severe and recurrent attacks and six for panic disorder. DSM-III criteria exclude a diagnosis of panic disorder if a person has major depression, schizophrenia, somatization disorder or agoraphobia. These exclusionary criteria were not employed in ECA analyses because they proved difficult to operationalize using DIS data.

The reliability of the diagnostic method used in this research has been evaluated. Robins *et al.* (1982) found that panic disorder had the lowest level of agreement of any of the DIS diagnoses (Kappa = 0.40). Burnham *et al.* (1983) also report a low level of reliability of the panic disorder diagnosis. These results suggest that more needs to be learned about the methodologic aspects of eliciting reports of panic attacks and that interpretation of panic disorder diagnostic data from an epidemiologic survey should be made with reasonable caution.

Population estimates of prevalence and incidence rates were made based on weighted data. The weights were estimated from sample selection probabilities adjusted on a post-stratification basis to 1980 census totals for each area by age, sex and race.

Prevalence rates

Table 3.1 shows prevalence rates of simple panic attacks, severe and recurrent attacks, and panic disorder by age, sex, race, educational attainment and marital status for the first three ECA sites. These results are generally consistent with other studies (Weissman *et al.*, 1978; Ilfeld, 1979) in that rates were highest for females, younger persons, and persons who were separated or divorced. These relationships were statistically significant and held after multivariate adjustment for covariates (Von Korff *et al.*, 1985).

Note that the prevalence of simple panic attacks tended to peak in the 18–24 year age group, while recurrent and severe attacks and panic disorder tended to peak in the 25–44 year age group. This observation is significant because it suggests the possibility that panic attacks are initiated at an earlier age than the full expression of panic disorder. We are able to pursue this issue in greater depth by examining the distribution of self-reported age of onset among persons who subsequently were identified as cases of panic disorder, severe and recurrent panic attacks, or simple panic attacks.

Age of onset of panic attacks

Subjects were asked to report the age at which they first experienced panic attacks. The distribution of age of onset of panic attacks is depicted in Figure 3.1. The modal age of onset was reported to be in the 15–19-year age group for persons with panic disorder, as well as persons with severe and recurrent or simple panic attacks not meeting full diagnostic criteria. Among persons with panic disorder, there was a modest elevation suggesting a second mode in the distribution of age of onset with increased onsets in the 25–34 year age group.

Comparing the distribution of prevalence by age with the distribution of age of onset of panic attacks indicates an appreciable difference between the peak age of initiation of panic attacks and the age range at which prevalence peaks. Like the difference in peak prevalence between simple attacks

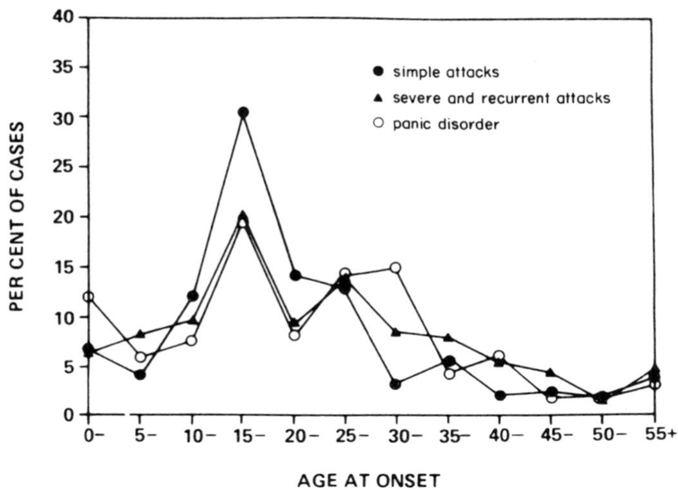

Figure 3.1 Percentage distribution of age (years) at onset for cases with simple panic attacks, severe and recurrent panic attacks, and panic disorder: New Haven CT, Eastern Baltimore MD, and St Louis MO Epidemiologic Catchment Area Program Surveys, 1980–82. From M.R. Von Korff, W.W. Eaton and P.M. Keyl, The epidemiology of panic attacks and panic disorders: results of three community surveys, *American Journal of Epidemiology*, **122** (1985). (Reproduced by permission of the *American Journal of Epidemiology*.)

and panic disorder, this suggests a prolonged incubation period between the initiation of panic attacks and the onset of panic disorder.

We are able to further explore the plausibility of a prolonged incubation period through analysis of longitudinal incidence data based on the one-year follow-up. If there was a prolonged incubation period, then most of the incident cases of panic disorder identified at the one-year follow-up interview should report a history of panic attacks at the first wave. If the full syndrome of panic disorder typically develops rapidly, then incident cases of panic disorder with no prior history of panic attacks at the first interview should be common.

Incidence rates

Table 3.2 shows two sets of age-specific incidence rates for panic disorder for all five ECA sites combined. The first set provides incidence rates per 1000 persons among individuals with no history of panic attacks at the first interview wave. There were 32 incident cases of panic disorder identified

Table 3.1 Prevalence per 1000 of simple panic attacks, severe and recurrent attacks, and panic disorder in three epidemiologic catchment area survey sites, 1980–82.

Total sampled	Simple panic attacks*			Severe and recurrent panic attacks**			Panic disorder		
Approx. 3000 per site	New Haven	E. Balt-imore	St Louis	New Haven	E. Balt-imore	St Louis	New Haven	E. Balt-imore	St Louis
Number of subjects in which panic was found	($n=40$)	($n=44$)	($n=59$)	($n=34$)	($n=33$)	($n=28$)	($n=26$)	($n=33$)	($n=33$)
Sex									
Male	9.4	4.5	8.6	3.6	3.7	4.4	3.0	7.9	7.4
Female	19.4	14.1	19.6	18.3	13.1	10.7	10.5	11.7	10.2
Age (years)									
18–24	30.3	9.4	32.7	4.2	7.4	7.7	3.5	10.1	8.7
25–44	16.9	16.4	15.8	19.7	8.3	13.5	10.7	12.5	13.2
45–64	4.5	5.7	7.9	5.8	9.9	2.5	4.3	11.8	7.1
65+	3.7	2.5	0.0	1.1	9.4	1.7	2.2	1.2	0.6
Education (years)									
0–8	5.9	6.6	7.4	14.2	13.6	11.0	2.8	13.2	20.7
9–11	12.2	15.0	20.7	11.4	11.2	8.1	8.9	14.4	4.4
12	7.4	9.5	18.1	13.5	5.2	10.4	7.0	4.9	6.9
13+	19.7	6.2	11.1	6.3	4.7	3.3	6.0	7.5	7.8

Marital status									
Married	8.4	8.0	11.9	9.5	9.7	5.8	4.3	6.5	7.6
Widowed	17.1	10.7	8.8	12.0	8.2	4.2	9.7	4.3	9.0
Separated/divorced	25.7	25.4	11.4	28.6	15.0	20.1	27.2	16.7	22.4
Never married	25.2	3.2	26.1	8.5	3.7	9.0	4.6	15.2	6.0
Race/ethnicity									
White	13.7	8.8	13.6	10.3	8.3	8.6	6.7	7.3	7.2
Other	20.0	11.1	17.7	17.3	9.7	4.8	8.1	14.9	9.0
All persons	13.3	9.7	14.5	10.1	8.8	7.7	6.3	10.0	8.9

*Does not include severe and recurrent attacks or panic disorder.

**Does not include panic disorder.

From M.R. Von Korff, W.W. Eaton and P.M. Keyl, The epidemiology of panic attacks and panic disorders: results of three community surveys, *American Journal of Epidemiology*, **122** (1985). (Reproduced by permission of the *American Journal of Epidemiology*.)

at the follow-up interview with no prior history of panic attacks reported at the baseline interview. The second set provides incidence rates among persons with no reported history of panic disorder at the first wave, but who may have had panic attacks prior to the first interview wave. There were 78 incident cases of panic disorder identified at the follow-up interview who reported no history of panic disorder at the baseline interview (these 78 incident cases include the 32 onsets with no prior history of panic attacks at the baseline interview).

Table 3.2 Cumulative incidence of panic disorder per 1000 adults by age: persons with no history of panic attacks or with no history of panic disorder at Wave 1.

Age at Wave 1	No prior attacks		No prior disorder		
	Rate	No. of cases	Rate	No. of cases	Total No.
18–24	1.1	(2)	1.9	(3)	2 256
25–34	2.9	(10)	8.4	(27)	4 058
35–44	2.8	(5)	8.4	(15)	2 459
45–54	6.0	(8)	10.7	(13)	1 732
55–64	0.9	(4)	4.3	(12)	2 356
65+	0.3	(3)	1.3	(8)	5 702
All ages	2.3	(32)	4.4	(78)	18 563

The crude incidence rate among persons with no prior history of panic attacks was 2.3 per 1000 per annum, while the rate for persons with no history of panic disorder (including persons with prior panic attacks) was 4.4. per 1000. Both incidence rate schedules are elevated in the 25–54 year age range and are lowest among persons below the age of 25 or older than age 55.

Of particular significance is that incidence rates were appreciably lower among persons with no history of panic attacks relative to persons with no history of panic disorder. Only about one-half of the incident cases were found to have reported no history of panic attacks at the first interview wave. Even among these cases, almost one-half (14 out of 32), when asked at follow-up when they first experienced a panic attack, reported that it occurred prior to the age of 18. Since these subjects had reported no prior history of panic attacks at the baseline interview, their report of panic attacks prior to age of 18 in the follow-up interview reflects poorly on the reliability of the recollection of panic attack history. However, it also suggests that very few persons have onset of a full panic disorder syndrome in close proximity to their first panic attack. Thus, longitudinal incidence data indicate an appreciable incubation period between the onset of panic attacks and meeting full criteria for panic disorder.

Prevalence data, age of onset data and incidence data from the ECA surveys all suggest an appreciable incubation period between the initiation of panic attacks and the expression of the full panic disorder syndrome. The limitations of DIS data collected within the context of a large scale community survey for addressing this question must be acknowledged. The interval between the initiation of panic attacks and onset of panic disorder could be established with more confidence within the context of longitudinal clinical investigation of persons experiencing initial panic attacks.

Sheehan *et al.* (1981) have reported age of onset data for panic attacks associated with endogenous phobic anxiety. In their study, the shape of the age of onset distribution was similar to that reported here, but the modal age of onset was in the 20–24 year age range. They reported that the mean latency period between the onset of panic attacks and the development of phobic avoidance was 3 months with a range of 1 day to 2 years. The mean latency between onset of panic attacks (mean age 24 years) and entering treatment (mean age 36.5 years) was reported to be 12.7 years.

While their data does suggest a relatively short incubation period for the development of avoidance behaviours after the onset of panic attacks, this issue deserves further investigation for several reasons. Their sample was limited to cases who had sought treatment and who suffered 'a significant degree of social and work impairment'. The broader spectrum of cases identified in a community survey may be found to have a longer interval from onset of panic attacks to the development of panic disorder. Since there was usually a long interval between the onset of panic attacks and seeking treatment, the report of the interval between onset of panic attacks and the development of avoidance behaviours was necessarily based on distant recollection. It is possible that the onset of panic attacks and the onset of phobic avoidance was telescoped in the patient's recollection. (H. Waring acknowledges the difficulty of retrospective reporting in the previous chapter.) It is also unclear whether the onset of phobic avoidance would be comparable to the onset of a fully developed clinical syndrome of panic disorder. The limitations of both epidemiologic survey data and of clinical data based on persons entering treatment point to the need for focused longitudinal study of persons who have recently experienced initial panic attacks to ascertain the progression of panic disorder over time.

If such research verified that panic disorder often requires an appreciable incubation period to develop, it would have considerable public health significance. The application of cognitive and behavioural interventions described elsewhere in this volume might have substantial value as interventions to prevent the promotion of panic disorder among persons experiencing panic attacks. In particular, one might expect greater efficacy

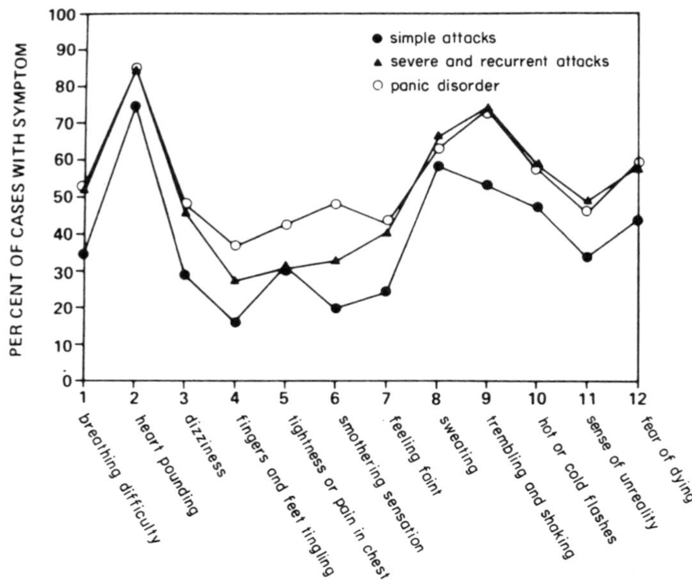

Figure 3.2 Percentage with specific autonomic symptoms among cases with simple panic attacks, severe and recurrent panic attacks and panic disorder: New Haven CT, Eastern Baltimore MD, and St Louis MO Epidemiologic Catchment Area Program Surveys, 1980–82. From M.R. Von Korff, W.W. Eaton and P.M. Keyl, The epidemiology of panic attacks and panic disorders: results of three community surveys, *American Journal of Epidemiology*, **122** (1985). (Reproduced by permission of the *American Journal of Epidemiology*.)

of behavioural interventions prior to the full development of avoidance behaviours and associated cognitions.

Symptom Profile

The epidemiologic data presented above suggest the possibility of a window of opportunity for prevention of promotion of the full syndrome of panic disorder among persons experiencing initial panic attacks. The data presented in Table 3.1 suggest that in a six-month prevalence period about 2 per cent of the adult population experiences simple panic attacks or severe and recurrent panic attacks without meeting full panic disorder criteria. In certain sociodemographic groups (e.g. females, young persons, persons who are separated or divorced) the occurrence of such panic attacks may affect 3 to 5 per cent of the population. These estimates do not support characterization of the panic attack as a normal phenomenon commonly experienced by a majority, or even a substantial minority, of adults. They do suggest that a substantial number of adults in the general population may be experiencing bouts of panic attacks, placing them at risk for development of a full panic disorder syndrome. This raises a significant question: What opportunities are there to identify these individuals and to initiate secondary preventive interventions before the dysfunctional behaviours and cognitions of panic disorder are fully developed?

Figure 3.2 presents the profile of the percentage of cases reporting specific symptoms among cases of simple panic attack, severe and recurrent panic attack and panic disorder. Panic attacks associated with panic disorder were reported to be similar to more benign panic attacks. Note that somatic symptoms such as breathing difficulty, dizziness, and chest pain are prominent manifestations of panic attacks. The symptom profile of the panic attack is of interest because the somatic symptoms of the panic attack might be interpreted by the affected individual either as a manifestation of psychological distress or as a possible symptom of physical disease or illness. The help seeking behaviours of the affected person may depend heavily on how they interpret their symptoms (Mechanic, 1972; Kleinman, 1980).

Epidemiologic research and clinical observation in a variety of health care settings suggests that panic symptoms are often identified by patients as possible indications of physical disease (Katon *et al.*, 1987; Katon, 1984; Sheehan, 1982; see also Table 2.3 of Waring's chapter). These symptoms are presented to the physician with the concern expressed or implied that they are caused by a physical disease process. The presentation of these symptoms often necessitates diagnostic evaluation to determine whether or not a significant physical disease is present. This diagnostic evaluation may further sensitize the patient to panic symptoms, support a cognitive appraisal of panic attacks as potentially harmful, and may provide social sanction for avoidance behaviours by the affected person. Despite these risks that accompany physical diagnostic evaluation, all too often the work-up does not include evaluation of possible psychiatric diagnoses that should be ruled out before further tests or treatments are considered.

Even in those cases where 'stress' is identified as a cause of panic attacks, intervention is often limited to brief counselling or non-specific anti-anxiety medications, rather than positive biologic and cognitive-behavioural treatment of the patient's presenting illness. Thus, on the one hand, many physicians do not treat panic attacks as a psychological illness because they may not know how to efficiently differentiate psychiatric from physical causes of autonomic symptoms. While, on the other hand, many physicians do not learn how to carry out an efficient differential diagnosis of panic attacks because they are not confident in their ability to effectively manage the patient experiencing panic attacks once identified.

It is now well recognized that the primary care physician is the modal provider of mental health services for persons seeking treatment for mental disorders (Regier, 1978; Shapiro *et al.*, 1984). Primary care physicians also treat large numbers of persons who are experiencing a mental disorder but who present their psychological distress in the form of physical symptoms as well illustrated by Waring, Table 2.1 in the previous chapter and also documented by others (e.g. Katon *et al.*, 1984; Mechanic, 1972). In the case of panic disorder, a prolonged incubation period and the salience of the symptom profile of panic disorder to health care concerns may afford significant opportunities for preventive intervention. The physician who identified panic attacks as a psychophysiologic syndrome could initiate a number of interventions that might reduce risks of panic attacks evolving into a full panic disorder syndrome. First, positive biologic treatment to control panic attacks might reduce risks of promotion of panic disorder. Second, implementation of behavioural intervention strategies might reduce risks of the entrenchment of avoidance behaviours. Third, the physician could offer a benign interpretation of panic attacks reducing the level of threat of a panic attack to the affected person. The patient's interpretations of panic attacks in terms of loss of control or in terms of life-threatening disease might be superseded with an interpretation of the panic attack as an unpleasant but time-limited physical sensation indicative of stress. Fourth, counselling or referral for psychologic treatment might be beneficial for management of any psychological or social precipitants implicated in the production of panic attacks.

We can only speculate that such early interventions by health care workers could prevent the promotion of panic disorder among persons experiencing initial panic attacks. However, the efficacy of early intervention in preventing the growth of dysfunctional avoidance behaviours and associated cognitions merits further evaluation through controlled clinical research. While the relatively crude epidemiologic data presented in this chapter cannot shed light on the efficacy of early intervention, it does suggest that the natural history of panic disorder may, in an appreciable percentage of cases, afford enough time to implement interventions of this nature if panic attacks can be recognized and treated expeditiously.

SUMMARY

We have presented basic epidemiologic data on panic attacks and disorder to improve understanding of the natural history of this disorder, and to consider possible strategies for preventive intervention. The limitations of epidemiologic data on panic disorder collected by lay interviewers in large scale surveys must be acknowledged. The possibility of prevention of behavioural sequelae of panic attacks, while an interesting possibility, is an area that requires further empirical evaluation through controlled clinical research.

As mental disorder epidemiologists turn their attention from estimation of prevalence rates to studies of the natural history of panic and other mental disorders, we expect a clearer picture of the developmental aspects of panic disorder over the lifespan to emerge. The complexity of epidemiologic investigation of mental disorder syndromes in terms of a staged model of development should not be underestimated. Such studies will require longitudinal investigation of subjects, a significant undertaking. They will require approaches to collection of psychiatric data better suited to describing the evolution of complex psychophysiologic, cognitive, emotional and behavioural components of mental disorder than provided by existing diagnostic schedules. However, we suspect that longitudinal investigation will yield epidemiologic data that is more relevant to answering questions about the etiology, prevention and control of panic disorder and other mental disorders than has been afforded to date by cross-sectional survey data.

REFERENCES

American Psychiatric Association (1980) *Diagnostic and Statistical Manual: Third Edition*, APA, Washington DC.

Bowlby, J. (1973) *Separation: Anxiety and Anger*, Basic Books, New York.

Brown, J.T., Mulrow, C.D. and Stoudmire, G.A. (1984) The anxiety disorders, *Annals of Internal Medicine*, **100**, 558–64.

Burnham, M.A., Karno, M., Hough, R.L. *et al.* (1983) The Spanish Diagnostic Interview Schedule: reliability and comparison with clinical diagnoses, *Archives of General Psychiatry*, **40**, 1189–96.

Cobb, S., Miller, M. and Wald, N. (1959) On the estimation of the incubation period in malignant disease, *Journal of Chronic Disease*, **9**, 385–93.

Crowe, R.R., Noyes, R., Pauls, D.L. *et al.* (1983) A family study of panic disorder, *Archives of General Psychiatry*, **40**, 1065–9.

Eaton, W.W., Holzer, C.E., Von Korff, M. *et al.* (1984) The design of the ECA surveys: the control and measurement of error, *Archives of General Psychiatry*, **41**, 942–8.

Eaton, W.W. and Kessler, L.G. (1985) *Epidemiologic Field Methods in Psychiatry*, Academic Press, New York.

Hopkins, P.N. and Williams, R.R. (1986) Identification and relative weight of cardiovascular risk factors, *Cardiology Clinics*, **4**, 3–31.

Ilfeld, F.W. (1979) Persons at risk for anxiety. In *Clinical Anxiety Tension in Primary Medicine: Proceedings*, Elsevier, New York.

Katon, W. (1984) Panic disorder and somatization: review of 55 cases, *American Journal of Medicine*, **77**, 101–6.

Katon, W., Ries, R.K. and Kleinman, A. (1984) The prevalence of somatization in primary care, *Comprehensive Psychiatry*, **25**, 208–15.

Katon, W., Vitalliano, P.P., Russo, J. *et al.* (1987) Panic disorder: spectrum of severity and somatization, *Journal of Nervous and Mental Diseases*, **175**, 12–19.

Klein, D.F. (1980) Anxiety reconceptualized, *Comprehensive Psychiatry*, **21**, 411–27.

Kleinman, A. (1980) *Patients and Healers in the Context of Culture*, University of California Press, Berkeley.

Lilienfeld, A.M. and Lilienfeld, D.E. (1980) *Foundations of Epidemiology, 2nd Edition*, Oxford University Press, New York.

Marks, I. and Lader, M. (1973) Anxiety states (anxiety neurosis): a review, *Journal of Nervous and Mental Diseases*, **156**, 3–18.

Mechanic, D. (1972) Social psychologic factors affecting the presentation of bodily complaints, *New England Journal of Medicine*, **286**, 1132–9.

Morris, J.N. (1975) *Uses of Epidemiology*, 3rd Edn, Churchill Livingstone, London.

Regier, D.A., Goldberg, I.D. and Taube, C.H. (1978) The de facto US mental health services system: a public health perspective, *Archives of General Psychiatry*, **38**, 685–93.

Regier, D.A., Myers, J.K., Kramer, M. *et al.* (1984) The NIMH Epidemiologic Catchment Area Program: historical context, major objectives and study population characteristics, *Archives of General Psychiatry*, **41**, 934–41.

Robins, L.N., Helzer, J.E., Croughan, J. *et al.* (1981) National Institute of Mental Health Diagnostic Interview Schedule: its history, characteristics and validity, *Archives of General Psychiatry*, **38**, 381–9.

Robins, L.N., Helzer, J.E., Ratcliff, K.S. *et al.* (1982) Validity of the Diagnostic Interview Schedule, Version II: DSM-III Diagnoses, *Psychological Medicine*, **12**, 855–70.

Shapiro, S., Skinner, E.A., Kessler, L.G. *et al.* (1984) Utilization of health and mental health services: three catchment area sites. *Archives of General Psychiatry*, **41**, 971– 8.

Sheehan, D.V. (1982) Panic attacks and phobias, *New England Journal of Medicine*, **307**, 156–8.

Sheehan, D.V., Ballenger, J. and Jacobsen, G. (1980) Treatment of endogenous anxiety with phobic, hysterical and hypochondrical symptoms, *Archives of General Psychiatry*, **37**, 51–9.

Sheehan, D.V., Sheehan, K.E. and Minichiello, W.E. (1981) Age of onset of phobic disorders: a reevaluation, *Comprehensive Psychiatry*, **22**, 544–53.

Uhlenhuth, E.H., Balter, M.B., Mellinger, G.D. *et al.* (1983) Symptom checklist syndromes in the general population: correlations with psychotherapeutic drug use, *Archives of General Psychiatry*, **40**, 1167–73.

Von Korff, M.R., Eaton, W.W. and Keyl, P.M. (1985) The epidemiology of panic attacks and panic disorder: results of three community surveys, *American Journal of Epidemiology*, **122**, 970–81.

Von Korff, M. and Parker, R.D. (1980) The dynamics of the prevalence of chronic episodic disease, *Journal of Chronic Disease*, **33**, 79–85.

Weissman, M.M. (1985) The epidemiology of anxiety disorders: rates, risks and familial patterns. In A.H. Tuma and J.D. Maser (eds), *Anxiety and the Anxiety Disorders*, Erlbaum Associates, Hillsdale, New Jersey.

Weissman, M.M., Myers, J. K. and Harding, P.S. (1978) Psychiatric disorders in a US urban community: 1975–76, *American Journal of Psychiatry*, **315**, 459–62.

Chapter 4

Ambulatory Monitoring Findings on Panic

ROBERT R. FREEDMAN

INTRODUCTION

Panic disorder is characterized by sudden attacks of fear or apprehension in conjunction with a variety of physical symptoms, including vertigo, faintness, chest pain, palpitations, dyspnoea, hot and cold flashes, and sweating. Although panic attacks may be provoked in the laboratory using sodium lactate as well as a variety of adrenergic drugs, such as isoproterenol and yohimbine, spontaneous panic attacks occur relatively infrequently in the laboratory. In order to better understand the pathophysiology of panic disorder, it would be desirable to obtain physiological measurements of panic attacks occurring spontaneously and in the patient's natural environment. The development of a variety of 'ambulatory monitoring' devices has made such research possible. In the present chapter, published investigations utilizing ambulatory monitoring procedures to record panic attacks will first be reviewed. The findings of these studies will then be compared and contrasted with those in which physiological recordings of panic attacks were performed in laboratory settings. The relative advantages and disadvantages of the procedures will then be discussed.

AMBULATORY MONITORING INVESTIGATIONS

Studies from the Behavioral Medicine Laboratory, Detroit

The first controlled investigation of ambulatory monitoring of panic disorder was performed relatively recently (Freedman *et al.*, 1985). Twelve

Panic Disorder: Theory, Research and Therapy. Edited by Roger Baker

patients with panic disorder and eleven control subjects received 24-hour ambulatory monitoring of heart rate, finger temperature, ambient temperature, and self-rated anxiety. Physiological measures were continuously recorded using a Medilog cassette recording system. Subjects wore the recorder from 10:00 a.m. to 10:00 p.m. on two consecutive days. Patients with panic disorder were instructed to press an event marker button on the recorder if a panic attack occurred and to make a diary entry for each attack. This included a 0 – 100 rating of anxiety experienced at the time of the attack, the patient's activities at that time, and the cause, time, and place of attack. Also at the end of each recording hour all subjects had to complete an event diary describing the activities of the preceding hour, and rate their anxiety on a 0 – 100 scale. The DSM-III criteria for panic attacks were reviewed with each patient at an initial interview, immediately before they went home with the recorder and on returning to the laboratory two days later, to ensure that only panic attacks meeting DSM-III criteria were coded as such.

Data were replayed at high speed using an Oxford Medilog PB2 playback system and were manually scored from analogue chart recordings. All parameters were measured hourly and for the five minutes preceding and the five minutes following each panic attack event mark and for control periods having high anxiety ratings but during which attacks did not occur. These periods were chosen using the hourly anxiety rating that matched the ratings of the panic attacks as closely as possible. The effects of ambient temperature on finger temperature were controlled for by subtracting each ambient temperature measurement from each finger temperature measurement.

Table 4.1 shows the average heart rate, temperature, and anxiety rating data for the panic disorder patients and normal subjects. Analyses of variance showed that there were no significant differences between the two groups on any measure or in the patterns of variation of these measures across time. Another set of analyses of variance was used to compare the hourly data of the five patients with panic disorder who had panic attacks during recordings and those of the seven patients who did not. There were again no significant effects from any analysis.

Table 4.1 Heart rates, finger-ambient temperature differences, and anxiety ratings (means ± SD)

	Heart rate (BPM)	Temperature Difference (°C)	Anxiety rating (0 – 100 scale)
Patients	78.3 ± 11.9	4.10 ± 2.34	17.4 ± 16.1
Controls	78.4 ± 8.4	3.14 ± 3.91	13.3 ± 15.1

Eight panic attacks were recorded in five patients; three patients each had two attacks, while the remaining two patients each had one attack. The heart rate data in Figure 4.1 show that seven of eight panic attacks were accompanied by heart rate increases ranging from 16 to 38 beats per minute. In contrast, the heart rate increase during the control periods ranged from 7 to 13 beats per minute. Since the second attack in patient 3 (W.T.) did not appear to show a heart rate increase, the data were reanalysed in six-second blocks. This analysis showed that heart rate actually increased to 100 beats per minute 51 seconds prior to the event mark. In contrast, heart rate during the control period increased to only 80 beats per minute during one six-second epoch. Thus all panic attacks were accompanied by larger heart rate increases than those that occurred during high anxiety control periods.

The finger temperature data usually showed a pattern of vasodilatation prior to the event mark followed by vasoconstriction at the event mark and a subsequent vasodilatation (Figure 4.2). The magnitude of the initial vasodilatation ranged from 0.3 to 2.3 °C for the eight panic attacks compared to 0 to 0.6 °C during the control periods.

A detailed description of the panic attacks for Case 1 (L.W.) has already been published (Freedman *et al.*, 1985). Descriptions of attacks for the remaining patients follow.

Case 2

Patient I.A. had spent the day visiting friends and relatives. She reported anxiety ratings of 20 and 30 while visiting friends. She reported an anxiety rating of 40 while visiting her niece at 6 p.m. At 7 p.m. she went to her fiance's house. At 7:20 p.m. and 9:20 p.m. she had two panic attacks with no reported causes. She reported anxiety ratings of 80 during both attacks. The control sample came from the 8 p.m. time period which occurred between the two panic attacks. The anxiety rating during the control period was 80.

Figure 4.1 shows that during the first attack (solid line) her heart rate remained steady (101–103 bpm) during the five minutes preceding the event mark. Heart rate did not increase until three minutes after the event mark when it reached 111 bpm. During the second attack, heart rate was 80 bpm five minutes prior to the event mark. It increased to a peak of 115 bpm at the event mark and then slowed to 77 bpm five minutes later. During the control period, heart rate ranged from 74 to 82 bpm. The changes were more gradual than those found during the panic attacks.

During the first attack (solid line) finger temperature difference increased from 4.7 °C five minutes before to 5.9 °C at the event mark and then

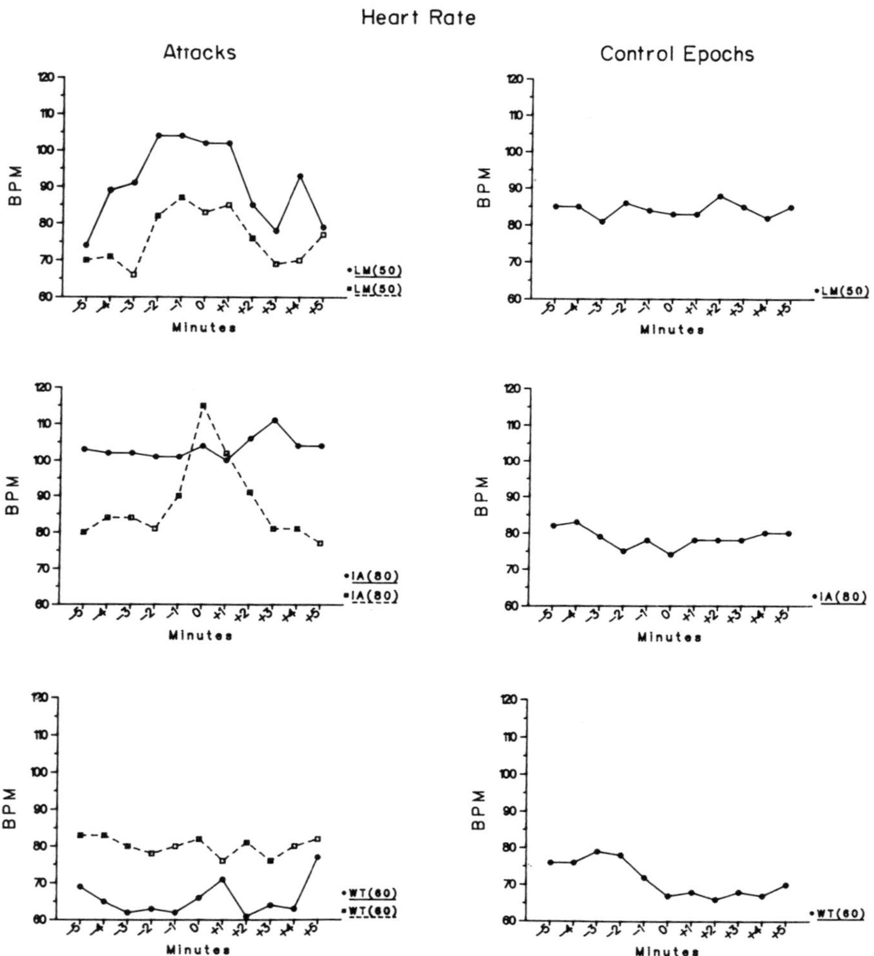
Heart Rate
Attacks
Control Epochs
BPM
Minutes
LM(50)
IA(80)
WT(60)

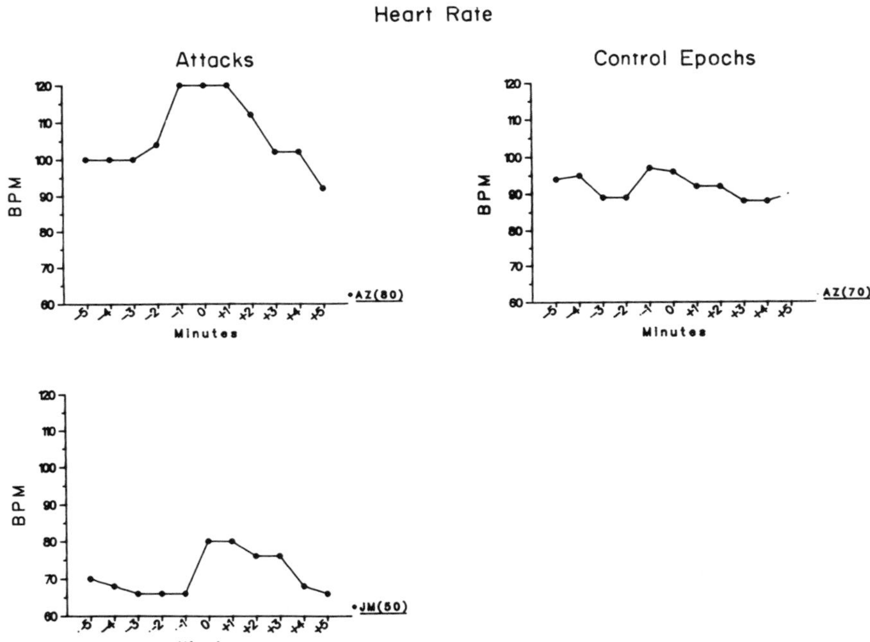

Figure 4.1 Heart rates during panic attacks and high-anxiety control periods. Anxiety ratings are shown in parentheses after initials. Solid lines represent first attack; dotted lines, second attack. (Copyright 1985, American Medical Association. Reprinted, with permission, from Freedman *et al.*, 1985)

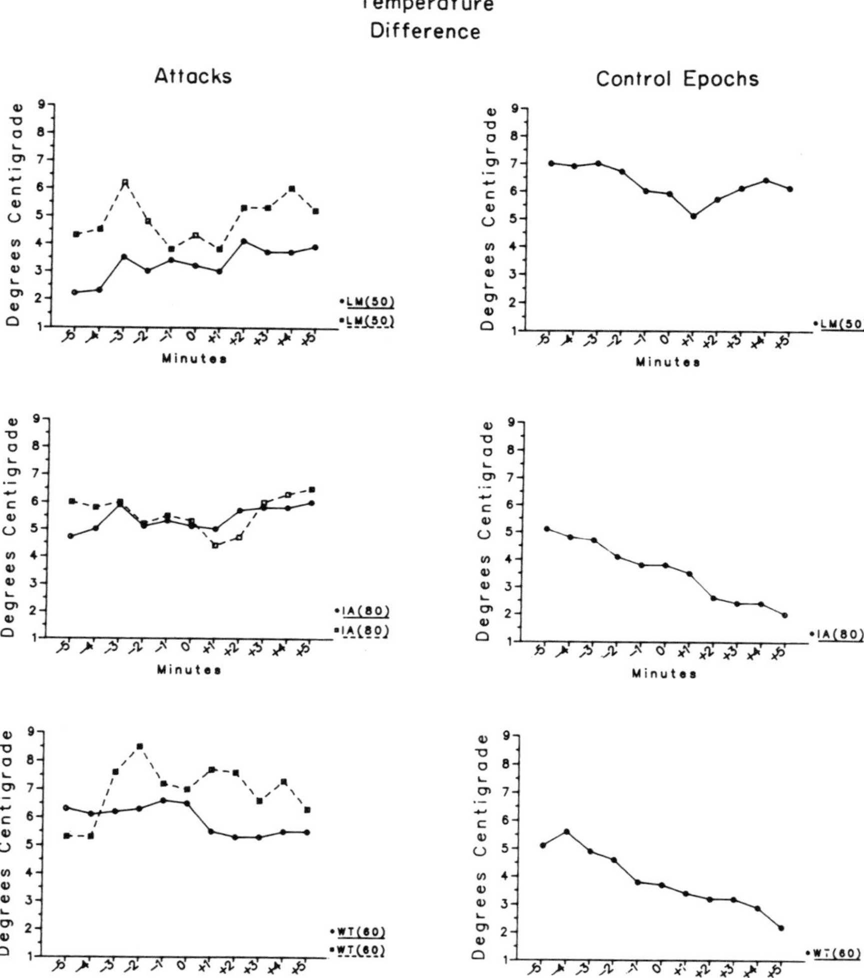
Temperature
Difference
Attacks
Control Epochs
Degrees Centigrade
Minutes
LM(50)
LM(50)
IA(80)
IA(80)
WT(60)
WT(60)

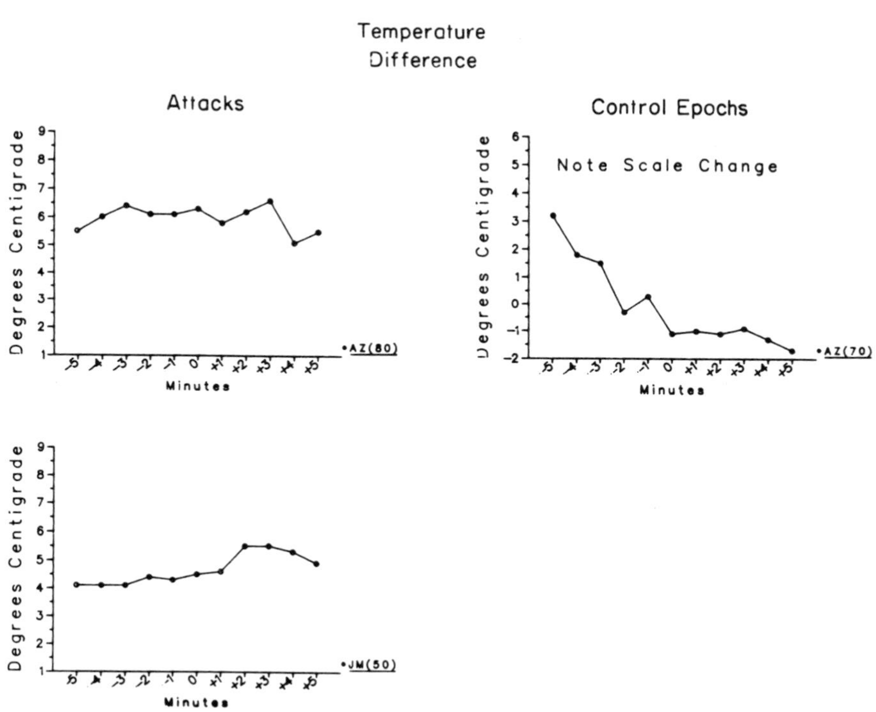

Figure 4.2 Finger–ambient temperature differences during panic attacks and high-anxiety control periods. Anxiety ratings are shown in parentheses after case numbers. Solid lines represent first attack; dotted lines, second attack. (Copyright 1985, American Medical Association. Reprinted, with permission, from Freedman *et al.*, 1985)

decreased to 5.0 °C during the minute following the event mark. It then increased to 6.0 °C over the next four minutes. Thus there was a pattern of vasodilatation followed by vasoconstriction and subsequent vasodilatation. During the second attack, finger temperature differences decreased from 6.0 °C to 4.4 °C and then increased to 6.5 °C. Thus there was a pattern of vasoconstriction followed by vasodilatation. In contrast, during the control period, finger temperature difference showed only a pattern of vasoconstriction beginning at 5.1 °C and ending at 2.0 °C. Thus the high anxiety control period lacked the vasodilatation pattern found during the panic attacks.

Case 3

W.T. had just had a telephone conversation with his homosexual lover whom he had been arguing with. This occurred just after he had begun the Medilog recording. At 10:25 a.m. he pressed the event marker to indicate a panic attack. He reported an anxiety rating of 60 and stated that the attack was caused by thinking about his conversation with his lover. The next day, W.T. had another attack during a phone conversation while his lover was criticizing him. W.T.'s anxiety rating was 60 and he reported the attack was caused by the conversation. During the control period at 5 p.m. the second day, W.T. again reported an anxiety rating of 60 during another phone conversation with his lover.

For the first attack (solid line), heart rate slowed from 69 to 61 bpm during the five minutes prior to the event mark, then increased to 71 bpm during the next two minutes. Heart rate then slowed to 61, 64 and 63 bpm until five minutes after the event mark when it increased to 77 bpm. For the second attack, heart rate changes were generally less pronounced and fluctuated between 76 and 83 bpm. However, during a six-second sample in minute −1, heart rate increased to 100 bpm. During the control period, heart rate tended to slow from 76 to 67 bpm.

Finger temperature difference during the first attack (solid line) showed some dilatation during the five minutes before activation of the event mark (from 6.1 to 6.6 °C). Vasoconstriction then lowered the difference to 5.3 °C for the next three minutes. This was followed by some vasodilatation to 5.5 °C. The second attack's event mark was preceded by vasodilatation from 5.3 °C to 8.5 °C and vasoconstriction to 7.0 °C. From there, finger temperature difference increased to 7.7 °C and then vacillated between vasodilatation and vasoconstriction. Thus the common feature of both attacks was a pattern of vasodilatation followed by vasoconstriction at the event mark and subsequent vasodilatation. The control period, in contrast, showed steady vasoconstriction from 5.1 °C to 2.2 °C.

Case 4

A.Z. was working in his office. He had spent the morning doing routine work and reported anxiety ratings of 30 and 40 at 10 a.m. and 11 a.m. respectively. Shortly after noon he went for a walk and reported an anxiety rating of 60. At 1 p.m. he returned to his desk to face some tougher problems and reported an anxiety rating of 60. At 2 p.m. he began feeling more anxious and at 2:30 p.m. he activated the event marker while reporting an anxiety rating of 80. He felt the attack was caused by working on a difficult problem. The 2 p.m. sample, with an anxiety rating of 70, was used as the control period.

Figure 4.1 shows that heart rate began at 100 bpm. When A.Z. activated the event marker, he was experiencing tachycardia (120 bpm) which lasted for three minutes. Heart rate then decreased to 102 bpm. The control period began with a heart rate of 94 bpm. Thus the magnitude of heart rate change was much greater during the panic attack than during the control period.

Finger temperature difference increased from 5.5 °C to 6.4 °C and then decreased to 5.8 °C immediately after the event mark indicating the attack. Then it increased to 6.6 before decreasing to 5.1 °C. Thus there was a pattern of vasodilatation, followed by vasoconstriction and subsequent vasodilatation which was followed by further vasoconstriction. During the control period, finger temperature difference decreased by +3.2 °C to −1.7 °C, suggesting an overall pattern of vasoconstriction.

Case 5

Patient J.M. had spent the day at home resting, watching TV and doing minor chores. She reported anxiety ratings of 20 throughout the day. Shortly after 8 p.m., her daughter came home from school and told her that another girl in school had threatened to kill her. J.M. became very upset about this and, at 8:15 p.m., indicated she was having a panic attack. She reported an anxiety rating of 50 and stated that she 'felt like her heart was beating fast'. A control period could not be extracted because all other anxiety ratings were 20.

Figure 4.1 shows that her heart rate slowed from 70 to 66 bpm during the five minutes preceding the event mark. When J.M. pressed the event mark, she was experiencing tachycardia (80 bpm). This lasted about four minutes and then her heart rate subsided to 66 bpm.

Finger temperature difference was 4.1 °C five minutes before the event mark. This increased to 5.5 °C during the next seven minutes and then declined. Thus there was a pattern of gradual vasodilatation followed by vasoconstriction.

In summary, panic attacks were accompanied by pronounced physiological changes, in comparison to control periods. All eight attacks had heart rate peaks which were not found during control periods. During six out of eight attacks, the finger temperature difference data suggested a pattern of vasodilatation followed by vasoconstriction prior to the event mark; this was followed by additional vasodilatation. There were no differences in average levels of heart rate, peripheral temperature, or self-reported anxiety between panic disorder patients and normal subjects or between patients who experienced attacks and those who did not.

Studies from other centres

Two investigations have been reported by Taylor *et al.* (1983, 1986) in which panic disorder patients had heart rate and physical activity data recorded using a Vitalog solid state device. In the first study, ten patients were recorded for a single 24-hour period while heart rate was recorded in one minute epochs with a precision of 10 bpm and physical activity was coded in one of eight levels. The latter measure was recorded using a mercury switch motion sensor attached to the lateral thigh with an elastic band. Subjects also completed a diary every 15 minutes consisting of levels of anxiety, panic, and physical activity.

Seven of the 10 patients reported panic attacks during the 24-hour recording period with one patient reporting two attacks. Four of the panic attacks occurred with elevated heart rates, greater than 110 bpm. In three of these attacks, the heart rate increases were significant in relation to level of physical activity; the fourth was not because the subject was physically active at the time of the attack.

In a subsequent investigation (Taylor *et al.*, 1986) 12 patients and 12 control subjects were recorded for six days using the same apparatus. In this study, the Vitalog was programmed to record heart rate with a precision of about 2 beats per minute. On one recording day, a Medicomp ECG monitor was simultaneously used to validate the Vitalog recordings and to determine if the patient was having any arrhythmias. Patients and control subjects also received a treadmill test at four metabolic equivalents. The stored Vitalog data were subsequently replayed on a computer and scored by three observers who were blind to the patient's status and diary data. Heart rate/activity patterns during self-reported panic attacks were compared with those during periods lasting the same intervals as the attacks but exactly 24 hours before or later.

Thirty-three panic attacks were reported by the patients in their diaries. Nineteen (58 per cent) occurred at heart rates disproportionate to activity levels and sufficiently different from surrounding heart rates to indicate a distinct physiologic state. These attacks occurred at a significantly higher heart rate (116.8 ± 24.6 bpm) than the matched heart rates that occurred 24 hours before or after (97.4 ± 21.8). The average heart rate increase was 38.6 ± 4.2 bpm. Six panic attacks occurred during simultaneous ECG monitoring; when elevated the heart-rate rhythm represented sinus tachycardia.

Baseline heart rates were not significantly different for patients (72.1 bpm) and control subjects (68.9 bpm) nor were maximum heart rates during the treadmill test (121.3 and 120.1 bpm, respectively). No panic attacks were reported by the control subjects.

Similar findings were reported in a subsequent study of cardiac rate and rhythm in panic patients (Shear *et al.*, 1987). Twenty-three panic disorder patients received two-channel continuous ECG recordings for one 24-hour period. Tapes were replayed on an Avionics scanner and scored by an experienced electrocardiographer. Ventricular premature complexes (VPC) were graded using the system of Lown and Wolf. Patients also recorded their anxiety levels, thoughts, and feelings in diaries throughout the ambulatory ECG recording period.

Five patients had full-blown panic attacks during the recordings. Average heart rate during the intervals of the reported panic attacks was 108 ± 14 bpm. This was significantly higher than the mean heart rate for the intervals immediately preceding the panic interval in these patients (91 ± 13 bpm). The average daily heart rate for all patients was 79 ± 12 bpm. There were no significant differences between the five patients who had attacks and the 18 who did not with respect to mean daily heart rate or minimum or maximum daily heart rate. Patients who had panic attacks did have a higher daily mean density of VPCs and a higher peak Lown grade during the period of recording than patients who did not have panic attacks.

The authors concluded that 'clinically important ventricular arrhythmias were distinctly uncommon in these patients' and that most symptomatic periods were free of arrhythmias. Thus, although panic disorder may represent an autonomic nervous disturbance, there is no evidence of underlying cardiovascular abnormality in these patients.

Finally, it was of interest to determine if blood pressure elevations occurred during panic attacks in the natural environment. White and Baker (1987) recorded blood pressure and heart rate every 15 minutes in 12 panic disorder patients. Nine of the 12 patients had 13 panic attacks during the 24-hour ambulatory monitoring period; two patients had two attacks, one had four attacks, and the rest had one attack.

Mean heart rate increased from 78 ± 20 bpm prior to the attack to 92 ± 24 bpm during the 15-minute interval containing the attack. Mean systolic blood pressure increased from 126 ± 14 mmHg before the attack to 152 ±

24 mmHg during the attack. Mean diastolic blood pressure increased from 85 ± 10 mmHg pre-attack to 90 ± 11 mmHg during the attack. The increase in systolic blood pressure was significantly correlated with the increase in heart rate.

Like the previous studies, the present investigation confirmed the increase in heart rate seen during panic attacks and adds the fact that blood pressure increases as well. Additionally, normal heart rates and blood pressures were obtained in these patients during non-attack periods.

Comment

Highly consistent findings emerge from the investigations described above. First, it is clear that significant heart rate increases occur during most but not all panic attacks. The magnitude of heart rate increase is dependent in part on the time interval used to analyse the heart rate data and the precision with which heart rate was recorded; analysis of heart rates over shorter time intervals yields heart rate elevations of larger magnitude. In those studies where ECG tracings were examined by an electrocardiographer, the ECG pattern during panic attacks was generally one of sinus tachycardia. Clinically significant cardiac arrhythmias were found to be rare in these patients. The average daily heart rates in panic patients were generally around 78 bpm and did not differ from those of control groups in those studies employing such groups.

Additional evidence suggesting a pattern of increased autonomic activation during panic attacks was obtained. White and Baker (1987) showed that systolic and diastolic blood pressure increased significantly during panic attacks in their patients. Freedman *et al.* (1985) found a pattern of peripheral vasodilatation and vasoconstriction which was not evident during control periods. Diary data generally showed increased anxiety ratings during panic attacks relative to control periods when such ratings were obtained. A number of interesting clinical anecdotes were present in the diary data and suggest that psychological triggers may be present for many panic attacks.

LABORATORY PHYSIOLOGICAL INVESTIGATIONS

Many investigations have been conducted in which heart rate, blood pressure, and other physiological measures were recorded on panic attack patients in the laboratory. Table 4.2 summarizes the results of studies in which physiological measurements were performed on panic disorder patients and control subjects during baseline conditions. The results of these comparisons are considerably less clear than the comparisons of average heart rate and blood pressure data obtained during ambulatory monitoring. The laboratory investigations are inconclusive regarding the issue of whether panic disorder patients show higher levels of physiological activity than normal subjects during baseline conditions. It has been hypothesized previously that anticipatory anxiety regarding the subsequent occurrence of panic attacks in the laboratory accounted for the increased physiological arousal found during baseline conditions. However, three of the investigations in Table 4.2 employed baseline recording sessions in which no drug infusions or other provocative procedures were employed (Roth *et al.*, 1986; Villacres *et al.*, 1987; Roth *et al.*, 1988). The Roth *et al.* studies found higher levels of physiological arousal in patients than in controls despite the absence of such procedures. Conversely, several other studies found no basal differences between the two groups even though provocative measures were subsequently employed. It is possible that anxiety regarding the laboratory situation in general may account for increased physiological arousal in some studies although this remains to be demonstrated.

Table 4.2 Do patients show significantly higher levels of physiological activity than controls during laboratory baseline conditions?

Study	Measure				
	Heart rate	Systolic bp	Diastolic bp	Skin conductance	Panic attacks
Kelly *et al.* (1971)	Y				Y
Freedman *et al.* (1984)	Y			N	Y
Roth *et al.* (1986)	Y			Y	N
Liebowitz *et al.* (1986)	Y	N	Y		Y
Woods *et al.* (1987)	N	Y	N		Y
Villacres *et al.* (1987)	N		N*		N
Cowley *et al.* (1987)	N	Y	Y		Y
Roth *et al.* (1988)	Y			Y	N
Gaffney *et al.* (1988)	N		N*		Y

*Mean arterial pressure.

Table 4.3 summarizes the results of studies in which physiological measures were recorded during non-pharmacological procedures, such as placebo infusions (Freedman *et al.*, 1984; Yeragani *et al.*, 1987) or behavioural provocations (Woods *et al.*, 1987). The results of these investigations are consistent with those of the ambulatory monitoring studies in demonstrating elevated autonomic activity during panic attacks relative to non-attack periods. Additional evidence of increased autonomic activity during panic attacks was found in the Lader and Mathews (1970) and Freedman *et al.* (1984) studies, both of which found increased peripheral vasoconstriction during panic attacks.

Table 4.3 Do patients show elevated levels of physiological activity during non-pharmacological attacks in the laboratory?

Study	Measure			
	Heart rate	Systolic bp	Diastolic bp	Skin conductance
Lader and Mathews (1970)	Y			Y
Freedman *et al.* (1984)	Y			Y
Woods *et al.* (1987)	Y	Y	N	
Yeragani *et al.* (1987)	Y			

CONCLUSION

Ambulatory monitoring studies have been consistent in demonstrating moderate heart rate increases during the majority of panic attacks. Finger temperature fluctuations (Freedman *et al.*, 1985) and blood pressure elevations (White and Baker, 1987) were also found during panic attacks in the two studies where these measures were recorded. These findings are generally consistent with those of non-pharmacological laboratory studies in demonstrating increased autonomic activity during panic attacks. However, no physiological marker has yet emerged which will reliably differentiate panic attacks from non-attack periods. The physiological changes found thus far are generally modest in magnitude and will occur during a variety of activities, such as exercise. It is possible that a physiological marker could be developed using patterns of change of several parameters, an approach that has not yet been tried. Such research will be aided by the recent development of ambulatory monitors capable of recording eight or more physiological parameters simultaneously.

As reviewed above, ambulatory monitoring studies have consistently found no basal differences between patients and controls on any measure, whereas the laboratory findings have been contradictory. Ambulatory monitoring offers the obvious advantages of recording patients in their natural environments over long time periods. The 'demand characteristics' of this technique are no doubt different from those of laboratory procedures and may explain the differences in results.

These advantages must be balanced against the lack of experimental control (e.g. ambient temperature, posture, physical activity level) inherent in ambulatory monitoring and the inability to obtain invasive or technically difficult measures. Ambulatory monitoring equipment is also expensive and not found in many laboratories. In our hospital, we have addressed this problem by sharing the equipment among three laboratories. Patient compliance has not been a problem in our experience of several hundred recordings.

Thus ambulatory monitoring has been a valuable research tool in the investigation of the pathophysiology of panic disorder, but has not yet developed as a routine clinical procedure. Additional knowledge will no doubt be gained by recording additional physiological measures on greater numbers of patients.

REFERENCES

Cowley, D.S., Hyde, T.S., Dager, S.R. and Dunner, D.L. (1987) Lactate infusions: the role of baseline anxiety, *Psychiatry Research*, **21**, 169–79.

Freedman, R.R., Ianni, P., Ettedgui, E., Phol, R. and Rainey, J.M. (1984) Psychophysiological factors in panic disorder, *Psychopathology*, **17**, 66–73.

Freedman, R.R., Ianni, P., Ettedgui, E. and Puthezhath, N. (1985) Ambulatory monitoring of panic disorder, *Archives of General Psychiatry*, **42**, 244–8.

Gaffney, F.A., Fenton, B.J., Lane, L. D. and Lake, C. R. (1988) Hemodynamic, ventilatory, and biochemical responses of panic patients and normal controls with sodium lactate infusion and spontaneous panic attacks, *Archives of General Psychiatry*, **45**, 53–60.

Kelly, D., Mitchell-Meggs, N., and Sherman, D. (1971) Anxiety and the effects of sodium lactate assessed clinically and physiologically, *British Journal of Psychiatry*, **119**, 129–41.

Lader, M. and Mathews, A. (1970) Physiological changes during spontaneous panic attacks, *Journal of Psychosomatic Research*, **14**, 377–82.

Liebowitz, M.R., Gorman, J.M., Fyer, A., Dillon, D., Levitt, M. and Klein, D.F. (1986) Possible mechanisms for lactate's induction of panic, *American Journal of Psychiatry*, **143**, 495–502.

Roth, W.T., Telch, M.J., Taylor, C.B., Sachitano, J.A., Gallen, C.C., Kopell, M.L., McClenahan, K.L., Agras, W.S. and Pfefferbaum, A. (1986) Autonomic characteristics of agoraphobia with panic attacks, *Biological Psychiatry*, **21**, 1133–54.

Roth, W.T., Telch, M.J., Taylor, C.B. and Agras, W.S. (1988) Autonomic changes after treatment of agoraphobia with panic attacks, *Psychiatry Research*, **24**, 95–107.

Shear, M.K., Kligfield, P., Harshfield, G., Devereux, R.B., Polan, J.J., Mann, J.J., Pickering, T. and Frances, A.J. (1987) Cardiac rate and rhythm in panic patients, *American Journal of Psychiatry*, **144**, 633–7.

Taylor, C.B., Telch, M.J. and Havvik, D. (1983) Ambulatory heart rate changes during panic attacks, *Journal of Psychiatric Research*, **17**, 261–6.

Taylor, C.B., Sheikh, J., Agras, W.S., Roth, W.T., Margraf, J., Ehlers, A., Maddock, R.J. and Gossard, D. (1986) Ambulatory heart rate changes in patients with panic attacks, *American Journal of Psychiatry*, **143**, 478–82.

Villacres, E.C., Hollifield, M., Katon, W.J., Wilkinson, C.W. and Veith, R.C. (1987) Sympathetic nervous system activity in panic disorder, *Psychiatry Research*, **21**, 313–21.

White, W.B. and Baker, L.H. (1987) Ambulatory blood pressure monitoring in patients with panic disorder, *Archives of Internal Medicine*, **147**, 1973–5.

Woods, S.W., Charney, D.S., McPherson, C.A., Gradman, A.H. and Heninger, G.R. (1987) Situational panic attacks, *Archives of General Psychiatry*, **44**, 365–75.

Yeragani, V.K., Balon, R., Pohl, R., Ortiz, A., Weinberg, P. and Rainey, J.M. (1987) Do higher preinfusion heart rates predict laboratory-induced panic attacks? *Biological Psychiatry*, **22**, 554–8.

Chapter 5

Personal Accounts of Panic

ROGER BAKER

INTRODUCTION

Panic attacks are highly emotive experiences, often changing the course of a person's life. In the previous chapter, Robert Freedman focused our attention on changes in physiological functioning which occur during panic attacks. Whilst physiological and behavioural measures are essential in the study of panic phenomena, the most fundamental impact for the person involved is the subjective experience of the event. For a full understanding of panic attacks we must somehow tap into this area of subjective experience, laying our findings alongside more objective sources of data. 'Personal accounts' refers to what a person says about his or her experiences, ordered in various ways; it is derived from Allport's usage of 'personal documents' (1951). Primarily it would refer to autobiographies, and the use of research interviews and case studies. It could also include cognitive assessment methods.

In this chapter I will briefly outline these four different approaches to personal accounts. This will be followed by a more extensive discussion of the benefits of personal accounts data, emphasising autobiographical accounts of panic. Lastly a critique of the scientific value of personal accounts data will be presented.

DIFFERENT TYPES OF PERSONAL ACCOUNTS

Cognitive assessment

Cognitive assessment attempts to elicit aspects of a person's ideation using some standardized procedure. It is usually specific and often related closely in time to the event of interest. It is included under 'personal

Panic Disorder: Theory, Research and Therapy. Edited by Roger Baker

accounts' because it does provide a window into the person's subjective world, but under controlled conditions. The most commonly used type of cognitive assessment is the psychometrically designed self-report inventory. Chambless's Agoraphobic Cognitions Questionnaire (Chambless *et al.*, 1984) is an example of one of the more popular and better validated scales. It lists the most common catastrophic thoughts that people have during panic attacks, such as 'I will not be able to control myself', or 'I am going to pass out'. The patient rates the frequency with which such thoughts occur. There are many other scales based on ratings by the patient about their own thoughts, somatic sensations, symptoms or behaviour. The use of structured diary measures is likewise fairly popular in both phenomenological (e.g. Mavissakalian, 1988), and treatment studies (Waddell *et al.*, 1984). Think aloud techniques (Genest and Turk, 1981), thought listing (Cacioppo and Petty, 1981) and imaginal assessment (Anderson, 1981) would seem to offer promise in that they are techniques which are both structured but able to generate a more spontaneous record of thought content than, say, self-report scales. Last *et al.* (1985) conducted an interesting study in which she compared three different assessment methods. Four agoraphobic patients assessed their experience of a five-minute session at a local shopping mall by 'think aloud' techniques (talking into a lapel microphone during the experience), 'thought listing' (immediately recording in writing thoughts that were recalled during the exposure period) and 'imaginal assessment' (visually imagining a scene at the mall and speaking the thoughts into a tape recorder). Last was somewhat disappointed by the lack of convergence of the three methods, though Clark (1988) regards the variability as acceptable. The use of personal construct methodology (Neimeyer and Neimeyer, 1981) differs from other techniques in trying to elicit the patients' constructs for assessment rather than using the constructs as predefined by the investigator. It could potentially reveal useful information about a person's perception of themselves and panic, though there are few, if any, studies reporting its use in panic anxiety.

Case studies

Individual case studies have provided some important data on panic attacks. Cohen *et al.* (1985), for instance, in reporting two instances of patients' reporting panic during relaxation exercises, not only created clinical awareness of this phenomenon but the existence of the phenomenon itself poses some interesting questions about panic. Many clinicians prior to this finding would have expected relaxation to reduce the probability of panic, not actually induce it in some patients. Likewise, Margraf *et al.*'s (1987) single case study in which a patient reported having a panic attack after receiving false heart rate feedback, was theoretically significant in demonstrating the crucial role cognition can play in the generation of panic. Lesser *et al.* (1985) happened to be physiologically monitoring the sleep of an agoraphobic woman when she had a night-time panic attack; during a normal sleep recording for most of the night, relatively late in the night during Delta sleep, the woman suddenly awoke, expressed that she was very frightened and experienced palpitations, shortness of breath, and other panic symptoms. She was not confused, could not recall any dream content and had good recall of the event later. While patients often report night-time panic, the recording of a naturally occurring event helps to validate this phenomenon. The ambulatory monitoring studies of Freedman as reported in Chapter 4 are particularly important as case study material; they manage to capture naturally occurring panic attacks, using controlled measurement (physiological and subjective) and with potentially large samples of patients.

However, in turning to another type of case study, that involving a detailed case history, although these can be found for agoraphobic patients (Goldstein, 1970; Wolpe, 1970; Goldstein and Palmer, 1975) the author could not find one substantial study for a panic disorder patient. Since this is usually regarded as primary clinical data—for instance Westphal's delineation of agoraphobia used case studies—its omission from the literature is rather curious.

Research interviews

Interviews have the advantage of being able to fully use the skills of the clinician interviewer in order to clarify and explore a person's self-report. They vary from structured to open-ended formats, and can be symptomatically, cognitively or phenomenologically based. They can be audio or video taped to allow assessment by others and structured in such a way as to elicit comparable information from a number of subjects.

There have been several studies employing research interviews to explore patients' account of panic, often cognitively oriented. Those of Beck *et al.* (1974) and Hibbert (1984) are particularly useful in providing standard summarized case data on each patient. Several important findings emerge from these studies. Firstly, they clearly indicate that during a panic attack, panic disorder patients really believe that they are in danger (Beck *et al.*, 1974; Hibbert, 1984). They believe that the danger is in the process of occurring (Argyle, 1988). They are terrified of the *outcome* of the experience—fainting, death, losing control, going crazy, etc. (Franklin, 1987). Cognitions are not nearly as dramatic in anxiety patients who have never experienced a panic attack, nor in panic disorder patients during episodes of gradual onset anxiety (Hibbert, 1984; Argyle, 1988).

Secondly, Hibbert's study (1984) indicates that during a panic attack, not only does the content of thought change but so also it would appear that the form of thought does. The danger ideation of panic disorder patients was reported as more intrusive, clearer, harder to exclude from the mind, and more credible during panic than at other times. This channelling of attentional focus could be conceptualized as an abnormal physiological response or as some dysfunctional thought process, although it could equally well be part of a normal response to danger (perceived danger in this case). Additionally, Beck found that 90 per cent of his sample of anxiety patients reported extremely emotive visual imagery during anxiety attacks. Hibbert (1984) only found 32 per cent of his sample who described such visual imagery, cognitions in verbal form being more common.

Thirdly, the interview studies have indicated three levels of antecedents to panic attacks. At the most general level many studies suggest that patients experience a single or a number of stressful life events in the months preceding the first panic attack (Beck *et al.*, 1974; Hibbert, 1984; Breier *et al.*, 1986, Uhde *et al.*, 1985; Faravelli, 1985). At a more temporally proximal level, Hibbert (1984) has identified that for 60 per cent of his sample there was an immediately identifiable period of physiological disturbance at the time of the first panic attack (e.g. delayed air flight causing exhaustion, menopausal flushing and irregular periods, inner ear inflammation). At the most molecular level, somatic sensations have been thought to act as immediate cues to so-called 'spontaneous panic' (Barlow *et al.*, 1985; Ley, 1985). Barlow *et al.* comment that 'our own impression is that cues for panic in both agoraphobics with panic and PD's are usually associated with mild exercise, sexual relations, sudden temperature changes, stress or other cues which alter physiological functioning in some discernible way, albeit out of the patient's awareness', a point also made by several authors in this book.

Undoubtedly studies utilizing research interviews have provided useful data for our understanding of panic. However they all rely on the retrospective recall of subjects about their experiences, suggesting the need for further validational studies.

Autobiographies

Autobiographies—whether comprehensive, topical or edited by another person—are a rather special medium for allowing us to share experiences from the writer's perspective; to get a glimpse of someone else's subjective world. Sustained attention to a single case provides us with a wealth of detailed information, focuses us on concrete examples, and gives a rounded and interrelated picture of an individual's life and experiences. They can be used effectively to teach the basic principles of psychology, enhancing interest in psychology amongst undergraduates (Allport, 1929). As Allport points out (1951) it is curious that autobiographies should be so absorbing to read, quoting Bergson's assertion that such idiographic material has preferential value for the human mind.

The interesting point in examining the autobiographies of panic disorder patients is that none exist!—or at least not in the academic literature that the author has examined; it is possible that popular magazines carry many stories in autobiographical vein. There are however several autobiographies of agoraphobic subjects in which panic attacks often feature very largely. It may be that the concept of 'panic disorder' has not yet sufficiently passed into public consciousness to be used by sufferers as a description of their problem. Alternatively, as Breier *et al*. (1986) suggest, panic disorder might represent an acute stage of what later becomes agoraphobia, and since autobiographies are invariably long-term accounts they may emphasize agoraphobia. In view of the lack of autobiographical data on panic disorder and that substantial case histories are rare, I have mainly drawn illustrations from studies of agoraphobic patients with panic attack. This introduces an obvious bias towards panic attacks rather than panic disorder which should be borne in mind. The reference section indicates the sample of the nine studies that have been used.

THE BENEFITS OF PERSONAL ACCOUNTS DATA

In this section I wish to examine the advantages of personal accounts data using illustrations from autobiographical accounts of panic, some case study data and the findings of research interviews.

Appreciating the suffering

The first important feature offered by personal accounts data is that they help us to appreciate the degree of human suffering involved in panic; concentrating on more objective studies or focusing on the behavioural aspects of panic can take the edge from our sensitivity. Panic is agony.

> I would gladly have sold my soul to the devil for just one day of complete health. I would unhesitatingly have given away everything I had personally and professionally to anyone who could have guaranteed just twenty-four hours of normal health. (Vose, 1981)

> I see a man hobbling past my house on crutches, a cripple for life, and I actually envy him. At times I would gladly exchange places with the humblest day-labourer who walks unafraid across the public square or saunters tranquilly over the viaduct on his way home after the day's work. (Vincent, 1919)

Most autobiographies stress how difficult it is to explain how painful panic is to 'outsiders'—'likened to trying to describe the colour red to a blind person' (Clarke and Wardman, 1985). Frequently writers express the bewilderment that other people show towards their problem, often including their medical practitioner, and several writers report how they resort to lying to hide their problem from others, even though it is out of character.

Law (1975) describes a fairly typical first panic attack which occurred after a prolonged period of hard work and frightening experiences of being blitzed during the Second World War. He had recently married and was taking a much needed holiday in Wales.

> On the morning of the fifth day I went for a haircut and shampoo, arranging to meet my wife later by the big clock near the pier. I had to wait some forty minutes before my turn came to occupy the chair, and I began to feel uneasy. For the first twenty minutes I felt no more than a pleasant langour, a not uncomfortable and unnatural feeling for someone on holiday. This sensation slowly dispersed to be replaced by a growing rigidity I couldn't understand. I began to long for the procedure to be over, I longed to get outside again. I felt I would be all right once I got out into the sparkling sunlight.
>
> Yet to get up and leave would have seemed absurd, especially after waiting so long. The haircut itself went off all right, the barber chatting away blithely. I bent over the bowl for the shampoo, and the tension began to build up again. With tremendous relief I sat back and waited for my hair to be dried. Usually, of course, an electric hot-air blower was used for this purpose, but this establishment didn't seem to boast such modern luxuries. The man picked up a towel and rubbed away vigorously.
>
> . . . sensations stronger and stranger than any I had previously known charged through my body. My throat seemed on fire; it screamed for water; gasping, my heart thundering away, I thought my hour had come. I jumped up, threw money towards the barber, and stumbled into the street.
>
> Trembling violently, I staggered towards the clock at the head of the pier. Desperately I looked around for my wife; at that moment I felt only the appearance of Joyce would save me. There was no sign of her, and another seizure, even more powerful, came swiftly upon me. I tried to walk away, but I couldn't. I held myself rigidly, my legs seemed fastened to lead weights, but I managed to move a yard or so. My whole body jerked as though subjected to an electric shock. Coiled up like steel wire, I turned and twisted to try to remove the devilish feelings that possessed me. I closed my eyes, but this made matters worse. Head swimming, a flash of light seemed to flood into me increasing in power and evil.

> Almost screaming, collapsing to my knees, I shook my head violently. Everything seemed to disintegrate. Twitching and trembling, I tried to thrust the evil sensations from me. The taking of breath was almost impossible and my heart was racing. My throat was burning, it closed like a vice, and each time I moved a fear-riddled spasm charged through me.
>
> Gasping hard, I staggered to my feet in an effort to escape from this evil thing that threatened to rob me of my identity, of my life. Through glazed eyes I frantically searched round for Joyce, but all I could see was the ghostly outline of people passing to and fro and past me.
>
> Heart thudding, my body pouring sweat, I made a final effort in a grotesque struggle for air and for life. Despairingly, I threw myself into the road. Then someone was trying to lift me, speaking to me and supporting me.
>
> 'What's the matter?' said a man's voice. 'What's the matter?'

Accounts obviously differ in detail but invariably illustrate the fear, confusion and despair engendered in the sufferer.

Understanding minutiae of experience

Secondly, personal accounts data help to provide us with a more detailed account of the experience of sufferers. They provide the minutiae of experience that is necessary to get a real 'feel' of the phenomenon, and details suggesting the way in which experience and behaviour relate.

Wayne Wardman was a general practitioner who was successfully treated for panic-anxiety and agoraphobia (Clarke and Wardman, 1985). The following extract is an illustration of the sort of detail personal reports data can provide. He is describing one way in which concentration can be affected by anxiety. (Wardman's 'internal sentences' are in parentheses.)

> Friend: ' Hi! How are you?'
> Self: 'I'm very well, thanks. Are you?' (Boy, it's hard enough being over this side of the hospital alone, without bumping into an obstacle like this? I hope he doesn't notice how nervous I am.)
> Friend: 'Yes. Have you come to see that new patient?'
> Self: (My car is too far away!) 'Yes, she needs some more investigating.' (My pulse is racing and my hands are shaking— *I know* it's obvious.)
> Friend: 'Are you going to the party tonight?'
> Self: (I know where my car is but it's a long way—I don't like being held up like this.) 'Um . . . I beg your pardon?'

A similar sort of interchange is quoted in *The Autobiography of David —* (Raymond, 1946, p. 92).

Sufferers often report how the weather or time of day or year affects their panic anxiety. Vincent (1919) reports 'some of the most stormy days of the hard winters of this region stand out as bright spots in my life,' and how 'darkness has a quieting effect on me.' 'I love a snowstorm, a regular blizzard, and feel much less discomfort in going about the town or riding on a train on such days, probably because one's view is obstructed.' Likewise Mrs F.H. (1952) reports 'At night I could go about more freely than in daylight without the dread fear that I couldn't get home, because . . . in the dark I couldn't see the things that prevented me from going home.' On the other hand Wardman (1985) found his condition worse in winter, and 'the greatest difficulty was a night when there was the added loss of visual access to "safety."' Likewise Vose (1981) reports, 'Winter was particularly hard to bear, since there were no leaves on the trees or hedges, and no high banks of weed in ditches to retreat to if panic struck. I was noticeably worse with agoraphobia in winter than in summer, and the simple reason was the lack of foliage.' All four patients were motivated by a fear of a panic striking. However Wardman and Vose needed to see 'safety' signals to be at ease, while Vincent and Mrs F.H. were helped by not seeing the 'blockages' that kept them from the safety of home. Owing to the selection bias inherent in autobiographies and (often) in case histories it is important to place these observations against more systematically derived information such as in a well constructed survey. Burns and Thorpe (1977) for instance found 56 per cent of their agoraphobic sample were averse to cloudy overcast weather. Despite the useful degree of systematization yielded by a survey, minutiae of experience and behaviour are not always present in a survey.

In most autobiographies there is one link between experience and behaviour that shouts out quite loudly; that is the amount of extraneous behaviour that develops around a panic. There are, for instance, escape routes—'going shopping bears all the resemblance to planning a train robbery. Lines of escape must be worked out all the way, and as long as the "rabbit runs" exist on any outing it can usually be tolerated' (Vose, 1981). The actual nature of escape routes can be quite unusual.

> On one occasion while walking up a very steep incline in the street I was seized with panic on noticing a space ahead. Could I negotiate it? My limbs trembled and a cold sweat broke over me as I glanced about for some refuge or 'cover'. Suddenly my eye lighted on a barrow with a large awning. It was heavily laden, and the hawker was pushing it uphill with great difficulty. Here was my chance to secure a 'shelter' in which to go 'over the top', as it were, across the space. I dashed at the barrow with what must have seemed furious zeal and shoved like a Trojan. Together we went up the hill at record speed; and the amazed hawker when he got to the top seized my hand and thanked me in terms full of gratitude, remarking, in a confidential way, that the war had made a big difference, and that there was a real feeling of comradeship now. I thought it best not to disillusion him.

Sufferers often develop their own individual methods to save themselves from the feared consequences of a panic attack, once it begins—such as holding on to people or objects, distracting themselves, deep breathing, repeated thoughts 'nothing's going to happen to me; nothing's going to happen to me', drinking water, taking tablets, lying down, running etc. The many unusual covert and overt habits that patients engage in through fear of a panic can be reasonably well understood from personal accounts data.

Though detailed current aspects of behaviour may be understood from an account, this does not mean that it is easy to trace the fundamental etiology of a condition through personal accounts. Etiology is difficult to assess under almost any circumstances (e.g. Harris and Brown, 1985), including personal accounts. Though Leonard (1928) attempts to trace the basic etiology for his agoraphobia in his autobiography, he has to admit defeat; though it may be possible for others who read his account to make hypotheses about etiology in an individual case (as Taylor and Culler did, 1929). Most of the writers of the present sample of autobiographies advance no ultimate theory about the development of their problem, restricting themselves to a description of its form and development and to more obvious and concrete explanations about specific aspects of behaviour.

Developmental continuity

Thirdly, personal accounts in the form of autobiographies, case histories and to some extent research interviews and survey data, provide a historical continuity and sense of development of panic which a single 'slice' from an experimental study usually cannot. The patient's life setting, relationships and personality help provide a fuller backdrop to the development of panic. For instance, in reading Raymond's excellent account *The Autobiography of David* — or Leonard's rather over-inclusive but fascinating *The Locomotive-God* one gets a vivid impression of the childhood and adolescence of the writers which is congruent with the emergence of panic in their lives. In case studies one does not get such a sense of a pattern unfolding in time since the interviewer has already made various connections between personal background and symptomatology, and presents these before us. Vines (1987) in *Agoraphobia: the Fear of Panic* lays out three case histories conducted in a uniform manner which help to illustrate the complex interaction of a number of factors in the development of panics and phobias. Goldstein and Palmer (1975), in the case of Veronica F. likewise systematically present the phenomenology, past history and course of treatment which emphasizes the significance of the person's background in the development of panic.

Another sense in which personal accounts data provide a developmental continuity is in the stage after the first few panic attacks, when the problem begins to elaborate and seriously affect the lifestyle of the person, the 'incubation' period described by M. Von Korff•and W. Eaton in Chapter 3. In this respect there are several interview-based studies which examine the relationship between the first panic attack and subsequent psychological disturbances. Breier *et al.* (1986) found that for agoraphobic and panic disorder patients anticipatory anxiety, agoraphobia and generalized anxiety disorder started after the first panic attack. The development of depression, obsessive compulsive disorder, and alcoholism did not closely relate to the initial panic attack. The studies of Uhde *et al.* (1985), Franklin (1987) and Thyer and Himle (1985) confirm the finding that pathological degrees of anxiety and avoidance behaviour develop after, rather than before, panic attacks in most patients. Raskin *et al.* (1982) additionally confirm that episodes of depression do not relate as clearly to initial panic attacks. Breier *et al.*'s (1986) study suggests that the patient's cognitive appraisal of the first panic attack relates to the later development of agoraphobic avoidance. According to self-report, patients who perceived their first panic attack as a form of anxiety (25 per cent) had a significantly longer interval before the onset of agoraphobic avoidance than those who perceived it as a life-threatening event (75 per cent). Breier illustrates the role of attribution with this example:

> two patients who were pregnant at the time of their first panic attacks were told by their obstetricians that the attacks were a 'normal' part of pregnancy and not to worry about them. Both patients accepted this explanation as plausible. No further panic attacks occurred at that time, and no phobic behaviour developed until later (11 months and 10 years respectively) when panic attacks recurred when they were not pregnant. At this point, the patients had no explanation for the attacks and immediately developed agoraphobia.

Franklin (1987) examined the changing nature of three aspects of fear in agoraphobic patients; autonomic sensations, situational fears and fears about outcome (loss of control, dying, fainting or collapsing, etc). Patients reported outcome fears as the most important at the time of the first panic. Over time, situational fears had worsened and outcome fears proportionately lessened, so that by the time of Franklin's interview the situational fears were reported as almost as severe as the outcome fears.

Insights about treatment

The treatment process

Personal accounts can also help us to understand how patients perceive our treatment regimes and may provide clues about the treatment process. DuPr (1982) provides sequential diary extracts from 'Marie' whose agoraphobic symptoms were treated using graded exposure. There are concurrent reports by two therapists who directed her programme. It is interesting to note the different way in which the patient and therapists perceived the treatment. In retrospect Marie felt that for several weeks she had been 'groping around', not understanding the rationale of exposure. She wished 'it had been made clear to me that seeking the high levels (of anxiety), not necessarily hitting them, was the important thing', and also wished her therapist had been a former phobic patient. Other patients (e.g. Vose, 1981) likewise express initial confusion about the rationale of behavioural exposure, often emerging with their own idiosyncratic rules about why they are doing it and how it should best be achieved.

Strangely enough, some patients in searching towards a cure for their panic anxiety, spontaneously hit upon particular therapeutic techniques. The most devastatingly persistent application of exposure treatment is documented in detail two decades before exposure treatment was developed! Mrs F.H. (1952) had suffered from serious phobias of light, and agoraphobia, for twenty years, had seen many psychiatrists (psychoanalytically oriented), and had been in and out of psychiatric hospitals.

> In attempting to tell as precisely as possible just what did happen, I find I have no real explanation to offer about it. That part seems, even as I write of it, shrouded in mystery. But, one day, suddenly, without warning, a blob of buried stuff cut itself loose from its moorings in the hinterland of my unconscious, and came out into the open. What I saw, I saw clearly, and *without* fear.
>
> In the days that followed I took counsel with myself and argued that if a certain part of the content of my unconscious had broken out of its Pandora's box, then it was possible for more to be discovered. So I decided to get along with the job of trying to track down the horrid 'appearances' which troubled me, to find out what they were, and to rid myself of them. It was a challenge that I had to accept, and I accepted it . . . Since walking alone in broad daylight was my worst hazard I set myself the task of going out every day in order to bring up my fears in all their might.

Over a period of months Mrs F.H. threw herself without mercy into situations that would evoke the worst possible fears, keeping a written and spoken record of events. She relates how she completely recovered from her phobias and how with each different exposure to her fears she experienced memories, images or thoughts which helped her to piece together the origins and development of her disorder.

Stanley Law (1975) describes the system of treatment that he developed by trial and error during the 1950s and 1960s: 'I was convinced that my system of "applied imagination" during relaxation was effective and beneficial. I knew also, that "controlled breathing" was vitally necessary in helping to stabilize panic attacks. I had further proved to myself that "muscle contraction" exercises greatly diminished muscle tension and fatigue.' His 'applied imagination' is very similar to Wolpe's systematic desensitization (he seems to be unaware of Wolpe's work) except it focused more on imaginal control of feelings than the relationship of relaxation and fear stimuli—

> I learned to gradually create or quickly diminish the most intense feelings of peace or terror. I would, for example, concentrate on a particularly tranquil scene, concentrate on it intently for about ten minutes. A deep feeling of rest would result, a feeling of infinite relaxation of the soul and mind. Deliberately I would attain and then disturb this condition, introducing into the field of tranquillity a rampaging bull. With picture after picture I would tear the beatitude to shreds, gradually bringing on tremors and the usual physical and mental distress. I would then deliberately wipe away the disturbing visions, replacing them with the original scenes of serenity. And then, eventually, I became able to attain serenity almost at will.

Law, like Mrs F.H., is an account of complete recovery.

Not all accounts are of recovery. In *The Autobiography of David* — (Raymond, 1946) the subject relates how psychoanalytical therapy, through increased introspection, challenging his value system and presenting the idea that cure was dependent on unearthing his complex, worsened his condition.

> My greatest trouble was that I could not put the thought of psychoanalysis from my mind. It haunted me. 'Your complex has not been discovered . . . It is no use pretending to yourself that you are normal . . . You are abnormal . . . You cannot be cured without psychoanalysis . . . You are unable to stand analysis.' Such thoughts drove through my mind like balls of fire. I felt I was really going mad.

Likewise Leonard (1928) who tried a number of different approaches to treatment met with complete failure, eventually adjusting his life style around his phobic difficulties.

Vose's autobiographical account (1981) is perhaps the most complete gourmet guide to the treatment of anxiety. She personally seems to have gone through most existing therapies including drug treatment, behaviour therapy, psychotherapy, hypnotism, carbon dioxide therapy, herbal/dietary remedies, and the approach that resulted in her final recovery—OBD. Organic brain dysfunction therapy is practised by a private institute for neuro-physiological psychology. The (unproven) premise on which it operates is that the physiological symptoms of agoraphobia and panic disorder are the result of difficulties in functioning caused by small faults in the central nervous system; such difficulties may be overcompensated for, and these overcompensations can themselves cause problems. Vose, after intensive testing at the Institute, was told she had a 'spinal (galant) primitive reflex of the right-hand side of my spine, plus a defective labyrinthine righting reflex'. Her therapy involved certain exercises designed to remove incorrect compensations and promote the correct reflexes. Ruth Vose fortunately had a mechanically-minded husband who built several large pieces of equipment which would rotate or spin a human body in a variety of positions: prone, supine, sitting, moving up and down—so that complete vestibular stimulation of the semicircular canals in the inner ear became possible.

> The first time I was spun round on one of the pieces of equipment, within minutes I got all my agoraphobic symptoms: dizziness, nausea and the desire to vomit and defaecate. Gradually I managed to take longer periods of the exercises.

Day by day she persisted in the 'exercises'. This would appear to be a crucial point in her complete recovery. This approach closely resembles interoceptive exposure as described by Rapee and Barlow in Chapter 11, and it is more than likely that this rather than OBD with its somewhat doubtful premises, contributed so much towards Vose's recovery. Unfortunately Vose stresses OBD as a possible cure for agoraphobia which has to some extent influenced one of the UK self-help organizations (Neville, 1986). This illustrates the care with which we should approach an individual's interpretation about the cause of their recovery; it must be compelling to assume that when a treatment is so obviously effective it was effective for the reasons espoused by the therapist.

Communicating treatment concepts

Personal accounts data are also relevant to treatment in that they can help in communicating ideas to patients. Several autobiographies suggest there is a real need for professionals to properly communicate information about panic. McKinnon (1983), as with many sufferers, visited her local medical practitioner after her first panic attack.

> The local doctor assured me that there was nothing seriously wrong with me, and that I was over-tired and run down. As he knew the stresses we had been under within the family during those years, he emphasised these and said I just needed a good rest. He was inclined to insist jovially that my experience was just a simple faint due to fatigue and he did not seem able to explain any of the unpleasant sensations I had experienced. The word 'panic' was not mentioned at all . . . I wanted to know what caused an attack so that it could be prevented from happening again. The only answer forthcoming was the repeated phrase that I had nothing to worry about and that I was simply 'on edge'. I found this difficult to accept. How could being 'on edge' cause such a dreadful feeling of illness?

Earlier I mentioned that a clear presentation of therapeutic rationale seemed an important aspect of exposure treatment; likewise a clear and informed explanation about the nature of panic would appear to be one of the most important initial communications between a therapist and a patient. Indeed education comprises the first component of therapy in several approaches to panic as, for instance, described in the chapters by Rapee and Barlow, Durham, and McFadyen, in this book.

Concrete experiences of patients, personal details and personal accounts of problems loom large in most self-help booklets. The most immediate appeal of quoting personal reports is that they presumably help the patient absorb and understand the required concepts better. The more patients can identify with the illustrative descriptions the more compliance we assume there will be. Strangely, the written word, and possibly videos too, command an authority which sometimes the therapist does not. Having spent many sessions unsuccessfully trying to explain the principle of sensitization to a patient he returned, to my chagrin, in one session informing me that he had read Claire Weekes's book *Peace from Nervous Suffering*, and felt that his problem was sensitization! Dr Weekes's books, of course, contain many examples at the experiential level which the sufferer can readily recognize and identify with.

Generating new hypotheses

Fifthly, personal accounts provide the material for new ideas and hypotheses. Traditionally this has been viewed as their only point of scientific value although Runyan (1984) argues that personal accounts documents have scientific validity in their own right.

Patients themselves offer various hypotheses about their behaviour. They are most useful when fairly specific, and factual, but particularly weak when patients attempt to advance wider theories of the phenomenon, generalizing from their own experience. They are also weak when the subject has too passionately assimilated some psychological approach or theory, and an otherwise reasonably raw account becomes swamped with interpretation.

While hypotheses suggested by the subject have to be approached with caution, they are sometimes worth considering for further, more systematic, study. For instance, Vose felt that more appropriate understanding in handling of her own emotions led to a reduction in somatic symptoms—

> As I gradually became more self-aware, I noticed distinct correlations between my various physical and nervous symptoms. If I suppressed any aggression, I

> would get colitis, fear of cancer resulted in lumps, anger resulted in vomiting, repressed speech (fear of saying what I really felt) resulted in sore throats . . . I found that if I tackled the underlying problem (for example, let my anger out rather than keep it in), the physical symptoms would automatically disappear.

Interestingly the failure to recognize and express emotion is echoed in Wolpe and Lazarus's (1966) now famous *Behaviour Therapy Techniques*. Mrs M.S. was referred for hyperventilation, panic, feelings of depersonalization and depression. Wolpe describes the appallingly enclosed world in which she lived, dominated emotionally and financially by her father-in-law and enforced by her husband. Her panic was successfully treated, not just by systematic desensitization, but by Wolpe helping her 'to see that her submission and inhibited reactions were responsible for her recurrent bouts of depression and her attacks of panic'. Vines (1987) describes the treatment of one agoraphobic patient in detail—again it is interesting that a marked improvement appeared after one session in which

> I suggested that one way of getting in touch with the feelings of anger she had expressed so clearly was to sit down and write a letter to her parents indicating how she felt about them. The letter was to be as angry as she felt, allowing her to explore all the feelings she repressed. It was not to be a letter to put in the post, but one in which she could articulate the forbidden and hidden parts of herself as honestly as possible.

Wardman noted that after one panic attack in a day a subsequent panic was less likely. 'It is as though having expended energy on one panic the "reserve supply" of anxiety, as it were, were somehow depleted.' He makes specific suggestions for the spacing of exposure sessions based on his personal experiences.

Another aspect of this is that autobiographies in particular have an advantage in that they are not usually structured according to present theories and approaches, but the writer can determine his own structure and include and exclude according to his or her own constructs. While this can introduce bias it can also mean that phenomena or emphases, overlooked in the academic literature, emerge—and some rather surprisingly. What, for instance, do we make of this experience which occurred at the height of a panic attack?

> Attempting to summon strength for self-possession from the depths of my being . . . I chanced to sweep the heavens from above Eagle Height and Black Hawks Cave, past the glare of the sun, riding high over the ancient Winnebago Camping grounds. Was the impact from outer space of that great light on my eyeballs the fearful stimulus? I don't know. But the summer's cloud to the left of the sun, with all its arcs of white and gold, kaleidoscoped in one onrush, into a vision of two tremendous shining horses head on, before

> a canopied chariot, in which was a bearded man and a fair young woman, that *felt* to me like the Last Judgement. And over to the woods, farther to the left, on my side of the lake, pictured in the unclouded blue regions, stood a gigantic negress in a red-and-black plaid bodice. An apocalypse. To me it was not alone a vision but a destroying menace. The horses and chariots were dashing at me. *This* at last was no mere *feel* . . . this was complete hallucination in all three dimensions of space . . . Literally, the vision knocked me down. I collapsed to my knees. It lasted at most a few seconds—possibly but four or five. I cannot say. The negress lasted longest over the woods. I leapt up, chattering aloud: 'Miracles are impossible; miracles are impossible'.

The sufferer was not psychotic but was describing part of the sequence of his first major panic attack. True, he was a Professor of English (Leonard, 1928) and the language somewhat poetic, but he made considerable efforts to ensure that the memory of his experiences was accurate, according to a set of psychological criteria, checking details with eye witnesses and notes that he kept, and involving two psychologists in the process of memory recall (Taylor and Culler, 1929). Interestingly, a very similar illusion was described during a full panic in the case of Mrs M.F. (1952, p. 171).

CRITIQUE AND CONCLUSION

Personal accounts data in the different formats described in this chapter would appear to be illuminating and have a place in contributing to our understanding of panic. The case for the scientific validity of autobiographies and case histories has been ably presented elsewhere (respectively, by Allport, 1951; De Waele and Harre, 1979; Runyan, 1984; Bromley, 1986), but there are certain methodological issues which should be highlighted in assessing the status of personal accounts in panic disorder.

One of the most serious problems with personal accounts data is that they generally rely on retrospective recall of experiences, sometimes in the relatively short term, such as in 'thought listing' after an event, or in the longer term, such as the recollections about childhood in a lifetime autobiography. Both M. Von Korff and W. Eaton, and J. Margraf and A. Ehlers, in their respective chapters in this book, quote evidence of memory distortion when people recalled panic attacks. There is also evidence that autobiographical memories are distorted in depressed patients (Williams and Scott, 1988). Wittchen *et al.*, (1989) indicate that recall of the date of the first panic attack is unreliable. Obviously the longer the interval of time the more opportunity there is for distortion, loss or bias in recall, for over-simplification, *post hoc* rationalization, or imposing one's present viewpoint and values on earlier events. Indeed Meichenbaum and Cameron (1981), in presenting guidelines for self-reports, suggest that the enquiry should be conducted as soon as possible after the cognitive event of interest. Self-report inventories differ in relying on recognition rather than recall, and many investigators (e.g. Glass and Arnkoff, 1982) argue that item endorsement may not reflect actual thought content. Clark's (1988) review of cognitive assessment indicates that no single approach—*in vivo* versus delayed, recall versus recognition—was consistently superior to another, and that there was discordance between different methods.

Runyan (1984) has argued that retrospective recall is not intrinsic to case studies and case histories. He points out that case studies can, and often do, rely on systematic longitudinal studies, can use prospective 'follow up' methods, and use alternative data such as letters, diaries, observations by contemporaries, archival data, etc. (e.g. Levy's study on *Maternal Overprotection*, 1966). Allport (1951) does not consider memory errors too serious in autobiographies. Such errors 'are not especially troublesome, for the very fact that the subject structures and recalls his life in a certain manner is what we want to know. Furthermore, it is unlikely (barring repression) that individuals will forget the emotional, ego-charged, personality-forming experiences in their lives. Inaccurate as testimony often is in respect to detail, the memory for salient facts, for atmosphere, and for experiences most closely related to the self is trustworthy.' Certainly panic attacks are experiences that are often seared into a person's memory, and one is surprised at the detail the person may recall many years later.

The representativeness of the sample needs attention in personal accounts, particularly in autobiographies and case studies. In most of the interview studies quoted in this chapter, selection was by consecutive referral of patients to a specialist clinic: some operated exclusion or inclusion criteria. In the autobiographical studies quoted, one problem in sampling has already been mentioned; patients chose to label themselves 'agoraphobic', not as having 'panic disorder'. This particular sample is also unrepresentative in the number of journalists and writers amongst them (five out of nine accounts), and proportionally greater number of males than would be expected (five out of nine). It would be possible to control for non-representation by, for instance, asking a more representative group to prepare autobiographical material according to a predefined protocol.

There are also a number of problems which hinge upon one's accepted approach to psychological science. To say that personal accounts are not 'scientific' merely begs the question as to the nature of real science. Strict adherence to the view that scientific data must be objective would rule out the use of personal accounts, which by definition are subjective. However, it would virtually eradicate the study of panic disorder; how could a patient be diagnosed in the first instance without a personal account from him or her, and how could one determine the onset, intensity and duration of a panic? Some would criticize personal accounts on the ground that one cannot generalize from individual studies. One solution has already been mentioned—that is by the use of a series of case studies, research interviews or autobiographies collected in a uniform manner. However, the need to generalize is based on acceptance of a nomothetic approach to science; if one adopts an idiographic approach, which regards the study of the individual as 'the only possible way of obtaining the granite blocks of data on which to build a science of human nature' (Murray, 1955) one could equally argue that it is impossible to particularize from a group study. In practice, the greatest benefit is probably to be derived from using nomothetic and idiographic approaches reciprocally.

A number of steps can be taken to try to meet these and other criticisms. These might include:

—Giving subjects a set that promotes honest and full accounts, asking them to describe their experiences, not explain or provide motives.

—Using measures of self-report which are open to public scrutiny such as unedited video or audio tapes, or verbatim transcripts.

—Using other assessors/interviewers to provide an independent assessment.

—Combining as many different sources and types of data as possible, for instance interviewing significant others about events, using different types of psychological or behavioural assessment, and using correlative data from diaries and journals, archives, newspapers, reports, letters, etc.

—If possible constructing a prospective study.

—Ensuring that the event and the account of it is as close as possible in time, or at least using correlative data such as a daily diary to act as a memory prompt.

—Using a clearly predesigned protocol for data collection/recall, for editing and analysis, made public before the study begins and adhered to throughout the study. Also providing information about the background and orientation of the interviewers.

—Use of certain validity checks, which could include checking for internal consistency of the report (accuracy of time sequence, plausibility, probability) (Runyan, 1984), critically examining the organization of a case study against certain rudimentary rules (Bromley, 1986), attempting to refute the account with alternative explanations (Runyan, 1984), assessing motivation and degree of self-deception of reporter, checking the accuracy of the person's recall in experimental studies, use of norms for autobiographical memory (Borrini *et al* 1989), etc.

—Assuring anonymity for autobiographical data.

Interestingly the two autobiographies which stand out most in the present group as being the more complete and reliable records were those in which there was the most effort to adhere to proper standards of reporting. Leonard, in his autobiography, *The Locomotive-God* (1928) went to particular lengths to ensure accuracy of recall, claiming it was 'the most accurate autobiography ever written', and in *The Autobiography of David* — (1946), the subject asked a renowned journalist, Ernest Raymond, to construct his autobiography, providing him with a wealth of journal and diary material, newspaper articles, photographs, pamphlets, and letters to him from well-known and little known people over a forty-year period, and leaving all editorial decisions to Raymond, who clearly describes his editorial criteria.

There is a well-known anecdote of the man who had lost his keys on one side of the street at night. A passer-by saw him searching for the keys beneath the lamp-post on the *opposite* side of the street and enquired why he was looking for them there. 'Well the light is so much better here', was the reply. Although the problems of personal accounts data are many we should not abandon them because the 'light is better elsewhere', but attempt to develop and refine methodology to derive the fullest possible benefit. In particular, in panic and anxiety, we cannot afford to overlook the subjective dimension.

REFERENCES

Note: The references marked with an asterisk are those autobiographies referred to in this chapter.

Allport, G.W. (1929) The study of personality by the intuitive method: an experiment in teaching from the Locomotive God, *Journal of Abnormal and Social Psychology*, **24**, 14–27.

Allport, G.W. (1951) The use of psychological documents in psychological science, Social Science Research Council, New York.

Anderson, M.P. (1981) Assessment of imaginal processes: approaches and issues. In T.V. Merluzzi, C.R. Glass and M. Genest (eds), *Cognitive Assessment*, Guilford, New York.

Argyle, N. (1988) The nature of cognitions in panic disorder, *Behaviour Research and Therapy*, **26**, 261–4.

Barlow, D.H., Vermilyea, J., Blanchard, E.B., Vermilyea, B.B., DiNardo, P.A. and Cerny, J.A. (1985) The phenomenon of panic, *Journal of Abnormal Psychology*, **94**, 320–8.

Beck, A.T., Lande, R. and Bohnert, M. (1974) Ideational components of anxiety neurosis, *Archives of General Psychiatry*, **31**, 319–25.

Borrini, G., Dall'ora, P., Sala, S.D., Marinelli, L., and Spinnler, H. (1989) Autobiographical memory. Sensitivity to age and education of a standardized enquiry, *Psychological Medicine*, **19**, 215–24.

Breier, A. Charney, D.S. and Heninger, G.R. (1986) Agoraphobia with panic attacks: development, diagnostic stability, and course of illness, *Archives of General Psychiatry*, **43**, 1029–36.

Bromley, D.B. (1986) *The Case-study Method in Psychology and Related Disciplines*, John Wiley, Chichester.

Burns, L.E. and Thorpe, G.L. (1977) The epidemiology of fears and phobias, *Journal of International Medical Research*, **5** (supplement 5), 1–7.

Cacioppo, J.T. and Petty, R.E. (1981) Social psychological procedures for cognitive response assessment: the thought-listing technique. In T.V. Merluzzi, C.R. Glass and M. Genest (eds), *Cognitive Assessment*, Guilford, New York.

Chambless, D.L., Caputo, G.C., Bright, P. and Gallagher, R. (1984) Assessment of fear of fear in agoraphobics: the body sensations questionnaire and the agoraphobic cognitions questionnaire, *Journal of Consulting and Clinical Psychology*, **52**, 1090–7.

Clark, D.A. (1988) The validity of measures of cognition: a review of the literature, *Cognitive Therapy and Research*, **12**, 1–20.

Clark, J.C. and Wardman, W. (1985) *Agoraphobia: A Clinical and Personal Account*, Pergamon, Sydney.*

Cohen, A.S., Barlow, D.H. and Blanchard, E.B. (1985) Psychophysiology of relaxation associated panic attacks, *Journal of Abnormal Psychology*, **94**, 96–101.

De Waele, J.P. and Harré, R. (1979) Autobiography as a psychological method. In G.P. Ginsburg (ed.), *Emerging Strategies in Social Psychological Research*, Wiley, New York.

DuPont, R.L. (1982) Case study of an agoraphobic. In R.L. Dupont (ed.), *Phobia: A Comprehensive Summary of Modern Treatments*, Brunner/Mazel, New York.*

Faravelli, C. (1985) Life events preceding the onset of panic disorder, *Journal of Affective Disorders*, **9**, 103–5.

Mrs F.H. (1952) Recovery from a long neurosis, *Psychiatry*, **15**, 161–77.*

Franklin, J.A. (1987) The changing nature of agoraphobic fears, *British Journal of Clinical Psychology*, **26**, 127–33.

Genest, M. and Turk, D.C. (1981) Think-aloud approaches to cognitive assessment. In T.V. Merluzzi, C.R. Glass and M. Genest (eds), *Cognitive Assessment*, Guilford, New York.

Glass, C.R. and Arnkoff, D.B. (1982) Think cognitively: selected issues in cognitive assessment and therapy. In P.C. Kendall (ed.), *Advances in Cognitive Behavioural Research and Therapy* (Vol. 1), Academic Press, New York.

Goldstein, A.J. (1970) Case conference: some aspects of agoraphobia, *Journal of Behaviour Therapy and Experimental Psychiatry*, **1**, 305–13.

Goldstein, M.J. and Palmer J.O. (1975) The case of Veronica F.: the invisible net. In M.J. Goldstein and J.O. Palmer (eds), *The Experience of Anxiety: A Casebook* (2nd Edn), Oxford University Press, London.

Harris, T. and Brown, G.W. (1985) Interpreting data in aetiological studies of affective disorder: some pitfalls and ambiguities, *British Journal of Psychiatry*, **147**, 5–15.
Hibbert, G.A. (1984) Ideational components of anxiety: their origin and content, *British Journal of Psychiatry*, **144**, 618–24.
Last, C.G., Barlow, D.H. and O'Brien, G.T. (1985) Assessing cognitive aspects of anxiety: stability over time and agreement between several methods, *Behaviour Modification*, **9**, 72–93.
Law, S.N. (1975) *Inspired Freedom: Agoraphobia—a Battle Won*, Regency Press, London.*
Leonard, N.E. (1928) *The Locomotive-God*, Chapman & Hall, London.*
Lesser, I.M., Poland, R.E., Holcomb, C. and Rose, D.E. (1985) Electroencephalographic study of nighttime panic attacks, *Journal of Nervous and Mental Disease*, **173**, 744–6.
Levy, D.M. (1966) *Maternal Overprotection*, Norton, New York.
Ley, R. (1985) Agoraphobia, the panic attack and hyperventilation syndrome, *Behaviour Research and Therapy*, **23**, 79–81.
Margraf, J., Ehlers, A. and Roth, W.T. (1987) Panic attack associated with perceived heart rate acceleration: a case report, *Behaviour Therapy*, **18**, 84–9.
Mavissakalian, M. (1988) The relationship between panic, phobic and anticipatory anxiety in agoraphobia, *Behaviour Research and Therapy*, **26**, 235–40.
McKinnon, P. (1983) *In Stillness Conquer Fear*. Dove Communications, Blackburn, Victoria.*
Meichenbaum, D. and Cameron, R. (1981) Issues in cognitive assessment: an overview. In T.V. Merluzzi, C.R. Glass and M. Genest (eds), *Cognitive Assessement*, Guilford, New York.
Murray H.A., (1955) Introduction. In A. Burton and R. Harris (eds), *Clinical Studies of Personality* (Vol. 1). Harper & Row, New York.
Neimeyer, G.J. and Neimeyer, R.A. (1981) Personal construct perspectives on cognitive assessment. In T.V. Merluzzi, C.R. Glass and M. Genest (eds), *Cognitive Assessment*, Guilford, New York.
Neville, A. (1986) *Who's Afraid of Agoraphobia?* Arrow Books, London.
Raskin, M., Peeke, H.V.S., Dickman, W. and Pinsker, H. (1982) Panic and generalized anxiety disorders: developmental antecedents and precipitants, *Archives of General Psychiatry*, **39**, 687–9.
Raymond, E. (1946) *The Autobiography of David—*, Victor Gollancz, London.*
Runyan, W.M. (1984) *Life Histories and Psychobiography: Explorations in Theory and Method*, Oxford University Press, New York.
Taylor, W.S. and Culler, E. (1929) The problem of the Locomotive-God, *Journal of Abnormal and Social Psychology*, **24**, 342–99.
Thyer, B.A. and Himle, J. (1985) Temporal relationship between panic attack onset and phobic avoidance in agoraphobia, *Behaviour Research and Therapy*, **23**, 607–8.
Uhde, T.W., Boulenger, J-P., Roy-Byrne, P.P., Geraci, M.F., Vittone, B.J. and Post, R.M. (1985) Longitudinal course of panic disorder; clinical and biological considerations, *Progress in Neuro-Psychopharmacology and Biological Psychiatry*, **9**, 39–51.
Vincent (1919) Confessions of an agoraphobic victim, *American Journal of Psychology*, **30**, 295–9.*
Vines, R. (1987) *Agoraphobia: the Fear of Panic*, Fontana, London.
Vose, R.H. (1981) *Agoraphobia*, Faber & Faber, London.*

Waddell, M.T., Barlow, D.H. and O'Brien, G.T. (1984) A preliminary investigation of cognitive and relaxation treatment of panic disorder: effects on intense anxiety vs. "background" anxiety, *Behaviour Research and Therapy*, **22**, 393–402.

Williams, J.M.G. and Scott, J. (1988) Autobiographical memory in depression, *Psychological Medicine*, **18**, 689–95.

Wittchen, H.-U., Burke, J.D., Semler, G., Pfister, H. and Von Cranach, M. (1989) Recall and dating of psychiatric symptoms, *Archives of General Psychiatry*, **46**, 437–43.

Wolpe, J. (1970) Identifying the antecedents of an agoraphobic reaction: a transcript, *Journal of Behaviour Therapy and Experimental Psychiatry*, **1**, 299–304.

Wolpe, J. and Lazarus, A.A. (1986) *Behaviour Therapy Techniques: A Guide to the Treatment of Neuroses*, Pergamon, Oxford.

Section 2

Classifying and Conceptualizing Panic

Introduction: Classifying and Conceptualizing Panic

In 1980 the American Psychiatric Association's *Diagnostic and Statistical Manual* (DSM-III) operationally defined 'panic disorder' by the presence of three panic attacks within a three-week period, not just precipitated by exposure to a phobic stimulus, and having at least four (any four) of a list of 12 somatic or cognitive symptoms. This is the classification upon which most of the research in this book is based. In 1987, DSM-III was revised (DSM-IIIR) resulting in some changes in what constituted 'panic disorder'. Now, four panic attacks in a four-week period were required for diagnosis, and although at least four of the list of the somatic symptoms had to be present, the list had been changed, with additions (e.g. nausea, depersonalization) and new combinations of symptoms. Tables 1.1 and 1.2 in Chapter 1 show the 1980 and 1987 definitions for panic disorder in detail. The criteria given in DSM-IIIR for changing classifications are mostly positive ones—the incorporation of new research, responsiveness to critiques by researchers and clinicians, etc., although some criteria are decidedly double-edged—such as acceptability to clinicians and researchers of varying theoretical orientations and compatibility with ICD-9. Clearly what had changed between 1980 and 1987 in the definition of panic disorder was not the panic phenomena themselves but the nature of the classification system.

How good a system is it? Can panic disorder be regarded as a disorder separate from agoraphobia and general anxiety disorder? Has this classification of panic disorder been a scientific advance or a blind alley? Opinions diverge sharply. Some clinicians consider that there is a genuine disorder to be delineated, and although our initial definitions (e.g. DSM-III) may be crude, with each successive set of definitions (DSM-IIIR, DSM-IV, etc.) we more accurately elucidate the genuine phenomenon. On the other hand, there are many others, particularly amongst the ranks of clinical psychologists, who although cautious of the existence of a disorder as such, welcome the research focus it has created on panic and related anxiety problems. Also 'panic disorder' and the other anxiety disorders described in DSM-III are far more congruent with current psychological theory and practice than the 'disorder' used in any other diagnostic classification system. Certainly knowledge of panic has advanced markedly since DSM-III was published in 1980. Yet others consider that 'panic disorder' is an unhelpful invention. Gelder, in a 1986 article in the *British Journal of Psychiatry*, concluded that 'as yet (there exists) no strong evidence that panic attacks mark out a different disorder', a position which echoes that of many British psychiatrists.

In this section the first two distinguished writers, Richard Hallam and Isaac Marks, address many of the difficult issues that arise in classifying panic. Richard Hallam, a clinical psychologist, explores the adequacy of the classification of panic from the psychiatric perspective of a distinct 'mental disorder', and from a prevailing psychological viewpoint of Lang's three system theory. He finds both approaches conceptually inadequate, proposing instead that study of the complex psychological processes involved in panic anxiety would ultimately be more fruitful.

Isaac Marks, a psychiatrist, approaches the topic differently. He accepts the validity and need for the classification of mental disorders, but finds the particular disorder in question—'panic disorder'—inadequate in several respects. He proposes that the category of agoraphobia is more robust and should subsume panic except in the case of spontaneous panic without avoidance.

The last author of this section, Manuel Zane, is not so much concerned with classification of disorder as how best to conceptualize panic attacks. The concept of a single unitary phenomenon known as 'a panic attack' is just too crude; Zane, using fascinating extracts from a number of therapist–patient encounters, illustrates quite poignantly that what a therapist does or says changes the form a panic attack takes; by implication what a patient does and says to him or herself during a panic also significantly affects its form. Dr Zane clearly illustrates how imagination and cognitive appraisal synergistically interact with somatic sensations, indicating that panic is more profitably viewed as a dynamic or changing process than as a fixed entity in time. He proposes that the study of changes in panic phenomena in response to the context they occur in—what he calls 'a contextual approach'—is methodologically sounder than studying panic as a fixed object.

Chapter 6

Classification and Research into Panic

RICHARD HALLAM

INTRODUCTION

The phenomenon of panic and the new diagnostic category of Panic Disorder have provoked new interest in the anxiety problems and their causes. Research interest in panic has grown considerably. In this chapter, I will discuss two approaches to conceptualizing and classifying panic complaints and comment on their implications for research. That different research strategies have been adopted is obvious from the rich and varied contributions to this book. In discussing these approaches I will be sounding two cautions. First, whether panic is a useful and unifying construct for a focus of research activity, and second, whether the explanation of complaints of panic requires new etiological concepts. Feeding into these questions is a concern about the way certain kinds of classification can be counter-productive for research. For example, does the creation of a class of panic phenomena really advance research into anxiety complaints? Or does it retard progress by raising the mistaken prospect of discovering a set of causal determinants linked uniquely to this class? In raising these questions, my purpose is to open up issues not to close them. Whatever else it has done, the concept of panic has rejuvenated interest in the anxiety complaints and that is a very welcome development.

PREVIOUS INTEREST IN PANIC

The concept of a panic attack is by no means new, going back at least to Freud's excellent descriptive account of anxiety neurosis (Freud, 1894). Freud noted the variability of 'anxiety attacks' pointing out that sometimes

Panic Disorder: Theory, Research and Therapy. Edited by Roger Baker

they were associated with somatic sensations, sometimes with the idea of sudden death or approaching insanity, and that sometimes there were no associated threatening interpretations. He also observed that an anxiety attack, especially one involving dizziness and unsteadiness, could lead on to fears of entering public places. The clinical importance of sudden attacks of anxiety continued to be recognised in psychiatric description, especially in accounts of people exhibiting fears of public places. However, Roth's studies (Roth, 1959, Roth *et al.*, 1965) were among the first to examine statistical associations between the complaint of a panic attack and other psychiatrically defined phenomena such as depersonalisation and phobic anxiety. His principal component analysis of psychiatric ratings of subjects from a heterogeneous clinical population revealed that 'panic' was associated with the sudden onset of a set of complaints in persons who were otherwise of a previously stable disposition. This pattern contrasted with a cluster of features that indicated long-standing psychological difficulties including a life-long tendency to report anxiety.

That the report of panic attacks was related to the development of fears of public places was made explicit in Roth's writings but it was Klein (1964) who argued the case for assigning greater etiological significance to panic. In this period of anxiety classification, the main distinction made by psychiatrists was between 'elicited' anxiety (cued or related to specific threats) and 'non-elicited' anxiety (i.e. generalised and 'free-floating'). The old category of anxiety neurosis was therefore defined negatively by the absence of obvious elicitors. Klein (1964, 1981) essentially produced a positive conception of non-elicited anxiety, arguing that an attack of panic was a *type* of anxiety which responded to a certain class of pharmacological agent and that it was related to a discrete underlying biological mechanism. He postulated that the occurrence of a panic attack gave rise to a second type of anxiety (anticipatory anxiety) which was realistically generated by the threat of further unpleasant panic attacks. Given the unpredictable nature of panic attacks (which were assumed to occur at any time) a generalised form of anticipatory distress was produced.

An implication of Klein's hypothesis is that the occurrence of panic attacks is causally related to fears of public places. If, as is generally the case, panic attacks are more likely to occur in public places, such as in public transport systems and open spaces, the anticipatory fear of panic may be associated with an avoidance of these places. This line of argument is consistent with my own critique of the phobia conception of fears of public places ('agoraphobia') and my suggestion (Hallam, 1978) that a theoretical explanation should be produced that recognised the close association between a variety of fears and anxieties and the agoraphobic cluster of complaints. Accordingly, I suggested that avoidance of public places be renamed 'staying-at-home' behaviour to emphasise that this was a coping strategy rather than the avoidance component of a phobia.

The impetus the concept of panic-anxiety has given to these new theoretical accounts does not rest or fall on the demonstration of a biological explanation of panic attacks. If, as now seems likely, the history of some types of anxiety complaints begins with an episode (or series of episodes) of 'panic' then we have good grounds for inferring that panic attacks are etiologically important. However, at this stage of research, when the phenomena themselves are poorly understood, it would seem wise to entertain the possibility of a variety of mechanisms in the etiology of the cluster of complaints we may call panic-anxiety. Klein may be right in assuming that biological abnormalities are important in some forms of panic attack but the appearance of 'abnormality' that panic attacks possess—their suddenness, their intensity and seeming irrationality—should not lead us into proposing unique biological dysfunctions to account for them. We have no successful examples of explanatory models based on unitary etiologies in psychiatry. Moreover, we have no reason to believe that panic attacks could not be explained by normal psychological processes.

How then should we go about investigating panic complaints? I will now consider the merits of two popular approaches—the disorder model of psychopathology and the three systems conceptualization—and discuss their implications for classification.

PANIC DISORDER AS A PSYCHIATRIC ENTITY

The classification process

Recent attention to the phenomenon of panic came about through clinical observation and the results of statistical methods of clustering complaints. In Klein's case, the realignment of clinical description was accompanied by a new conceptualization of anxiety complaints. This was followed as is well known by a new typology of anxiety disorders, incorporated into the influential American Psychiatric Association's Diagnostic and Statistical Manuals. This sequence of events supports Roth's statement in a recent article that 'Novel classifications relating to groups of disorders in Psychiatry usually embody new hypotheses or theories about their character and etiological basis' (Roth, 1984). Apart from classifications based on empirical demonstrations of obvious practical value, the disorder model is justified when the pattern of observations that define the disorder can be interpreted theoretically by a unifying construct. Whether Klein's biological hypothesis is correct or not, the typology which includes panic disorder

(PD) must be shown to differentiate forms of distress in other than trivial ways. The fact that, descriptively, complaints look similar or different does not in itself guarantee that these surface characteristics are potentially explicable in terms of theoretically significant etiological processes.

While it is obvious that classification is essential for scientific progress, the criteria which define psychiatric typologies include concepts of morality, statistical deviation, and practical utility (Faust and Milner, 1986). Categories like PD are supposedly devised for the scientific study of causal processes. But as stated by psychiatrists themselves (Sartorius, 1981) there are other reasons for creating taxonomies such as the need for order in psychiatric practice, epidemiological research and cost effectiveness studies. Sartorius places scientific requirements in third place. Disorders are therefore stipulated into existence as much as they are hypothesised to exist. The process of psychiatric classification and its supposed validation can be likened to a bootstrap operation. Classes of disorder are proposed on various grounds (pragmatic and scientific) and then as time goes on either the grounds of pragmatism shift or research based itself on the classification reveals inadequacies within it and the obvious advantage of a new approach. For these two reasons (usually the first) frequent revisions in psychiatric classification have been made.

In essence, the research strategy which is based on the disorder model sets out to validate what is assumed, namely, in the case of PD, that it is constituted by a distinctive pattern of observations in the family of putative disorders with which it is contrasted. Subjects are chosen who satisfy predefined criteria. They have PD or can be said to be in a state of panic. The researcher looks for antecedents, consequents, or associated features which differentiate the putative disorders into coherent and unique patterns. In a penetrating critique of this methodology of supposed validation of putative disorders, Boyle (1988) has argued that the usual scientific procedures are reversed. Instead of inferring a scientific construct from a pattern of observations and validating the construct by prediction of new properties/relationships, the construct (in this case PD) is assumed and observations are made in an attempt to validate it. It is noteworthy that abandonment of Klein's etiological constructs (suggested in J. Margraf *et al.*'s 1986 paper but made more explicit in Margraf and Ehler's chapter in this book) is unlikely to lead to a discarding of panic disorder as a class of anxiety disorders.

Research using the disorder model

Research devised within this general approach has produced results which argue both for and against the idea of PD as a meaningful pattern of observations. On the negative side, panic attacks have a high incidence within all the anxiety disorders (Barlow *et al.*, 1985) and PD appears to exist on a continuum with panic-like phenomena in the general population (Norton *et al.*, 1985). This suggests that there is no natural demarcation between PD and other anxiety complaints although this cannot be established conclusively until a non-arbitrary definition of panic is produced. The absence of a theoretically validated concept of panic need not be a disadvantage for research purposes if the aim is to study typical or paradigmatic examples of a phenomenon. However, the doubt must remain as to whether the features of PD are the typical expression of a natural phenomenon or the artificial creation of circumstances surrounding the observation process. These might include the fact that the paradigmatic case has been observed in a psychiatric rather than say a medical or general population context; that the features are typical of chronicity/severity of the problem rather than its essential nature; that the observers are selectively observing features that satisfy preconceptions of the problem, and so on. Descriptions of the 'agoraphobic syndrome' provide examples of the tendency to perceive 'the typical case'. Marks (1969) notes that 'simply knowing that a patient fears going out into the street and crowded places enables one to predict that many of the other features of the syndrome will be present . . .'. This statement cannot be faulted but it begs the question whether 'agoraphobia' shades off in many different directions into other 'syndromes' and whether the perception of lines of demarcation represents anything more than the reification of existing categories. Diagnostic criteria inevitably eliminate ambiguity because that is what they are designed to do.

Multivariate statistical methods can also give false support to diagnostic divisions. This can happen if the selection of cases for analysis excludes subjects who might potentially demonstrate the phenomenon of interest. Thus it is not surprising that an agoraphobia factor is extracted from samples of subjects who either define their problem in terms of phobia or agoraphobia or are actually selected because they satisfy psychiatric criteria (e.g. Marks, 1967; Hallam and Hafner, 1978). Investigations of the factor structure of self-reported psychological symptoms in the general population in fact provide little support for more than one anxiety dimension (Lipman *et al.*, 1979; Derogaitis and Cleary, 1977). It can be objected that these studies too, reify existing categories by limiting the choice of items to those that conform with what the experimenter deems important, i.e. often items associated with the accepted diagnostic patterns.

Bearing in mind previous criticism, research adopting the disorder model has suggested that there are some clinical features of PD (as defined by DSM-III) which do seem to differentiate it from the disorder whose definition it most closely resembles—generalised anxiety disorder

(GAD). These include a sudden onset (previously noted by Roth, 1959), a lack of comprehension of the nature of the attack, and a sporadic course with frequent periods of remission. Moreover, unlike panic attacks in simple phobias and social anxieties, panic in PD often occurs as if spontaneously. Even when panic attacks are cued by specific situations, as in fears of public places, the cue appears to act as a setting condition for raising the probability of a panic attack and is not generally perceived as an object or source for the fear.

Thus, comparisons between PD and GAD have indicated that GAD has a more continuous course (Raskin *et al.*, 1982; Barlow *et al.*, 1986) and PD has a later sudden onset (Anderson *et al.*, 1984). PD is also more likely to be associated with complaints related to autonomic lability, dizziness and fears of going crazy or losing control (Barlow *et al.*, 1986). Of course, care must be taken to ensure that the differences between PD and GAD are not simply an elaboration and consequence of the criteria used to select the groups. Barlow notes that GAD is a residual category when other disorders have been excluded. It is quite rare as a primary diagnosis (11 per cent of a clinically anxious sample). Barlow suggests that GAD may not be a residual category if the content of the 'anxious expectation' characteristic of this group proves to be different from that in other groups (e.g. worry about multiple life circumstances versus expectation of panic or phobic encounters).

After studying the longitudinal course of PD, Uhde and his colleagues (1985) argue against the view that a panic attack represents a more severe form of generalised anxiety. Theirs was a retrospective analysis in which all the subjects who could not remember the first episode were excluded. In this group, the complaint of severe anxiety almost always followed the first episode of panic. Avoidance of public situations, when present, usually developed within six months. Of relevance too, was the observation that some subjects, all of them male, had panic attacks without associated complaints of anxiety or fears of public places. It would appear that the 'attacks' are not necessarily categorised by the sufferer as anxiety phenomena at all, especially in the early stages (see case studies in Hallam, 1985). In one individual, a drug abuser seen by the author, considerable 'phobic avoidance' was present without the perception of the problem as one of 'anxiety'. This raises the possibility that episodes of sensory disturbance (noted especially by Uhde and reported by many other authors as well), are separable from the secondary elaboration of the phenomena as threatening or as examples of 'fear'.

We may conclude that differences between PD and GAD do exist though these may in part be tautologous. One explanation of the episodic, rapid onset, escalation of distress in PD is that it involves 'fear-of-fear', a vicious cycle phenomenon.

Complexity of anxiety complaints

The hypothesis that the escalation of panic episodes into a severely disabling condition depends on interoceptive cueing of panic, perception of threat, and fear-of-fear has a long history (e.g. C.Weekes, Chapter 15); formal elaborations of the idea have now become more sophisticated (e.g. Goldstein and Chambless, 1978; Clark, 1986). If this general hypothesis proves to be correct, then 'panic' should not be regarded as a different 'type' of anxiety but as a reported experience with distinctive cueing and maintenance processes. Moreover, if the interoceptive cues are found to be related to endogenous processes having no intrinsic relationship to psychological processes associated with complaints of anxiety, then again, the difference between PD and GAD will be cast in a different light. However, the differences might still be regarded as sufficiently important to validate the diagnostic distinction between PD and GAD but from a research point of view the advantage of making this distinction resolves into a question of research strategy rather than the acceptance of the existence of two different 'disorders'.

The critical feature of panic is that the putative cue for the anxiety complaint is interoceptive. Escape and avoidance are literally impossible. The response to the interoceptive cue includes somatic reactions with their own interoceptive feedback so that a vicious cycle ensues. A wide range of physiological processes has already been implicated in the sensory cueing of panic (e.g. hyperventilation, vestibular dysfunction, CNS stimulation, cardiovascular irregularities). These processes may be subject to random changes which would account for the unpredictable nature of panic attacks and subjects' lack of comprehension of their cause. This scenario is probably far too simple, however, with the origins of the first episode left almost to chance. Authors such as Goldstein (1982) postulate additional psychological mechanisms to account for a lack of awareness of the determinants of panic. The occurrence of intrusive thoughts or images is another more 'psychological' explanation of cueing. I have raised elsewhere the possibility of disinhibition of learned mechanisms of autonomic control (Hallam, 1985). These proposals are speculative at present. Investigation of the patterning of panic attacks and periods of remission may be the avenue to resolving these and other competing accounts.

Researchers who adopt psychological models seem united in the view that the etiology of anxiety complaints is multidimensional. While the putative anxiety disorders such as PD and GAD have distinctive features, the research strategy based on the disorder model has severe weaknesses as noted above. The investigation of a few separate anxiety disorders does not do justice to the complexity of anxiety complaints and it downgrades the value of psychological constructs which can be inferred from patterns of observation common to all the anxiety disorders.

CLASSIFICATION AND EMPIRICAL RESEARCH INTO PANIC

Difficulties with the three systems approach to anxiety

A panic attack is a cluster of concomitant changes in motoric, physiologic, and verbal/cognitive systems. The panicking individual *may be* saying that he is intensely fearful, *may be* reporting unpleasant somatic sensations, is *probably* physiologically aroused, and *may be* attempting to escape to a safer place. In qualifying these statements, I am recognising that when a person says they are panicking they are not using a precise concept in a precise manner. I suggest also that there is little point at this stage of our understanding in agreeing on an arbitrarily precise definition. As noted above, a few individuals demonstrate some but not all features of the panic-anxiety cluster of complaints. This raises several problems for researchers who want to make an empirical study of the pattern of observations we call a panic attack or more generally, panic-anxiety. The word panic, like anxiety in most of its uses, is a polysemous, summarising term. According to Delprato and McGlynn (1985) it is an intervening variable rather than a hypothetical construct, but even this may amount to an overestimate of its scientific status.

Some theorists do of course treat anxiety as a hypothetical construct—using it to characterise a motivational/emotional state. However, it was on account of failure to make successful predictions from this kind of construct that anxiety has come to be viewed less theoretically. Lang (1968), Rachman and Hodgson (1974) and Rachman (1978) were influential in pointing out that when we refer to fear (or anxiety or panic) we are dealing with several independently measurable but loosely coupled response systems. Rachman popularised this view with the succinct phrase that 'fear is not a lump'. Consequently, a lack of concordance between activity in these systems is no longer regarded as a sign of the construct's internal inconsistency but as an empirical fact of theoretical interest in its own right.

Unfortunately, the advent of the three systems approach to conceptualising anxiety phenomena has not always added clarity to research investigation. To reason that assessment in each response mode is important and to be aware that each mode may enter functional relationships independently of the other modes, is not the same as saying that 'anxiety' is composed of three components. So long as anxiety is still understood as an underlying existent or organising principle (i.e. as a hypothetical construct) new theoretical models for organising the data will not be developed. Moreover, if any one of the three system components is thought to indicate 'anxiety' and the components are not perfectly correlated, logical problems ensue (Hugdahl, 1981). In practice, 'anxiety' does frequently creep into research reports as an explanatory concept.

The three systems approach does not recommend itself as a taxonomy either. Evans (1986) has pointed out several problems, including the fact that the boundaries between the response modes are arbitrary and sometimes misinterpreted. Measurements of the different response modes are often confounded. More importantly, the three modes do not correspond with physiological reality or with other worthwhile schemes of behavioural organisation. Evans therefore makes a plea for developing alternative models of behavioural organisation so that response interrelationships can be conceptualised. Classification would follow as a theory-driven exercise. For example, a systems approach offers one such model for looking at structure and function within a behavioural repertoire (e.g. Hallam, 1976). A systems model could be used to generate a classification in terms of patterns of feedback relationships. Classification of problem behaviour as exemplifying types of approach and avoidance conflicts is another long familiar though rarely used organising principle.

How then can the three systems approach to empirical enquiry develop our understanding of panic? Clearly *not* by measuring as much as we can and by defining panic in some arbitrary way as, let us say, high activity in all three systems. In practice we have a variety of different responses in anxiety complaints and no doubt a host of contextual determinants. We observe freezing and fleeing, very high heart-rates and very low heart-rates, pallor and flushing, great lamentations of distress and complete 'denial'. Until we understand the meaning of the interactions between the systems (and this is coming with advances in psychophysiology) there is little point in developing arbitrary operational definitions of panic phenomena.

A contextual and functional approach

When adequate constructs of behavioural organisation have been developed, the clinician will not ask whether the problem in front of him or her is an example of such and such a disorder (e.g. agoraphobia or social phobia) but will ask a more general question of the form 'What is the pattern of elicitation or maintenance here?' or 'What is the structure and organisation of the response repertoire?' and follow this up with an empirical enquiry. In this way, we may avoid the creation of separate and unrelated disorders. Instead, we set up a frame of reference for apprehending the similarities and differences between much more clearly specified patterns of complaint. Consequently, if a client reports that they have acute attacks of somatic distress and a feeling of doom, this is not regarded as the verbal/subjective component of a panic disorder but an item of behaviour that should be interpreted structurally (in relation to the presence or absence of other behaviour in the repertoire) contextually (as an act whose meaning derives from a specific context) and functionally (in relation to eliciting and maintaining events). It may turn out that a person who expresses his/her problem in this way may have a great deal in common with persons who describe their distress in different ways. In a recent article, Stockwell and his colleagues wondered whether reports of the 'dry shakes' in alcohol abusers have anything in common with 'panic attacks' (Stockwell *et al.*, 1983). The dry shakes occur in abstinent periods when it is unlikely that they represent withdrawal symptoms. The point I am making is that we will never in fact know if they have anything in common if we regard them as separate clinical phenomena and do not develop constructs of behavioural organisation through which they can be related together.

This last point raises the question of whether any one response system is 'primary' in defining panic phenomena. After all, if individuals do not use fear-related terms, should the problem they are expressing be classified as one of panic? Conversely, if the term panic is used so freely that in any minor distressing circumstance, an individual claims to be panicking, should the self-report be discounted? It should be apparent by now that this issue does not become an empirical or definitional question until some theoretical construct has been developed which relates together a pattern of observations. For example, it is conceivable that through techniques of ambulatory monitoring of panic attacks, a behavioural/physiological construct will make more sense of the data than a verbal/cognitive one. Likewise, it may be discovered that the propensity to use 'panic' as a self-descriptor is related to observations from entirely different domains (e.g. sex-role identification, denial defence mechanisms) in which case the panic attack would be subsumed by and classified according to a different set of theoretical constructs.

The problem of defining panic is nicely illustrated in a study by Ehlers and her colleagues (1986). These authors investigated the hypothesis that panic attacks produced by infusion of sodium lactate provide an adequate model for panic attacks in patients diagnosed as having PD. They compared panic attacks produced in this way with spontaneous panic attacks monitored subjectively and by ambulatory EKG recording in the previous week. They also studied the response of normal volunteers. Lactate infusion (but not saline) led to an increase in anxious mood and somatic symptoms in all subjects. Controls and panickers were equally reactive but because the latter started out with a higher baseline, their absolute level of responding was greater. Four out of 10 panickers asked to terminate the infusion before the end of the infusion period of 20 minutes whereas none of the controls requested this. The questions of interest here are:

1. Whether the 'panic attacks' produced by lactate in PD subjects are different in kind from the anxiety episodes produced in the control subjects? (This is relevant to the hypothesis that lactate-induced panic is a biological marker for PD.)
2. Whether the 'panic attacks' produced by lactate are similar in kind to spontaneous panics? (This is relevant to the question whether lactate-induced panic is a good experimental analogue for natural panic.)

In answer to the first question, it would seem that the volunteers (control subjects) experienced panic (even if this term was not used in self-description) in a similar way but to a lesser degree. The only notable differences (apart from intensity) were, first, a tendency for the panickers to report more somatic symptoms of a kind not normally associated with lactate infusion or catecholamine response and, second, they showed a more rapid rise in systolic blood pressure during the infusion. This suggests slight differences in response between the groups but the authors argued that the response to lactate was so similar in the two groups that lactate does not produce 'true panic'. They concluded that response to lactate cannot be used as biological marker for a proneness to spontaneous panic attacks. In order to answer the second question, panic during lactate infusion was compared with previous spontaneous panics or, for the volunteers, their 'most extreme anxiety episode'. The majority of subjects in each group reported the experiences as similar. Mean heart rate levels in natural and spontaneous panic were comparable. Moreover, 'anticipatory anxiety' experienced by the panic subjects in a pre-infusion test session was rated as high as 'anxiety' at the end of the infusion period. From these data it would be difficult to argue for any qualitative distinctions in anxiety. Indeed, if there were such differences one might expect the English language to contain finer distinctions than it in fact does in the anxiety domain. The only clear difference between lactate panic and 'natural panic' seems to be the obvious one that spontaneous panic is not apparently elicited whereas lactate panic is.

This study illustrates how difficult it is to say that one 'type' of anxiety is similar or dissimilar to another. This sort of question, based as it is on the formist or structuralist approach to science, may be the wrong one to ask in attempts to classify experience and behaviour. It has been argued elsewhere (Sarbin, 1964; Hallam, 1985) that the term anxiety is a lay construct whose origins lie in figurative language. If this is the case, a contextual and functional approach may have more to offer in ordering our observations of panic phenomena.

ACKNOWLEDGEMENTS

I am indebted to Mary Boyle for her comments on the manuscript and for helping me to be as consistent in my views as their logic permits.

REFERENCES

Anderson, D.J., Noyes, R. and Crowe, R.R. (1984) A comparison of panic disorder and generalised anxiety disorder, *American Journal of Psychiatry*, **141**, 572–5.

Barlow, D.H., Blanchard, E.B., Vermilyea, J.A., Vermilyea, B.B. and DiNardo, P.A. (1986) Generalised anxiety and GAD; description and reconceptualisation, *American Journal of Psychiatry*, **143**, 40–4.

Barlow, D.H., Vermilyea, J.A., Blanchard, E.B., Vermilyea, B.B., DiNardo, P.A. and Cerny, J.A. (1985) The phenomenon of panic, *Journal of Abnormal Psychology*, **94**, 320–8.

Boyle, M. (1988) Schizophrenia: a scientific delusion? Doctoral thesis, North East London Polytechnic (unpublished).

Clark, D.M. (1986) A Cognitive approach to panic, *Behaviour Research and Therapy*, **24**, 461–70.

Delprato, D.J. and McGlynn, F.D., (1984) Behavioral theories of anxiety disorders. In S.M. Turner (ed.), *Behavioral Theories and Treatments of Anxiety*, Plenum, New York.

Derogatis, L.R. and Cleary, P.A. (1977) Confirmation of the dimensional structure of the SCL-90. A study in construct validation, *Journal of Clinical Psychology*, **33**, 981–9.

Ehlers, A., Margraf, J., Roth, W.T., Taylor, C.B., Maddock, R.J., Sheikh, J., Kopell, M.L., McClenahan, K.L., Gossard, D., Blowers, G.H., Agras, W.S. and Kopell, B.S. (1986) Lactate infusions and panic attacks: do patients and controls respond differently? *Psychiatry Research*, **17**, 295–308.

Evans, I.M. (1986) Response structure and the triple response mode concept. In R.O. Nelson and S.C. Hayes (eds), *Conceptual Foundations of Behavioral Assessement*, Guilford, New York.

Faust, D. and Milner R.A. (1986) The empiricist and his new clothes: DSM III in perspective, *American Journal of Psychiatry*, **143**, 962–7.

Freud, S. (1894) The justification for detaching from neurasthenia a particular syndrome: The anxiety neurosis. In J. Strachey (ed.), *The Complete Works of Sigmund Freud (Vol. 3)*. Hogarth, London (originally published, 1894).

Goldstein, A.J. and Chambless, D.L. (1978) A reanalysis of agoraphobia, *Behavior Therapy*, **9**, 47–59.

Goldstein, A.J. (1982) Agoraphobia: treatment successes, treatment failures, and theoretical implications. In D.L. Chambless and A.J. Goldstein (eds), *Agoraphobia: Multiple Perspectives on Theory and Treatment*, John Wiley, New York.

Hallam, R.S. (1976) A complex view of simple phobias. In H.J. Eysenck (ed.), *Case Studies in Behaviour Therapy*, Routledge & Kegan Paul, London.

Hallam, R.S. (1978) Agoraphobia: a critical review of the concept, *British Journal of Psychiatry*, **133**, 314–19.

Hallam, R.S. (1985) *Anxiety: Psychological Perspectives on Panic and Agoraphobia*. Academic Press, London.

Hallam, R.S. and Hafner, R.J. (1978) Fears of phobic patients: factor analyses of self-report data, *Behaviour Research and Therapy*, **16**, 1–6.

Hugdahl, K. (1981) The three systems model of fear and emotions: a critical examination, *Behaviour Research and Therapy*, **19**, 75–85.

Klein, D.F. (1964) Delineation of two drug-responsive anxiety syndromes, *Psychopharmacologia*, **5**, 397–408.

Klein, D.F. (1981) Anxiety reconceptualised. In D.F. Klein and J. Rabkin (eds), *Anxiety: New Research and Changing Concepts*, Raven Press, New York.

Lang, P.J. (1968) Fear reduction and fear behavior: problems in treating a construct. In J.M. Schlien (ed.), *Research in Psychotherapy* Vol. III, A.P.A., Washington, DC..

Lipman, R.S., Covi, L. and Shapiro, A.K. (1979) The Hopkins Symptom Checklist (HSCL), *Journal of Affective Disorders*, **1**, 9–24.

Margraf, J., Ehlers, A. and Roth, W.T. (1986) Panic attacks: theoretical models and empirical evidence. In I. Hand and H.-U. Wittchen (eds), *Panic Attacks and Panic Disorder: The Need for a Behavioural Perspective*, Springer, Heidelberg.

Marks, I.M. (1967) Components and correlates of psychiatric questionnaires, *British Journal of Medical Psychology*, **40**, 261–71.

Marks, I. M. (1969) *Fears and Phobias*, Academic Press, London.

Norton, G.R., Harrison, B., Hauch, J. and Rhodes, L. (1985) Characteristics of people with infrequent panic attacks, *Journal of Abnormal Psychology*, **94**, 216–21.

Rachman, S. (1978) *Fear and Courage*, Freeman, San Francisco.

Rachman, S. and Hodgson, R. (1974) I Synchrony and desynchrony in fear and avoidance, *Behaviour Research and Therapy*, **12**, 311–18.

Raskin, M., Peeke, H.V.S., Dickman, W. and Pinsku, H. (1982) Panic and generalised anxiety disorders, *Archives of General Psychiatry*, **39**, 687–9.

Roth, M. (1959) The phobic anxiety depersonalisation syndrome, *Proceedings of the Royal Society of Medicine*, **52**, 587–95.

Roth, M. (1984) Agoraphobia, panic disorder, and generalised anxiety disorder: some implications of recent advances, *Psychiatric Developments*, **2**, 31–52.

Roth, M., Garside, R.F. and Gurney, C. (1965) Clinical and statistical enquiries into the classification of anxiety states and depressive disorders. In *Proceedings of Leeds Symposium on Behavioural Disorders*. May and Baker, London.

Sarbin, T.R. (1964) Anxiety: reification of a metaphor, *Archives of General Psychiatry*, **10**, 630–8.

Sartorius, N. (1981) Interview with Dr N. Sartorius, *Medicographia*, **3**, 42–4.

Stockwell, T., Smail, P., Hodgson, R. and Canter, S. (1983) Alcohol dependence and phobic anxiety states II: a retrospective study, *British Journal of Psychiatry*, **144**, 58–63.

Uhde, T.W., Boulenger, J-P., Roy-Byrne, P.P., Garaci, M.F., Vittone, B.J. and Post, R.M. (1985) Longitudinal course of panic disorder: clinical and biological considerations, *Progress in Neuro-Pharmacology and Biological Psychiatry*, **9**, 35–51.

Chapter 7

Agoraphobia and Panic Disorder

ISAAC MARKS

INTRODUCTION

With the advent of the DSM-III category of panic disorder in 1980 a change seemed to appear in human emotions. Frightened people ceased to complain of fear, and began to speak only of panic. As happens so often, the variable labels which can be given to the same mental event have swung to the prevailing ethos, which currently emphasizes panic rather than fear or anxiety. In fact, however, the phenomenology of agoraphobia has not changed since it was described by Westphal in 1871.

Situational panic

The DSM-III terminology has led to some confusion about the nature of panic in agoraphobia. At least two types of panic need to be distinguished in so-called 'panic disorder'. The first occurs in the great majority of cases, i.e. those who have both panic disorder and agoraphobia. This is *phobic (situational) panic* that is predictably triggered by a characteristic cluster of agoraphobic situations which mainly involve public places (*agora* = Greek for market-place), e.g. going in the street, stores, crowds, public transport, theatres and enclosed spaces. Agoraphobics may not panic in all those situations but always do in some of them—multiple fears from within that cluster of cues are pathognomonic.

The situations that evoke phobic panic in agoraphobics may be real or imagined, i.e. it can be brought on either by actually going into those situations or by merely thinking about entering them. The latter is *anticipatory* phobic *panic* similar to the panic that will strike a severe cat phobic

Panic Disorder: Theory, Research and Therapy. Edited by Roger Baker

on thinking about cats or a normal mother on thinking her child has had an accident.

Situational (phobic) panic, including anticipatory panic, is a hallmark of *all* phobics, not merely of the agoraphobia that is present in most cases of panic disorder. The subjective, behavioural and physiological features of phobic panic are similar across the various types of phobia, and indeed in normal panic, as in soldiers under bombardment. Moreover, in agoraphobics, as in all phobics, relevant cues evoke discomfort that ranges from anxiety in milder cases to panic in severe ones. There is no sharp divide between differing degrees of situational anxiety and situational panic—they fall on a continuum of severity shading into one another. (Henceforth 'panic' will include lesser degrees of anxiety too.) By definition situational panic is not found in non-phobics.

Given that the panic ensuing from contact with the phobic situation is so similar across all types of phobia, is there anything distinctive about the situational panic of agoraphobia/panic disorder? The answer is the *particular constellation of situations that bring it on*. Agoraphobics are not frightened on encountering real or imagined cats, thunderstorms, or dirt, but are terrified when in the street, crowds, theatre or subway. In contrast, cat phobics are not frightened of public places, only cats, while thunderstorm phobics fear not public places but thunderstorms.

A critical concomitant of phobic panic in all phobias, including agoraphobia, is *avoidance* of those cues that regularly trigger panic. This leads to handicap if the avoided situations are frequent in everyday life, which is the case in agoraphobia. It is easier for a cat phobic to carry on normal life while avoiding cats than it is for an agoraphobic who avoids going into the street, stores and other public places. This avoidance leads many agoraphobics to become completely housebound.

Spontaneous panic

Leaving situational (phobic) panic, the second type of panic is found in all cases of panic disorder, whether or not they have agoraphobia. This panic occurs with no clear trigger, and has been called *spontaneous*, non-situational, non-phobic, unpredictable, uncued, or free floating panic. In so far as everything has a cause there must be some hidden trigger for spontaneous panic, but that trigger is not a particular external situation or thought about such a situation. Speculations about possible precipitants of spontaneous anxiety range from discharges in the locus ceruleus to unconscious fantasies. Those speculations are splendid Rorschachs of the proposer, but cannot be evaluated in the absence of good controlled data.

There is a continuum between spontaneous anxiety and spontaneous panic corresponding to that in situational (phobic) anxiety, both with respect to duration and intensity of the phenomenon. Tonic tension and surges of spontaneous panic merge into one another and are highly correlated.

Spontaneous panic may occur without agoraphobia (yielding the DSM-III category of panic disorder without agoraphobia), and is also common in major depression. Most agoraphobics have spontaneous as well as situational panic. This separates them from other phobics, in whom spontaneous panics are unusual. Another feature separating agoraphobics from most other phobics is the high frequency with which they get depressed mood. Agoraphobia can thus be distinguished from other phobias by the fact that:

1. its phobic panic is brought on by a characteristic cluster of situations,
2. within that cluster the fears are multiple rather than specific,
3. agoraphobics more often have non-phobic symptoms, including spontaneous panics, tonic tension, depression and depersonalization.

Although many believe that agoraphobics always start with a series of spontaneous panics, in fact quite a few begin to avoid the place where panic began from the very outset, so that only the very first panic is spontaneous (cf. Table 2.4 of H. Waring's chapter). Thereafter escape reduces panic and so reinforces further escape and ultimately avoidance. What initiates the original discomfort is still obscure. Dysphoria for whatever reason can potentiate it, but some agoraphobics deny ever having been substantially depressed.

THE STATUS OF AGORAPHOBIA AND PANIC DISORDER

Separating agoraphobia and panic disorder

In the DSM-III agoraphobia is both a subset of panic disorder (panic disorder with agoraphobia) and an entity outside it (agoraphobia without panic attacks). This is a rather spurious division with little to commend it. There is no evidence that agoraphobia with subpanic levels of situational or spontaneous anxiety differs substantively from agoraphobia in which such anxieties reach an intensity warranting the label of panic. After all, mild and severe rheumatoid arthritis are not separate disorders.

There is good reason, however, to separate agoraphobia from panic disorder without agoraphobia. Unlike pure panic disordered cases, agoraphobics not only panic in certain situations but also tend to avoid them, and it is this *avoidance* par excellence which gives rise to their disability—their gradual confinement to the home because places outside bring on panic. Agoraphobics may even have panics at home, but much less so. Rarely agoraphobics actually avoid sleeping in their bed once they have had a panic there, but these are great exceptions. Avoidance is far more likely to develop to outside than home situations in which panic has been experienced. As a species we may be more prepared to link panic to places outside our home territory than inside it, though this is probably not the whole story. It is hard to discern a common theme in the agoraphobic cluster. Saying that agoraphobics seek safety begs the question of why home seems so much safer than outside it even when panic occurs.

We do not know why the spontaneous panic of panic disorder often gets conditioned to the situations in which it occurs, becoming transformed into the situational (phobic) panic and avoidance so typical of agoraphobia, while a minority of cases remain pure panic disorder without developing agoraphobia. A prospective follow-up of cases from the start might clarify that conundrum, but would be expensive to complete.

Agoraphobics with a stuttering onset remind us of the phenomenon of kindling in animals, whereby intermittent electrical stimulation of the amygdala eventually elicits a seizure, after which even previously subthreshold levels of stimulation trigger a fit. It may take a massive panic in an actual store to precipitate avoidance of that store the first time round, but after many trials even just thinking of that situation will precipitate panic.

Agoraphobia as more robust

There are strong reasons to retain the diagnostic category of agoraphobia that Westphal coined well over a century ago. Though the syndrome is rather protean, the exact cluster of phobias varying from one patient to the next, the agreement about its 'fuzzy set' of features has been impressive in many multivariate analyses in the USA and Europe. Simply knowing that someone fears going into the street and stores predicts her liability to show many other phobic and non-phobic aspects of that syndrome.

The same firm research base does not underlie the DSM-III introduction of the label 'panic disorder', and it could be argued that the term should be abandoned as it covers such a wide range of conditions. Intense phobic panic is found in all phobics in contact with their phobic stimulus, while spontaneous panic is usual in major depression and withdrawal from alcohol or opiates. Only a handful of cases have spontaneous panics without these other features, and it has not been conclusively shown that they differ from generalized anxiety disorder other than in severity. Hundreds of articles uninformatively refer to 'panic disorder' without telling us whether the patients are agoraphobic. It is not terribly informative to say that someone has panic—is it phobic panic and if so of what type? Is it spontaneous panic? Is it part of depression or alcohol withdrawal, or even of obsessive-compulsive disorder?

TREATMENT BY BEHAVIOURAL EXPOSURE

Self-help applications of exposure

Agoraphobia, which constitutes the lion's share of panic disorder, responds well to the treatment of live exposure. Controlled trials in the US and Europe have repeatedly found that agoraphobia does well after exposure therapy, and have also demonstrated that improvement persists up to four to seven years follow-up, which is far longer than anything shown after drugs have stopped. Moreover, this improvement does not require the clinician to devote more time to the patient than is customary with drugs and other widely used forms of psychiatric treatment. Within days of instruction many clinicians become able to find ways of helping agoraphobics in routine clinics by fairly simple advice about the exposure principle.

This encouraging development partly arises from the recent move away from the idea of behavioural treatment as something done to patients towards a realization that behavioural methods form a system of self-help that the patient learns from a clinician who largely acts as coach and monitor. In the majority of agoraphobics there is no need to practise exposure with them in the phobic situation, only to guide them on what to do there.

The more usual pattern of a behavioural session in the clinic takes a different form, the practice part of the treatment now being mainly carried out by the patient without a clinician being present. The first step in the assessment interview is to carefully unravel the patient's avoidance profile in detail. What does she avoid because it evokes anxiety or panic? Next, the clinician explains to the patient (and a relative too if one is available as a cotherapist) how she can overcome the problem by an exposure self-help programme that will deal with each part of the avoidance profile in detail. The therapist also asks the patient to use a suitable manual as a guide in the self-exposure programme and to record every day in a structured but simple diary the exposure tasks carried out and their outcome. Patients then leave the clinic to practise the suggested exposure tasks as homework between sessions while keeping a daily record of this homework and its results. They bring this exposure-homework diary back to the therapist in the next session for discussion and suggestions how to proceed further. Sometimes it is also helpful for patients to phone the therapist once or twice between sessions to make an interim report on progress and setbacks and to get ideas on how to deal with these. The patient is taught to anticipate setbacks and how to manage them.

Minimal intervention

Even severe agoraphobia can respond with very little therapist investment, merely appropriate advice. An example is a woman of 40 who was enduringly helped by only 1½ hours of my time. She had been virtually housebound for eight years, and managed to attend my clinic for assessment by a heroic effort and by being escorted by her husband. She gave a history of classic agoraphobia. After she, her husband and I delineated her avoidance profile—which situations she avoided regularly because they evoked panic, we worked out an exposure-homework programme that she could gradually carry out as she slowly habituated to one situation after another. I explained how she should keep a diary of her exposure homework exercises, and asked her to post them to me. This she did, weekly at first and then at lengthening intervals. She diligently carried out her exposure programme and within weeks was mobile for the first time in years. She kept up her progress without seeing me again for four years, but then had some family difficulties which depressed her, and she quickly relapsed back to square one. Seeing her once more for an hour encouraged her to revive her original exposure homework programme. On doing this she recovered her gains, to six years follow-up when last heard of. That is a gratifying result for 2½ hours of time from a clinician.

Such accounts can be given by many clinicians who have adopted exposure treatment. It is not a story of miracle cures. Far from it. Though little time is needed from the clinician, the patient has to work hard to implement the exposure programme worked out together with the therapist; improvement is only hard-won by systematic self-implementation over many days and weeks and perhaps even months. The story illustrates what might be achieved by means of minimal intervention *of the right kind for the right type of problem*. This cannot be stressed too much. We are not talking about a general placebo effect in which saying almost anything soothing might do the trick. Any old advice just will not do. Anti-exposure instructions, for example, do not help phobics, nor does advice to relax. When such patients were advised to take a break from panic and to avoid whatever was upsetting them they did not improve, though these same cases did improve on being asked to embark on an exposure programme. (Greist *et al.*, 1980).

We are talking of a touch of the rudder, but the touch must be in the right direction. Touch the rudder the wrong way, and the patient goes off course. Even simple procedures have to be executed properly. Psychotherapeutic interventions can be as specific in their effects as are drugs.

Cases responding to brief exposure guidance of the kind we have just seen are not rare. A clinician who is alert to the possibilities of behavioural psychotherapy will frequently find agoraphobics who can benefit from detailed exposure advice which is individually tailored to their particular problem.

The amount of behavioural help that agoraphobics need from a clinician varies enormously. Many sufferers merely lack the knowledge of what principle to apply, and on learning what to do from a clinician or on reading a suitable self-exposure manual can then go off and apply it successfully without further help, devising and completing a methodical self-exposure programme entirely on their own. Detailed manuals and diaries to record exposure homework help sufferers to execute their programme properly. In planning a self-exposure programme phobics have to remember that long exposure periods reduce panic more than do shorter ones.

Some agoraphobics need a bit of prompting to start a self-exposure programme and can then take off on their own. Others require a bit more help from the clinician in monitoring their progress at intervals. Clinicians need to teach patients to expect setbacks and rehearse dealing with them alone, but be available for the odd brief booster session that some people require. A few cases want indefinitely continuing therapist-aided exposure despite having repeatedly improved during sessions; the long-term outcome in such cases is dubious, as eventually the therapist must fade out of the scene.

Experimental evidence for self-exposure

At least 15 controlled studies have found self-exposure to be helpful for agoraphobia and only one found no benefit from self-exposure (reviewed by Marks, 1987). In the largest controlled study (Ghosh and Marks, 1987) marked gains from self-exposure occurred despite patients having no interaction with a clinician beyond initial screening. Forty chronic agoraphobics were randomized to get self-exposure instructions over 10 weeks from a self-help book (*Living With Fear*—Marks, 1978), a psychiatrist, or a computer. Apart from a 1½-hour initial assessment, mean clinician time per patient in the three groups was respectively only 0, 1.6, and 1.5 hours. All three groups improved markedly and equally up to 6 months follow-up

(Ghosh and Marks 1987). Neither the clinician nor the computer conferred any advantage over the manual.

An obvious question is whether all three treatment conditions in the above study were doing anything more than placebo. The answer is that in other controlled studies phobics who expected to improve with another procedure—anti-exposure—failed to get better (Greist *et al.*, 1980), and indeed anti-exposure almost abolished gains from imipramine in agoraphobics (Telch *et al.*, 1985). So improvement from self-exposure has little to do with the mere expectation of improvement and more to do with the component of exposure that causes panic to subside.

Exposure by the book

Self-exposure seems to have better results when patients use an appropriate manual and diary that records homework tasks for regular review. Still to be tested is the value of reading a manual without any prompting from a clinician. Two patients in the book-instructed condition of Ghosh and Marks (1987) had in fact previously bought the book *Living With Fear* on their own initiative but failed to follow its directions until they were asked to do so by the psychiatrist in the trial, so initial contact with a clinician is an important motivator for some people. This raises critical theoretical issues that affect many fields. Why should certain people who know exactly what to do need a guru before they can do it? Some can learn a language, tennis or carpentry by self-practice with the aid of books and tapes without any coaching, while others, even if highly intelligent, find such tasks a losing battle despite intensive skilled teaching. Many ill-understood variables affect this process.

The need for therapist-aided exposure for agoraphobics has diminished as self-exposure manuals have been refined. This is welcome as therapist-aided exposure is time-consuming and thus expensive. Patients on the author's waiting list are asked to first try treating themselves using *Living With Fear* as a manual, and not infrequently improve enough therewith to obviate the need for a therapist. For most of the remaining cases the clinician's role is to assess the problem and to teach people to help themselves better.

Drugs and exposure therapy

Is there a role for drugs as well as for exposure therapy? There is little doubt that antidepressants help agoraphobics who are dysphoric, at least in the short term (this issue still has to be examined for benzodiazepines), but there is disagreement about whether antidepressants help agoraphobics who have normal mood. The few direct comparisons that are possible between the size of effect of antidepressants and of live exposure show these to be comparable.

Can behavioural treatment offer anything to the minority of cases of panic disorder who have no agoraphobia? In theory habituation might occur in a programme of exposure to fantasies of internal cues of panic. Such an approach remains to be tested in systematic controlled trials with adequate follow-up. Research on this point is long overdue.

SUMMARY

In so-called 'panic disorder' we should distinguish between phobic and spontaneous panic. The chief handicap comes from avoidance of a particular cluster of agoraphobic situations. It is moot whether the problem is best labelled as *panic* disorder. The category of agoraphobia is more viable. Behavioural treatment delineates the agoraphobic avoidance profile and encourages a self-exposure programme to produce habituation. Self-exposure with only minimal time from the clinician has encouragingly durable efficacy. In the presence of dysphoria the addition of antidepressant drugs can be helpful; these do not interfere with exposure, though they may give troublesome side-effects. Two important questions need more research—whether benzodiazepines interfere with exposure, and whether behavioural treatment can help panic in the absence of avoidance.

REFERENCES

Ghosh, A. and Marks, I.M. (1987) Self-treatment of agoraphobia by exposure, *Behavior Therapy*, **18**, 3–16.

Greist, J.H., Marks, I.M., Berlin, F. and Noshirvani, H. (1980) Avoidance versus confrontation of fear, *Behavior Therapy*, **11**, 1–14.

Marks, I.M. (1978) *Living with Fear*, McGraw-Hill, New York.

Marks, I.M. (1987) *Fears, Phobias and Rituals*, Oxford University Press, New York.

Telch, M., Agras, W.S., Taylor, C.B. *et al.* (1985) Imipramine and behavioural treatment for agoraphobia, *Behaviour Research and Therapy*, **23**, 325–35.

Chapter 8

A Contextual Approach to Panic

MANUEL D. ZANE

INTRODUCTION

Panic disorder, with and without agoraphobia, is characterized by panic attacks that meet the criteria of the APA DSM-IIIR *Diagnostic and Statistical Manual* (1987). A panic attack is manifested by the sudden onset of inexplicable, widespread bodily and mental feelings of distress and the rising expectation of some uncontrollable, imminent disaster. Panic attacks also occur in simple phobias and other mental disorders. However, the nature of the panic attack, the phenomenon which all therapies for panic disorder seek to affect, is not yet sufficiently understood.

Klein (Klein *et al.*, 1987), largely from his studies of panic provoked by sodium lactate injections and treated with imipramine, seems to regard panic mainly as a fixed pathophysiologic state that derives from some hypothesized biochemical imbalance and results secondarily in the development of agoraphobia. Sheehan (1983) likewise embraces this fundamentally unitary biological concept which dominates the contemporary, largely pharmacologic therapeutic approach to panic and leaves insufficiently considered many facts readily available to clinicians who, during exposure treatment, have directly observed patients experiencing panic undergoing changes in its contexts.

Thus, Shear (1986) notes that lactate provocation studies of panic have been done 'dichotomously' on a 'present or absent basis' and raises these important questions:

1. Are panic episodes physiologically uniform or heterogeneous?
2. What are the mechanisms of action of physiologic and psychologic treatment?

Panic Disorder: Theory, Research and Therapy. Edited by Roger Baker

3. What are the cognitive and behavioural aspects of pharmacologic provocative treatment?

She then suggests that panic be studied more fully, not just in the laboratory, but also in its natural settings and that attention be paid to the psychologic aspects of panic, to the physiologic effects of fearful imagery and to the fact that panic and its underlying physiologic disturbance are not present all day.

In trying to understand human behaviour which is so complex and constantly changing (Boulding, 1980) and is so remarkably affected by imagery, fantasy and ideas many (Herrick, 1956; Bronowski, 1978; Engel, B.T. 1986; Rice and Greenberg, 1984) have called for the study of the actual transactions that constitute the process of change, in order to investigate the individual directly and to include disciplined introspective information (Mead, 1976; Marmor, 1982; Bridgman, 1961; Brain, 1965). Roger Baker's chapter on personal accounts of panic in this volume makes practical suggestions for gathering 'disciplined introspective information'. Tinbergen (1974) in his Nobel Prize Lecture, notes that direct, open-minded observation, 'of watching and wondering', which he calls a basic scientific method, though especially important in human beings, is too often 'looked down on by those blinded by the glamour of apparatus, by the prestige of tests and by the temptation to turn to drugs'. Engel, G.L. (1977) has long spoken of a crisis in both psychiatry and medicine because of adherence to the limited bio-medical model and has proposed a 'biopsychosocial' or systems approach in recognition of the profound effects upon behaviour of psychological and social factors in addition to biological factors. Recently Freedman, D.X. and Glass (1984) have stated, similarly, that 'elucidating the complex relationships of biology, subjective experience and behaviour is a major but increasingly realizable goal for both research and clinical activities in psychiatry'.

When a clinician observes and tries to influence a patient's state of panic as it is occurring, i.e. during exposure treatment and also in the office, an unusual opportunity is created to study and identify in many people under many conditions, factors in the context (psychological, physiological, affective, social and environmental) that make the panic *change*—get better and worse—in natural settings. It then becomes apparent that panic is *not* a fixed entity, psychologic or physiologic, but can,in response to changing conditions in the context, change in quality and quantity. Clearly, such behavioural changes in the present must be explained by something changing in the present. Psychoanalytic and behavioural therapy theories and biochemical hypotheses, which largely ascribe current behavioural disturbances to the effects of some fixed condition in the past or present, are not able to explain current *changes* in a phenomenon, particularly a series of changes. To comprehend observed changes in present behaviour we must adopt a systems approach and identify current factors and relationships changing in the present context and then conceptualize the processes determining the changes in behaviour. Such validatable concepts might then make it possible to achieve some integration of currently conflicting biological and psychological theories and therapies of panic.

Once *changes* in a piece of behaviour become the object of observation and study, as advocated by a host of important clinical investigators (Agras *et al.*, 1979; Bandura, 1978, Goldstein *et al.*, 1966; Lazarus, 1978; Parloff, 1982; Engel, B.T., 1986; Strupp, 1973; Herrick, 1956; Singer, 1974), many critical advances in the study and understanding of human behaviour become possible. The changes themselves can then, often, be recorded in their immediate contexts and such public data become available (1) for hypothesizing the processes that determine change and (2) for public validation and invalidation of any hypothesis. Thus scientific methodology (Mead, 1976) may finally be applied to the study of an important form of disturbed human behaviour—to changes in panic with, eventually, all of its inestimable benefits for the clinician, the researcher, the patient and possibly for society itself.

This presentation is concerned with offering a hypothesized conception of the mechanisms and processes by which the phenomenon of panic changes in its contexts as observed directly during a form of exposure therapy that I have called 'contextual analysis and treatment (CAAT)' or 'contextual therapy' for short (Zane, 1978). To illustrate the method and the results of studying such changes, a few recorded clinical examples of panic undergoing changes or recalled by patients during CAAT will be presented. From a multitude of such observations in many people under many conditions, a clinically-based verifiable psychophysiological concept of panic will be hypothesized as an alternative to the biological model of Klein and Sheehan and some answers will be attempted to the kinds of penetrating questions raised by Shear.

RECORDED CLINICAL EXAMPLES IN WHICH CHANGES IN PANIC AND PHOBIC BEHAVIOUR WERE OBSERVED

The following tape recordings were edited to isolate a series of changes in panic and phobic behaviour and their immediate contexts (Zane, 1965). Since these recording were made at different points over the years, the methodology of study for each recording varies though all are focused on observable changes in their internal and external contexts.

Tape 1: Sarah

This first tape shows Sarah, a forty-year-old woman with severe agoraphobia with panic, in my office. She had been making good progress when two unexpected recent panic attacks created a setback and disturbed her deeply. She was now terrified of re-experiencing them. I was trying to help her learn to accept and cope with her automatic panicky feelings rather than to try vainly to stop them from coming or to run away to avoid them.

Recording (2′ 27″)

Therapist: Now you've got to accept your ability to feel anything.

Patient: Right.

Therapist: But the feelings are not . . .

Patient: Dr Zane, I think I'm going to have to go out for a minute or two.

Therapist: Now wait a minute, honey, you can go out if you want to but please explain to me what's happening . . .

Patient: Suddenly that wave of fear coming over me . . . it just makes me relive the panic attack and I fear it's coming on again. My mind slipped away from what you were saying and I was kind of focusing again on the two panic attacks I've had recently and that kind of feeling came over me.

Therapist: Why do you want to leave?

Patient: I just felt it would make me more comfortable.

Therapist: That's the automatic way of dealing with it, you see, but there's another way of dealing which is what I'm doing now . . . getting you to stop and think with me. Doesn't that affect it a little bit?

Patient: Yeah, it does in fact because the feeling has ebbed.

Therapist: It ebbed.

Patient: The same feeling—that kind of a sensation in the palm of the hand, prickly sensation.

Therapist: Came in? (*He feels her palms*) Kind of moist too.

Patient: Yeah.

Therapist: Why are they moist?

Patient: Because I'm so frightened, I guess.

Therapist: Right.

Patient: And that sort of fuzzy feeling in the ears.

Therapist: What else do you feel?

Patient: Like a pressure suddenly coming onto one's head and ears.

Therapist: Right. Did you have a panic attack just now?

Patient: No, but if I wasn't here and I hadn't focused on you that first wave would have built up by, 'Now what if this is going to happen and this is going to happen?' (*Her voice quickens*) And then a second wave would have come up and then probably I would have hit a full-fledged panic which I am terribly frightened of.

Therapist: Of course.

Patient: That basically is what happens each time.

Therapist: What do you mean?

Patient: That is what creates the panic attack, a sort of wave that comes over me of fear. And then, when I start adding the ominous meaning, further feelings arise and then I'm away. It's so terrifying.

Therapist: Let me feel your hand now. Yeah, a little bit moist.

Patient: (*She sighs and laughs*) It's incredible, isn't it?

Therapist: Isn't it in a way sort of exciting to see this?

Patient: Yeah, today it has been a little exciting, actually. That is really interesting, that is really interesting.

Therapist: What do you mean?

Patient: How something as simple as getting involved, as it happened with you at that point could make that feeling drop down. That is really incredible.

Comments on observed changes

In this tape we see how, automatically, her fear began, triggered probably by automatic, disturbing bodily reactions to her immediate, private, fearful perception of what I was saying about her having to allow herself to feel anything, including panic (which I believe necessary for one to learn to gain control). She immediately recalled and bodily felt a little of her two previous panic attacks, regarded that as a 'first wave', anticipated that it would get worse by focusing on future endangering expectations and wanted to flee before the terrifying 'full-fledged panic' would hit again as the 'second wave'. As she spoke with me her panicky feelings dropped and came under control. What is interesting, as with many phobic and panicky people, is how some successful involvement, i.e. effective communication with me, promptly dropped her fear, averted her anticipated panic, and restored her bodily functions.

An additional noteworthy element is her excitement in recognizing the emergence of some understandable pattern to her otherwise, inexplicable and bewildering reactions. Recognizing the cause of one's changing behaviour can lessen, while not knowing, can intensify fear. Alone, unquestioned, it is highly unlikely that she would have been able to identify and relate the many, almost instantaneous elements that comprised the bases of her experience and her panic might have appeared as 'spontaneous'. Her panic included many automatic, fearful reactions to what she was feeling bodily and to what she anticipated. Also, in addition to her recognizing something of the structure of her panicky experience, she was able to sense the therapeutic value of her realistic involvement, in this case effective communication with her therapist.

Tape 2: Thomas

Thomas, severely agoraphobic for most of his life but still remarkably accomplished, had become panicked the day before while walking with his son in the park. Thomas and I decided to go there together to help him confront and study his problem. At the same spot where he had panicked the day before, he talked into a microcassette recorder.

(A), (B), (C) etc = points at which phobic and panic behaviour changed. (*Note*: 'Manny' refers to Dr 'Manny' Zane.)

Recording (45")

Patient: Here is where I began to feel—ooh—I'm getting elements of it. Manny! (A)

Therapist: That's all right. Stay with it. Talk and connect to me. But try not to lose yourself.

Patient: Yeah—oh! Just looking around—Manny!! Manny!! (B)

Therapist: That's good. That's all right. Just stay with it.

Patient: Oh Manny!!! (C)

Therapist: Stay with me.

(*Tapping is heard*)

Therapist: Feel my hand.

Patient: Yeah.

Therapist: Talk into the tape-recorder. You don't have to get out to recover. You're all right. (*Tapping continues to be heard*) You're connected but you can't stop the feeling.

Patient: Yeah. (D) ooh—it's gone down . . . (*Tapping continues to be heard*) . . . somewhat from that . . .

Therapist: All right. Don't worry about it.

Patient: . . . I'm going into my head, feeling that I could do anything because there were thoughts and feelings coming in that I didn't know how to handle . . . you know . . . What'll I do? How'll I hold onto myself? (E)

Figure 8.1 illustrates the changes in his levels of fear on a scale from 0 to 10 where 10 signifies an almost unbearable degree of fearful distress (i.e. panic) and 0 means no fear. The levels of fear, estimated by the patient, were determined by my questioning him afterwards about his feelings and thoughts at the observed points of change.

Observations at points of change

0, A, B, C etc. = Points of change in phobic and panicky behaviour

0 (score = 0) In my presence and talking together he was able to enter the very area where he had panicked the day before with his son.

A (score = 2) His level rose automatically and unexpectedly when, as he told me later, he looked ahead and saw how far he was from the exit gate.

B (score = 4) His level rose further, despite my words of assurance and my continued presence, in automatic response to his private thoughts, feelings and expectations of personally perceived dangers.

C (score = 10) (*Panic*) His level rose sharply and reached panicky levels, manifested by the audible terror in his voice, despite my best efforts.

D (score = 3) Intuitively I began *tapping* his arm while I spoke to him. His level promptly began to drop.

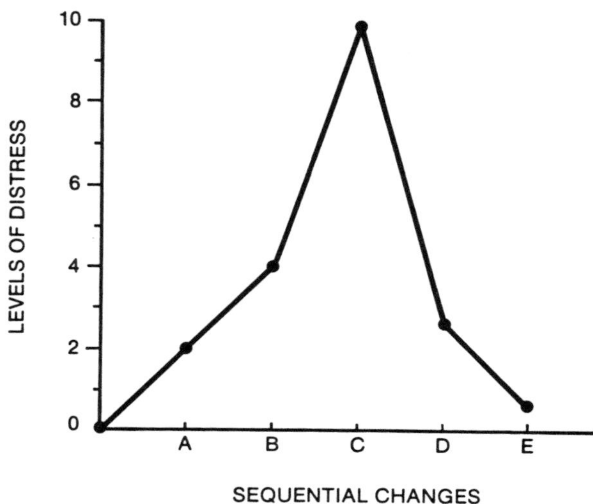

Figure 8.1 Changes in Thomas's phobic behaviour in open field. (Reproduced with permission.)

E (score = 1) His levels dropped still more as he talked and communicated what he was experiencing within when he became panicky and how he was feeling now.

Comments on observed changes

As Marmor (1982) has noted, the systems approach recognizes that the impact of all stimuli—internal and external—'depends on the specific context in which they are experienced and the context itself is a relative matter changing at different times and in different settings'. In this recording the physical setting remained the same, I was always there and talking as before and yet these remarkable changes occurred. As soon as the sight of the distant gate triggered, automatically and involuntarily, a low level of fear in that setting, he immediately became increasingly involved, within his head, i.e. with endangering thoughts of what would be and what was happening. His bodily and mental states rapidly changed. My presence and my talking then no longer had any influence on the swift rise of fear. Apparently, as his focus of attention went inwards so completely (onto swiftly escalating, dreaded expectations), much as occurs during hypnosis (Frankel and Orne, 1976), his responsiveness to the real environment faded. The more primitive physical contact created by my tapping, however, apparently quickly reoriented him and activated integrated responses to, for him, comforting physical and cognitive realities and removed him from the kinds of frightening thoughts, feelings and expectations that had created a rapidly spiralling fear experienced as a rising, terrifying panic.

Hypothesized processes affecting change

Here we can hypothesize a *pathogenic process* that creates increasing fear and rising panic as a result of automatic responses to rapidly growing numbers of privately perceived, unmanageable dangers (Breier *et al.*, 1987) and a *therapeutic process* which increases his orientation and effective responses to manageable realities. These pathogenic and therapeutic processes causing phobic behaviour to change seem common to all phobic and panic disorders: fear rises or falls in the situation depending on whether the person is responding then more to factors in the context that are being personally perceived and responded to as unmanageable and endangering or as manageable and comforting. Clinically, fear and panic, though qualitatively different, seem linked quantitatively as are water and steam passing from one phase to the other as a result of an overpowering preoccupation with and responses to increasing numbers of imagined and felt dangers.

Tape 3: Tess

Since simple phobias can also be associated with panic, the phenomenon of panic—a sudden, inexplicable, overwhelming, terrifying state of generalized disorganization—can be studied directly in the office as it changes in the simple phobias by bringing in the feared object. As Bandura (1978) has noted, the snake phobia is an excellent model for investigating the mechanism of changes in phobic behaviour.

Because changes in phobic behaviour, including panic, can be readily identified and controlled in the simple phobias, it is possible, when the patient is questioned as fearful behaviour changes, to detect the existence at times of conflict and of concordance between two aspects of her behaviour, the externally observable (E) and the internally felt (I) reactions.

The following symbols will be used in this case study:

Change A, Change B, etc. = sequential changes in phobic behaviour.
Task 1, *Task* 2, etc. = sequential tasks confronted.

(E) = external reactions
(I) = internal reactions
(+) = phobic behaviour got better (more appropriate to the task)
(−) = phobic behaviour got worse (less appropriate to the task)
( ) = no change in phobic behaviour when external situation changed

In 1960, Tess, a 28-year-old graduate student was in psychotherapy for social difficulties. As an added problem she had a snake phobia. She was afraid to open up new magazines or books lest she see a picture of a snake. Even the sinuous block letter 'S' at the beginning of some chapters could frighten her. We started a programme of gradually increasing exposure to the phobic stimulus. Eventually she could view a book of coloured snake pictures while I held it. I then asked:

Recording (3′ 38″)

Task 1

Therapist: Can you open the book up?

Patient: I just never would do this under normal circumstances (*She agreed to attempt the task*) So that I'm a little . . . you know . . . uneasy about it. (*Change* A: E+I−)

Task 2: (Therapist holds the book and describes some pictures, trying to prepare her for holding and looking at the pictures herself)

Therapist: You may come across a big snake that's coiled, with highlights, with a mouth, with scales, you know, that's shining.

Patient: I can really picture it, by the way, when you talk like that.

Therapist: Uh huh.

Patient: When you say 'scales' or '*tongue*' and '*rattlers*'.

Therapist: Uh huh.

Patient: And for that second I see only that. I want to run away. (*Change B*: E+I−)

Task 3

Therapist: You're going to hold it now.

Patient: Umh! (*She holds book and looks at pictures inside*) Mmn!

Therapist: What is it?

Patient: It's such a miserable experience to look at those things. (*Change C*: E+I−)

Therapist: Yes, in what way?

Patient: I don't know exactly except that . . . (*she continues to look through pages of book*) It just scares me somehow.

Therapist: Well, what do you feel?

Task 4

Patient: Shit! Now why can't I handle the book? Mmn. (*She lowers the book*)

Therapist: What happened when you put it down? What did you feel?

Patient: I just, I just couldn't stand to be that close to it and got away from it. (*Change D*: E−I−)

Therapist: Was it doing something to you?

Patient: Maybe. I tell you I didn't hold it long enough to let it do it to me. I think they did get some movement. I got some feeling that they were moving or something like that. I thought it was just a nest of them.

Task 5

Patient: (*She resumes looking at the book*) They're simply pictures on pages, pictures on pages . . . Well, that's not so bad. (*Change E*: E+I+)

Therapist: You said 'pictures on pages'. What were you doing there?

Patient: Well, I somehow tried to drill into myself that it's paper basically with colour on it, to make sure I don't let them move or that I don't think they're moving, they're alive.

Task 6

She kept on looking through the pages

Therapist: And if they do move, what?

Patient: Well, then I get scared, you know, and I forget that they're on paper (*Change F*: E+I−)

Therapist: I see.

Task 7

Patient: Umh. (*She sighs. Kept looking through pages*) I think it's much better if I don't focus too much on them . . . I just keep, sort of, moving my eyes around the page and I don't get kind of hypnotized by one of them. (*Change* G: E+I+)

Therapist: What does that mean?

Task 8

Patient: Well, if I begin to focus on it very carefully, then those scales just . . . just come real. I tell you another feature about that one . . . it's faced towards me. When it moves, it moves this way. (*Change H*: E+I−)

Therapist: Uh huh.

Task 9

Patient: Should I try to flip through a few more pages?

Therapist: Yes, if you wish.

Patient: Okay. Paper, paper, paper, paper . . . I really . . . I'm really doing my best to kind of control my reaction and . . . uh . . . (*Change I*: E+I+)

Therapist: Well, why?

Task 10

(She continues to look through pages. Suddenly throws the book to the floor . . . noise!!) (*Change J*: E−I−)

Therapist: All right, what happened there? You threw it down.

Patient: (*Long pause*) Something . . .

Therapist: Now you're picking it up again. Your face got flushed and you pulled all the way back. A little later you recovered and picked it up.

Task 11

Patient: At that second, this one seemed real. (*She points to coiled snake picture on the back cover*) I was so . . . fixed on . . . on telling myself that they're 'pages, paper, not real snakes' and

> . . . I forgot all about the cover on the book with the snakes, saw the cover on the book and (*snaps her fingers*) it just threw away all that good sense. (*Change K*: E+I+)

Comments on observed changes

Change A (E+I−): Even as she agreed to confront the task she felt uneasy indicating the simultaneous operation of opposing modes of reacting —externally (E) and internally (I).

Change B (E+I−): As she continued to contemplate confronting the task, she imagined scary details of a snake (i.e. 'tongue', 'rattlers') *that I never mentioned*. These self-created scary images 'spontaneously' increased her disturbed feelings and impulses to run but, objectively, she stayed with our task.

Change C (E+I−): Involuntarily and inexplicably to her, negative, scary feelings arose again and continued as she successfully looked at other pictures of snakes in the book.

Change D (E−I−): As she viewed more pictures her negative feelings intensified, involuntarily, until she felt compelled to stop and lowered the book. In reporting her reactions she first realized that as she kept looking she had begun to feel a snake was starting to move like it was alive and automatically she broke off contact.

Change E (E+I+): Spontaneously, altogether on her own, she reinforced her realistic perception and behaviour and her appropriate feelings by repeating aloud, 'pictures on pages', 'pictures on pages'.

Change F (E+I−): As she continued to look at more pictures at random, she reported again that she was struggling hard to keep the snakes from moving, scaring her and making her actually forget that they were on paper.

Change G (E+I+): She discovered by herself that when she moved her eyes around a page and didn't dwell on any snake picture, her fear dropped and she wouldn't get 'hypnotized'. (*Her words*).

Change H (E+I−): She observed also that her focusing 'very carefully' on scary details of the snake picture actually made it come 'alive' and move towards her. None the less she was able to stay with the task.

Change I (E+I+): As she flipped pages she kept saying aloud, 'paper, paper, paper'. This verbal activity, reinforcing the reality, apparently kept her disturbing perceptions and reactions under the control desired and needed for the task.

Change J (E−I−): While reporting her successful struggle to maintain control in the face of inner difficulties, she abruptly threw the book down without, for the moment, knowing why (e.g. a moment of panic).

Change K (E+I+): Slowly and silently, and in response to Z's questioning, she recovered, regaining her realistic orientation and picked up the book again. Then, feeling better and responsive to comforting, realistic information, she reviewed what had happened. She then realized that, while successfully carrying out our task, she had caught sight of an unexpected, coiled snake picture on the back cover. Immediately, she felt endangered by a 'real' snake, panicked and automatically broke away. For that moment, all information from the comforting realities including my presence and what she was learning vanished for her.

Tape 4: Harold

Once changes in panicky behaviour have been studied at first hand, it becomes possible to ask helpful questions and to better comprehend the patient's reports.

In the next tape, because of this patient's remarkable ability to describe his complex, inner experiences, we gain a closer and more comprehensible look at the processes that generated, for this man, the overwhelming exponentially increasing fear and disturbance that constitute panic.

Harold, a forty-year-old man, greatly handicapped as a result of severe agoraphobia with panic, was deeply disturbed about his mental and physical states. He tells how an episode of panic had developed the day before in a public place.

Recording (2′ 12″)

Patient: All of a sudden, I begin to get a, a feeling that I can't breathe, that I, that I'm having a coronary, though I have no pain. And, uh, my head begins to feel heavy, I begin to feel like I'm going to fall over. My legs feel like they can't carry me. In the meantime, I'm trying to hide them from the world. I'm frightened that I'm going to faint or collapse and before you know it, I'm shaking like a leaf and I don't know what's going to happen next. I'm certain that this is the end.

Therapist: Now you haven't talked much about your mind, how it works at that time. Can you do that?

Patient: Well, I have two minds at that time. One mind is this awareness of these terrible feelings and the other mind is trying to stay in the reality of the room and what's going on in the room with respect to the other people in the room. The fear is that I'm going crazy, I'm going mad, that this is going to be the worst attack I ever had. And that this attack can be so bad that I can never recover from it and I will have a complete, uh, just plunge into the depths of total black madness, you know, from which there is no recall. And I'm taking very short, rapid breaths (*he breathes rapidly and audibly*) I'm breathing like that and you know the world is closing in on me and this is the end, you know, there's no way out. I just want to run and get the hell out of there. Somehow, I don't know if I can make it back to the car and if I make it back to the car, how will I ever drive back home feeling this way, all the way back?

Therapist: How many things are going on for you?

Patient: Oh, it's, it's, that's why I call it a kaleidoscope or a calamity. They're all going on.

Therapist: What do you mean?

Patient: The whole thing is going on, the breathing, the head, the legs, the . . . when it really reaches the panic stage, it's all going on at one time. But I can't control it any more. They've just gone off like a rocket, you know. It's out of control. It's just going to go wherever it's going to go.

Therapist: In one direction?

Patient: No, it's more like a, like the fourth of July where it goes off in all directions. You know, the bang, and everything lets loose. And I don't know how to control, you know, I didn't know how, in the past, to control this at all.

Comment on these recalled changes

Figure 8.2 depicts, schematically, in this man the operation of the pathogenic 'phobogenic' or 'panicogenic' process. In his phobic situation, presumably because of past experiences there, he reacted automatically with some discomfort in breathing. Then, with astonishing rapidity, this minor disturbance increased, expanded and accelerated, exponentially, leaving him in a panic, feeling overwhelmingly distressed, bewildered, helpless and incapacitated.

My hypothesis is that while he still tried to react appropriately to the public place his organism automatically also responded, physiologically

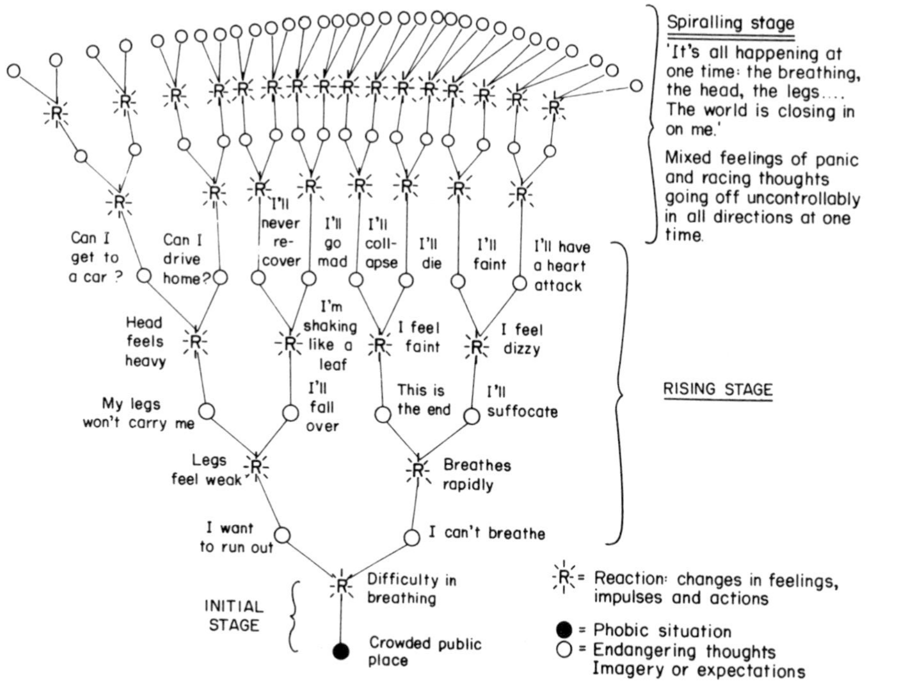

Figure 8.2 Schematic diagram of phobogenic process causing Harold's panic. (Reproduced with permission.)

to increasing and accelerating numbers of imagined, unmanageable dangers resulting in growing conflict and the spiralling disorganization and distress that we call panic. Others have also described this phenomenon as a positive feedback, snowballing, catastrophizing, pyramiding process, escalating mental and physical crisis and vicious circle (Margraf *et al.*, 1986; Beck *et al.*, 1985; Wilson, 1986; Zane, 1978, 1984).

Tape 5: Steve

The anti-panic effects of drugs, such as Xanax and the antidepressants, may become comprehensible from statements of patients who are taking such drugs if they are questioned about changes in their subjective experiences in their usually panicking situations. The following is an example of the kinds of observations such patients have made during therapy.

Steve, a 28-year-old man with agoraphobia and panic, often in traffic and on bridges, was reporting to me how the addition of three milligrams of Xanax daily to his treatment was now helping him deal more successfully with a usually panic-producing situation. I asked how he felt the drug was helping him and how he thought it affected him.

Recording: (46")

Patient: It gives me more time to think. OK? Let's say I was in the traffic. All of a sudden, like ten, not even ten, in five seconds I would see myself stuck in the traffic, never getting out, getting stuck on the bridge, all these disasters happening. OK? Now with Xanax I felt I was in the traffic but I had time in my mind. It like slowed everything down, where I had time to think. 'Well, I'm in the traffic. It'll move eventually.' It slowed down, rather than spiralling up in, in, in five seconds. I had a longer time to think about it and try to keep it under control. I don't know. I'm just saying. That's my theory. It might have been I was lucky.

Comments on reported changes

From such observations and comments by patients it is possible to hypothesize that these anti-panic drugs may affect the brain chemistry and the neurotransmitters so as to inhibit mainly the overwhelmingly rapid expansion and acceleration of imagined dangers and/or their bodily reactions that are typical of the exponentially spiralling 'phobogenic' or 'panicogenic' process. In this case, actually, Steve still seemed able to think, immediately, of the imagined dangers but apparently, because of the drug, did not react bodily to them and so, because the dangers did not *feel* real he did not experience panic. We may infer that, in exposure and other effective psychologic treatments, people learn likewise to prevent or keep under control the bodily disturbances characteristic of the panicogenic process, not by means of drugs but by getting increasingly involved with manageable, organizing realities instead of with fear-generating thoughts and imaginings. In Tape 3, spontaneously, Tess used her organizing verbalizations, e.g. 'paper, paper, pictures on pages' to reinforce the manageable realities, so as not to dwell on her imagery and so to maintain control over her tendency to develop a burst of panicky reactions to the imagined 'live' snake.

Tape 6: Rachel

A very important factor in the development of inexplicable panic—and, I believe, much, much too little appreciated in contemporary psychiatry and psychology—is the physiologic effects of frightening reactions to hosts of purely imagined past experiences. Apparently, these reactions, like experiences with realities (Kandel, 1983; Pardes, 1986; Freedman, A.M., 1974) have been stored away over the years as synaptic connections in the brain and can be automatically activated by association in the present and contribute greatly to the current state of panic.

The next tape will illustrate this phenomenal role in present panicky experiences of past frightening *imagined*, experiences.

The following material was taken, unedited, from a continuous video-taped recording of a person exposed in individually graded steps to her snake phobia stimuli during CAAT while measurements were made of changes in her heart rate, skin temperature, GSR and her subjective self-estimated levels of fear (Zane *et al.*, 1985).

Rachel was a 40-year-old artist with a snake phobia. Five years earlier, in her garden, she had picked up what she thought was a black hose which turned out to be a black snake. Quickly, terrified but unharmed, she dropped the snake and ran into her house. For five years thereafter, whenever she thought of going into her garden which she loved, she pictured herself encountering a snake, becoming frozen and helpless with fear while the imagined snake came at her, crawled up her body and wrapped itself around her neck and choked her. This, of course, never actually happened, but she *imagined and felt* it countless numbers of times. Now, she stated, whenever she anticipates encountering a snake she panics and feels terrified, starts to shake, feels cold, tense and anxious, her mouth becomes dry and her face feels tight, her heart palpitates rapidly, her chest feels constricted and her breathing becomes fast and heavy.

To both help and study her, during CAAT over three sessions she was videotaped and exposed gradually first, to snake pictures and then, in turn to small and larger plastic snakes. Continuous pulse rates and subjective levels of fear on a 0 – 10 scale were recorded. (Skin temperatures and GSR were also recorded but will not be considered here.) At her third session she held a life-sized plastic snake on her knee. Her pulse rate was 76 and her fear level was 2 at this point. Then, knowing her history, I asked if she could put that plastic snake around her neck. She promptly became anxious, her heart rate quickly rose to 96 and her fear level to 8. Her feet started to move involuntarily, associated with an expressed desire to leave. She remarked, 'I want to quickly put it around my neck and you see I still can't do it, though . . . It's so confusing, so out of control . . . It's still that crazy feeling . . . I can't believe I didn't put it around my neck.' As she kept speaking her heart rate fell to 83 and rose again to 96. She then seemed to be giving up and her heart rate fell to 75 and she reported a feeling of nausea. I then commented that she had to make up her mind whether to follow her feelings or her head as to what was best for her. She then said, 'I've got to follow my head'. Then, with many expressions of repugnance and increased levels of fear, her heart rate rose to 98 and she quickly raised the plastic snake from her knee and flung it around her neck stating, 'This is what it would look like if I had a snake around my neck . . . Now that I did it, it immediately became plastic and it looks artificial.' Her levels of fear promptly dropped to 2 and her heart rate to 75. Afterwards, she volunteered that she could not have done this if the therapist's same suggestion had been made on the telephone.

Comments about observed changes

From these videotaped observations we can infer that:

1. The neuronal patternings laid down in her brain as a consequence of her many, many involuntary reactions to the endangering snake *imagery* over the five years, were automatically activated by association and gave rise to conflicting, highly disturbing, otherwise inexplicable, physiological and psychological experiences in the present which largely determined her unrealistic phobic and panicky behaviour. Her cognitive awareness of reality, clearly, was not enough by itself for her to overcome the private effects on her behaviour and expectations of what she had experienced as a result of just her imaginings and thoughts over the five years.

2. Her automatic, physiologically-based highly distressing feelings when confronting the task may well have blocked out realistic information

(Hernandez-Peon *et al.*, 1956; Schatzman, 1984) and reinforced her unrealistic perceptions of the plastic snake as being truly real, endangering and 'not so plastic'. This is similar to what occurs in hypnosis, nightmares and florid psychosis where the imagined is experienced as reality with the excluding of information from existing realities.

3. The support and reinforcement for her realistic reactions from the therapist's presence, actions and words tipped the balance and enabled her eventually to make the choice to follow her public realistic views and desires despite her concomitant, very strong, private, unrealistic, fearful feelings, expectations and inclinations.
4. Once the snake was around her neck the manageable and comforting realities were automatically reinforced by the new factually harmless experience and then, immediately completely dominated her perceptions and her behaviour. Before that her bodily and felt reactions shifted several times depending on the relative strengths of her prevailing, conflicting perceptions that were based on her focus and on her objectives for that moment. But until, with the therapist's verbal and active encouragement, guidance and support, she actually raised the snake and confronted the reality, her involuntary, negative, unrealistic reactions to her private expectations predominated involuntarily.

DISCUSSION

From these and many other clinical observations of changes in panicky behaviour, it is hypothesized that panic is the psychophysiologic product of a disorganizing 'phobogenic process' made up of automatic, bodily reactions to exponentially increasing and accelerating numbers of mainly privately imagined dangers that conflict with each other and with the person's realistically integrated responses. Years ago Cannon (1939) stated, 'Reactions to new situations must remain harmonious with the internal integration necessary for life'. In panicky states, the growing numbers of conflicting reactions lead to functional disturbances throughout the organism and the person then feels gravely and incomprehensibly endangered even though the disturbances, though real, are almost always reversible (as with Sarah in Tape 1, and Thomas in Tape 2). However, once experienced, whether the triggers are identified or not, it seems likely that panic can be reproduced 'spontaneously' merely by association or memory.

Since, in panicky situations, the nature of the dangers imagined may keep changing, even from moment to moment, it is reasonable to assume that their associated physiological responses also vary in kind and degree.

Thus, this hypothesis predicts changing and varied physiological disturbances in states of panic and may explain the widely reported 'desynchrony' and inconstancy of physiological reactions found in panic and anxiety (Wiener, 1985; Curtis *et al.*, 1978; Woods, 1987; Aronson and Logue, 1988).

Panic comes automatically under greater control in what I have called the 'therapeutic process' when reactions to imagined dangers drop as the person shifts focus and reacts increasingly to manageable tasks and involvements which restores greater body integration. All effective therapies, cognitive, psychoanalytic, behavioural, exposure (Marks, 1987), inspirational or pharmacologic, albeit by different routes, probably are able to control panic when they enable the person to shift from responding to expanding numbers of imagined unmanageable dangers, which is disorganizing, to relatively fixed, manageable involvements, which is organizing. The problem is that what one thinks and especially what one feels in the panicky situation has developed from years of private, scary reactions in that situation. These automatic reactions must recur and must be accepted by the patient (Weekes, 1972) until sufficient new experiences over time enable that individual to respond predominantly in that same situation to other available information which makes possible a contrary, more realistic and manageable reaction and view. The gathering and cultivation of such experiences by the panicky patient, guided and supported by the therapist, and the development of such integrating, veridical beliefs over the time needed by the individual, is the ultimate objective of CAAT and many other exposure therapies.

The disorganizing and organizing effects of the phobogenic and therapeutic processes, respectively, can be related to familiar, elemental observations of all living creatures. Thus, in experiencing environments, both external and internal, that are felt as unmanageable, all organisms may become disturbed, physiologically, feel endangered and seek contact with the familiar and comforting (Hofer, 1975; Harlow and Zimmerman, 1959; Bowlby, 1969, 1988). Bowlby (1969) terms this innate tendency in the human being 'attachment behaviour' and states: 'In conditions of sudden danger or disaster a person will almost certainly seek proximity to another known and trusted person.' In early recognition of this same principle, but more generally, Claude Bernard (1865) stated: 'The mind like the body needs a primary point of support. The body's point of support is the ground which the foot feels, the mind's point of support is the known . . . Man can learn nothing except by going from the known to the unknown.' In the panicking person we witness how the fabulous human mind and imagination, in the absence of knowledge of what is happening, can create readily and almost instantaneously, hosts of unmanageable hypothesized unknowns to which the organism reacts automatically. Clearly, the operation of the psychophysiologic phobogenic or panicogenic process, in a few moments, as described so vividly by Harold in Tape 4, can do exactly the opposite of what the human being needs for a sense of safety and for organized mental and physical functioning.

In the future, it seems necessary to conduct studies of *changes* in panic occurring in natural settings (Engel, B.T., 1986) that combine simultaneous investigations in the person of *both* psychological and physiological factors that are associated with the changes. Such combined studies can be done with phobic people who experience changes in their panic behaviour in the phobic situations (Zane, 1978, 1982). Thus, people with simple phobias, like the snake phobia, can be studied and recorded in the office, while agoraphobic people can be observed and recorded as sequential changes occur in the field using telemetric and other elegant instrumental studies. Not only will the professions then learn more of the relationships of body and mind under varied conditions and be able to communicate better with each other but the patient, also, will acquire understandable and demonstrable reasons for the bewildering, otherwise inexplicable, experience that is panic. Such methodologically sound investigations will require the joint efforts and contributions of the clinician, the patient (who alone has access to his or her thoughts, imagery, and feelings), and the laboratory investigator to get the information in the system essential to develop a more scientific understanding of observed changes in phobic and panicky behaviour and to make research clinically meaningful (Barlow, 1981).

REFERENCES

Agras, W.S., Kazdin, A.E. and Wilson, G.T. (1979) *Towards an Applied Clinical Science*, W.H. Freeman, San Francisco.

APA DSM-IIIR (1987) *Diagnostic and Statistical Manual of Mental Disorders* (Third edition, Revised), American Psychiatric Association, Washington, DC.

Aronson, T.A. and Logue, C.M. (1988) Phenomenology of panic attacks: a descriptive study of panic disorder patient's self-reports, *Journal of Clinical Psychiatry*, **49**, 8– 13.

Bandura, A. (1978) On paradigms and recycled ideologies, *Cognitive Therapy and Research*, **2**, 79–103.

Barlow, D.H. (1981) Empirical practice and realistic research: new opportunity for clinicians, *Journal of Consulting and Clinical Psychology*, **49**, 147–55.

Beck, A.T., Emery, G. and Greenberg, R.L. (1985) *Anxiety Disorders and Phobias*, Basic Books, New York.

Bernard, C. (1865, Reprinted 1949) *An Introduction to the Study of Experimental Medicine*, Henry Schuman, New York.

Boulding, K.E. (1980) Our common heritage, *Science*, **207**, 831–6.

Bowlby, J. (1969) *Attachment and Loss: Attachment* (Volume 1), Basic Books, New York.

Bowlby, J. (1988) Developmental psychiatry comes of age. *American Journal of Psychiatry*, **145**, 1–10.
Brain, W.P. (1965) Science and antiscience, *Science*, **48**, 192–8.
Breier, A. *et al*. (1987) Controllable and uncontrollable stress in humans: alteration in mood and neuroendocrine and psychophysiologic function, *American Journal of Psychiatry*, **144**, 1419–25.
Bridgman, P.W. (1961) *The Way Things Are*, The Viking Press, Compass Books Edition, New York.
Bronowski, J. (1978) *The Origins of Knowledge and Imagination*, Yale University Press, New Haven.
Cannon, W.B. (1939) *The Wisdom of the Body*, W.W. Norton, New York.
Curtis, G.C. *et al*. (1978) Anxiety and plasma cortisol at the crest of the circadian cycle: reappraisal of a classical hypothesis, *Psychosomatic Medicine*, **40**, 368–77.
Engel, B.T. (1986) Presidential address: psychosomatic medicine, behavioral medicine, just plain medicine, *Psychosomatic Medicine*, **48**, 466–79.
Engel, G.L. (1977) The need for a new medical model—a challenge for biomedicine, *Science*, **196**, 129–36.
Frankel, F.H. and Orne, M.T. (1976) Hypnotizability and phobic behavior, *Archives of General Psychiatry*, **33**, 1259–61.
Freedman, A.M. (1974) Presidential address: creating the future, *American Journal of Psychiatry*, **131**, 749–54.
Freedman, D.X. and Glass, R.M. (1984) Psychiatry, *Journal of the American Medical Association*, **252**, 2223–8.
Goldstein, A.P., Heller, K. and Sechrest, L.B. (1966) *Psychotherapy and the Psychology of Behavior Change*, John Wiley and Sons, New York.
Harlow, H. and Zimmerman, R.R. (1959) Affectional responses in the infant monkey, *Science*, **130**, 421–32.
Hernandez-Peon, R., Scherrer, H. and Jouvet, M. (1956) Modification of electrical activity in cochlear nucleus during attention in unanesthetized cats, *Science*, **123**, 331.
Herrick, C.J. (1956) *The Evolution of Human Behavior*, Harper Torchbooks, The Science Library, Harper Brothers, New York.
Hofer, M.A. (1975) Studies on how early maternal separation produces behavioral change in young rats, *Psychosomatic Medicine*, **37**, 245–64.
Kandel, E.R. (1983) From metapsychology to molecular biology: exploration into the nature of anxiety, *American Journal of Psychiatry*, **140**, 1277–93.
Klein, D.F. *et al*. (1987) Panic and avoidance in agoraphobia, *Archives of General Psychiatry*, **44**, 377–85.
Lazarus, R.S. (1978) A strategy for research on psychological and social factors in hypertension, *Journal of Human Stress*, **4**, 35–40.
Margraf, J., Ehlers, A. and Walton, P.R. (1986) Panic attacks: theoretical models and empirical evidence. In I. Hand and H.W. Wittchen (eds), *Panic and Phobias*, Springer-Verlag, Berlin, New York.
Marks, I.M. (1987) *Fears, Phobias and Rituals*, Oxford University Press, New York, Oxford.
Marmor, J. (1982) Psychoanalysis, psychiatry and systems thinking, *Journal of the American Academy of Psychoanalysis*, **10**, 337–50.
Mead, M. (1976) Towards a human science, *Science*, **191**, 903–9.
Pardes, H. (1986) Neuroscience and psychiatry: marriage or coexistence? *American Journal of Psychiatry*, **143**, 1205–12.

Parloff, M.B. (1982) Psychotherapy research. Evidence and reimbursement decisions: Bambi meets Godzilla, *American Journal of Psychiatry*, **139**, 718–27.

Rice, L.N. and Greenberg, L.S. (1984) The new research paradigm. In L.N. Rice and L.S. Greenberg (eds), *Patterns of Change*, Guilford Press, New York.

Schatzman, M. (1984) Ghosts in the machine, *Psychology Today*, 99.

Shear, M.K. (1986) Pathophysiology of panic: a review of pharmacologic provocative tests and naturalistic monitoring data, *Journal of Clinical Psychiatry*, **47**, Supplement, 18–26.

Sheehan, D.V. (1983) *The Anxiety Disease*, Charles Scribner and Sons, New York.

Singer, M.T. (1974) Presidential address: Engagement-involvement: a central phenomenon in psychophysiological research, *Psychosomatic Medicine*, **36**, 1–17.

Strupp, H.H. (1973) *Psychotherapy: Clinical Research and Theoretical Issues*, Jason Aronson, New York.

Tinbergen, N. (1974) Ethology and stress diseases. Nobel Prize Lecture, 12 December, 1973, *Science*, **185**, 20–7.

Weekes, C. (1972) *Peace From Nervous Suffering*, Hawthorn Books, New York.

Wiener, H. (1985) The psychobiology and pathophysiology of anxiety and fear. In A.H. Tuma and J. Maser (eds), *Anxiety and the Anxiety Disorders*, Lawrence Erlbaum, Hillside, New Jersey.

Wilson, R.R. (1986) *Don't Panic*, Harper and Row, New York.

Woods, S.W. *et al.* (1987) Situational panic attacks, *Archives of General Psychiatry*, **44**, 365–75.

Zane, M.D. (1965) How one psychiatrist utilizes his tape recorder with patients, *Roche Reports*, **6**, 1.

Zane, M.D. (1978) Contextual analysis and treatment of phobic behavior as it changes, *American Journal of Psychotherapy*, **32**, 338–56.

Zane, M.D. (1982) A method to study and conceptualize changes in phobic behavior. In R.L. DuPont (ed.), *Phobia—A Comprehensive Summary of Modern Treatments*, Brunner Mazel, New York.

Zane, M.D. (1984) Psychoanalysis and contextual analysis of phobias, *Journal of the American Academy of Psychoanalysis*, **12**, 553–68.

Zane, M.D., Weinstein, S. and Drozdenko, R. (1985) *Towards a Scientific Assessment of Contextual Changes in Phobia Treatment*, presented at a full meeting of the Phobia Society of America, Dallas, Texas.

Section 3

The Etiology of Panic

Introduction: The Etiology of Panic

There are numerous etiological models for panic. Rather than having different writers proposing their models separately what to my mind was more profitable was to attempt to integrate, compare and evaluate the validity of the different models. This basically would have to be done by a single person (or team). There are few people with a sufficiently widespanning and intimate knowledge of the world literature who might be able to attempt such an integration. Jürgen Margraf and Anke Ehlers are exceptional in this respect; their substantial reviews of biological models of panic disorder and agoraphobia (1986a), of theoretical models of panic attacks (1986b), of the sodium lactate literature (1986c) and the mitral valve prolapse literature (1988) (written with W.T. Roth) demonstrate an outstanding ability for critical evaluation of substantial areas of panic research. Apart from such reviews they have presented a number of their own researches which have been quite significant (e.g. Margraf *et al.*, 1987a, 1987b).

In this section they review etiological models of panic. The different models broadly fall into two categories; medical/biological models and psychological models. Drs Margraf and Ehlers have prepared two chapters for this section addressing respectively the two types of model. They also present their own psychophysiological model of panic derived from their various reviews and researches, which might well prove significant in shaping future research.

REFERENCES

Margraf, J., Ehlers, A. and Roth, W.T. (1986a) Biological models of panic disorder and agoraphobia—a review, *Behaviour Research and Therapy*, **24**, 553–67.

Margraf, J., Ehlers, A. and Roth, W.T. (1986b) Panic attacks: theoretical models and empirical evidence. In I. Hand and H.V. Wittchen (eds), *Panic and Phobias* Springer, Berlin.

Margraf, J., Ehlers, A. and Roth, W.T. (1986c) Sodium lactate infusion and panic attacks: a review and critique. *Psychosomatic Medicine*, **48**, 23–51.
Margraf, J., Taylor, C.B., Ehlers, A., Roth, W.T. and Agras, W.S. (1987a) Panic attacks in the natural environment, *Journal of Nervous and Mental Disease*, **175**, 558–65.
Margraf, J., Ehlers, A. and Roth, W.T. (1987b) Panic attack associated with false heart rate feedback, *Behavior Therapy*, **18**, 84–9.
Margraf, J., Ehlers, A. and Roth, W.T. (1988) Mitral valve prolapse and panic disorder: a review of their relationship, *Psychosomatic Medicine*, **50**, 93–113.

Chapter 9

Etiological Models of Panic—Medical and Biological Aspects

JÜRGEN MARGRAF AND ANKE EHLERS

INTRODUCTION

The models that we construe to explain the origins and causes of psychological disturbances have a major impact on research and treatment. Empirical research guided by such etiological models will prove more systematic than simple *ad hoc* gathering of data. In the same vein, it is usually assumed that a thorough understanding of the causes of a disturbance may lead to more successful treatments addressing the underlying causes of the disorder rather than simply trying to alleviate symptoms that may prove to be superficial. We have earlier attempted to explicate the main constituents of two of the major competing etiological models for panic attacks and review the evidence for them (Margraf *et al.*, 1986a, 1986b). Since the completion of these articles in 1985 there have been a number of new developments. In the present chapter we will focus on recent results related to biological or medical illness models of panic. We will first briefly present the central assumptions of these etiological models. Then we will review the empirical evidence for these assumptions as well as other research on possible biological correlates of panic attacks. New developments in psychophysiological or cognitive models of panic will be dealt with in a separate chapter.

First, however, we have to clarify what type of patients this chapter is concerned with since the nosology of panic disorder and agoraphobia is still not well established. Recent studies show that the relationship between panic and avoidance behavior is more complex than often assumed (Rachman, 1987; Rachman and Levitt, 1985; Rachman and Lopatka, 1986; Arntz and van den Hout, 1988). While most agoraphobic patients seen in clinical settings have panic attacks (e.g. Thyer and

Panic Disorder: Theory, Research and Therapy. Edited by Roger Baker

Himle, 1985) the picture looks quite different in nonclinical samples. In epidemiologic studies (Weissman *et al.*, 1986; Wittchen, 1986) only a small percentage of agoraphobics also exhibit panic disorder (ranging from 6 to 16% in the various study sites) or limited panic symptoms (another 17% to 50%). We have argued elsewhere that such results speak for the influence of sampling bias in patients from clinical series (Margraf and Ehlers, 1988). In addition, it is still an open question whether panic disorder, agoraphobia, and generalized anxiety disorder can be strictly separated from one another or from depression (Roth and Mountjoy, 1982; Tyrer, 1984, 1986; Hallam, 1985; Stavrakaki and Vargo, 1986; Marks, 1987a). Since a complete discussion of these topics would be beyond the scope of this chapter we will restrict our contribution to those patients that meet DSM-III-R criteria for panic disorder with or without agoraphobia.* For a thorough discussion of the classification of panic and its relation to other anxiety disorders the reader is referred to the chapters by R. Hallam and I. Marks in the present volume.

EARLY ETIOLOGICAL ASSUMPTIONS

Early assumptions about the causes of panic attacks have primarily been a function of the discipline of the particular theoretician. We will not repeat the customary long list of diagnoses given to patients whose essential complaint was sudden episodes of anxiety (see Cohen and White, 1950 for a list). Instead, let us just present a few illustrative examples. Cardiologists tended to call the problem 'neurocirculatory asthenia' or 'irritable heart' and attributed its origin to a cardiac dysfunction. Westphal (1870) discussed the role of epilepsy, Benedikt (1870) focused on impairment of the visual system. Freud (1895a, 1895b) ascribed what he called 'anxiety neurosis' to a sexual mechanism that he conceived as totally biological: 'Its specific etiology is the accumulation of genital tension provoked by abstinence or frustrated genital irritation (. . . by the effects of coitus interruptus, relative impotence of the husband, excitement without satisfaction among fiances, forced abstinence, etc.)' (Freud, 1895b/1952, p. 352, translation by the author). However, all of these ideas were based on just a few cases or even single observations. As a rule, they could not be confirmed by subsequent research if such attempts were made at all. For instance, Cohen *et al.* (1946,

*In the following we will use the term 'panic patients' for patients fulfilling the DSM-III criteria for panic disorder or for agoraphobia with panic attacks. Only when important differences are present will we distinguish between these two disorders.

quoted in Cohen and White, 1950) did not find differential rates of coitus interruptus in patients and controls. More recent critical accounts of the Freudian approach can be found in Roth (1984) and Michels *et al.* (1985).

An example of the first experimentally based formulations is the lactate theory of anxiety by Pitts (1969). Based on reports that patients with anxiety neurosis are exercise 'intolerant' and produce excessive sodium lactate during exercise testing (reviewed by Ackerman and Sachar, 1974), Pitts and McClure (1967) developed the idea that the lactate ion itself could produce anxiety attacks in vulnerable subjects. They then decided to infuse anxiety neurotics and normal controls with sodium lactate using a placebo-controlled double-blind design. Thirteen of 14 patients but only two of 10 controls responded with anxiety attacks. This led Pitts (1969) to theorize that 'anxiety symptoms may ultimately be expressed through a common biochemical mechanism: the complexing of calcium ions by lactate ions. If this binding occurs in the intercellular fluid at the surface of excitable membranes such as nerve endings, an excess of lactate could interfere with the normal functioning of calcium in transmitting nerve impulses' (p. 73). For the next few years this theory received great attention until it was refuted on a number of grounds. It was argued, for example, that anxiety occurs without excessive lactate levels and that high levels of lactate occur without anxiety (Grosz and Farmer, 1969, 1972; Ackerman and Sachar, 1974, cf. Ehlers *et al.*, 1986a, Margraf *et al.*, 1986c). None the less, as we will discuss below the past few years have witnessed a revival of interest in the response to lactate infusions as a possible marker for panic attacks. Today, etiological models of panic attacks are more complex. They have stimulated a fascinating body of research growing at a tremendous rate. We will now review this research and the theoretical models guiding it.

MEDICAL-ILLNESS MODELS

The major impetus for the revival of interest in panic attacks has come from medical-illness models (MI models) of the disorder. The proponents of this approach use either the term MI model (e.g. Sheehan, 1982a, p. 156; Klein *et al.*, 1985, p. 510) or biological model. However, as Weiner (1978) argued, a truly biological model of disease needs to incorporate data from levels of organization as diverse as the cultural, evolutionary, and molecular. Modern neuroscience has accepted many levels of analysis as appropriate for mental phenomena (Uttal, 1987). In the same vein, van Praag (1985) has recently asserted that it would be unfortunate to use 'biological' as a synonym for 'physiological'. For these reasons MI model seems the more appropriate term to us. An excellent discussion of the underlying assumptions and problems of the medical-illness approach to anxiety is given by Hallam (1985).

The central assumption in MI models of panic is a *qualitative* difference between panic attacks and other types of anxiety. The hallmark of panic disorder is seen in the apparent 'spontaneity' of many panic attacks. It is admitted that everybody experiences discrete episodes of intense anxiety in acutely dangerous or stressful situations (Klein *et al.*, 1985). However, intense states of anxiety suddenly arising without clear-cut precipitants are considered biologically different from the anxiety normal people can experience or even the 'anticipatory' anxiety that patients with panic disorder show in between panic attacks. Thus, the lack of stimuli outside of the central nervous system that could explain the patient's anxiety is a major basis for all MI models of panic attacks. From this basis it is assumed 'that in contrast to stress-related situational anxiety, panic disorder is associated with a biochemical abnormality in the nervous system, to which there is a genetic vulnerability' (Sheehan, 1982a, p. 156).

Klein's and Sheehan's approaches

The most influential model of panic attacks was proposed by Klein (e.g. 1980, 1981). He suggests that both animals and humans have an innate biological mechanism that controls separation anxiety. Normally this unlearned alarm mechanism is activated by separation from specific social stimuli to which attachment had developed. There are two components of the mechanism related to protest (active, help-seeking behavior) or despair (passive behavior) analogous to Bowlby's (1969, 1973) first two stages of the response to separation. Klein proposes an abnormally lowered threshold in the 'protest' component due to some biological, genetically determined dysfunction as the underlying cause of panic attacks. With such a chronically lowered threshold activation of the mechanism could occur even without triggers. The experience of such 'spontaneous' panic attacks is then assumed to lead to other psychopathology characteristic for panic disorder, e.g., avoidance behavior (agoraphobia). A schematic representation of Klein's model is given in Figure 9.1.

In the same vein, Sheehan (1982a, 1984; Sheehan and Sheehan, 1983) sees 'spontaneous' panic attacks as the manifestation of an 'endogenous' subtype of anxiety that is simply a 'metabolic disease' (Carr and Sheehan, 1984). 'Exogenous' anxiety, on the other hand, is associated with external stimuli and is supposed to depend on different physiological mechanisms. Sheehan (1982a) strongly emphasizes that his patients describe 'spontaneous panic attacks as a special kind of anxiety never before experienced, even under stress' (p. 156). Secondary to this metabolic

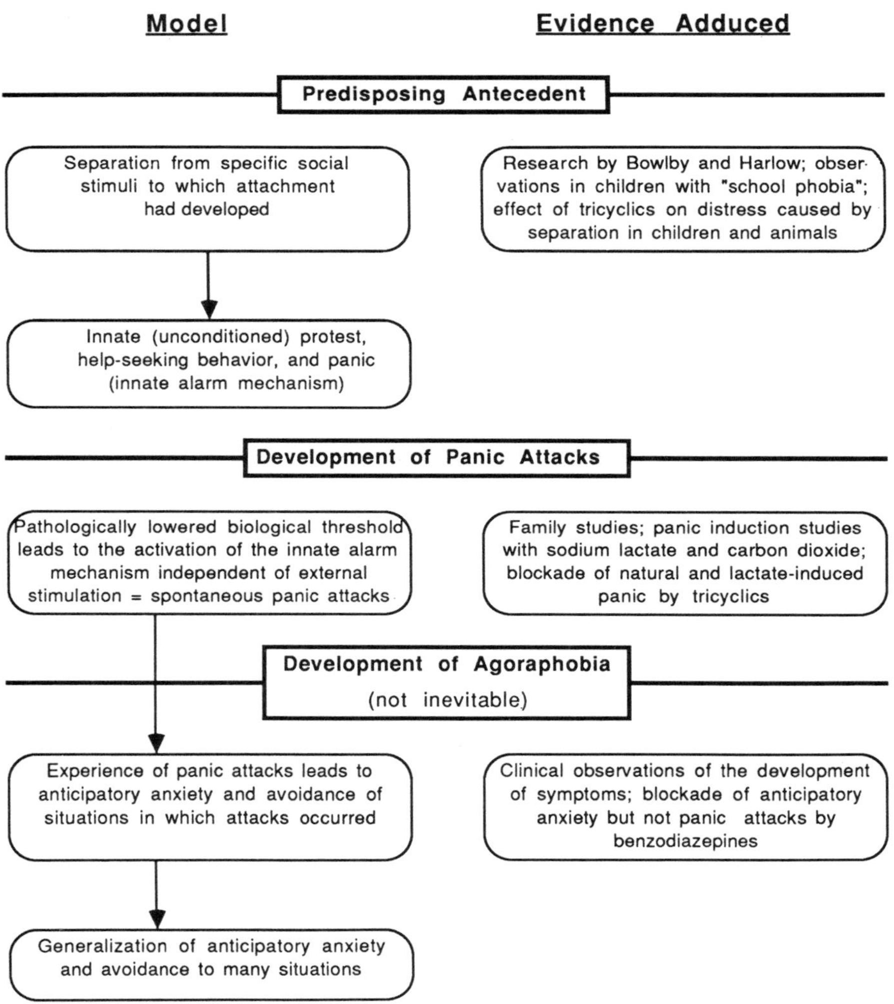

Figure 9.1 Schematic representation of Klein's model of panic disorder and agoraphobia (modified from Margraf *et al.*, 1986a).

core disease and superimposed on it, learning processes may lead to phobic avoidance behavior or even the generalized clinical picture of agoraphobia. As possible stages in the natural history of the disorder Sheehan and Sheehan (1983) name limited symptoms attacks, full blown panic attacks, hypochondriasis, phobic avoidance, and finally reactive depression. Stressors are given a non-specific exacerbating rather than a causal role in this approach. In contrast to Klein, separation anxiety is not considered necessarily related to panic.

Proponents of the MI models forward the following main arguments for their approach:

(a) *Treatment specificity*. Different drugs are therapeutic for panic attacks and other types of anxiety. Tricyclic antidepressants and monoamine oxidase (MAO) inhibitors treat panic but not 'anticipatory' anxiety, sedatives and minor tranquilizers (especially benzodiazepines) treat 'anticipatory' but not panic anxiety.
(b) *Experimental panic induction*. Panic attacks can be induced by specific biological agents in panic patients but not in other patients or normal controls.
(c) *Spontaneity of panic attacks*. The majority of panic attacks especially at the onset of the disorder occur spontaneously, that is, not in response to specific stimuli.
(d) *Genetic specificity*. There is a strong genetic factor for panic that is transmitted independently of the risk for other anxiety disorders.
(e) *Separation anxiety*. Childhood separation anxiety is a precursor to panic attacks that shows similar clinical characteristics and response to tricyclic treatment. This argument is relevant only to Klein's model.

Klein's and Sheehan's models have been presented more extensively in our earlier publication (Margraf *et al.*, 1986a). We shall now review the empirical evidence for the arguments listed above.

Empirical support for Klein's and Sheehan's models

Treatment specificity

Different drugs are therapeutic for panic attacks and other types of anxiety. Tricyclic antidepressants and MAO inhibitors treat panic but not 'anticipatory' anxiety, sedatives and minor tranquilizers (especially benzodiazepines) treat 'anticipatory' but not panic anxiety.

This is the most important argument for the MI models and the one that initiated their development. When we finished our earlier reviews (Margraf *et al.*, 1986a, 1986b) a major problem was that this argument had not been adequately tested by empirical research. The available findings, however, pointed to a highly critical appraisal. Since then, a number of studies have appeared that not only support our earlier conclusions but make it possible to state that the drug specificity argument in its original form is wrong. Tricyclic antidepressants such as imipramine and clomipramine been shown to reduce generalized or 'anticipatory' anxiety in patients with other primary diagnoses (Beaumont, 1977; Marks *et al.*, 1980; Sheehan *et al.*, 1980; Munjack *et al.*, 1985; Charney *et al.*, 1986a; Kahn *et al.*, 1986; Buigues and Vallego, 1987). There were also clear-cut anxiolytic effects in the only controlled study of imipramine in patients with a DSM-III diagnosis of generalized anxiety disorder (Kahn *et al.*, 1986). Thus, the specificity of tricyclics to panic anxiety has been refuted. In addition, it is well established now that benzodiazepines have powerful effects on both the intensity and frequency of panic attacks if prescribed in a way similar to the usual prescription for imipramine. If constantly high blood levels of the drugs are maintained over a prolonged period of time, diazepam (Noyes *et al*,. 1984; Dunner *et al.*, 1986; Dager *et al.*, 1987), alprazolam (Chouinard *et al.*, 1982; Charney *et al.*, 1986a; Dunner *et al.*, 1986; Rickels and Schweizer, 1986; Rizley *et al.*, 1986; Dager *et al.*, 1987) and halazepam (Fann *et al.*, 1982) all have panic-reducing effects similar to those of imipramine. In addition to these controlled studies, lorazepam (Schweizer, 1986, quoted in Rickels and Schweizer, 1986), clonazepam (Fontaine and Chouinard, 1984; Spier *et al.*, 1986), and a number of other benzodiazepines have had similar effects in uncontrolled studies. The earlier claims of specificity of benzodiazepines that were based on clinical experience (e.g. Klein, 1980; Sheehan, 1982b; Klein *et al.*, 1985) are thus clearly contradicted by systematic empirical studies.

We cannot address in depth here the difficult issue whether or not panic attacks should regularly be treated pharmacologically. The chapter by L. Walker and G. Ashcroft concentrates on the pharmacological approach in more detail. Of interest is the theoretical point that the claim of differential efficacy for antidepressants and benzodiazepines has been proven wrong. In order not to give a too uncritical account, however, let us mention that there are a number of problems with the drug treatments. First, the long-term outcome of these therapies is not well known (Grunhaus *et al.*, 1981; Matuzas and Glass, 1983; Telch *et al.*, 1983; Klein, 1984). Relapse rates after discontinuation may be high (Pohl *et al.*, 1982; Keefe and Agras, 1983; Marks, 1983; Ballenger, 1986; Pecknold and Swinson, 1986; Fyer *et al.*, 1987). Follow-up studies have usually involved patients treated with drugs plus some kind of psychological therapy. In one such study Mavissakalian and Michelson (1986) found no difference between agoraphobics treated with behavior therapy plus imipramine or placebo two years after treatment. Tyrer and Steinberg (1975) reported a one-year follow-up of 26 agoraphobics. Blind comparisons showed no significant differences between patients treated with phenelzine or placebo. Despite the intention to stop all drugs at the end of treatment, 10 of 13 phenelzine patients continued to take it and three (23%) were still taking it at follow-up because of a return of symptoms on stopping or reducing the drug. Difficulties in discontinuing the drug are especially frequent in the case of the benzodiazepines (Dupont and Pecknold, 1985; Pecknold and Swinson, 1986; Fyer *et al.*, 1987). In a partial analysis of the Upjohn cross-national collaborative panic disorder study, Pecknold and Swinson (1986) found that only 57% of their alprazolam patients completed regular withdrawal. Among those who did, the proportion of patients with 'zero' panic attacks dropped from roughly 60% at peak dose to about 40% two weeks after discontinuation of the drug. In contrast, among the 43% placebo-treated patients who completed 'withdrawal', the number of panic-free patients rose from about 40 to 50% two weeks after stopping the drug. Thus, placebo-treated patients did significantly worse only at peak drug dose, but significantly better at two-week follow-up. While the mechanism of action of drug therapy remains unknown, the relatively high proportion of positive responses to placebo (e.g. Pecknold and Swinson, 1986; Dager *et al.*, 1987; Mavissakalian, 1987) points to a significant contribution of non-pharmacological effects.

In an extension of our earlier reviews we have called the argument discussed here 'treatment' rather than 'drug specificity.' This takes into account that Klein and Sheehan also made statements about non-pharmacological therapies. Specifically, they assume that behavioral treatment affects phobic anxiety related to avoidance of external phobic stimuli but not panic anxiety. However, in the past few years a number of studies have shown that cognitive behavioral treatments can strongly reduce or totally eliminate panic attacks even in patients without agoraphobic avoidance behavior (Barlow *et al.*, 1984; Clark *et al.*, 1985; Salkovskis *et al.*, 1986a; Griez and van den Hout, 1986; Öst, 1988; Klosko *et al.*, 1988; Shear *et al.*, 1988). The results are not only maintained during follow-up (up to two years) but often improve further after the end of therapy. Similar to the drug treatments there seems to be no treatment specificity for behavior therapy. The therapeutic techniques include exposure to feared stimuli, cognitive restructuring, relaxation, and breathing training, all of which are also used in the treatment of phobic anxiety. The main difference seems to be that they are aimed internal (primarily bodily) stimuli rather than external phobic situations. In conclusion, recent research has refuted the treatment specificity argument.

Experimental panic induction

Panic attacks can be induced by specific biological agents in panic patients but not in other patients or normal controls.

The list of 'successful' and presumably 'biological' challenges has grown quite long over the past few years. It now includes lactate infusion, carbon dioxide inhalation, and hyperventilation as well as oral or intravenous yohimbine, isoproterenol, (nor-)epinephrine, caffeine, beta-carboline ligands for benzodiazepine receptors, and gamma-aminobutyric acid (GABA). We will mainly focus here on the results of standard sodium lactate infusion studies since this is the first and by far the most frequently used method to induce panic attacks. However, our conclusions apply to the other challenges as well. After a review of the argument for the MI models we will examine methodological problems and the validity of response to lactate as a laboratory model for panic. We will then present the evidence for differences between panic patients and controls, discuss whether any necessary or sufficient physiological conditions for panic have been identified, and present evidence for the influence of cognitive variables. We have reviewed the panic induction literature earlier (Ehlers *et al.*, 1986a; Margraf *et al.*, 1986c). In addition, there are reviews by Guttmacher *et al.* (1983), Gorman *et al.* (1985a), Shear (1986), and Ley (1988). In order to avoid redundancy we will rely as much as possible on these reviews.

Earlier claims. The usual claim with respect to lactate infusion has been that 65–100% of all panic patients respond with panic attacks, while controls never or only very rarely do so (Klein, 1981; Shader *et al.*, 1982; Carr and Sheehan, 1984; Fyer *et al.*, 1985; Dager *et al.*, 1987). While it was originally thought that response to such challenges could be a specific marker for panic disorder more recent studies have shown approximately similar rates of 'panic' responses in all patients with a history of (even infrequent) panic attacks regardless of whether their primary diagnosis is panic disorder, generalized anxiety disorder, depression, or bulimia. Lower frequencies essentially comparable to those of normal controls are reported for patients with obsessive-compulsive disorder, social phobia, generalized anxiety disorder, or depression without a history of panic attacks (Gorman *et al.*, 1985a, 1985b; Liebowitz *et al.*, 1985a; Cowley *et al.*, 1986; Dager *et al.*, 1987; McGrath *et al.*, 1985; Walsh *et al.*, quoted by Gorman *et al.*, 1985a). Thus, response to lactate seems to be more related to the phenomenon of panic attacks than to the clinical syndrome of panic disorder. The critical point for the MI models is whether the results of panic induction studies show a *qualitatively distinct* response of panic patients that can only be explained by a purely biological mechanism. As we will see, this is not the case for a number of reasons.

Methodological problems. We have earlier documented severe methodological problems in most lactate infusion studies including inadequate control of demand characteristics, expectancy effects, and other cognitive variables as well as the influence of baseline levels of anxiety and arousal (Margraf *et al.*, 1986c). The critical relevance of such variables is underlined by recent research. Studies using lactate (van der Molen *et al.*, 1986) and CO_2 (van den Hout and Griez, 1982) in healthy non-anxious volunteers and hyperventilation (Margraf *et al.*, 1989) and CO_2 (Rapee, in press) in panic patients have clearly established that the effects of panic challenges can be strongly altered by manipulating expectancy experimentally. In addition, it has been firmly established that those subjects that reach the highest levels of anxiety and/or autonomic arousal during panic induction already have heightened levels during the baselines preceding the challenge in lactate-induced (Kelly *et al.*, 1971; Freedman *et al.*, 1984; Ehlers *et al.*, 1986b; Liebowitz *et al.*, 1985b; Yeragani *et al.*, 1987; Dillon *et al.*, 1987; Balon *et al.*, 1988; Cowley *et al.*, 1987), CO_2-induced (Ehlers *et al.*, 1988a; Margraf, 1988), or phobic exposure-induced panics (Rachman, 1987).

A general problem in evaluating the results of panic induction studies is that most of them inappropriately dichotomize the subjects' complex responses simply into panic or not panic. However, this distinction is difficult since panic attacks show considerable variation across and within individuals (Margraf *et al.*, 1987a) and there are no generally accepted objective criteria for panic attacks (Ehlers *et al.*, 1986c; Margraf *et al.*, 1986c; Shear, 1986). Different criteria result in widely different percentages of panic attacks as illustrated by data from a CO_2-study (Margraf, 1988) in Figure 9.2.

Neither the consensus of expert clinicians nor patient reports about panic can be taken at face value. Ehlers *et al.* (1986b) showed that patients and controls differ systematically in their response styles to questions about somatic symptoms. A demand to stop the challenge is not a useful criterion of panic either, since it is determined by a combination of baseline levels, reactivity, response bias, and avoidance behavior (Ehlers *et al.*, 1986c). In our lactate infusion study, all four patients who asked to stop had clinical diagnoses of avoidance behavior and high baseline levels, but average reactivities (Ehlers *et al.*, 1986b). Similarly, having a rater determine the occurrence of a panic attack is subject to bias. There are now two published reports showing that the rate of lactate-induced 'panic' drops considerably in patients and increases in control subjects if raters are blind to diagnostic status and/or infusion content (73% vs. 51% in panic patients and 0% vs. 13% in normal controls, Gorman *et al.*, 1985a, 70% to 42% in anxious depressives, McGrath *et al.*, 1985). In addition to being prone to biases, relying on the artificial dichotomous variable 'panic/not panic' entails a considerable loss of information compared to the measurement of continuous variables.

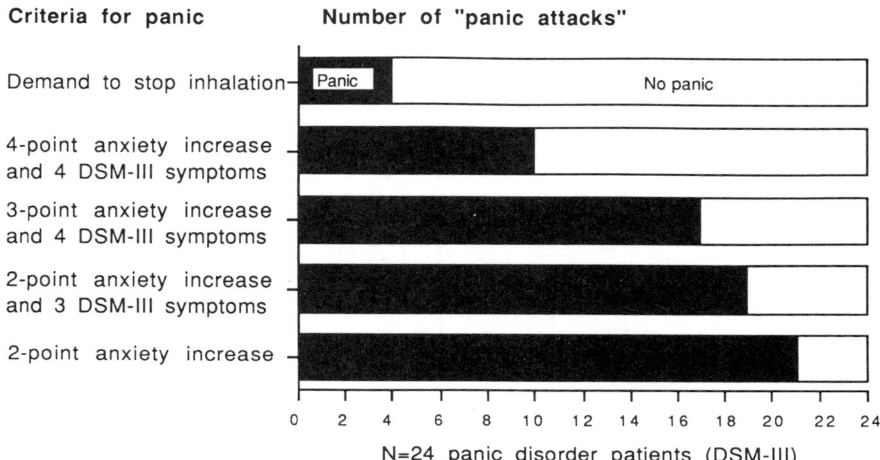

Figure 9.2 The proportion of panic attacks induced by CO_2 depends on the criteria used to determine the presence of panic (modified from Margraf, 1988).

As Shear (1986) pointed out, it is very well 'possible that assessing lactate-induced panic attacks on a dimensional severity scale would produce different results' (p. 20). Finally, physiological measures do not offer a solution. The variable that shows the highest degree of covariation with subjective anxiety within and across studies is heart rate. But even here drastic desynchrony between subjective and physiological measures may occur. As an example, Figure 9.3 shows the heart rates of the two patients with the highest anxiety ratings in the lactate infusion study of Ehlers *et al.* (1986b). Both patients reported experiencing a panic attack and yet heart rate increased in only one of them. For all of the above reasons, the best approach is to record the effects of panic challenges in detail.

Validity of laboratory models. How similar are then the patients' responses to lactate and naturally occurring panic attacks? About 70% of all panic patients rate lactate-induced effects and naturally occurring panic as similar when asked directly (Rainey *et al.*, 1984; Ehlers *et al.*, 1986b; Margraf, 1988). However, the similarity generally does not achieve the degree of total identity. Moreover, the retrospective ratings of naturally occurring panic attacks on the 'tension-anxiety' scale of the Profile of Mood States (POMS, McNair *et al.*, 1981), on the STAI, and on the panic symptoms of DSM-III are significantly higher than the scores during lactate or CO_2 (Ehlers *et al.*, 1986b; Margraf, 1988). The maximal anxiety that the average

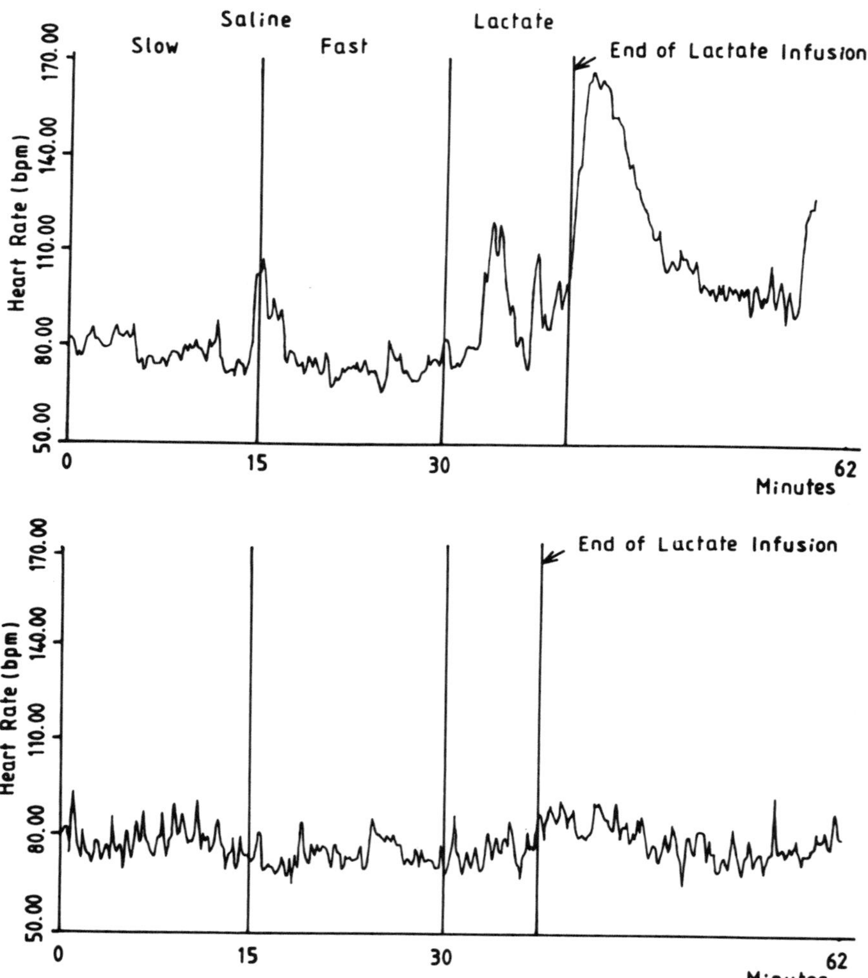

Figure 9.3 Desynchrony between heart rate and subjective anxiety in the two subjects with the highest anxiety ratings in the lactate infusion study of Ehlers *et al*. (1986b).

patient reaches under lactate or CO_2 varies in the published studies from 5 to 7.9 on a 0 to 10 scale with an average across studies of 6.3 (adjusted for sample size, calculated from Kelly *et al.*, 1971; Lapierre *et al.*, 1984; Ehlers *et al.*, 1986b; Margraf, 1988). Similarly, the results on the psychometric State-Trait Anxiety Inventory (STAI, state form, Spielberger *et al.*, 1970) vary from 54 to 62.5 with an average of 59.7 (calculated from Rainey *et al.*, 1984; Ehlers *et al.*, 1986b, Margraf, 1988). These values are not as high as one usually associates with the term 'panic.' They are within a standard deviation of the mean of a general sample of neuropsychiatric patients at rest (Spielberger *et al.*, 1970).

In the same way psychophysiological or biochemical variables show changes of only moderate intensity. The variable consistently yielding the largest effect is the heart rate response to lactate. The maximal heart rate of panic patients under lactate is on the average 100–110 beats per minute (bpm), the increase about 20 bpm (calculated from nine studies reviewed by Ehlers *et al.*, 1986a). In comparison, actors during monologue or inexperienced parachutists before a jump show values of 145–150 bpm (Fenz and Epstein, 1967). Thus, the findings from panic induction studies show that challenges such as lactate, CO_2, or yohimbine do not provoke 'maximal' anxiety. This led us at first to believe that there was only limited similarity between these experimental models and naturally occurring panic. A firm conclusion on this question, however, has to be based on systematic information on naturally occurring panic.

Laboratory observations of spontaneously occurring panics are very rare (Lader and Mathews, 1970; Cohen *et al.*, 1985; Cameron *et al.*, 1987). More informative are ambulatory monitoring studies in the patients' natural evironment. The first reports of such studies were given by Taylor *et al.* (1983, 1986), Freedman *et al.* (1985), Harbauer-Raum (1987), Margraf *et al.* (1987a), and Shear *et al.* (1987, submitted), (see chapter by R.B. Freedman in this volume and Shear (1986) for reviews.) Of importance to our topic is the finding of Margraf *et al.* (1987a) that the average anxiety during 175 diary recorded panic attacks was only 5.6 (0–10 rating scale). Many attacks were not accompanied by heart rate increases and those that did occur were rather small (mean of only 10 bpm during situational panics, less during spontaneous attacks). These results resemble the effects of lactate or other experimental panic induction procedures. With respect to the pattern of symptoms, however, there were clear-cut differences. While the same overall group of symptoms were observed during natural and experimentally induced panic, the patterns were very different as shown in Figure 9.4. The rank correlation between the average symptoms under lactate infusion and during natural panic was less than 0.10 and not significantly different from zero.

Another important finding in this context is the patients' tendency to retrospectively distort their descriptions of panic attacks. Figure 9.5 shows the frequency of 14 panic symptoms during 175 attacks recorded on a diary immediately after each attack (concurrent measurement) and the results of two retrospective assessment methods, namely a highly reliable questionnaire (Symptom questionnaire, Ehlers *et al.*, 1986b) and a clinical interview (Margraf *et al.*, 1987a). The differences between concurrent

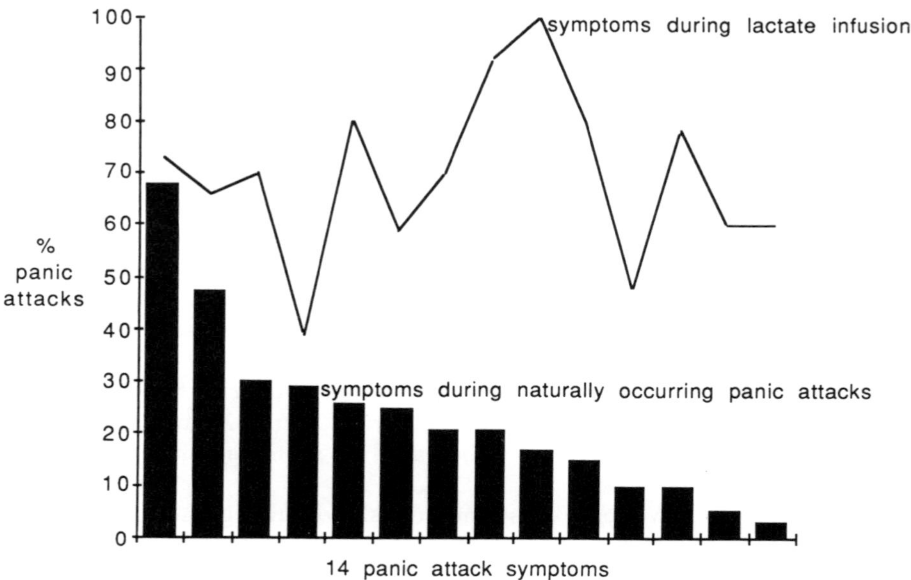

Figure 9.4 The frequency of 14 panic attack symptoms during 175 naturally occurring attacks (Margraf *et al.*, 1987a) and in response to lactate infusion (averaged across four studies reviewed in Margraf, 1988). Symptoms are (from left to right): palpitations, dizziness/lightheadedness, dyspnea, nausea/abdominal distress, sweating, chest pain/discomfort, fear of going crazy or losing control, trembling/shaking, hot or cold flashes, derealization/depersonalization, faintness, paresthesias, choking or smothering, fear of dying.

and retrospective assessment were highly significant (Wilcoxon tests; diary vs. questionnaire: $z = 3.297$, $p < 0.001$; diary vs. interview: $z = 3.296$, $p < 0.001$). Thus, panic attacks retrospectively appear much more severe than at their actual time of occurrence. R. Baker's suggestion in Chapter 5, that descriptions of panic by patients should be collected as soon as possible after the event, would appear to be a useful guideline.

Taking the ambulatory monitoring data into account, we can conclude that the results of experimental panic induction methods appear to have reasonable similarity but not total identity with naturally occurring panic. If this is accepted, however, panic attacks on the average appear to have only average severity. Thus, they are not characterized by the intense anxiety normally associated with the term 'panic'. It may therefore be more appropriate to use the term 'anxiety attack' as was already proposed by Freud (1895a).

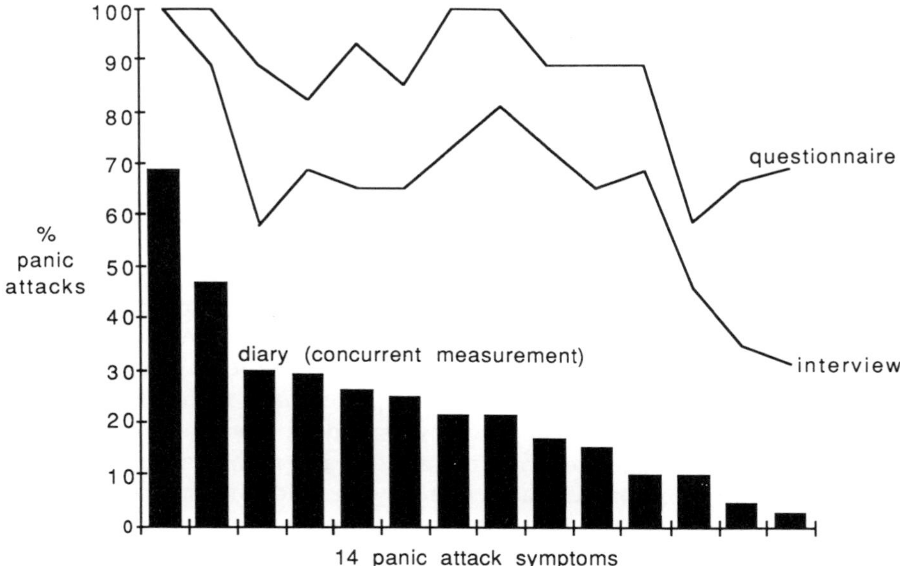

Figure 9.5 Proportion of all panic attacks accompanied by 14 panic symptoms as assessed concurrently by diary or retrospectively by questionnaire or interview (Margraf *et al.*, 1987a). The sequence of symptoms is the same as in Figure 9.4

Differences between panic patients and controls. Now that we have established a reasonable validity for this experimental model of panic let us investigate how different the responses of panic patients and normal controls are. Some studies have attempted to show differential reactivities in patients and controls by first defining subgroups of 'panicking' and 'non-panicking' patients (e.g. Liebowitz *et al.*, 1985b). However, this type of analysis is circular (cf. Ehlers *et al.*, 1986c). The patient group is split *post hoc* into responders and nonresponders, and it is then demonstrated that responders among the patients react stronger or faster than the controls as a whole. It is justifiable to form subgroups for such purposes as looking for predictors of reactivity. But in this case it is logical and indeed necessary to create subgroups among both controls and patients. Since this has not been done so far, we will focus on the comparison of the complete patient and control groups.

Significant qualitative differences would exist if core psychological or physiological changes occurred exclusively in patients, or if clearly different patterns of changes were observed. However, our earlier reviews (Ehlers *et al.*, 1986a; Margraf *et al.*, 1986c) showed that this is not the case. All symptoms as well as subjective, psychophysiological, or biochemical changes occur in both patients and controls and the patterns of changes are very similar. It is possible that increases in some variables may be stronger in panic patients than in controls. However, only some studies report this (and only for some variables) whereas others find equal increases. The variable that most often shows a steeper increase in patients is the number or intensity of bodily symptoms. As discussed above, however, patients have a systematic bias of over-reporting somatic symptoms which renders this type of measure less valid.

In a lactate infusion study we had found similar (phasic) responses of panic patients and normal controls although overall (tonic) levels of anxiety and arousal were significantly different (Ehlers *et al.*, 1986b). We have replicated and extended these findings using inhalation of 5.5% CO_2 following Gorman *et al.*'s (1984a) protocol. We again found no significant differences between the responses of 24 panic patients and 18 normal controls (Margraf, 1988; preliminary results in Ehlers *et al.*, 1988a). Moreover, the effects of two standard stress tests not usually considered panic challenges (cold pressor test and mental arithmetic) were comparable to those of CO_2, a presumably specific panic challenge. As in our earlier study, we did find significant differences in baseline levels of anxiety and arousal. Using discriminant analyses it was obvious that tonic (baseline) levels differentiated much better between patients and controls than reactivity measures. The best discrimination was obtained using the baseline anxiety rating (0–10 scale), STAI score (83.3% correct classifications for both), or heart rate (78.9% correct classifications). Reactivity measures did hardly better than chance. The 'best' discrimination here was with the responses to CO_2 on anxiety ratings and heart rate (each yielding 63.4% correct classifications).

Differential responses of patients and controls could be caused not only by an innate vulnerability of panic patients as suggested by the MI models but also by cognitive mediating variables such as expectancy. It is likely that panic patients and normal controls enter panic induction studies with very different expectations. We have recently shown that the amount of increase in panic patients' anxiety and arousal strongly depends on whether they were told that they were undergoing a 'biological panic attack test' or a 'fast paced breathing task'. This effect did not occur in normal controls. Figure 9.6 shows the results of a study using hyperventilation as the challenge in 73 panic patients and 46 normal controls (Margraf *et al.*, in press). It is important to note that the patients' anxiety response to this challenge could not only be enhanced but could also be almost completely abolished by manipulating their expectancies. This result would not be expected if the patients' responses were primarily due to a biological vulnerability.

Similar results have been obtained in lactate and CO_2 studies manipulating instructions in normal volunteers and panic patients (van den Hout

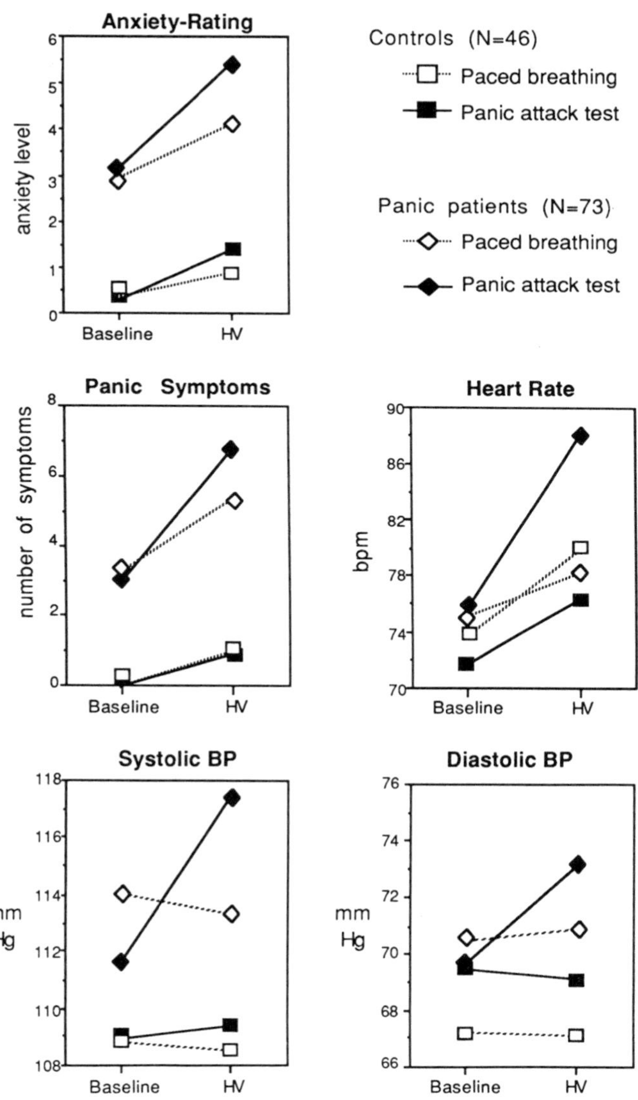

Figure 9.6 Panic patients' response to mild hyperventilation challenge depends on instruction: one instruction called hyperventilation a 'biological panic attack test,' the other called it 'fast-paced breathing' (Margraf *et al.*, 1989). Reproduced from Margraf and Ehlers in *Handbook of Anxiety*, Vol III. (eds G.D. Burrows, R. Noyes, M. Roth) by permission of Elsevier Science Publishers.

and Griez, 1982; van der Molen *et al.*, 1986; Rapee *et al.*, 1988). Together, these studies suggest that differential reactivities, if found at all, may result from differential expectations rather than from physiological vulnerability. One could speculate that some studies (e.g. Ehlers *et al.*, 1986b; Margraf, 1988) did not obtain greater reactivities because they were conducted in an experimental setting that stimulated the expectation of experiencing a panic attack less than other studies that for instance gave different instructions to panic patients and controls (e.g. Appleby *et al.*, 1981).

Necessary or sufficient conditions. Are there central or peripheral physiological changes investigated to date that are sufficient or necessary conditions for lactate-induced panic? Our earlier negative answer (Margraf *et al.*, 1986c) has now been corroborated by additional research. Several new studies intensively searching for specific neuroendocrine, cardiologic, or psychophysiologic characteristics of lactate-induced panic have yielded essentially negative results. The list of variables measured is rather impressive. It includes hemoglobin, hematocrit, beta-endorphin immunoactivity, cortisol, luteinizing hormone, prolactin, growth hormone, L-lactate, D-lactate, epinephrine, norepinephrine, 3,4-dihydroxyphenylglycol, 3-methoxy-4-hydroxyphenylglycol (MHPG), prostacyclin, thromboxane B_2, platelet factor 4, insulin, blood sugar, pyruvate, calcium, phosphate, bicarbonate, phosphate, sodium, potassium, chloride, protein, respiratory volume and rate, pH, pCO_2, oxygen uptake, carbon dioxide release, heart rate, systolic and diastolic blood pressure, mean arterial pressure, cardiac output, stroke volume, and total peripheral resistance (Gorman *et al.*, 1984a, 1984b, 1984c, 1986a; Carr *et al.*, 1986; Liebowitz *et al.*, 1985b and 1986; Gaffney *et al.*, 1988; van der Molen and van den Hout, submitted). Many of these variables did not change at all during 'panic'. Others changed in all patients and control subjects regardless of whether a 'panic' was rated to have occurred. An exception was growth hormone that changed more strongly in patients than in controls (Carr *et al.*, 1986). Considering the multitude of variables measured, a single significant finding may simply represent a consequence of alpha-inflation, since no corrections for multiple comparisons were made. This finding clearly needs replication before it can be regarded as meaningful. Moreover, no variable showed specificity to panic in the sense that a change was observed in every panic and during no non-panic period. However, an interesting association emerged between the average response to lactate and hyperventilation. Panic patients showed clear signs of respiratory alkalosis indicative of hyperventilation before lactate infusion (Gorman *et al.*, 1986a). During lactate all subjects increased ventilation (Gorman *et al.*, 1986a; Gaffney *et al.*, 1988). The strongest increase occurred in 'panicking' patients (Gorman *et al.*, 1986a). These findings are clearly in agreement with Ley's (1988) interpretation that lactates' panicogenic effects can be explained at least partly by hyperventilation. Van der Molen and van den Hout (submitted) have shown that the respiratory response to lactate depends on the subject's expectation of anxiety and can be manipulated by instructions. We will address the relationship of hyperventilation and panic attacks again in our chapter on psychophysiological models of panic.

A special word may be in place on a recent finding using positron emission tomography (PET). Reiman *et al.* (1984, 1986) reported a blood flow asymmetry in the region of the parahippocampal gyrus in resting panic patients who subsequently 'panicked' in response to lactate. No such abnormality was observed in normal controls or panic patients who did not 'panic' under lactate. Interestingly, the authors claim a perfect relationship between the blood flow asymmetry and lactate-induced panic. Given the fact that criteria for lactate-induced panic are unreliable and subject to biasing influences as shown above, one wonders how a perfect correlation with a less than perfect measure could be obtained. It is stated that the left-to-right ratio asymmetry was not present in normals or non-panicking patients. However, the mean ratios for these groups vary from 0.97 to 1.03 with standard deviations of up to 0.12. This means that the asymmetry must have been present in some of the controls and non-panicking patients. Other problems with the study include a possible contribution of medication status to the results ('responders' were more often on medication), poor age and sex matching, and the failure to correct PET measures for brain-fluid tissue ratios. It is unclear whether the location of arterial and venous lines was constant across subjects and whether the classification of patients was *post hoc*. The authors fail to specify how many sets of statistical comparisons were made and whether they had an *a priori* hypothesis or simply obtained their results in one of many possible *post hoc* analyses. In addition, the fact that one of their control subjects was found to fit their diagnostic criteria for panic *after* examining the dependent variables makes one wonder about their selection procedures. Because of these problems we cannot accept this PET scan finding as relevant until it has been independently replicated in a better controlled study. To our knowledge, only one other PET study of lactate infusion exists. These authors (Stewart *et al.*, 1988) reported a marked increase following lactate in both panic patients and controls but no consistent regional blood flow differences at rest or during lactate in any of the cortical areas studied.

Conclusions. In conclusion, results from panic induction studies do not provide evidence for the MI models. Methodological problems limit the interpretability of most panic induction studies. Although the response to lactate infusion and similar challenges has reasonable validity as model for panic attacks, the anxiety observed in these models on the average is only moderately intense. No psychophysiological or biochemical variable studied so far is a necessary or sufficient condition for panic. Control subjects show responses that are qualitatively similar to those of panic patients. In addition, the rare quantitative differences found in some studies can easily be explained by cognitive or behavioral mechanisms whereas the results of the expectancy studies cannot be explained by the MI models (cf. the chapter on psychophysiological models). The same is true for the incidental observation of Bonn *et al.* (1973) and Kelly *et al.* (1971) that patients do not panic because of the physicians' presence. Another fact difficult to explain for the MI models is that a wide variety of non-pharmacologic challenges have recently been shown to produce similar panic attacks as do lactate infusion or CO_2-inhalation. These challenges include exposure to agoraphobic stimuli (Woods *et al.*, 1987), false heart rate feedback (Margraf *et al.*, 1987b; Ehlers *et al.*, 1988b), reading cards with combinations of bodily sensations and catastrophic consequences (Clark *et al.*, 1988), progressive muscle relaxation (Heide and Borkovec, 1983; Cohen *et al.*, 1985), or exposure to small enclosed rooms (Rachman and Levitt, 1985). Furthermore, repeated exposure to lactate infusion (Bonn *et al.*, 1971, 1973) or CO_2-inhalation (Griez and van den Hout, 1986; van den Hout *et al.*, 1987a) reduces anxiety and decreases the frequency of panic attacks. In the same vein, 'blocking' of lactate-induced panic has now been described not only for tricyclics, alprazolam, and to a lesser degree placebo (Carr *et al.*, 1986; Dager *et al.*, 1987) but also for behavioral treatment (Guttmacher and Nelles, 1984; Shear and Fyer, 1987).

Spontaneity of panic attacks

The majority of panic attacks especially at the onset of the disorder occur spontaneously, that is, not in response to specific stimuli.

At the time the MI models were formulated the claimed spontaneity of many panic attacks was not based on any systematic research. In their original publications neither Klein (1980, 1981) nor Sheehan (1982a, 1984) quoted any studies of the spontaneity of panic attacks. Both failed to specify the notion of spontaneity. A critique of Klein's implicit concept of spontaneity is given by Michels *et al.* (1985, pp. 606–8). Before discussing the empirical evidence we have to distinguish between the different ways the term 'spontaneity' is used. First, it refers to panic attacks that appear unpredictable or unexpected to the patient. Second, the term is used to indicate that at least some panic attacks are due to a biological dysfunction and represent an autonomic discharge that is independent of perceptual, evaluative, and situational factors. This notion of spontaneity has not been tested empirically by the proponents of the MI models. Another important distinction is whether we refer to panic disorder as a whole or to individual panic attacks.

Let us first examine the evidence with respect to panic disorder as a whole. There is little argument that psychosocial or physiological stressors can contribute to the overall frequency or severity of panic attacks (Klein, 1964; Brehony and Geller, 1981; Mathews *et al.*, 1981; Raskin *et al.*,1982; Last *et al.*, 1984; Tearnan *et al.*, 1984; Uhde *et al.*, 1985a; Roy-Byrne *et al.*, 1986a; Kleiner and Marshall, 1987; Lelliott *et al.*, in press). In addition to separation experiences discussed in the next section, other major life events and medical problems such as operations or drug-intake are frequently associated with the onset of panic attacks and their exacerbations. A certain degree of specificity of life events related to panic disorder is suggested by the findings of Finlay-Jones and Brown (1981). In this study the onset of anxiety or panic symptoms or their exacerbation were more frequently preceded by 'danger'-related events. In contrast, 'loss'-related events were more frequently related to depression. It remains to be determined why some people are resistant to stressors that may be pathogenic in others. In addition to these rather long-term influences events operating in a time frame of days or hours can be important. These precipitants can be feared situations or their anticipation, or non-specific stress. When panic attacks occur in feared situations, they can be said to be spontaneous or unpredictable only in the sense that their exact time of occurrence within the larger time frame or context cannot be predicted. In this sense, however, even the anxiety of simple or social phobics can be 'unpredictable' since phobic anxiety may not occur with every exposure to the phobic stimulus and is phenomenologically similar to 'spontaneous' panic (Roth, 1984; Marks, 1987b).

Most central to the validity of the MI models is whether immediate external or internal triggers for individual panic attacks exist. If such triggers are regularly present, the distinction between 'spontaneous' panic and other kinds of anxiety is vitiated. The appearance of unpredictable or unexpected panic attacks is confirmed by recent interview and diary data (Barlow *et al.*, 1985; Taylor *et al.*, 1986; Breier *et al.*, 1986; Margraf *et al.*, 1987a). However, it is very well possible that the patients do not make adequate connections between triggering events and their anxiety. Michels *et al.* (1985) point out that in clinical practice it is usually possible to find specific antecedents to a panic attack if one questions the patient carefully. More systematic evidence comes from diary studies showing that a significant proportion of 'spontaneous' panic attacks occur in standard phobic situations such as shopping or driving or following arguments with family members (Freedman *et al.*, 1985; Taylor *et al.*, 1986; Margraf *et al.*, 1987a).

Similarly, Lelliott *et al.* (in press) found that 93% of the first panic attacks of 59 agoraphobic patients occurred outside home (79% in situations from the agoraphobic cluster, the remaining 14% at work or in school). More important than these findings on external triggers for many supposedly 'spontaneous' attacks is research on internal cues as triggering events. As we will discuss in our chapter on psychophysiological or cognitive models of panic this research suggests certain bodily sensations and cognitive events as definite triggers for panic.

More recently, Klein *et al.* (1987, p. 378) have given another definition of spontaneity: 'By spontaneous we mean that there is no danger in the environment sufficient to engender sudden extreme fear. Furthermore, at the onset of the illness there are no specific phobic stimuli.' The second part of this definition is in line with the older formulation and thus inconsistent with the data of Lelliott *et al.* (in press) quoted above. The first part of the new definition represents a substantial broadening of the original notion. It is problematic since requiring a lack of sufficient real danger does not separate between panic and other anxiety disorders. In fact, situational inappropriateness is common to all types of what used to be called neurotic anxiety. Therefore, this broadened view of spontaneity seems to us to abandon the features of spontaneity that were postulated specifically for panic attacks by the original MI models.

Genetic specificity

There is a strong genetic factor for panic that is transmitted independently of the risk for other anxiety disorders.

In contrast to treatment specificity, there have been few new studies on genetic specificity since 1985. Thus, our earlier conclusions remain unchanged. A strong familial component to anxiety disorders has clearly been established (Marks, 1986). However, there are no adoption studies that would enable us to determine to what degree the familial transmission of these disorders is genetic. As we pointed out earlier (Margraf *et al.*, 1986a), there are major inconsistencies in the twin and family data. Siblings in the family studies usually have higher rates of psychopathology than dizygotic twins in twin studies even though they are at the same genetic risk. Furthermore, the majority of monozygotic twins is not concordant, an increased risk is usually found only or primarily in female relatives, and some family studies do not support an increased familial risk in agoraphobics. In addition, the criteria for determining concordance in twin studies have been quite loose. Carey and Gottesman (1981) found a higher incidence of psychiatric or general medical treatment for 'nervous' problems in the dizygotic (DZ) rather the monozygotic (MZ) twins of phobic probands (DZ 46% vs. MZ 25%). However, they were able to reverse this result by classifying the co-twins on a poorly defined looser criterion of being psychiatrically 'noteworthy' (DZ 38% vs. MZ 88%).

Most important, however, there is no convincing support for a specific transmission of the risk for panic. Family studies (Raskin *et al.*, 1982; Leckman *et al*; 1983; Angst *et al.*, in press) show that relatives of subjects with panic disorder have increased risks not only for panic but also for other psychopathology, especially depression and alcoholism. The Australian twin study (Jardine *et al.*, 1984; Kendler *et al.*, 1987) shows a non-specific disposition for all anxiety and depressive disorders. The authors conclude that environmental factors determine which type of symptoms prevails. Torgersen (1983) found a larger difference between the concordance rates of MZ and DZ twins for panic disorder and agoraphobia with panic attacks (15% in MZ vs. 0% in DZ) than for generalized anxiety disorder (0% vs. 5%). When two subjects with 'possible' panic disorder were included the concordance for panic-related disorders rose to 31% for MZ twins. This finding points towards a stronger genetic contribution in panic patients than in GAD patients. However, it does not support a genetic transmission of a risk for panic independent of the risk for other anxiety. In fact, co-twins of panic patients have a greater risk for GAD than for panic disorder or agoraphobia (MZ: 31% vs. 15%, DZ: 25% vs. 0%). This directly contradicts the specificity argument. Table 9.1 shows the probandwise concordance rates for panic disorder, agoraphobia with panic attacks, and generalized anxiety disorder.

This pattern of results can be better explained by the effect of differential severity than by genetic specificity. Familial loading may increase with raising severity of an anxiety disorder. Torgensen (1983) states that clinicians in his country consider generalized anxiety disorder as less severe than panic disorder. A higher familial loading may then simply be an expression of greater severity of panic disorder compared to less severe anxiety states. Additional evidence for this view is offered by the fact that chronic childhood anxiety is much more often a precursor for adult panic disorder than for adult generalized anxiety disorder (Torgersen, 1986). Furthermore, it is obvious from the table that conclusions about specific anxiety disorders are based on very small numbers. Concordances for panic attacks are due to only two pairs of twins with panic disorder and agoraphobia with panic attacks. Differences were not significant unless all probands with panic attacks were compared to all probands without panic attacks which seems rather arbitrary.

Finally, a more general problem in interpreting the family and twin data is that it is unknown what exactly is transmitted. For instance, panic patients have been shown to have high degrees of somatization (Fisher and Wilson, 1985; Cameron *et al.*,1986; King *et al.*, 1986). It is possible then that

Table 9.1 Probandwise concordance rates in Torgersen's (1983) twin study.

Proband diagnosis	Co-twin diagnosis			
	Panic disorder	Agoraphobia with panic attacks	Generalized anxiety disorder	Other psychiatric disorder
Panic disorder				
MZ ($N=5$)	0	1	2	0
DZ ($N=6$)	0	0	2	0
Agoraphobia with panic attacks				
MZ ($N=8$)	1	0	2	0
DZ ($N=10$)	0	0	2	0
Panic disorder and agoraphobia with panic attacks				
MZ ($N=13$)	1	1	4*	0
DZ ($N=16$)	0	0	4	0
Generalized anxiety disorder				
MZ ($N=12$)	0	0	0	2
DZ ($N=20$)	0	0	1	3

*Two of these were later rediagnosed as 'possible' panic disorder (Torgersen, 1983, p. 1087).
Abbreviations: MZ = monozygotic twins, DZ = dizygotic twins.

somatization which is also strongly familial (Guze *et al.*, 1986) represents the transmitted characteristic. A second example is depression which is familially related to panic (Leckman *et al.*, 1983). In conclusion, although a genetic component to the anxiety states is very likely the genetic specificity of panic attacks has not been demonstrated convincingly.

Separation anxiety

Childhood separation anxiety is a precursor to panic attacks that shows similar clinical characteristics and response to tricyclic treatment.

This argument is of special relevance to Klein's model. Klein considers 'school phobia' as an expression of pathological childhood separation anxiety and a precursor for agoraphobia. Consequently, Gittelman-Klein and Klein (1973, 1980) investigated the effects of doses of up to 200 mg imipramine on 'school phobia' and found a positive outcome. However,

Berney *et al*. (1981) found no effect of a lower dose of up to 75 mg of clomipramine. Since similar doses of clomipramine have been reported to reduce panic attacks in adults (Gloger *et al*., 1981; Caetano, 1985) the different result cannot simply be explained by a lower dose as Klein *et al*. (1985) suggested. Roth (1984) pointed out that school phobia generally has a benign long-term outcome if it starts before age 11. Only if it begins later in adolescence, there seems to be a chronic development into severe adult agoraphobia and these cases are rare (Warren, 1965; Tyrer and Tyrer, 1974; Roth, 1984). For a review of school phobia see Ollendick and Mayer (1984). Finally, Tearnan *et al*. (1984) and Margraf *et al*. (1986a) argued that it is problematic to equate school phobia with childhood separation anxiety.

It is therefore a better approach to directly compare the prevalence of current or past separation anxiety in agoraphobics and other anxiety disorders. This has so far only been done in retrospective studies. Separation experiences do seem to precede the development of panic attacks or agoraphobic behavior in a subgroup of patients (cf. Tearnan *et al*., 1984). In a retrospective interview study with non-blind interviewers Klein (1964) found a history of childhood separation anxiety in 50% of his agoraphobic patients. Breier *et al*. (1986) established a much lower prevalence of 18% using similar methods. Gittelman-Klein and Klein (1984) reported a higher prevalence of both childhood and current separation anxiety in agoraphobics than in simple phobics using an interview approach. With questionnaires that are less prone to experimenter/interviewer bias, we found significantly higher levels of current separation anxiety in patients with panic disorder with or without agoraphobia than in normal controls, alcoholics or medical outpatients (Margraf and Ehlers, 1987). Remotely related evidence comes from two animal studies (Scott *et al*., 1973; Suomi *et al*., 1978) that found imipramine to reduce 'distress vocalizations' caused by separation. However, this effect was not present in all species studied.

There are several lines of negative evidence, however. In all studies about 50% of agoraphobic patients showed no evidence for past or current separation anxiety. A history of separation anxiety does not correlate with the therapeutic success of imipramine in the treatment of agoraphobia (Gittelman-Klein and Klein, 1984). In addition, Gittelman-Klein (1975) and Berg (1976) found no evidence for a transmission of a vulnerability for separation anxiety from agoraphobic parents to their children. Furthermore, it can easily be argued that separation anxiety develops as a consequence of agoraphobia rather than vice versa. This problem can be avoided by studying people with panic attacks that have not yet developed the full-blown clinical syndrome. Margraf and Ehlers (1988) compared such infrequent panickers and non-panicking controls and found no difference in current separation anxiety determined by questionnaire. Also in contrast to Klein's argument, a whole series of studies from different research centers found no differences between agoraphobics and other anxiety patients in difficulties attending school, the death of a parent, or the frequency of long-term separation from the parents during childhood (Berg *et al.*, 1974; Solyom *et al.*, 1974; Buglass *et al.*, 1977; Raskin *et al.*, 1982; van der Molen *et al.*, submitted). Specifically, five recent studies comparing panic and agoraphobic patients with patients suffering from generalized anxiety, simple phobia, and non-panic neuroses all found no support for more separation anxiety or objective separation events in panic patients (Raskin *et al.*, 1982; Thyer *et al.*, 1985, 1986; Torgersen, 1986; van der Molen *et al.* submitted). Moreover, there was even some evidence to the contrary. Van der Molen *et al.* (submitted) found scores on a childhood separation anxiety scale significantly higher than in normal controls in non-panic neurotics but not in agoraphobics. Torgersen (1986) observed that patients with generalized anxiety disorder had lost their fathers and/or mothers before age 16 significantly more often than panic disorder patients, who had more often experienced chronic anxiety during childhood. Besides, childhood separation experiences seem to be associated more with adult depression than with anxiety (Tennant *et al.*, 1981, 1982).

In conclusion, separation is only one of many possible stressors associated with the onset or exacerbation of panic or other disorders. We can state even more firmly than only a few years ago that most research fails to support a specific relation of childhood separation anxiety to adult panic attacks.

If we take the empirical evidence for the main arguments for the MI models together, the results are either equivocal or contradict the models. Especially the treatment specificity argument that formed the starting point for these approaches has been falsified in its original form.

The locus coeruleus hypothesis

The only etiological model that actually attempts to specify a neuroanatomic substrate for panic attacks is the locus coeruleus (LC) hypothesis. This nucleus is located in the dorsolateral tegmentum of the pons and contains more than half of the cerebral noradrenergic neurons. It is named for the pigment the cells bear in man and some higher primates (Cooper *et al.*, 1982). It has ascending projections to numerous brain regions including the hippocampus, hypothalamus, limbic area, and forebrain. Its descending pathways primarily influence peripheral sympathetic activity.

Figure 9.7 gives a schematic representation of the locus coeruleus and its major projections in the human brain.

The hypothesis

The original LC hypothesis assumes a noradrenergic discharge due to either excessive stimulation or insufficient inhibition as the substrate of panic attacks (Redmond and Huang, 1979; Charney *et al.*, 1984; Gorman *et al.*, 1984a; Uhde *et al.*, 1984a; Gelder, 1986). Redmond and his colleagues (reviewed by Redmond, 1979; Redmond and Huang, 1979) conducted the basic research on the LC and anxiety in stumptail monkeys (macaca arctoides or speciosa). They reported an increase in LC activity after

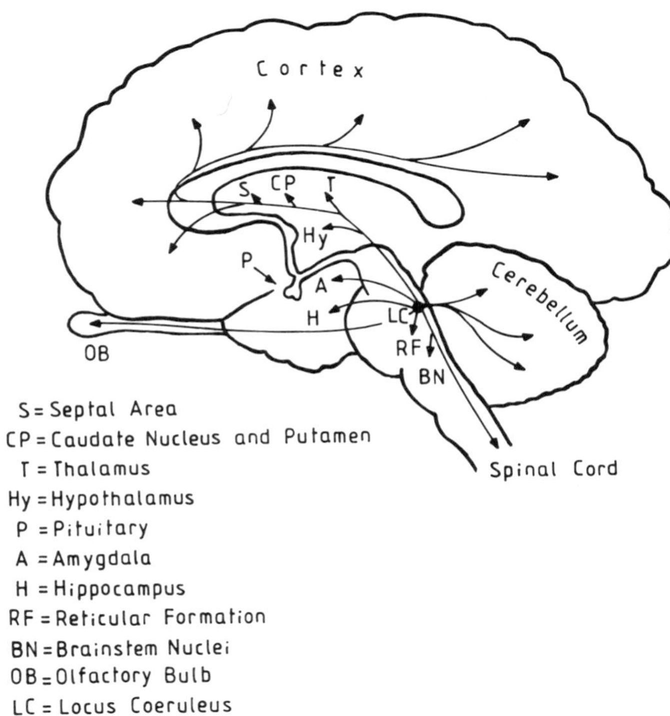

Figure 9.7 Schematic representation of the efferent projections of the locus coeruleus. Reproduced from Margraf and Ehlers in *Handbook of Anxiety*, Vol. III (eds G.D. Burrows, R. Noyes and M. Roth) by permission of Elsevier Science Publishers.

exposure to threatening situations. Electrical or pharmacologic stimulation of the LC led to increased brain, cerebrospinal fluid, and plasma levels of norepinephrine (NE) and MHPG (3-methoxy-4-hydroxyphenethylene), a major metabolite of norepinephrine, and to behaviors associated with fear in the wild (e.g. scratching, grimacing). Bilaterial surgical ablation of the LC decreased the occurrence of these behaviors in threatening situations. In addition, a number of drugs that increase LC firing are anxiogenic in humans, for instance caffeine (Boulenger *et al.*, 1984; Charney *et al.*, 1985) and yohimbine (Charney *et al.*, 1983, 1984). Conversely, the panic reducing drugs diazepam (Grant *et al.*, 1980), clonidine (Aghajanian, 1978), and the tricyclic antidepressants (Nybäck *et al.*, 1975; Svensson and Usdin, 1978) all inhibit locus coeruleus firing. The LC hypothesis also offers a possible common explanation for the panicogenic effects of lactate and CO_2, since CO_2 is a metabolic product of lactate that freely crosses the blood-brain barrier and increases firing of noradrenergic neurons in animals (Elam *et al.*, 1981). Alternatively, the panicogenic effects of lactate might be mediated through its capacity to reduce alpha-1 adrenergic receptor binding in rat and mouse brain tissue (Rick *et al.*, 1985).

A more specific formulation that avoids some of the pitfalls of the original LC hypothesis has recently been proposed by Charney and Heninger (1986a). These authors assume that an 'abnormally high responsivity of brain noradrenergic systems is etiologically related to the development of panic disorders' (p. 1042). Their main candidate for the localization of the NE abnormality is the alpha-2 adrenergic autoreceptor. They give up the global pretension of the original LC hypothesis by carefully stating that NE abnormalities 'may be identifying distinct neurobiological subgroups of patients and not a regulatory disturbance common to most patients with panic disorder' (p. 1049). Even though the reformulation no longer is a pure MI model we discuss it here since it evolved on the basis of the LC hypothesis. Support for an abnormal function of the central alpha-2 adrenal autoreceptor comes from Charney *et al.* (1984). These authors showed a stronger MHPG and blood pressure response to yohimbine stimulation in patients with frequent panic attacks than in normal controls and patients with fewer panic attacks. However, one could argue that this effect was mediated by the patients' perception and anxious appraisal of the bodily symptoms associated with yohimbine-induced arousal. This criticism does not apply to subsequent studies that found clonidine, an alpha-2 receptor agonist, to cause greater *decreases* in MHPG and blood pressure, but not in heart rate of panic patients (Charney and Heninger, 1986a; Nutt, 1986*). Similarly, Uhde *et al.* (1986) found a blunted growth

*The authors are indebted to Dr David M. Clark, Oxford, for drawing their attention to the study by Nutt (1986).

hormone response to clonidine stimulation in all of their panic and depressed patients, but in only half of their normal controls.

Problematic aspects

There are several problems with the LC hypothesis, however, that cast severe doubt on its validity. First, some of the basic research on the LC hypothesis has been criticized (Mason, 1981; van Dongen, 1981). Pharmacologically specific lesions of NE systems of the LC by 6-hydroxy-dopamine in rats do not impair their responses to anxiety provoking stimuli (File *et al.*, 1979; Mason and Fibiger, 1979a) nor do they alter the anxiolytic properties of chlordiazepoxide and ethanol (Koob *et al.*, 1981). In addition, the acquisition of one-way (Fibiger and Mason, 1978) or two-way active avoidance (Mason and Fibiger, 1979b), Sidman avoidance or conditioned suppression (Mason and Fibiger, 1979c) are not altered. Moreover, LC neurons are activated by a variety of stimuli not related to anxiety (Foote *et al.*, 1980; van Dongen, 1981; Cooper *et al.*, 1982), and other brain areas respond to anxiety stimuli as well (cf. Gray, 1982). Consistent with these problems is the fact that in humans disturbances in the LC and central NE transmission are associated with impaired perceptual organization and memory, disorientation, confusion, delusions, and hallucinations, whereas anxiety disorders are not a prominent feature of such disturbances (van Dongen, 1981).

Second, if the hypothesis is correct in its general form, all drugs that stimulate noradrenergic neurons in the LC should prove panicogenic and drugs that inhibit these neurons should block panic attacks. This is not the case. Both buspirone and the tricyclic anticonvulsant, carbamazepine, increase locus coeruleus firing (Olpe *et al.*, 1983; McMillen *et al.*, 1985; Sanghera *et al.*, 1983; van der Maelen *et al.*, 1986) and at the same time have anxiolytic effects in patients with generalized anxiety (Taylor *et al.*, 1985; Cohn and Wilcox, 1986) and panic attacks (Uhde *et al.*, 1984a, 1985b). Klein *et al.* (1985) pointed out that acute administration of mianserin blocks the alpha-2 autoreceptor, but that there have been no reports of mianserin-induced panic. These authors even saw one panic patient benefit from the drug. With respect to drugs inhibiting LC firing, it must be noted that the panic reducing effect of clonidine wears off within a few weeks and it may even worsen anxiety (Hoehn-Saric *et al.*, 1981; Liebowitz *et al.*, 1981; Uhde *et al.*, 1985b). Furthermore, clonidine may act on neurotransmitters outside the NE system. Also opposite to the LC hypothesis is an early report that imipramine worsens, rather than attenuates, yohimbine-induced anxiety (Holmberg and Gershon, 1961).

A third problem of the original LC hypothesis is the prediction that panic attacks should be accompanied by increased levels of the catecholamine metabolite MHPG. Support for this comes from an uncontrolled pilot study of six patients with agoraphobia with panic attacks (Ko *et al.*, 1983). In this study, plasma MHPG levels were significantly higher on days when a panic attack had occurred than on days without a panic. Clonidine and imipramine treatments both decreased MHPG and 'patients also anecdotally reported some decrease in the frequency and severity of spontaneous panic attacks, as well as some side effects . . .' (p. 428). Subsequent research assessing MHPG in 'spontaneously' occurring panic attacks (Cameron *et al.*, 1987) or panic induced experimentally by exposure to feared situations (Woods *et al.*, 1987), 5% CO_2-inhalation (Woods *et al.*, 1988), or lactate infusion (Carr *et al.*, 1986) could not confirm this preliminary report. In none of these studies were there uniform increases or decreases in MHPG associated with panic attacks. While CO_2 did not affect MHPG, lactate infusion on the average led to small decreases in MHPG. When studied, normal controls showed MHPG responses similar to panic patients. Moreover, diazepam reverses yohimbine-induced anxiety in normal subjects without reducing plasma-free MHPG (Charney *et al.*, 1983). This indicates that diazepam probably has an anxiolytic effect without decreasing NE turnover which is consistent with the apparently low density of benzodiazepine receptors on LC neurons (Speth *et al.*, 1980; Young and Kuhar, 1980).

Another problem for the LC hypothesis comes from the observation that relaxation may in some patients induce panic attacks (Heide and Borkovec, 1983, 1984; Cohen *et al.*, 1985). Some of these episodes were characterized by very strong autonomic responses (Cohen *et al.*, 1985). However, Matthew *et al.* (1981) found a decrease in plasma NE and epinephrine following relaxation treatment. As Shear (1986) has argued, relaxation is likely to be associated with parasympathetic activation and the sudden, fast rises in heart rate seen in some relaxation-induced panics are more consistent with a parasympathetic withdrawal mechanism than the sympathetic activation postulated by the LC hypothesis.

Whatever differences have been found apply only to subgroups, never to all panic patients. In the same vein, not even the most frequent sympathomimetic concomitants of panic are present in all attacks, and the same changes appear in a substantial group of subjects that do not panic. These facts are very difficult to reconcile with a MI model that proposes a specific neuroanatomic substrate for the disorder *in toto* and does not take into account other critical variables such as cognitive factors, learning experiences, or environmental demands.

The specificity of any differences between panic patients and controls is not established since with one exception the studies quoted above have not involved other clinical control groups. The only study with a clinical comparison group actually found no difference between panic and depressed patients' growth hormone response to clonidine stimulation (Uhde *et al.*, 1986). In this context, it is interesting to note that disinhibition of the LC system has also been implicated in a model for depression (Weiss and Simson, 1986). In addition to depression, other important comparison groups would include patients with generalized anxiety disorder and severely stressed normal subjects since both conditions may influence the noradrenergic system (Uhde *et al.*, 1984a). As long as such data have not been provided, differences between panic patients and normals cannot be firmly linked to the clinical problem of panic attacks. Another important deficiency of almost all studies is the failure to consider physical activity as a confounding variable. Exercise has strong effects on the catecholamines (Dimsdale and Moss, 1980; Dimsdale, 1986) and panic patients and normals differ with respect to physical fitness (Ehlers *et al.*, 1988c; Taylor *et al.*, 1987). Any difference between panic patients and normals in catecholamine metabolites might therefore reflect differential physical activity and fitness rather than effects associated with anxiety.

One last critical point is that one cannot simply generalize from short-term studies of acute stimulation or drug administration to long-term conditions such as panic disorder or its pharmacological treatment in clinical practice. It is very well conceivable that different mechanisms operate in prolonged and acute drug trials.

Conclusion

The LC hypothesis in its original, global form cannot account for much of the available data and is actually contradicted by a number of findings. Rather than being a specific substrate for (pathological) anxiety, the LC seems to be involved in a more general noradrenergic 'alarm' system, whereas 'anxiety' may be more specifically related to benzodiazepine/GABA-systems (Mason and Fibiger, 1979a; van Dongen, 1981; Insel *et al.*, 1984; Uhde *et al.*, 1984a). This would be consistent with the proposed global function of the brain NE system in the amplification of the effects of sensory information in the brain (Cooper *et al.*, 1982; Foote *et al.*, 1983). Studies in untreated, awake, behaviorally responsive rats and monkeys have shown that LC units are highly responsive to many non-noxious stimuli and that this responsiveness varies with the animal's level of behavioral vigilance (Cooper *et al.*, 1982). If such a NE system modulates the arousing and other behavioural effects of both environmental and internal bodily stimuli, it seems reasonable to assume that it would also be implicated in some way in anxiety processes. However, this is not the same as equating such processes with NE mechanisms or pathological anxiety with pathological LC function. As pointed out by Uhde *et al.*

(1984a), altered NE function may play an important, but not exclusive role in the neurobiology of anxiety.

The reformulated LC hypothesis avoids some of these criticisms. Nevertheless, the weakness of clonidine's anxiolytic effects, the effects of mianserin, the clear absence of signs of NE activity in many studies of panic attacks, the occurrence of relaxation-induced panic, the lack of data on specificity for panic patients and of longitudinal information as well as the problem of generalizing from short-term experiments to long-term phenomena all have not been resolved by the alpha-2 autoreceptor hypothesis. Moreover, it admittedly cannot serve as an etiological model for panic disorder as a whole.

Conclusions on MI models

Recent research shows that the MI models are not able to account for all the relevant data on panic attacks and in fact are contradicted by many results. Their narrow biological approach has to be broadened by taking into account the influence of psychological factors and their interaction with biological factors. In rejecting biological reductionism we have to take care not to go to the other extreme and deny the importance of biological research on panic. There have been numerous studies on biological correlates in the past few years. The results of these studies have contributed to our understanding of panic and may have implications for the conceptualization of emotions in general. We will review the most important findings of this research in the next section.

POSSIBLE BIOLOGICAL CORRELATES OF PANIC ATTACKS

Two main areas of research on biological correlates of panic attacks are ambulatory monitoring and experimental panic induction studies. Their results have already been discussed earlier in this chapter and in the chapter by R.R. Freedman. We will now review the findings of studies investigating a possible relationship between panic disorder and mitral valve prolapse, the dexamethasone suppression test, and various other possible correlates of potential relevance to etiological models of panic.

Mitral valve prolapse and panic attacks

There has been considerable speculation about a possible relationship between panic disorder and mitral valve prolapse syndrome (MVP). MVP is a cardiac condition characterized by a bowing of the mitral valve back into the left atrium during systole. This leads to the typical sounds that were originally used to diagnose the syndrome. Today the diagnosis is usually based on echocardiography which allows non-invasive visualization and measurement of the mitral valve (Devereux *et al.*, 1987). Clinical descriptions of various diagnoses on the borderline of psychiatry and cardiology such as 'Da Costa's syndrome', 'soldier's heart', 'effort syndrome', or 'neurocirculatory asthenia' bear many similarities to current diagnostic criteria for panic disorder. The same applies to today's MVP syndrome, the heir of these cardiological 'diseases of yesteryear' (Wooley, 1976). Surprisingly, empirical studies have yielded highly inconsistent results. We have reviewed this literature extensively elsewhere (Margraf *et al.*, 1988) demonstrating several methodological problems as possible reasons for this inconsistency. Another recent review was published by Dager *et al.* (1986).

Our review of 17 studies of the prevalence of MVP in panic patients revealed one group of studies reporting low frequencies of 0–8% and another group reporting high frequencies of 24–35% 'definite' MVP (average across all studies: 18% of panic patients, 1% of normal controls). Elevated prevalences of MVP were also reported for generalized anxiety disorder, bipolar affective disorder, and anorexia nervosa. Studies of MVP patients, on the other hand, generally failed to find an elevated prevalence of panic compared to other cardiac patients or normal controls (averages across eight studies: 14, 10, and 7% respectively). The inconsistency of these results may be due to widely different diagnostic criteria for MVP, a low reliability of this diagnosis, 'non-blind' ratings for panic or MVP, inadequate control groups, and sampling bias in both patient and control groups.

Gorman *et al.* (1986b) had two experienced echocardiogram readers rate the same 15 recordings of patients with panic disorder. While one reader diagnosed MVP in 9 patients, the other did not make the diagnosis in any patient. Similarly poor interrater reliability was obtained by another study (Dager *et al.*, submitted for publication). This study also showed a very low retest reliability after 10 months (kappa: 0.41–0.45). Other studies reviewed by Margraf *et al.* (1988) have shown that reliability can be better if very stringent and conservative criteria are used. However, this has not been the case in most studies of MVP in panic patients. The importance of blind ratings is emphasized by the study of Gorman *et al.* (1981) in which one blind rater found 35% MVP, while the non-blind rater found 50% MVP among their panic patients.

In addition to diagnostic problems, the selection of patients and controls has a strong influence on the results. None of the studies reviewed were based on community surveys. The patient samples were always drawn from referral populations in clinical settings that most probably represent a selection of highly symptomatic individuals. This has been termed 'ascertainment bias' by Motulsky (1978). People with two disorders are more likely to seek treatment or be detected in diagnostic screenings than people with one disorder alone. Thus, we may be dealing with a problem of co-morbidity rather than a true association between panic and MVP. Several researchers have tried to circumvent the problem of biased selection by studying special control groups. One such group involves 'cardiac controls', i.e. subjects that had sought professional help but did not show any identifiable disease (termed the 'worried well' by Uretsky, 1982). These subjects show rates of panic similar to MVP patients who had sought professional help (Uretsky, 1982; Bowen *et al.*, 1985). A second elegant strategy involves family members of MVP patients who had not sought professional help themselves and thus presumably represented a group with less selection bias. Family members with MVP had the same prevalence of panic as family members without MVP. Both groups had fewer panic attacks than the original samples of MVP patients who had been referred to the clinic (Hartman *et al.*, 1982; Devereux *et al.*, 1986). These results are consistent with the lack of significant cardiovascular symptoms (including many typical panic attack symptoms) in subjects with MVP found in large community surveys such as the Framingham Heart Study (Savage *et al.*, 1983). They clearly illustrate the relevance of ascertainment bias and control group selection for studying the relationship between panic and MVP. If this bias is eliminated or controlled, the prevalence of panic attacks or psychiatric symptoms is not higher in subjects with MVP than among all patients in cardiologic practice. It is possible, however, that all of these groups have a higher prevalence of panic attacks than normal control subjects who are not searching for professional help, although the family studies of Hartman *et al.* (1982) and Devereux *et al.* (1986) do not support this notion.

We can conclude then that the evidence for a higher prevalence of MVP in panic disorder patients is weak. If there is an overlap between the two syndromes, it is small, affecting less than 8% of MVP and less than 20% of clinical and thus highly selected samples of panic disorder patients. As discussed in our review (Margraf *et al.*, 1988) such an overlap must consist primarily of subjects with milder variants of MVP that represent functional and perhaps reversible rather than anatomical and permanent abnormalities since the former are more numerous and only a low proportion of panic attack patients show both auscultatory and echocardiographic signs of MVP. The reversibility of MVP is supported by recent data showing that evidence for MVP often disappears after remission in patients with panic attacks (Gorman, 1986) or anorexia nervosa (Meyers *et al.*, 1986). At present it seems more justified to assume that the low correlation between panic and MVP represents co-morbidity in highly symptomatic individuals rather than a functional relationship.

Dexamethasone suppression test in panic patients

The dexamethasone suppression test (DST) is the most widely evaluated potential laboratory test in psychiatric diagnosis (Berger and Klein, 1984; Arana *et al.*, 1985). In its standard application, one milligram of dexamethasone is given orally at 23:00 hours. Failure of dexamethasone to suppress cortisol secretion is given if serum cortisol levels at 16:00 hours on the following day are above 5 micrograms/deciliter (Carroll *et al.*, 1981). After much initial enthusiasm it is clear today that the test is not suitable as a routine diagnostic tool (Ross, 1986). Its results are influenced by a wide variety of factors including severity of the disorder, weight loss, sleep disturbances, situational stress, drug and alcohol withdrawal, and the pharmacokinetics of dexamethasone (Berger and Klein, 1984; Arana *et al.*, 1985; Ceulemans *et al.*, 1985). However, even though the DST is not a specific test for depression (or any subtype of depression) it still is an interesting probe of the hypothalamic–pituitary–adrenal (HPA) axis which is highly sensitive to psychological stimuli (Sachar, 1970). For all of these reasons it is interesting to study the responses of panic patients to the DST. Table 9.2 gives an overview of 13 published studies of this topic.

It is clear from the table that the large majority of panic patients shows normal suppression of cortisol secretion following the DST. The average rate of non-suppression was only 15.2% in panic patients without concurrent major depressive disorder. Moreover, there were no differences in the responses of patients with primary major depressive disorder with and without panic attacks. In two out of three comparisons there was no significant difference between panic patients and normal controls. In the study reporting a difference the patients were hospitalized whereas controls were not (Coryell *et al.*, 1985). While hospitalization may affect the DST, the rate of 18% non-suppression described in the study is similar to that found in most other studies. It is interesting to note that patients with GAD also had comparable or even higher rates of non-suppression. Schweizer *et al.* (1986) have reported a rate of 24% non-suppression in 79 GAD patients that is almost identical to the one found by Avery *et al.* (1985) quoted in Table 9.2. In order to interpret the results of these studies we need to consider the effects of stress on the DST. Ceulemans *et al.* (1985) have recently shown a rate of 47.5% non-suppression in 40 presurgical subjects without a history of psychiatric disturbances. Careful control of potential physical illnesses or other variables influencing the DST and internal standardization of the assays (0% non-suppression in 20 healthy

Table 9.2 Dexamethasone suppression test and panic disorder.

Study	Blind assays[1]?	DST[2]	Per cent positive DST (5 micrograms/dl) and sample size[3]					Comments[4]
			PD/AG	PD/AG with MDD	MDD	GAD	Controls	
Avery *et al.*, 1985	yes	1, 23, 13–16	14.3 *N*=35	—	8.3 *N*=60	23.1 *N*=26	—	Age and sex matching only fair: 33/39/42 years, 71/42/45 % female
Bridges *et al.*, 1986	?	1,23, 16	13 *N*=15	—	—	—	25 *N*=8	Only partial control for medications
Bueno *et al.*, 1984	?	1,23, 11+16	—	46.7 *N*=15	0 *N*=15 secondary depression	—	—	Multiple non-anxious and non-depressive primary diagnoses of depressed patients
Coryell *et al.*, 1985	?	1, 23, 16	18 *N*=50	—	24.3 *N*=37	—	4.4 *N*=23	Both clinical groups hospitalized, normal control not
Cottraux and Claustrat, 1984	?	1,23, 16	16.7 *N*=30	—	—	—	—	43% of the patients were depressed, DST + had higher depression
Curtis *et al.*, 1982	?	1, 23, 16	15 *N*=20	—	—	—	—	16 patients were on medication or alcohol
Faludi *et al.*, 1986	?	1, 22, 8+15	16.7 *N*=30	—	56.7 *N*=30	—	—	All inpatients, poor age matching (38 vs. 54 years)

1987		16+23		N=16	N=16			whether matched for sex
Lieberman *et al.*, 1983	?	1, 23, 16	0 N=10	—	40.9 N=22	—	—	Most patients were on medication
Peterson *et al.*, 1985	?	1, 23, 16	12.4 N=97	—	—	—	—	36% were depressed but correlation with DST
Roy-Byrne *et al.*, 1985b	?	1, 23, 16	25 N=16	—	—	—	14 N=22	Sex matching only fair (56 vs. 73% female), 11 patients were inpatients
Sheehan *et al.*, 1983	yes	1, 23, 16	11.8 N=51	—	—	—	—	Cortisol correlated −0.37 with weight
Whiteford and Evans, 1984	?	1,22, 15+22	28.6 N=21	—	64.3 N=28	—	—	Half of the abnormal DSTs in PD/AG normal at 3 p.m.; 12 of 50 other psychiatric patients had abnormal DST
Average (adjusted for sample size)			15.2 57 of 375	51.6 16 of 31	31.7 66 of 208 includes secondary depression	23.8 6 of 26	9.4 5 of 53	

1 Blind assays: 'Yes' means that the person evaluating the cortisol assay did not know what experimental group the subjects were belonging to.
2 DST: The three numbers refer to the amount of DST given (1 = one milligram), to the time of application on a 24-hour scale (e.g. 23 = at 23.00 hours), and to the time the blood sample for the cortisol assay was taken (e.g. 16 = at 16.00 hours), respectively.
3 % positive DST and sample size: For each experimental group, the upper line gives the percentage of subjects that displayed a positive DST (more than 5 micrograms/deciliter cortisol on the following day) and the lower line gives the total sample size.
4 Comments: Methodological problems or additional results of special interest.

controls) give validity to the authors' interpretation of a stress effect. In the light of diagnostic non-specificity of the DST in the studies reviewed in Table 9.2 it seems at present justified to conclude that any elevated rate of non-suppression in panic patients most probably reflects a non-specific stress effect associated with a disabling psychological disturbance.

Other possible biological correlates

Negative results

A number of candidates for biological correlates of panic attacks have been investigated with essentially negative results. This includes studies with metabolites or precursors of neurotransmitters as well as studies of hormones and receptor binding. No differences between panic patients and normal controls have been found with respect to baseline plasma levels of prolactin (Charney and Heninger, 1986b; Roy-Byrne *et al.*, 1986b), growth hormone (Nesse *et al.*, 1984; Uhde *et al.*, 1986), MHPG (Roy-Byrne *et al.*, 1986c), or the dopaminergic metabolite homovanillic acid (HVA) (Roy-Byrne *et al.*, 1986c). Similarly, pain sensitivity (Roy-Byrne *et al.*, 1985a), and in vitro immune function as measured by lymphocytic proliferative response to mitogen stimulation (Surman *et al.*, 1986) were the same in panic patients and normal controls. Serotonergic function as investigated by infusion of the serotonin precursor tryptophane or by platelet serotonin levels was similar in panic patients and normal controls (Charney and Heninger, 1986b; Balon *et al.*, 1987a). Both groups showed similar prolactin levels before, during, and after tryptophane infusion and this was not altered by alprazolam treatment in the panic group.

Inconsistent results

Platelet MAO is an enzyme suspected to be involved in the breakdown of catecholamines and indoleamines. Yu *et al.* (1983) found significantly higher platelet MAO activity in 29 agoraphobics than in 64 normal controls or 17 depressed patients. Possible problems with the study were that many patients were on medication and that all agoraphobics were inpatients which is unusual for this disorder. Higher MAO activity in 20 panic patients than in 20 normal controls was also reported by Gorman *et al.* (1985c). In this study the sum of plasma epinephrine and norepinephrine correlated significantly negatively ($r = 0.45$) with MAO activity. Already a few years earlier, Matthew *et al.* (1981) had found higher platelet MAO levels in patients with generalized anxiety disorder than in normal controls. Results of this study have to be interpreted with caution because MAO activity is higher in females (Fowler *et al.*, 1982; Khan *et al.*, 1986) and patients and controls were not matched for sex (70% vs. 40% females). In all of these studies, the differences between the various clinical and non-clinical groups were rather small, all the means being within one standard deviation of each other. It is not surprising then that there are negative results as well. In a study without a normal control group Sheehan *et al.* (1984) reported no elevation in baseline MAO activity in their agoraphobic patients. Balon *et al.* (1987b) found no difference between 21 panic patients and 12 healthy controls. Khan *et al.* (1986) compared patients with panic disorder and agoraphobia ($N=74$), GAD ($N=25$), and major depression ($N=64$) as well as normal controls ($N=34$), the largest sample studied yet. There were no significant differences between these groups. Since the authors carefully controlled confounding variables such as sex, medication, and medical illnesses as well as because of its large sample size this study casts doubt on the earlier positive results. In this context it is interesting to note that results on possibly altered MAO activity in other clinical groups such as schizophrenia, alcoholism, and depression have been inconsistent as well (cf. Gorman *et al.*,1985c; Khan *et al.*, 1986).

The number of imipramine binding sites on blood platelets is interesting with respect to the role of tricyclic antidepressants and the possible relationship between panic and depression. A number of studies have reported fewer binding sites in depressed patients than in normal controls (Asarch *et al.*, 1980; Briley *et al.*, 1980; Paul *et al.*, 1981; Raisman *et al.*, 1981; Baron *et al.*, 1983; Suranyi-Cadotte *et al.*, 1983; Lewis and McChesney, 1985; Schneider *et al.*, 1985; Wagner *et al.*, 1985). However, there are conflicting results (Mellerup *et al.*, 1982; Whitaker *et al.*, 1984; Gentsch *et al.*, 1985; Tang and Morris, 1985) and other evidence suggests that ^{3}H-imipramine binding may reflect a state rather than a trait (Berreltini *et al.*, 1982; Suranyi-Cadotte *et al.*, 1982). Using both the maximal concentration of binding sites (B_{max}) and the dissociation constant (K_d), Lewis *et al.* (1985) recently reported reduced platelet imipramine binding in 28 panic patients compared to 25 normal controls. This effect was not related to depression (Lewis, 1986). Two subsequent studies, however, could not confirm this finding. Uhde *et al.* (1987) found no difference for B_{max} and K_d between 17 panic patients and 14 normal controls. Similarly, Schneider *et al.* (1987) found no differences between 52 panic patients, 55 GAD patients, and 26 normal controls. This was true despite the presence of significant depressive symptomatology in the panic patients. Moreover, there was no relationship between B_{max} or K_d and severity of depression or family history of affective disorder. Thus, the weight of the evidence is against reduced imipramine binding in panic patients.

Sleep parameters have been studied extensively in depressed patients. Together with the reports of night-time panic attacks (Taylor *et al.*, 1986;

Margraf *et al.*, 1987a) this gives a rationale for studying the sleep of panic patients. The results have been inconsistent or negative. One well controlled study found no differences between panic patients and normal controls on any of the sleep parameters studied (Dubé *et al.*, 1986). Moreover, patients with both panic attacks and major depression were more similar to normals than to patients with depression alone. This is consistent with Grunhaus *et al.* (1986) who also found less disturbed sleep in patients with both major depression and panic than in patients with depression alone. In contrast to these findings of rather normal sleep in panic patients, Uhde *et al.* (1984b) and Hauri *et al.* (1986) reported increased movement time in panic patients in the sleep laboratory. In our ambulatory monitoring studies, however, we found no differences in night-time physical activity between panic patients and normal controls (Taylor *et al.*, 1986; Margraf *et al.*, 1987a). Uhde *et al.* (1984b) also reported shorter REM latency and REM density and a negative correlation between the number of panic attacks and the amount of delta sleep of $r=0.73$. These findings were not replicated by Dubé *et al.* (1986) although Grunhaus *et al.* (1986) found shorter REM latency in depressed patients with panic than in those without panic. Considering the large number of parameters studied, the number of significant findings reported appears small. Together with the lack of replication across studies and the preliminary nature of some of the studies, it seems justified at present to retain the null hypothesis of normal sleep in the average panic patient.

One last area of conflicting results concerns the thyroid hormones. Two uncontrolled studies found no signs of abnormal thyroid function (T_3, T_4, TSH) in panic patients compared to general population norms (Pariser *et al.*, 1979; Fishman *et al.*, 1985). Kathol and Delahunt (1986) noted panic attacks in 13 of 26 patients referred with hyperthyroidism. Adams *et al.* (1985) compared 51 panic patients with 41 other psychiatric patients. They found no difference in total triiodothyronine (T_3) and total thyroxine (T_4), but higher baseline values for free T_3 and T_4 in the panic group. The authors concluded that even though clinically euthyroid and biochemically within the normal range of thyroid function, panic patients may have their hypothalamic – pituitary – thyroid function 'set' at a higher level than other patients. Roy-Byrne *et al.* (1986b), however, recently obtained no differences between levels of peripheral thyroid hormones (total T_3, total T_4, and free T_4) in 12 panic patients and 10 normal controls. Panic patients had a reduced thyroid stimulation hormone (TSH) response to a thyroid-releasing hormone (TRH) stimulation test. Female patients also showed a reduced prolactin response. These responses were not related to past history or current level of depression. A confounding variable in this study was that all patients but none of the controls were hospitalized. A reduced TSH response to TRH is often seen in depressed patients. In an extensive review Loosen and Prange (1982) concluded that the pathophysiological significance of the finding remains uncertain.

Positive results

There are a number of isolated positive findings using biological tests in panic patients. McIntyre *et al.* (1986) studied plasma melatonin levels in 13 panic patients and 18 controls. They found lower mean levels at midnight in the patient group. Roy-Byrne *et al.* (1986d) reported lower ACTH and cortisol responses to a corticotropin releasing hormone stimulation test as well as a lower ratio of ACTH to cortisol response in eight panic patients than in 30 normal controls. The patients also had higher baseline levels of ACTH and cortisol measured between 19:15 and 20:00 hours. The study is limited by poor age matching (33 vs. 24 years) and the fact that only patients were hospitalized. In another study with poor age and sex matching, Nesse *et al.* (1984) reported elevated afternoon levels of cortisol in panic patients that were about to undergo an isoproterenol infusion. However, patients that were studied at rest only had cortisol levels similar to controls and significantly lower than the other patients. Patients before infusions also had higher state anxiety scores before the test protocol than patients without infusions. These results suggest that the cortisol response was a short-term stress response. This interpretation is consistent with the sensitivity of cortisol to expectancy effects and the fact that panic patients show stronger expectancy effects before possible panic challenges (cf. the section on panic induction above).

Conclusions on possible biological correlates

Although some interesting leads exist, most of the results reviewed in this section have been negative or inconclusive. Most of the positive findings were not specific to panic disorder but have also been obtained in other clinical groups such as depressed or anorexic patients. This generally unsatisfactory outcome may be due to technical as well as theoretical problems. Most studies used small samples and lacked control of important confounding variables. However, we have to be careful in interpreting negative results, since they can be due to artifacts or insensitive measures. Even if the findings can be replicated in better controlled studies we will not know whether the hormonal findings represent short-term responses to the laboratory environment and the test procedure as in the case of the cortisol results, whether they are a function of a more enduring response associated with the stress of the disorder, or whether they document a permanent trait characteristic or vulnerability factor of these patients. There have been no studies of these hormonal parameters in the natural environment of panic patients. Repeated 24-hour urine/plasma studies or ambulatory monitoring of blood parameters are needed to interpret the meaning of differences obtained in the laboratory. Moreover, environmental variables will have to be carefully monitored and experimentally manipulated in both laboratory and ambulatory monitoring studies in order to evaluate their impact. A basic problem is that most studies gathered data rather unsystematically since they were not undertaken within a firm theoretical framework. Research guided by etiological models might have yielded more informative results.

A final discussion of etiological models of panic disorder is given at the end of the next chapter which reviews the psychophysiological or cognitive models that have been put forward as an alternative to MI models.

ACKNOWLEDGEMENTS

Preparation of this chapter was supported by German Research Foundation Grants Ma 1116/1-1 and Eh 97/1-3.

REFERENCES

Ackerman, S. and Sachar, E. (1974) The lactate theory of anxiety: a review and reevaluation, *Psychosomatic Medicine*, **36**, 69–81.

Adams, J.R., Wahby, V.S., Giller, E.L. and Mason, J.W. (1985) Free thyroid hormone levels in patients with panic disorder, Paper presented at the Annual Meeting of the American Psychosomatic Society, Washington, DC, March 1985.

Aghajanian, G.K. (1978) Tolerance of locus coeruleus neurons to morphine and suppression of withdrawal response by clonidine, *Nature*, **276**, 186–8.

Angst, J., Vollrath, M., Merinkangas, K.R. and Ernst, C. Comorbidity of anxiety and depression in the Zurich Cohort Study of Young Adults. In *Proceedings of the Conference on Symptom Comorbidity in Anxiety and Depressive Disorders*, Tuxedo NY, September 1987, in press.

Appleby, I.L., Klein, D.F., Sachar, E. and Levitt, M. (1981) Biochemical indices of lactate-induced panic. A preliminary report. In D.F. Klein and J.G. Rabkin (eds), *Anxiety: New Research and Changing Concepts*, Raven Press, New York.

Arana, G.W., Baldessarini, R.J. and Ornsteen, M. (1985) The dexamethasone suppression test for diagnosis and prognosis in psychiatry. Commentary and Review, *Archives of General Psychiatry*, **42**, 1193–1204.

Arntz, A. and van den Hout, M.A. (1988) Generalizability of the match/mismatch model of fear. *Behaviour Research and Therapy*, **26**, 207–23.

Asarch, K.B., Shih, J.C. and Kulcsar, A. (1980) Decreased ^{3}H-imipramine binding in depressed males and females, *Communications in Psychopharmacology*, **4**, 425–32.

Avery, D.H., Osgood, T.B., Ishiki, D.M., Wilson, L.G., Kenny, M. and Dunner, D.L. (1985) The DST in psychiatric outpatients with generalized anxiety disorder, panic disorder, or primary affective disorder, *American Journal of Psychiatry*, **142**, 844–8.

Ballenger, J.C. (1986) Pharmacotherapy of the panic disorders, *Psychopharmacology Bulletin*, Supplement **6**, 47, 27–32.

Balon, R., Pohl, R., Yeragani, V., Rainey, J.M. and Oxenkrug, G.F. (1987a) Platelet serotonin levels in panic disorder. *Acta Psychiatrica Scandinavica*, **75**, 315–17.

Balon, R., Rainey, J.M., Pohl, R., Yeragani, V., Oxenkrug, G.F. and McCauley, R.B. (1987b) Platelet monoamine oxidase activity in panic disorder, *Psychiatry Research*, **22**, 37–41.

Balon, R., Pohl, R., Yeragani, V., Weinberg, P. and Rainey, J.M. (1988) Comparison of lactate-induced panic attacks in panic disorder patients and controls, *Psychiatry Research*, **22**, in press.

Barlow, D.H., Cohen, A.S., Waddell, M.T., Vermilyea, B.B., Klosko, J.S., Blanchard, E.B. and DiNardo, P.A. (1984) Panic and generalized anxiety disorders: nature and treatment, *Behavior Therapy*, **15**, 431–49.

Barlow, D.H., Vermilyea, J., Blanchard, E.B., Vermilyea, B.B., DiNardo, P.A. and Cerny, J.A. (1985) The phenomenon of panic. *Journal of Abnormal Psychology*, **94**, 320–28.

Baron, M., Barkai, A., Gruen, R., Kowalik, S. and Quitkin, F. (1983) ^{3}H-imipramine platelet binding sites in unipolar depression, *Biological Psychiatry*, **18**, 1403–9.

Beaumont, G. (1977) A large open multicentre trial of clomipramine (anafranil) in the management of phobic disorders. *Journal of International Medical Research* Supplement **55**, 116–23.

Benedikt, V. (1870) Über 'Platzschwindel'. *Allgemeine Wiener Medizinische Zeitung*, **15**, 488–92.

Berg, I. (1976) School phobia in the children of agoraphobic women, *British Journal of Psychiatry*, **128**, 86–9.

Berg, I., Butler, A. and Pritchard, J. (1974) Psychiatric illnesses in the mothers of school-phobic adolescents, *British Journal of Psychiatry*, **125**, 466–7.

Berger, M. and Klein, H.E. (1984) The dexamethasone suppression test: a biological marker for endogenous depression? *European Archives of Psychiatry and Neurological Sciences*, **234**, 137–46.

Berney, T., Kolvin, I., Bhate, S., Garside, R., Jeans, J., Kay, B. and Scarth, L. (1981) School phobia: a therapeutic trial with clomipramine and therapeutic outcome, *British Journal of Psychiatry*, **138**, 110–18.

Berreltini, W.H., Nurnberger, J.I., Post, R.M. and Gershon, E.S. (1982) Platelet ^{3}H-imipramine binding in euthymic bipolar patients, *Psychiatry Research*, **7**, 215–19.

Bonn, J.A., Harrison, J. and Rees, W. (1971) Lactate-induced anxiety: therapeutic application, *British Journal of Psychiatry*, **119**, 468–70.

Bonn, J.A., Harrison, J. and Rees, L. (1973) Lactate infusion in the treatment of free-floating anxiety, *Canadian Psychiatric Association Journal,*, **18**, 41–5.

Bonn, J.A., Readhead, C.P.A. and Timmons, B.A. (1984) Enhanced adaptive behavioral response in agoraphobic patients pretreated with breathing retraining, *Lancet*, 665–9.

Boulenger, J.-P., Uhde, T.W., Wolff, E.A. and Post, R.M. (1984) Increased sensitivity to caffeine in patients with panic disorders, *Archives of General Psychiatry*, **41**, 1067–71

Bowen, R.C., Orchard, R.C., Keegan, D.L. and D'Arcy, C. (1985) Mitral valve prolapse and psychiatric disorders, *Psychosomatics*, **26**, 926–32.

Bowlby, J. (1969) *Attachment and Loss. Vol. 1: Attachment*, Basic Books, New York.

Bowlby, J. (1973) *Attachment and Loss. Vol. 2: Separation Anxiety and Anger*, Basic Books, New York.

Brehony, K.A. and Geller, E.S. (1981) Appraisal of research and proposal for an integrative model. In M. Hersen, R. Eisler and P. Miller (eds), *Progress in Behavior Modification*, Vol. 12, Academic Press, New York.

Breier, A., Charney, D.S. and Heninger, G.R. (1986) Agoraphobia with panic attacks. Development, diagnostic stability, and course of illness, *Archives of General Psychiatry*, **43**, 1029–36.

Bridges, M., Yeragani, V.K., Rainey, J.M. and Pohl, R. (1986) Dexamethasone suppression test in patients with panic attacks, *Biological Psychiatry*, **21**, 853–5.

Briley, M.S., Langer, S.Z., Raisman, R., Sechter, D. and Zarifian, E. (1980) Tritiated imipramine binding sites are decreased in platelets of untreated depressed patients, *Science*, **209**, 303–5.

Bueno, J.A., Sabanes, F., Gascon, J., Gasto, G. and Salamero, M. (1984) Dexamethasone suppression test in patients with panic disorder and secondary depression, *Archives of General Psychiatry*, **41**, 723–4.

Buglass, D., Clarke, J., Henderson, A.S., Kreitman, N. and Presley, A.S. (1977) A study of agoraphobic housewives, *Psychological Medicine*, **7**, 73–86.

Buigues, J. and Vallejo J. (1987) Therapeutic response to phenelzine in patients with panic disorder and agoraphobia with panic attacks, *Journal of Clinical Psychiatry*, **48**, 55-9.

Caetano, D. (1985) Treatment for panic disorder with clomipramine (anafranil): An open study of 22 cases. Ciba-Geigy reprint, *Journao Brasileiro de Psiquiatria*, **34**, 123–32.

Cameron, O.G., Lee, M.A., Curtis, G.C. and McCann, D.S. (1987) Endocrine and physiological changes during 'spontaneous' panic attacks. *Psychoneuroendocrinology*, **12**, 321–31.

Cameron, O.G., Thyer, B.A., Nesse, R.M. and Curtis, G.C. (1986) Symptom profiles of patients with DSM-III anxiety disorders, *American Journal of Psychiatry*, **143**, 1132–7.

Carey, G. and Gottesman, I.I. (1981) Twin and family studies of anxiety, phobic, and obsessive disorders. In D.F. Klein and J.G. Rabkin (eds), *Anxiety: New Research and Changing Concepts*, Raven Press, New York.

Carr, D.B. and Sheehan, D.V. (1984) Evidence that panic disorder has a metabolic cause. In J.C. Ballenger (ed.), *Biology of Agoraphobia*, APA Press, Washington, DC.

Carr, D.B., Sheehan, D.V., Surman, O.S., Coleman, J.H., Greenblatt, D.J., Heninger, G.R., Jones, K.J., Levine, P.H. and Watkins, W.D. (1986) Neuroendocrine correlates of lactate-induced anxiety and their response to chronic alprazolam therapy, *American Journal of Psychiatry*, **143**, 483–94.

Carroll, B.J., Feinberg, M., Greden, J.F., Tarika, J., Albala, A.A., Haskett, R.F., James, N.M., Kronfol, Z., Lohr, N., Steiner, M., de Vigne, J.P. and Young, E. (1981) A specific laboratory test for the diagnosis of melancholia, *Archives of General Psychiatry*, **38**, 15–22.

Ceulemans, D.L.S., Westenberg, H.G.M. and van Praag, H.M. (1985) The effects of stress on the dexamethasone suppression test, *Psychiatry Research*, **14**, 189–95.

Charney, D.S., Heninger, G.R. and Redmond, D.E. (1983) Yohimbine induced anxiety and increased noradrenergic function in humans: effects of diazepam and clonidine, *Life Sciences*, **33**, 19–29.

Charney, D.S., Heninger, G.R. and Breier, A. (1984) Noradrenergic function in panic anxiety, *Archives of General Psychiatry*, **41**, 751.

Charney, D.S., Heninger, G.R. and Jatlow, P.I. (1985) Increased anxiogenic effects of caffeine in panic disorders, *Archives of General Psychiatry*, **42**, 233–43.

Charney, D.S. and Heninger, G.R. (1986a) Abnormal regulation of noradrenergic function in panic disorders, *Archives of General Psychiatry*, **43**, 1042–54.

Charney, D.S. and Heninger, G.R. (1986b) Serotonin function in panic disorders. The effect of intravenous tryptophan in healthy subjects and patients with panic disorder before and during alprazolam treatment, *Archives of General Psychiatry*, **43**,1059–65.

Charney, D.S., Woods, S.W., Goodman, W.K., Rifkin, B., Kinch, M., Aiken, B., Quadrino, L.M. and Heninger, G.R. (1986a) Drug treatment of panic disorder: the comparative efficacy of imipramine, alprazolam, and trazodone, *Journal of Clinical Psychiatry*, **47**, 580–6.

Chouinard, G., Annable, L., Fontaine, R. and Solyom, L. (1982) Alprazolam in the treatment of generalized anxiety and panic disorders: A double-blind placebo-controlled study, *Psychopharmacology*, **77**, 229–33.

Clark, D.M., Salkovskis, P.M. and Chalkley, A.J. (1985) Respiratory control as a treatment for panic attacks, *Journal of Experimental Psychiatry and Behavior Therapy*, **16**, 23–30.

Clark, D.M., Salkovskis, P.M., Gelder, M., Koehler, K., Martin, M., Anastasiades, P., Hackmann, A., Middleton, H. and Jeavons, A. (1988) Tests of a cognitive theory of panic. In I. Hand and H.-U. Wittchen (eds), *Treatments of Panic and Phobias—Modes of Application and Variables Affecting Outcome*, Springer, Berlin.

Cohen, A.S., Barlow, D.H., Blanchard, E.B. (1985) Psychophysiology of relaxation-associated panic attacks, *Journal of Abnormal Psychology*, **94**, 96–101.

Cohen, M.E. and White P.D. (1950) Life situations, emotions, and neurocirculatory asthenia (anxiety neurosis, neurasthenia, effort syndrome), *Proceedings of the Association for Research on Nervous and Mental Diseases*, **29**, 832–69.

Cohn, J.B. and Wilcox, C.S. (1986) Low-sedation potential of buspirone compared with alprazolam and lorazepam in the treatment of anxious patients: a double-blind study, *Journal of Clinical Psychiatry*, **47**, 409–12.

Cooper, J.R., Bloom, F.E. and Roth, R.H. (1982) *The Biochemical Basis of Neuropharmacology*. 4th edn, Oxford University Press, New York.

Coryell, W., Noyes, R., Clancy, J., Crowe, R. and Chaudhry, D. (1985) Abnormal escape from dexamethasone suppression in agoraphobia with panic attacks, *Psychiatry Research*, **15**, 301–11.

Cottraux, J. and Claustrat, B. (1984) Agoraphobie avec attaques de panique. Interet du test a la dexaméthasone, *La Presse Médicale*,**13**, 2582.

Cowley, D.S., Dager, S.R. and Dunner, D.L. (1986) Lactate-induced panic in primary affective disorder, *American Journal of Psychiatry*, **143**, 646–9.

Cowley, D.S., Hyde, T.S., Dager, S.R. and Dunner, D.L. (1987) Lactate infusions: the role of baseline anxiety. *Psychiatry Research*, **21**, 169–79.

Curtis, G.C., Cameron, O.G. and Nesse, R.M. (1982) The dexamethasone suppression test in panic disorder and agoraphobia, *American Journal of Psychiatry*, **139**, 1043–6.

Dager, S.R., Comess, K.A., Saal, A.K. and Dunner, D.L. (1986) Mitral valve prolapse in a psychiatric setting. Diagnostic assessment, research, and clinical implications, *Integrative Psychiatry*, **4**, 211–23.

Dager, S.R., Cowley, D.S. and Dunner, D.L. (1987) Biological markers in panic states: lactate-induced panic and mitral valve prolapse, *Biological Psychiatry*, **22**, 339–59.

Dager, S.R., Unacceptable reliability of M-mode echocardiography for detecting mitral valve prolapse. Submitted for publication.

Dealy, R.S., Ishiki, D.M., Avery, D.H., Wilson, L.G. and Dunner, D.L. (1981) Secondary depression in anxiety disorders, *Comprehensive Psychiatry*, **22**, 612–17.

Devereux, R.B., Kramer-Fox, R., Brown, W.T., Shear, M.K., Hartman, N., Kligfield, P., Lutas, E.M., Spitzer, M.C. and Litwin, S.D. (1986) Relation between clinical features of the mitral valve prolapse syndrome and echocardiographically documented mitral valve prolapse, *Journal of the American College of Cardiology*, **8**, 763–72.

Devereux, R.B., Kramer-Fox, R., Shear, M.K., Kligfield, P., Pini, R. and Savage, D.D. (1987) Diagnosis and classification of severity of mitral valve prolapse: methodologic, biologic, and prognostic considerations, *American Heart Journal*, **113**, 1265–80.

Dillon, D.J., Gorman, J.M., Liebowitz, M.R., Fyer, A.J. and Klein, D.F. (1987) The measurement of lactate-induced panic and anxiety, *Psychiatry Research*, **20**, 97–105.

Dimsdale, J.E. (1986) New dimensions in studying sympathetic nervous system responses to stressors. In T.H. Schmidt, T.M. Dembrowski and G. Blümchen (eds), *Biological and Psychological Factors in Cardiovascular Disease*, Springer, Berlin.

Dimsdale, J.E. and Moss, J. (1980) Plasma catecholamines in stress and exercise, *Journal of the American Medical Association*, **243**, 340–42.

Dubé, S., Jones, D.A., Bell, J., Davies, A., Ross, E. and Sitaram, N. (1986) Interface of panic and depression: Clinical and sleep EEG correlates, *Psychiatry Research*, **19**, 119–33.

Dunner, D.L., Ishiki, D., Avery, D.H., Wilson, L.G. and Hyde, T.S. (1986) Effect of alprazolam and diazepam on anxiety and panic attacks in panic disorder: a controlled study, *Journal of Clinical Psychiatry*, **47**, 458–60.

Dupont, R.L. and Pecknold, J.C. (1985) Symptoms after stopping alprazolam: relapse or withdrawal? Paper presented at the 138th Annual Meeting of the American Psychiatric Association, Dallas, Texas, May 1985.

Ehlers, A., Margraf, J. and Roth, W.T. (1986a) Experimental induction of panic attacks. In I. Hand and H.-U. Wittchen (eds), *Panic and Phobias*, Springer, Berlin.

Ehlers, A., Margraf, J., Roth, W.T., Taylor, C.B., Maddock, R.J., Sheikh, J., Kopell, M.L., McClenahan, K.L., Gossard, D., Blowers, G.H., Agras, W.S. and Kopell, B.S. (1986b). Lactate infusions and panic attacks: do patients and controls respond differently? *Psychiatry Research*, **17**, 295–308.

Ehlers, A., Margraf, J. and Roth, W.T. (1986c) Letter to the editor, *Psychiatry Research*, **19**, 165–7.

Ehlers, A., Margraf, J. and Roth, W.T. (1988a) Interaction of expectancy and physiological stressors in a laboratory model of panic. In D. Hellhammer, I. Florin and H. Weiner (eds), *Neurobiological Approaches to Human Disease*, Huber, Toronto.

Ehlers, A., Margraf, J., Roth, W.T., Taylor, C.B. and Birbaumer, N. (1988b) Anxiety induced by false heart rate feedback in patients with panic disorder, *Behavior Research and Therapy*, **26**, 2–11.

Ehlers, A., Margraf, J., Taylor, C.B. and Roth, W.T. (1988c) Cardiovascular aspects of panic disorder. In T. Elbert, W. Langosch, A. Steptoe, and D. Vaitl (eds), *Behavioural Medicine in Cardiovascular Disorders*, Wiley, London.

Elam, M., Yao, T., Thoren, P. and Svensson, T.H. (1981) Hypercapnia and hypoxia: Chemoreceptor-mediated control of locus ceruleus neurons and splanchnic, sympathetic nerves, *Brain Research*, **222**, 373–81.

Faludi, G., Kasko, M., Perényi, A., Arato, M. and Frecska, E. (1986) The dexamethasone suppression test in panic disorder and major depressive episodes, *Biological Psychiatry*, **21**, 1008–14.

Fann, W.E., Richman, B.W. and Pitts, W.M. (1982) Halazepam in the treatment of recurrent anxiety attacks in chronically anxious outpatients: a double-blind placebo controlled study, *Current Therapeutic Research*, **32**, 906–10.

Fenz, W.D. and Epstein, S. (1967) Gradients of physiological arousal of experienced and novice parachutists as a function of an approaching jump, *Psychosomatic Medicine*, **29**, 33–51.

Fibiger, H.C. and Mason, S.T. (1978) The effect of dorsal bundle injections of 6-OHDA on avoidance responding in rats, *British Journal of Pharmacology*, **64**, 601–6.

File, S.E., Deakin, J.F.W., Longden, A. and Crow, T.J. (1979) An investigation of the role of the locus coeruleus in anxiety and agonistic behavior, *Brain Research*, **169**, 411–20.

Finlay-Jones, R. and Brown, G.W. (1981) Types of stressful life event and the onset of anxiety and depressive disorders, *Psychological Medicine*, **11**, 801–15.

Fisher, L.M. and Wilson, G.T. (1985) A study of the psychology of agoraphobia, *Behaviour Research and Therapy*, **23**, 97–107.

Fishman, S.M., Sheehan, D.V. and Carr, D.B. (1985) Thyroid indices in panic disorder, *Journal of Clinical Psychiatry*, **46**, 432–3.

Fontaine, R. and Chouinard, G. (1984) Antipanic effect of clonazepam, *American Journal of Psychiatry*, **141**, 149.

Foote, S.L., Ashton-Jones, G. and Bloom, F.E. (1980) Impulse activity of locus coeruleus neurons in awake rats and monkeys is a function of sensory stimulation and arousal, *Proceedings of the National Academy of Sciences of the USA*, **77**, 3033–7.

Foote, S.L., Bloom, F.E. and Ashton-Jones, G. (1983) Nucleus locus coeruleus: new evidence of anatomical and physiological specificity, *Physiological Review*, **63**, 844–914.

Fowler, C.J., Tipton, K.F., Mackay, A.V.P. and Youdim, M.B.A. (1982) Human platelet monoamine oxidase. A useful enzyme in the study of psychiatric disorders? *Neuroscience*, **7**, 1577–94.

Freedman, R.R., Ianni, P., Ettedgui, E., Pohl, R. and Rainey, J.M. (1984) Psychophysiological factors in panic disorder, *Psychopathology*, Supplement **1**, 17, 66–73.

Freedman, R.R., Ianni, P., Ettedgui, E. and Puthezhath, N. (1985) Ambulatory monitoring of panic disorder, *Archives of General Psychiatry*, **42**, 244–8.

Freud, S. (1895a) Obsessions et Phobies. *Revue Neurologique*, 3. Also in *Gesammelte Werke, Band I*. Imago, London, 1952 (pp. 345–55).

Freud, S. (1895b) Über die Berechtigung, von der Neurasthenie einen bestimmten Symptomenkomplex als 'Angstneurose' abzutrennen. *Neurologisches Zentralblatt*, 2. Also in *Gesammelte Werke, Band I*. Imago, London, 1952 (pp. 315–42).

Fyer, A.J., Liebowitz, M.R., Gorman, J.M., Davies, S.O. and Klein, D.F. (1985) Lactate vulnerability of remitted panic patients, *Psychiatry Research*, **14**, 143–7.

Fyer, A.J., Liebowitz, M.R., Gorman, J.M., Campeas, R., Levin, A., Davies, S.O., Goetz, D. and Klein, D.F. (1987) Discontinuation of alprazolam treatment in panic patients, *American Journal of Psychiatry*, **144**, 303–8.

Gaffney, F.A., Fenton, B.J., Lane, L.D. and Lake, C.R. (1988) Hemodynamic, ventilatory, and biochemical responses in panic patients and normal controls during sodium lactate infusion and spontaneous panic attacks, *Archives of General Psychiatry*, **45**, 53–60.

Gelder, M.G. (1986) Panic attacks: new approaches to an old problem, *British Journal of Psychiatry*, **149**, 346–52.

Gentsch, C., Lichsteiner, M., Gastpar, M., Gastpar, G. and Feer, H. (1985) ^{3}H-imipramine binding sites in platelets of hospitalized psychiatric patients, *Psychiatry Research*, **14**, 177–87.

Gittelman-Klein, R. (1975) Psychiatric characteristics of the relatives of school phobic children. In A. Sankar (ed.), *Mental Health in Children*, Vol. I, PDJ Publications, New York.

Gittelman-Klein, R. and Klein, D.F. (1973) School phobia: diagnostic considerations in the light of imipramine effects, *Journal of Nervous and Mental Disease*, **156**, 199–215.

Gittelman-Klein, R. and Klein, D.F. (1980) Separation anxiety in school refusal and its treatment with drugs. In A. Hersov and I. Berg (eds), *Out of School*, Wiley, London.

Gittelman-Klein, R. and Klein, D.F. (1984) Relationship between separation anxiety and panic and agoraphobic disorders, *Psychopathology*, Supplement **1**, 17, 56–65.

Gloger, S., Grunhaus, L., Birmacher, B. and Troudart, T. (1981) Treatment of spontaneous panic attacks with clomipramine, *American Journal of Psychiatry*, **138**, 1215–17.

Gorman, J.M. (1986) Panic disorder: Focus on cardiovascular status. Paper presented at the 139th Annual Meeting of the American Psychiatric Association, Washington, DC, May 1986.

Gorman, J.M., Fyer, A.J., Glicklich, J., King, D.L. and Klein, D.F. (1981) Mitral valve prolapse and panic disorders: Effect of imipramine. In D.F. Klein and J.G. Rabkin (eds), *Anxiety: New Research and Changing Concepts*, Raven Press, New York.

Gorman, J.M., Askanazi, J., Liebowitz, M.R., Fyer, A.J., Stein, J., Kinney, J.M. and Klein, D.F. (1984a) Response to hyperventilation in a group of patients with panic disorder, *American Journal of Psychiatry*, **141**, 857–61.

Gorman, J.M., Martinez, J.M., Liebowitz, M.R., Fyer, A.J. and Klein, D.F. (1984b) Hypoglycemia and panic attacks, *American Journal of Pyschiatry*, **141**, 101–2.

Gorman, J.M., Liebowitz, M.R., Stein, J., Fyer, A.J. and Klein, D.F. (1984c) Insulin levels during lactate infusion, *American Journal of Psychiatry*, **141**, 1621–2.

Gorman, J.M., Dillon, D., Fyer, A.J., Liebowitz, M.R. and Klein, D.F. (1985a) The lactate infusion model, *Psychopharmacology Bulletin*, **21**, 428–33.

Gorman, J.M., Liebowitz, M.R., Fyer, A.J., Dillon, D., Davies, S.O., Stein, J. and Klein, D.F. (1985b) Lactate infusions in obsessive-compulsive disorder, *American Journal of Psychiatry*, **142**, 864–6.

Gorman, J.M., Liebowitz, M.R., Fyer, A.J., Levitt, M., Baron, M., Davies, S. and Klein, D.F. (1985c) Platelet monoamine oxidase activity in patients with panic disorder, *Biological Psychiatry*, **20**, 852–7.

Gorman, J.M., Cohen, B.S., Liebowitz, M.R., Fyer, A.J., Ross, D., Davies, S.O. and Klein, D.F. (1986a) Blood gas changes and hypophosphatemia in lactate-induced panic, *Archives of General Psychiatry*, **43**, 1067–71.

Gorman, J.M., Shear, M.K., Devereux, R.B., King, D.L. and Klein, D.F. (1986b) Prevalence of mitral valve prolapse in panic disorder: effects of echocardiographic criteria, *Psychosomatic Medicine*, **48**, 167–71.
Grant, S.J., Huang, Y.H. and Redmond, D.E. (1980) Benzodiazepines attenuate single unit activity in the locus ceruleus, *Life Sciences*, **27**, 2231–6.
Gray, J.A. (1982) *The Neuropsychology of Anxiety*, Oxford University Press, New York.
Griez, E. and van den Hout, M.A. (1986) CO_2 inhalation in the treatment of panic attacks, *Behaviour Research and Therapy*, **24**, 145–50.
Grosz, H. and Farmer, B. (1969) Blood lactate in the development of anxiety symptoms, *Archives of General Psychiatry*, **21**, 611–19.
Grosz, H. and Farmer, B. (1972) Pitts' and McClure's lactate-anxiety study revisited, *British Journal of Psychiatry*, **120**, 415–18.
Grunhaus, L., Gloger, S. and Weissturb, E. (1981) Panic attacks, A review of treatments and pathogenesis, *Journal of Nervous and Mental Disease*, **169**, 608–13.
Grunhaus, L,. Rabin, D., Harel, Y., Greden, J.F., Feinberg, M. and Hermann, R. (1986) Simultaneous panic and depressive disorders: clinical and sleep EEG correlates, *Psychiatry Research*, **17**, 251–9.
Gruhaus, L., Flegel, P., Haskett, R.F. and Greden, J.F. (1987) Serial dexamethasone suppression tests in simultaneous panic and depressive disorders, *Biological Psychiatry*, **22**, 332–8.
Guttmacher, L.B. and Nelles, C. (1984) In vivo desensitization alteration of lactate-induced panic: a case study, *Behavior Therapy*, **15**, 369–72.
Guttmacher, L.B., Murphy, D.L. and Insel, T.R. (1983) Pharmacologic models of anxiety, *Comprehensive Psychiatry*, **24**, 312–26.
Guze, S.B., Cloninger, C.R., Martin, R.L. and Clayton, P.J. (1986) A follow-up and family study of Briquet's syndrome, *British Journal of Psychiatry*, **149**, 17–23.
Hallam, R.S. (1985) *Anxiety. Psychological Perspectives on Panic and Agoraphobia*, Academic Press, London.
Harbauer-Raum, U. (1987) Wahrnehmung von Herzschlag und Arrhythmien — Eine Labor-Feldstudie an Patienten mit Herzphobie. In D.O. Nutzinger, D. Pfersman, T. Welan and H.-G. Zapotoczky (eds), *Herzphobie*, Enke, Stuttgart.
Hartman, N., Kramer, R., Brown, W.T. and Devereux, R.B. (1982) Panic disorder in patients with mitral valve prolapse, *American Journal of Psychiatry*, **139**, 669–70.
Heide, F.J. and Borkovec, T.D. (1983) Relaxation-induced anxiety: paradoxical anxiety enhancement due to relaxation training, *Journal of Consulting and Clinical Psychology*, **51**, 171–82.
Heide, F.J. and Borkovec, T.D. (1984) Relaxation-induced anxiety: mechanisms and theoretical implications, *Behaviour Research and Therapy*, **22**, 1–12.
Hoehn-Saric, R., Merchant, A.F., Keyser, M.L. and Smith, V.K. (1981) Effects of clonidine on anxiety disorders, *Archives of General Psychiatry*, **38**, 1278–81.
Holmberg, G. and Gershon, S. (1961) Autonomic and psychic effects of yohimbine hydrochloride, *Psychopharmacologia*, **2**, 93–106.
Insel, T.R., Ninan, P.T., Aloi, J., Jimerson, D.C., Skolnik, P. and Paul, S.M. (1984) A benzodiazepine receptor-mediated model of anxiety, *Archives of General Psychiatry*, **41**, 741–50.
Jardine, R., Martin, N.G. and Henderson, A.S. (1984) Genetic covariation between neuroticism and the symptoms of anxiety and depression, *Genetic Epidemiology*, **1**, 89.

Kahn, R.J., McNair, D.M., Lipman, R.S., Covi, L., Rickels, K., Downing, R., Fisher, S. and Frankenthaler, L.M. (1986) Imipramine and chlordiazepoxide in depressive and anxiety disorders, *Archives of General Psychiatry*, **43**, 79–85.

Kathol, R.G. and Delahunt, J.W. (1986) The relationship of anxiety and depression to symptoms of hyperthyroidism using operational criteria, *General Hospital Psychiatry*, **8**, 23–8.

Keefe, P. and Agras, W.S. (1983) Letter to the editor, *New England Journal of Medicine*, **308**, 341.

Kelly, D., Mitchell-Heggs, N. and Sherman, D. (1971) Anxiety and the effects of sodium lactate assessed clinically and physiologically, *British Journal of Psychiatry*, **119**, 129.

Kendler, K.S., Heath, A.C., Martin, N.G. and Eaves, L.J. (1987) Symptoms of anxiety and symptoms of depression. Same genes, different environment? *Archives of General Psychiatry*, **44**, 451.

Khan, A., Lee, E., Dager, S.R., Hyde, T., Raisys, V., Avery, D. and Dunner, D.L. (1986) Platelet MAO-B activity in anxiety and depression, *Biological Psychiatry*, **21**, 847–9.

King, R., Margraf, J., Ehlers, A. and Maddock, R.J. (1986) Panic disorder—overlap with symptoms of somatization disorder. In I. Hand and H.-U. Wittchen (eds), *Panic and Phobias*, Springer, Berlin.

Klein, D.F. (1964) Delineation of two drug-responsive anxiety syndromes, *Psychopharmacologia*, **5**, 397–408.

Klein, D.F. (1980) Anxiety reconceptualized, *Comprehensive Psychiatry*, **21**, 411–27.

Klein, D.F. (1981) Anxiety reconceptualized. In D.F. Klein and J.G. Rabkin (eds), *Anxiety: New Research and Changing Concepts*, Raven Press, New York.

Klein, D.F. (1984) Psychopharmacological treatment of panic disorder, *Psychosomatics*, Supplement, **25**, 32–6.

Klein, D.F., Rabkin, J.G. and Gorman, J.M. (1985) Etiological and pathophysiological inferences from the pharmacological treatment of anxiety. In A.H. Tuma and J.D. Maser (eds), *Anxiety and the Anxiety Disorders*, Lawrence Erlbaum, Hillsdale, NJ.

Klein, D.F., Ross, D.C. and Cohen, P. (1987) Panic and avoidance in agoraphobia. Application of path analysis to treatment studies, *Archives of General Psychiatry*, **44**, 377–85.

Kleiner, L. and Marshall, W.L. (1987) The role of interpersonal problems in the development of agoraphobia with panic attacks, *Journal of Anxiety Disorders*, **1**, 313–23.

Klosko, J.S., Barlow, D.H., Tassinari, R.B. and Cerny, J.A. (1988) Comparison of alprazolam and cognitive behavior therapy in the treatment of panic disorder: A preliminary report. In I. Hand and H.-U. Wittchen (eds), *Treatments of Panic and Phobias—Modes of Application and Variables Affecting Outcome*, Springer, Berlin.

Ko, G.N., Elsworth, J.D., Roth, R.H., Rifkin, B.G., Leigh, H. and Redmond, D.E. (1983) Panic-induced elevation of plasma MHPG levels in phobic-anxious patients, *Archives of General Psychiatry*, **40**, 425–30.

Koob, G., Strecker, R., Roberts, D. and Bloom, F.E. (1981) Failure to alter anxiety or the anxiolytic properties of chlordiazepoxide and ethanol by destruction of the dorsal noradrenergic system. *Society for Neuroscience Abstracts*, **6**, 108 (Abstract 40.6).

Lader, M. and Mathews, A.M. (1970) Physiological changes during spontaneous panic attacks, *Journal of Psychosomatic Research*, **14**, 377–80.

Lapierre, Y.D., Knott, V.J. and Gray, R. (1984) Psychophysiological correlates of sodium lactate, *Psychopharmacology Bulletin*, **20**, 50–57.

Last, C.G., Barlow, D.H. and O'Brien, G.T. (1984) Precipitants of agoraphobia: role of stressful life events, *Psychological Reports*, **54**, 567–70.

Leckman, J.F., Weissman, M.M., Merinkangas, K.R., Pauls, D.L. and Prusoff, B.A. (1983) Panic disorder and major depression, *Archives of General Psychiatry*, **40**, 1055–60.

Lelliott, P., Marks, I. and McNamee, G. The onset of panic disorder with agoraphobia, *Archives of General Psychiatry*, in press.

Lewis, D.A. (1986) Letter to the editor. *Psychiatry Research*, **18**, 191–2.

Lewis, D.A. and McChesney, C. (1985) Tritiated imipramine binding distinguishes among subtypes of depression. *Archives of General Psychiatry*, **140**, 485–8.

Lewis, D.A., Noyes, R., Coryell, W. and Clancy, J. (1985) Tritiated imipramine binding to platelets is decreased in patients with agoraphobia, *Psychiatry Research*, **16**, 1–9.

Ley, R.A. (1988) Hyperventilation and lactate infusion in the production of panic attacks, *Clinical Psychology Review*, **8**, 1–18.

Lieberman, J.A., Brenner, R., Lesser, M., Coccaro, E., Borenstein, M. and Kane, J.M. (1983) Dexamethasone suppression tests in patients with panic disorder, *American Journal of Psychiatry*, **140**, 917–19.

Liebowitz, M.R., Fyer, A.J., McGrath, P. and Klein, D.F. (1981) Clonidine treatment of panic disorder. *Psychopharmacology Bulletin*, **17**, 122–3.

Liebowitz, M.R., Fyer, A.J. and Gorman, J.M. (1985a) Specificity of lactate infusions in social phobia versus panic disorder, *American Journal of Psychiatry*, **142**, 947–50.

Liebowitz, M.R., Gorman, J., Fyer, A., Levitt, M., Dillon, D., Levy, G., Appleby, I., Anderson, S., Palij, M., Davies, S. and Klein, D.F. (1985b) Lactate provocation of panic attacks: II. Biochemical and physiological findings, *Archives of General Psychiatry*, **42**, 709–19.

Liebowitz, M.R., Gorman, J.M., Fyer, A., Dillon, D., Levitt, M. and Klein, D.F. (1986) Possible mechanisms for lactate's induction of panic, *American Journal of Psychiatry*, **143**, 495–502.

Loosen, P.T. and Prange, A.J. (1982) Serum thyrotropin response to thyrotropin-releasing hormone in psychiatric patients: A review, *American Journal of Psychiatry*, **139**, 405–16.

Margraf, J. (1988) Psychophysiologische Untersuchungen bei Panikanfällen. In H. Hippius, M. Ackenheil and R. Engel (eds), *Angst—Leitsymptom psychiatrischer Erkrankungen*, Springer, Berlin.

Margraf, J. and Ehlers, A. (1986) Erkennung und Behandlung von akuten Angstanfällen. In J.C. Brengelmann and G. Bühringer (eds), *Therapieforschung für die Praxis 6*, Röttger, München.

Margraf, J. and Ehlers, A. (1987) Fear of fear in panic disorder and agoraphobia: the panic and agoraphobia profile (PAP). Paper presented at the 17th Annual Meeting of the European Association for Behaviour Therapy, Amsterdam, August 1987.

Margraf, J. and Ehlers, A. (1988) Panic attacks in nonclinical subjects. In I. Hand and H.-U Wittchen (eds), *Panic and Phobias 2*, Springer, Berlin.

Margraf, J. Ehlers, A. and Roth, W.T. (1986a) Biological models of panic disorder and agoraphobia—A review, *Behaviour Research and Therapy*, **24**, 553–67.

Margraf, J. Ehlers, A. and Roth, W.T. (1986b) Panic attacks: theoretical models and empirical evidence. In I. Hand and H.-U. Wittchen (eds), *Panic and Phobias*, Springer, Berlin.

Margraf, J., Ehlers, A. and Roth, W.T. (1986c) Sodium lactate infusions and panic attacks: a review and critique, *Psychosomatic Medicine*, **48**, 23–51.
Margraf, J., Taylor, C.B., Ehlers, A., Roth, W.T. and Agras, W.S. (1987a) Panic attacks in the natural environment, *Journal of Nervous and Mental Disease*, **175**, 558–65.
Margraf, J., Ehlers, A. and Roth, W.T. (1987b) Panic attack associated with false heart rate feedback, *Behavior Therapy*, **18**, 84–9.
Margraf, J., Ehlers, A. and Roth, W.T. (1988) Mitral valve prolapse and panic disorder: a review of their relationship. *Psychosomatic Medicine*, **50**, 93–113.
Margraf, J., Ehlers, A. and Roth, W.T. (1989) Hyperventilation and expectancy as laboratory stressors. In D. Hellhammer, I. Florin, and H. Weiner (eds), *Frontiers of Stress Research*, Huber, Toronto.
Marks, I. (1983) Are there anticompulsive or antiphobic drugs? Review of evidence, *British Journal of Psychiatry*, **143**, 338–47.
Marks, I. (1986) Genetics of fear and anxiety disorders, *British Journal of Psychiatry*, **149**, 406–18.
Marks, I. (1987a) Agoraphobia, panic disorder and related conditions in the DSM-IIIR and ICD-10, *Journal of Psychopharmacology*, **1**, 6–12.
Marks, I. (1987b) *Fears, Phobias, and Rituals. Panic, Anxiety, and their Disorders*. Oxford University Press, New York.
Marks, I., Stern, R.S., Mawson, D., Cobb, J., and McDonald, R. (1980) Clomipramine and exposure for obsessive-compulsive rituals: I, *British Journal of Psychiatry*, **136**, 1–25.
Mason, S.T. (1981) Norepinephrine in the brain. Progress in theories of behavioral function, *Progress in Neurobiology*, **16**, 263–303.
Mason, S.T. and Fibiger, H.C. (1979a) Current concepts. I. Anxiety: the locus coeruleus disconnection, *Life Sciences*, **25**, 2141–7.
Mason, S.T. and Fibiger, H.C. (1979b) Noradrenaline and avoidance learning in the rat, *Brain Research*, **161**, 321–34.
Mason, S.T. and Fibiger, H.C. (1979c) Noradrenaline, fear and extinction, *Brain Research*, **165**, 47–56.
Mathews, A.M., Gelder, M.G. and Johnston, D.W. (1981) *Agoraphobia: Nature and Treatment*, Guilford Press, New York.
Matthew, R.J., Ho, B., Kralik, P., Taylor, D. and Claghorn, J. (1981) Catecholamines and monoamine oxidase activity in anxiety, *Acta Psychiatria Scandinavia*, **63**, 245–52.
Matuzas, W. and Glass, R.M. (1983) Treatment of agoraphobia and panic attacks, *Archives of General Psychiatry*, **40**, 220–22.
Mavissakalian, M. (1987) The placebo effect in agoraphobia, *Journal of Nervous and Mental Disease*, **175**, 95–9.
Mavissakalian, M. and Michelson, L. (1986) Two-year follow-up of exposure and imipramine treatment of agoraphobia, *American Journal of Psychiatry*, **143**, 1106–12.
McGrath, P.J., Stewart, J.W., Harrison, W., Quitkin, F.M. and Rabkin, J. (1985) Lactate infusion in patients with depression and anxiety, *Psychopharmacology Bulletin*, **21**, 555–7.
McIntyre, I.M., Marriott, P.F., Jefferys, D., Burrows, G.D., Judd, F.K. and Norman, T.R. (1986) Melatonin in panic disorder, *Biological Psychiatry*, **21**, 1438–9.
McMillen, B.A., Matthews, R.T., Sanghera, M.K., Shepard, P.D. and German, D.C. (1983) Dopamine receptor antagonism by the novel antianxiety drug, buspirone, *Journal of Neuroscience*, **3**, 733–8.

McNair, D.M., Lorr, M. and Droppleman, L.F. (1981) *Profile of Mood States*. EDITS, San Diego.

Mellerup, E.T., Plenge, P. and Rosenberg, R. (1982) ^{3}H-imipramine binding sites in platelets from psychiatric patients, *Psychiatry Research*, **7**, 221–7.

Meyers, D.G., Stark, H., Pearson, P.H. and Wilken, D.E.L. (1986) Mitral valve prolapse in anorexia nervosa, *Annals of Internal Medicine*, **105**, 384–6.

Michels, R., Frances, A. and Shear, M.K. (1985) Psychodynamic models of anxiety. In A.H. Tuma and J.D. Maser (eds), *Anxiety and the Anxiety Disorders*, Lawrence Erlbaum, Hillsdale, NJ.

Motulsky, A.G. (1978) Biased ascertainment and the natural history of diseases, *New England Journal of Medicine*, **298**, 1196–97.

Munjack, D.L., Rebal, R., Shaner, R., Staples, F., Braun, R. and Leonard, M. (1985) Imipramine vs. propanolol for panic attacks: a pilot study, *Comprehensive Psychiatry*, **26**, 80–89.

Nesse, R.M., Cameron, O.G., Curtis, G.C., McCann, D.S. and Huber-Smith, M.J. (1984) Adrenergic function in patients with panic anxiety, *Archives of General Psychiatry*, **41**, 771–6.

Noyes, R., Anderson, D., Clancy, J., Crowe, R., Slymen, D., Ghoneim, M. and Hinrichs, J. (1984) Diazepam and propanolol in the treatment of panic disorder, *Archives of General Psychiatry*, **41**, 287–92.

Nutt, D.J. (1986) Increased central alpha$_2$-adrenoreceptor sensitivity in panic disorder, *Psychopharmacology*, **90**, 268–9.

Nybäck, H., Walters, J.R., Aghajanian, G.K. and Roth, R.H. (1975) Tricyclic antidepressants: effects on the firing rate of brain noradrenergic neurons, *European Journal of Pharmacology*, **32**, 302–12.

Ollendick, T.H. and Mayer, J.A. (1984) School phobia. In S.M. Turner (ed.), *Behavioral Theories and Treatment of Anxiety*, Plenum Press, New York.

Olpe, H.R., Jones, R.S.G. and Steinman, M.W. (1983) The locus coeruleus: actions of psychoactive drugs, *Experientia*, **39**, 242–9.

Öst, L.-G. (1988) Applied relaxation vs. progressive relaxation in the treatment of panic disorder. *Behaviour Research and Therapy*, **26**, 13–22.

Pariser, S.F., Jones, B.A., Pinta, E.R., Young, E.A. and Fontana, M.E. (1979) Panic attacks: diagnostic evaluations of 17 patients, *American Journal of Psychiatry*, **136**, 105–6.

Paul, S.M., Rehavi, M., Skolnick, P., Ballenger, J.C. and Goodwin, F.K. (1981) Depressed patients have decreased binding of tritiated imipramine to platelet serotonin 'transporter,' *Archives of General Psychiatry*, **38**, 1315–17.

Pecknold, J.C. and Swinson, R.P. (1986) Taper withdrawal studies with alprazolam in patients with panic disorder and agoraphobia, *Psychopharmacology Bulletin*, **22**, 173–6.

Peterson, G.A., Ballenger, J.C., Cox, D.P., Hucek, A., Lydiard, R.B., Laraia, M.T. and Trockman, C. (1985) The dexamethasone suppression test in agoraphobia, *Journal of Clinical Psychopharmacology*, **5**, 100–2.

Pitts, F.N. (1969) The biochemistry of anxiety, *Scientific American*, **220**, 69–75.

Pitts, F.N. and McClure, J. (1967) Lactate metabolism in anxiety neurosis, *New England Journal of Medicine*, **277**, 1329–36.

Pohl, R.P., Berchou, R. and Rainey, J.M. (1982) Tricyclic antidepressants and monoamine oxidase inhibitors in the treatment of agoraphobia, *Journal of Clinical Psychopharmacology*, **2**, 399–407.

Rachman, S. (1987) Panics and their consequences—A review and prospect.

In S. Rachman and J.D. Maser (eds), *Panic: Psychological Perspectives*, Lawrence Erlbaum, Hillsdale, NJ.

Rachman, S. and Levitt, K. (1985) Panics and their consequences, *Behaviour Research and Therapy*, **23**, 585–600.

Rachman, S. and Lopatka, C. (1986) Match and mismatch in the prediction of fear—I, *Behaviour Research and Therapy*, **24**, 387–93.

Rainey, J.M., Pohl, R.B., Williams, M., Knitter, E., Freedman, R.R. and Ettedgui, E. (1984) A comparison of lactate and isoproterenol anxiety states, *Psychopathology*, Supplement **1**, 17, 74–82.

Raisman, R., Sechter, D., Briley, M.S., Zarifian, E. and Langer, S.Z. (1981) High affininty ^{3}H-imipramine binding in platelets from untreated and treated depressed patients compared to healthy volunteers, *Psychopharmacology*, **75**, 368–71.

Rapee, R., Mattick, R. and Murrell, E. (1988) Cognitive mediation in the affective component of spontaneous panic attacks, *Journal of Behavior Therapy and Experimental Psychiatry*, **17**, 245–53.

Raskin, M., Peeke, H.V.S., Dickman, W. and Pinsker, H. (1982) Panic and generalized anxiety disorder, *Archives of General Psychiatry*, **39**, 687–9.

Redmond, D.E. (1979) New and old evidence for the involvement of a brain norepinephrine system in anxiety. In W.E. Fann, I. Karacan, A.D. Pokorny and R.L. Williams (eds), *Phenomenology and Treatment of Anxiety*, Spectrum Press, New York.

Redmond, D.E. and Huang, Y. (1979) Current concepts. II. New evidence for a locus coeruleus-norepinephrine connection with anxiety, *Life Sciences*, **25**, 2149–62.

Reiman, E.M., Raichle, M.E., Butler, F.K., Herscovitch, P. and Robins, E. (1984) A focal brain abnormality in panic disorder, a severe form of anxiety, *Nature*, **310**, 683–5.

Reiman, E.M., Raichle, M.E., Robins, E., Butler, F.K., Herscovitch, P., Fox, P. and Perlmutter, J. (1986) The application of positron emission tomography to the study of panic disorder, *American Journal of Psychiatry*, **143**, 469–77.

Rick, S., Beckman, H. and Müller, W.E. (1985) DL-sodium lactate reduces alpha$_1$-adrenergic receptor binding in rat and mouse brain, *Psychiatry Research*, **16**, 241–7.

Rickels, K. and Schweizer, E.E. (1986) Benzodiazepines for treatment of panic attacks: a new look, *Psychopharmacology Bulletin*, **22**, 93–9.

Rizley, R., Kahn, R.J., McNair, D.M. and Frankenthaler, L.M. (1986) A comparison of alprazolam and imipramine in the treatment of agoraphobia and panic disorder, *Psychopharmacology Bulletin*, **22**, 167–72.

Ross, C.A. (1986) Biological tests for mental illness: their use and misuse, *Biological Psychiatry*, **21**, 431–5.

Roth, M. and Mountjoy, C.Q. (1982) The distinction between anxiety states and depressive disorders. In E. Paykel (ed.), *Handbook of Affective Disorders*, Guilford, New York.

Roth, M. (1984) Agoraphobia, panic disorder, and generalized anxiety disorder: some implications of recent advances, *Psychiatric Developments*, **2**, 31–52.

Roy-Byrne, P.P., Uhde, T.W., Post, R.M., King, A.C. and Buchsbaum, M.S. (1985a) Normal pain sensitivity in patients with panic disorder, *Psychiatry Research*, **14**, 75–82.

Roy-Byrne, P.P., Bierer, L.M. and Uhde, T.W. (1985b) The dexamethasone suppression test in panic disorder: comparison with normal controls, *Biological Psychiatry*, **20**, 1237–40.
Roy-Byrne, P.P., Geraci, M. and Uhde, T.W. (1986a) Life events and course of illness in patients with panic disorder, *American Journal of Psychiatry*, **143**, 1033–5.
Roy-Byrne, P.P., Uhde, T.W., Rubinow, D.R. and Post, R.M. (1986b) Reduced TSH and prolactin responses to TRH in patients with panic disorder, *American Journal of Psychiatry*, **143**, 503–7.
Roy-Byrne, P.P., Uhde, T.W., Sack, D.A., Linnoila, M. and Post, R.M. (1986c) Plasma HVA and anxiety in patients with panic disorder, *Biological Psychiatry*, **21**, 849–53.
Roy-Byrne, P.P., Uhde, T.W., Post, R.M., Gallucci, W., Chrousos, G.P. and Gold, P.W. (1986d) The corticotropin-releasing hormone stimulation test in patients with panic disorder, *American Journal of Psychiatry*, **143**, 896–9.
Sachar, E.J. (1970) Psychological factors relating to activation and inhibition of the adrenocortical stress response in man: A review. In D. de Wied and J.A. van Weijnen (eds), *Progress in Brain Research, Vol. 32,* Elsevier, Amsterdam.
Salkovskis, P.M., Jones, D.R.O. and Clark, D.M. (1986a) Respiratory control in the treatment of panic attacks: Replication and extension with concurrent measurement of behaviour and pCO_2, *British Journal of Psychiatry*, **148**, 526–32.
Sanghera, M.K., McMillen, B.A. and German, D.C. (1983) Buspirone, a non-benzodiazepin anxiolytic, increases locus coeruleus noradrenergic neuronal activity, *European Journal of Pharmacology*, **86**, 106–10.
Savage, D.S., Devereux, R.B., Garrison, R.B., Castelli, W.P., Anderson, S.J., Levy, D., Thomas, H.E., Kannel, W.B. and Feinleib, M. (1983) Mitral valve prolapse in the general population. 2. Clinical features: The Framingham Study, *American Heart Journal*, **106**, 577–81.
Schneider, L.S., Severson, J.A. and Sloane, R.B. (1985) Platelet ^{3}H-imipramine binding in depressed elderly patients, *Biological Psychiatry*, **20**, 1232–4.
Schneider, L.S., Munjack, D., Severson, J.A. and Palmer, R. (1987) Platelet ^{3}H-imipramine binding in generalized anxiety disorder, panic disorder, and agoraphobia with panic attacks, *Biological Psychiatry*, **22**, 59–66.
Schweizer, E.E., Swenson, C.M., Winokur, A., Rickels, K. and Maislin, G. (1986) The dexamethasone suppression test in generalized anxiety disorder, *British Journal of Psychiatry*, **149**, 320–2.
Scott, J.P., Stewart, J.M. and DeGhett, V.J. (1973) Separation in infant dogs. Emotional response and motivational consequences. In J.P. Scott and E.C. Senay (eds), *Separation and Depression: Clinical and Research Aspects*, American Association for the Advancement of Science, Washington, DC.
Shader, R., Goodman, M. and Gever, J. (1982) Panic disorders: current perspectives, *Journal of Clinical Psychopharmacology*, Supplement, **2**, 2–10.
Shear, M.K. (1986) Pathophysiology of panic: A review of pharmacologic provocative tests and realistic monitoring data, *Journal of Clinical Psychiatry*, Supplement, **47**, 18–26.
Shear, M.K. and Fyer, A.J. (1987) Effects of cognitive-behavioral treatment on sodium lactate response of panic patients: Preliminary results. Paper presented at the Symposium on Treatments of Panic and Phobias, Ringberg, Bavaria, October 1987.
Shear, M.K., Kligfield, P., Harshfield, G., Devereux, R.B., Polan, J.J., Mann, J.J., Pickering, T. and Frances, A.J. (1987) Cardiac rate and rhythm in panic patients, *American Journal of Psychiatry*, **144**, 633–7.

Shear, M.K., Ball, G.G., Josephson, S.C. and Gitlin, B.C. (1988) Cognitive-behavioral treatment of panic. In I. Hand and H.-U. Wittchen (eds), *Treatments of Panic and Phobias—Modes of Application and Variables Affecting Outcome*, Springer, Berlin.

Shear, M.K., Polan, J.J., Harshfield, G., Pickering, T., Mann, J.J., Frances, A. and James, G. Ambulatory monitoring of blood pressure and heart rate in panic patients. Submitted for publication.

Sheehan, D.V. (1982a) Panic attacks and phobias, *New England Journal of Medicine*, **307**, 156–8.

Sheehan, D.V. (1982b) Current views on the treatment of panic and phobic disorders, *Drug Therapy*, **12**, 179–93.

Sheehan, D.V. (1984) Strategies for diagnosis and treatment of anxiety disorders. In R.O. Pasnau (ed.), *Diagnosis and Treatment of Anxiety Disorders*, APA Press, Washington, DC.

Sheehan, D.V. and Sheehan, K.H. (1983) The classification of phobic disorders, *International Journal of Psychiatry in Medicine*, **12**, 243–66.

Sheehan, D.V., Ballenger, J.C. and Jacobsen, G. (1980) Treatment of endogenous anxiety, *Archives of General Psychiatry*, **37**, 51–9.

Sheehan, D.V., Claycomb, J.B., Surman, O.S., Baer, L., Coleman, J. and Gelles, L. (1983) Panic attacks and the dexamethasone suppression test, *American Journal of Psychiatry*, **140**, 1063–4.

Sheehan, D.V., Coleman, J., Greenblatt, D.J., Jones, K.J., Levine, P.H., Orsulak, P.J., Peterson, M., Schildkraut, J.J., Uzogara, E. and Watkins, D. (1984) Some biochemical correlates of panic attacks with agoraphobia and their response to a new treatment, *Journal of Clinical Psychopharmacology*, **4**, 66–75.

Solyom, L., Beck, P., Solyom, C. and Hugel, R. (1974) Some etiological factors in phobic neurosis, *Canadian Psychiatric Association Journal*, **19**, 69–78.

Speth, R.C., Johnson, R.W., Regan, J., Reisine, T., Kobayashi, R.M., Bresolin, N., Roeske, W.R. and Yamamura, H.I. (1980) The benzodiazepine receptor of mammalian brain, *Federal Proceedings*, **39**, 3032–8.

Spielberger, C.D., Gorsuch, R.L. and Lushene, R.E. (1970) *State-Trait Anxiety Inventory*. Consulting Psychologists Press, Palo Alto.

Spier, S.A., Tesar, G.E., Rosenbaum, J.F. and Woods, S.W. (1986) Treatment of panic disorder and agoraphobia with clonazepam, *Journal of Clinical Psychiatry*, **47**, 238–42.

Stavrakaki, C. and Vargo, B. (1986) The relationship of anxiety and depression: a review of the literature, *British Journal of Psychiatry*, **149**, 7–16.

Stewart, R.S., Devous, M.D., Rush, A.J., Lane, L. and Bonte, F.J. (1988) Regional cerebral blood flow changes with sodium lactate infusion, *American Journal of Psychiatry*, in press.

Suomi, S.J., Seaman, S.F., Lewis, J.K., Delizio, R.D. and McKinney, W.T. (1978) Effects of imipramine treatment of separation-induced social disorders in rhesus monkeys, *Archives of General Psychiatry*, **35**, 321–5.

Suranyi-Cadotte, B.E., Wood, P.L., Nair, N.P.V. and Schwartz, C. (1982) Normalization of platelet ^{3}H-imipramine binding in depressed patients during recovery, *European Journal of Pharmacology*, **85**, 357–8.

Suranyi-Cadotte, B.E., Wood, P.L., Schwartz, C. and Nair, N.P.V. (1983) Altered platelet ^{3}H-imipramine binding in schizoaffective and depressive disorders, *Biological Psychiatry*, **18**, 923–7.

Surman, O.S., Williams, J., Sheehan, D.V., Strom, T.B., Jones, K.J. and Coleman, J. (1986) Immunological response to stress in agoraphobia and panic attacks, *Biological Psychiatry*, **21**, 768–74.

Svensson, T.H. and Usdin, T. (1978) Feedback inhibition of brain noradrenaline neurons by tricyclic antidepressants: alpha-receptor mediation, *Science*, **202**, 1089–91.

Tang, S.W. and Morris, J.M. (1985) Variation in human platelet ^{3}H-imipramine binding, *Psychiatry Research*, 141–6.

Taylor, C.B., Telch, M.J., and Havvik, D. (1983) Ambulatory heart rate changes during panic attacks, *Journal of Psychiatric Research*, **17**, 261–6.

Taylor, C.B., Sheikh, J., Agras, W.S., Roth, W.T., Margraf, J., Ehlers, A., Maddock, R.J. and Gossard, D. (1986) Ambulatory heart rate changes in patients with panic attacks, *American Journal of Psychiatry*, **143**, 478–82.

Taylor, C.B., King, R.J., Ehlers, A., Margraf, J., Clark, D., Roth, W.T. and Agras, W.S. (1987) Treadmill exercise test and ambulatory measures in patients with panic attacks, *American Journal of Cardiology*, **60**, 48J–52J.

Taylor, D.P., Eison, M.S., Riblet, L.A. and VanderMaelen, C.P. (1985) Pharmacological and clinical effects of buspirone, *Pharmacology, Biochemistry, and Behavior*, **23**, 687–94.

Tearnan, B.H., Telch, M.J. and Keefe, P. (1984) Etiology and onset of agoraphobia: a critical review, *Behaviour Research and Therapy*, **21**, 505–17.

Telch, M.J., Tearnan, B.H. and Taylor, C.B. (1983) Antidepressant medication in the treatment of agoraphobia: a critical review, *Behaviour Research and Therapy*, **21**, 505–17.

Tennant, C., Smith, A., Bebbington, P. and Hurry, J. (1981) Parental loss in childhood. Relationship to adult psychiatric impairment and contact with psychiatric services, *Archives of General Psychiatry*, **38**, 309–14.

Tennant, C., Hurry, J. and Bebbington, P. (1982) The relation of childhood separation experiences to adult depressive and anxiety states, *British Journal of Psychiatry*, **141**, 475–82.

Thyer, B.A. and Himle, J. (1985) Temporal relationship between panic attack onset and phobic avoidance in agoraphobia, *Behaviour Research and Therapy*, **23**, 607.

Thyer, B.A., Nesse, R.M., Cameron, O.G. and Curtis, G.C. (1985) Agoraphobia: a test of the separation anxiety hypothesis, *Behaviour Research and Therapy*, **23**, 75–8.

Thyer, B.A., Nesse, R.M., Curtis, G.C. and Cameron, O.G. (1986) Panic disorder: a test of the separation anxiety hypothesis, *Behaviour Research and Therapy*, **24**, 209–11.

Torgersen, S. (1983) Genetic factors in anxiety disorders. *Archives of General Psychiatry*, **40**, 1085–9.

Torgersen, S. (1986) Childhood and family characteristics in panic and generalized anxiety disorders, *American Journal of Psychiatry*, **143**, 630–2.

Tyrer, P. (1984) Classification of anxiety, *British Journal of Psychiatry*, **144**, 78–83.

Tyrer, P. (1986) New rows of neuroses—are they an illusion? *Integrative Psychiatry*, **4**, 25–31.

Tyrer, P. and Tyrer, S. (1974) School refusal, truancy and adult neurotic illness, *Psychological Medicine*, **4**, 416–21.

Tyrer, P. and Steinberg, D. (1975) Symptomatic treatment of agoraphobia and social phobias: a follow-up study, *British Journal of Psychiatry*, **127**, 163–8.

Uhde, T.W., Boulenger, J.-P., Post, R.M., Siever, L.J., Vittone, B.J., Jimerson, D.C. and Roy-Byrne, P.P. (1984a) Fear and anxiety: relationship to noradrenergic function, *Psychopathology*, Supplement **3**, 17, 8–23.

Uhde, T.W., Roy-Byrne, P.P., Gillin, J.C., Mendelson, W.B., Boulenger, J.-P., Vittone, B.J. and Post, R.M. (1984b) The sleep of patients with panic disorder: A preliminary report, *Psychiatry Research*, **12**, 251–9.

Uhde, T.W., Boulenger, J.-P., Roy-Byrne, P.R., Geraci, M.F., Vittone, B.J. and Post, R.M. (1985a) Longitudinal course of panic disorder: clinical and biological considerations, *Progress in Neuro-Psychopharmacology and Biological Psychiatry*, **9**, 39–51.

Uhde, T.W., Roy-Byrne, P.P., Vittone, B.J., Boulenger, J.-P. and Post, R.M. (1985b) Phenomenology and neurobiology of panic disorder. In A.H. Tuma and J.D. Maser (eds), *Anxiety and the Anxiety Disorders*, Lawrence Erlbaum, Hillsdale, NJ.

Uhde, T.W., Vittone, B.J., Siever, L.J., Kaye, W.H. and Post, R.M. (1986) Blunted growth hormone response to clonidine in panic disorder patients, *Biological Psychiatry*, **21**, 1081–5.

Uhde, T.W., Berrettini, W.H., Roy-Byrne, P.P., Boulenger, J.-P. and Post, R.M. (1987) Platelet ^{3}H-imipramine binding in patients with panic disorder, *Biological Psychiatry*, **22**, 52–8.

Uretsky, B.F. (1982) Does mitral valve prolapse cause nonspecific symptoms? *International Journal of Cardiology*, **1**, 435–42.

Uttal, W.R. (1987) The psychobiology of mind. In G.Adelman (ed.), *Encyclopedia of Neuroscience, Vol. II*, Birkhäuser, Boston.

van den Hout, M.A. and Griez, E. (1982) Cognitive factors in carbon dioxide therapy, *Journal of Psychosomatic Research*, **26**, 219–24.

van den Hout, M.A., van der Molen, M., Griez, E., Lousberg, H. and Nansen, A. (1987a) Reduction of CO_2-induced anxiety in patients with panic attacks after repeated CO_2 exposure, *American Journal of Psychiatry*, **144**, 788–91.

van Dongen, P.A. (1981) The human locus coeruleus in neurology and psychiatry, *Progress in Neurobiology*, **17**, 97–139.

van der Maelen, C.P., Taylor, D.P., Gehlbach, G. and Elson, M.S. (1986) Nonbenzodiazepine anxiolytics: Insights into possible mechanisms of action, *Psychopharmacology Bulletin*, **22**, 807–12.

van der Molen, G.M. and van den Hout, M.A. Effects of anxiety-instruction on respiration during lactate. Submitted for publication.

van der Molen, G.M., van den Hout, M.A., Vroemen, J., Lousberg, H. and Griez, E. (1986) Cognitive determinants of lactate-induced anxiety, *Behaviour Research and Therapy*, **24**, 677–80.

van der Molen, G.M., van den Hout, M.A., van Dieren, A.C. and Griez, E. Childhood separation anxiety: no specific precursor to panic disorders. Submitted for publication.

van Praag, H.M. (1985) Psychiatrists, beware of dichotomies! *Biological Psychiatry*, **21**, 247–8.

Wagner, A., Aberg-Wistedt, A., Asberg, M., Ekquist, B., Martensson, B. and Montero, D. (1985) Lower ^{3}H-imipramine binding in platelets from untreated depressed patients compared to healthy controls, *Psychiatry Research*, **16**, 131–9.

Warren, W. (1965) A study of adolescent psychiatric in-patients and the outcome six or more years later. II: Follow-up study, *Journal of Child Psychology and Psychiatry*, **6**, 141–60.

Weiner, H. (1978) The illusion of simplicity: the medical model revisited, *American Journal of Psychiatry*, **135**, July Supplement, 27–33.

Weiss, J. and Simson, P.G. (1986) Depression in an animal model: focus on the locus coeruleus. In Ciba Foundation (ed.), *Antidepressants and Receptor Function (Ciba Foundation Symposium 123)* Wiley, Chichester.

Weissman, M.M., Leaf, P.J., Blazer, D.G., Boyd, J.H. and Florio, L. (1986) The relationship between panic disorder and agoraphobia: an epidemiologic perspective, *Psychopharmacology Bulletin*, **22**, 787–91.

Westphal, C. (1870) Die Agoraphobie, eine neuropathische Erscheinung, *Archiv für Psychiatrie und Nervenkrankheiten*, **3**, 138–61.

Whitaker, P.M., Warsh, J.J., Stancer, H.C., Persad, E. and Vint, C.K. (1984) Seasonal variation in platelet ^{3}H-imipramine binding: comparable values in depressed and control populations, *Psychiatry Research*, **11**, 127–31.

Whiteford, H.A. and Evans, L. (1984) Agoraphobia and the dexamethasone suppression test, *Australian and New Zealand Journal of Psychiatry*, **18**, 374.

Wittchen, H.-U. (1986) Epidemiology of panic attacks and panic disorders. In I. Hand and H.-U. Wittchen (eds), *Panic and Phobias*, Springer, Berlin.

Woods, S.C., Charney, D.S., McPherson, C.A., Gradman, A.H. and Heninger, G.R. (1987) Situational panic attacks: behavioral, physiological, and biochemical characterization, *Archives of General Psychiatry*, **44**, 365–75.

Woods, S.C., Charney, D.S., Goodman, W.K. and Heninger, G.R. (1988) Carbon dioxide-induced anxiety: Behavioral, physiologic, and biochemical effects of 5% CO_2 in panic disorders patients and 5 and 7.5% CO_2 in healthy subjects, *Archives of General Psychiatry*, **45**, 43–52.

Wooley, C.F. (1976) Where are the diseases of yesteryear? DaCosta's syndrome, soldiers heart, the effort syndrome, neurocirculatory asthenia—and the mitral valve prolapse syndrome, *Circulation*, **53**, 749–51.

Yeragani, V., Pohl, R., Balon, R., Weinberg, P., Berchou, R. and Rainey, J.M. (1987) Pre-infusion anxiety predicts lactate-induced panic attacks in normal controls, *Psychosomatic Medicine*, **49**, 383–9.

Young, W.S. and Kuhar, M. (1980) Radiohistochemical localization of benzodiazepine receptors in rat brains, *Journal of Pharmacology and Experimental Therapy*, **212**, 337–46.

Yu, P.H., Bowen, R.C., Davis, B.A. and Boulton, A.A. (1983) Platelet monoamine oxidase activity and trace acid levels in plasma of agoraphobic patients, *Acta Psychiatrica Scandinavica*, **67**, 188–94.

Chapter 10

Etiological Models of Panic—Psychophysiological and Cognitive Aspects

JÜRGEN MARGRAF AND ANKE EHLERS

INTRODUCTION

The past few years have witnessed significant progress in theory and research on psychophysiological or cognitive models of panic. Until a few years ago, most behavioural or psychological theorists focused on the avoidance behaviour of agoraphobics and did not directly address the problem of panic attacks unrelated to external fear-arousing stimuli. We will not attempt to discuss this literature since it has been excellently reviewed before (e.g. Brehony and Geller, 1981; Mathews *et al.*, 1981; Foa *et al.*, 1984; Roth, 1984; Thorpe and Burns, 1983; Hallam, 1985; Marks, 1987). Instead we will focus on those approaches that explicitly attempted to give a theoretical model of panic attacks with or without agoraphobic behaviour.* We will present the central assumptions of these etiological models and review the empirical evidence for them. In addition, we will discuss a number of areas where psychophysiological and cognitive approaches to panic require further specification.

Alternatives to medical illness (MI) models vary with respect to the emphasis placed on the different mechanisms proposed to be involved, the directness with which they address the problem of panic, and their names. Thus, these models have been termed 'behavioral' (Goldstein and Chambless, 1978; Barlow, 1986a), 'psychological' (Hallam, 1985; van den Hout, 1987; Barlow, 1986b), 'cognitive psychophysiological' (Margraf *et al.*, 1986c), 'cognitive/physiological' (Rapee, 1987), 'psychophysiological'

*In the following we will use the term 'panic patients' for patients fulfilling the DSM-III criteria for panic disorder or for agoraphobia with panic attacks. Only when important differences are present will we distinguish between these two disorders.

Panic Disorder: Theory, Research and Therapy. Edited by Roger Baker

(Margraf and Ehlers, 1988; Margraf *et al.*, 1986a), 'cognitive' (Beck *et al.*, 1985; Clark, 1986, 1987) 'interoceptive-fear'(van den Hout *et al.*, 1987), 'hyperventilation' (Ley, 1985), and 'constructivist' (Hallam, 1985). In spite of their differences, these approaches share enough of their central characteristics to be considered variants of the same theme. In the following we will use the term 'psychophysiological models' (PP models) since we feel that it emphasizes best the interaction of psychological and physiological factors that most authors consider central to the etiology of panic attacks.

CENTRAL CHARACTERISTICS OF PSYCHOPHYSIOLOGICAL OR COGNITIVE MODELS

Psychophysiological models assume panic attacks to be *quantitatively* rather than *qualitatively* different from other types of anxiety on a number of dimensions. Some of the most important of these dimensions are the nature of the triggering events (internal vs. external), the nature (somatic vs. psychic) and time course (sudden vs. gradual) of the predominant symptoms, and the content of feared consequences (immediate bodily/mental catastrophes vs. other more long-term negative events). Panic attacks are not seen as spontaneous in the sense of being unrelated to triggering stimuli. They are explained as the consequence of a positive feedback loop between bodily sensations or cognitive events and the person's reaction to them. The association of internal or external cues with a perceived immediate threat is considered a necessary part of the development of panic. A schematic representation of the PP model of panic as proposed by Margraf and Ehlers (Margraf *et al.*, 1986b, 1986c, Ehlers *et al.*, 1988c, Ehlers and Margraf, in press) is given in Figure 10.1.

The central part of the model in Figure 10.1 shows a positive feedback loop (illustrated by black arrows) leading to a panic attack. Its components are physiological, cognitive, and emotional responses of the panicking person. The positive feedback may start with any of its following elements.

—Physiological or cognitive changes occur as a consequence of various causes such as physical effort, drug intake (e.g. caffeine), situational stressors (e.g. heat) or emotional responses (e.g. anxiety, anger).

—The person perceives these changes. Changes in body sensations may not accurately reflect actual physiological changes. For example, persons may feel that their heart has accelerated after going to bed because the change in body posture has increased their cardiac awareness.

—The bodily or cognitive changes are associated with danger. Clark (1986) emphasizes the immediate nature of the anticipated threat. This association can take various forms ranging from conditioning (Goldstein

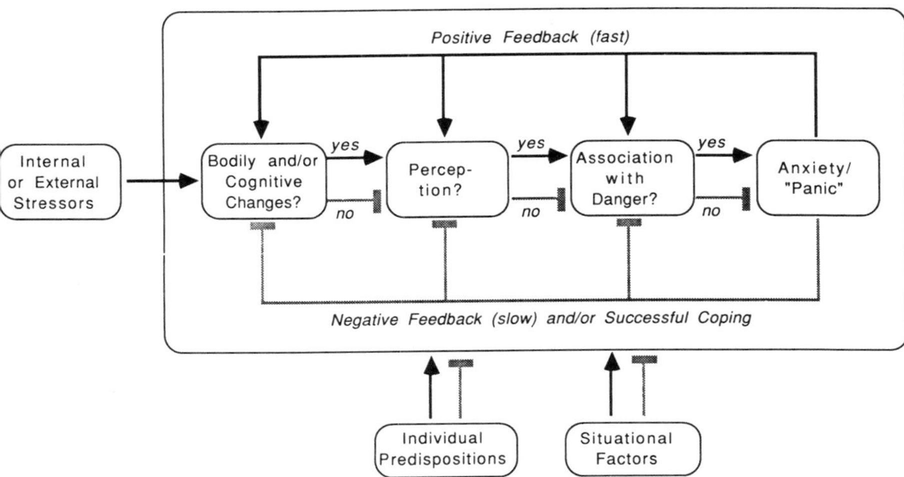

Figure 10.1 Schematic representation of the psychophysiological (PP) model of panic attacks. Black arrows indicate panicogenic effects, grey arrows indicate inhibitory effects. Reproduced from Ehlers *et al.*, 1986a, in *Panic and Phobias II* (I. Hand and H.-U. Wittchen, eds) by permission of Springer-Verlag.

and Chambless, 1978; Barlow, 1986a; Margraf *et al.*, 1986c; van den Hout, 1987) to catastrophic misinterpretations in conscious thoughts (Ottaviani and Beck, 1987; Clark, 1986; Goldstein and Chambless, 1978; Margraf *et al.*, 1986a). The positive feedback loop may start at this point without prior bodily changes if situational variables are associated with immediate threat. For example, simple phobics may experience panic attacks when confronted with their phobic stimulus. In agoraphobics, however, the phobic situations are probably only indirectly associated with danger via their relation with body sensations (Foa and Kozak, 1986).

—The person responds to the perceived threat with anxiety that in turn leads to physiological changes, body sensations, and/or cognitive symptoms (positive feedback). If these symptoms are again perceived and associated with danger, further anxiety increases occur. This positive feedback may escalate in a panic attack. Note that positive feedback is a fast process. It is unclear at what point anxiety may be called panic. Since panic attacks do not seem to be an all-or-none phenomenon (Margraf *et al.*, 1987a), this is probably a question of severity. The patient's perception and appraisal of their body sensations and of situational variables again influence whether they call their anxiety panic (see below).

—Simultaneously, negative feedback mechanisms operate that counterbalance the positive feedback (grey arrows). These mechanisms influence all of the components of the positive feedback loop and lead to a reduction in anxiety. The negative feedback operates more slowly than the positive feedback. Thus, a panic attack may rapidly develop, but anxiety will decrease with time. Examples for negative feedback processes are habituation and fatigue, both of which decrease physiological responses or self-limiting homeostatic mechanisms in hyperventilation. Another example is that persons may notice after some time that no catastrophic consequences of their palpitations have occurred and thus may alter the association between this symptom and danger.

—Parallel to negative feedback, the perceived availability of coping strategies will decrease anxiety. Again coping attempts may influence any of the elements of the positive feedback loop. An example for coping strategies influencing physiological symptoms is paced breathing. Distraction strategies, for example focusing the attention on external cues, operate at the perceptual level. Cognitive strategies such as reattribution of bodily sensations affect the association with danger. A very common coping strategy is avoidance or help-seeking behaviour that changes the situational context in which the anxiety occurred. Failure of coping on the other hand may increase anxiety. When patients notice that they experience dizziness or palpitations or feel anxious in spite of attempts to control these sensations, this usually feeds into the positive feedback loop.

A number of variables affect the probability of experiencing a panic attack. These factors are shown outside the central box in Figure 10.1.

—Internal or external stressors may increase the probability of physiological or cognitive events that may trigger the positive feedback loop.

—Individual predispositions include biological and psychological diatheses that increase the likelihood of bodily sensations, their perception, and their association with immediate bodily/mental threat. Other predispositions like the patients' learning history (reinforcement and modeling) with reports of somatic symptoms and emotional experiences influence whether they report panic attacks and seek help for them.

—Situational factors have an impact on whether body sensations are perceived and associated with danger. In addition, situational variables can in themselves be associated with danger and thus directly trigger a panic attack.

Some of the consequences of having experienced panic attacks act as maintaining factors. Most patients worry about having another attack.

This worry leads to a tonically heightened level of anxiety and bodily arousal which in turn make the occurrence of panicogenic body sensations and their catastrophic misinterpretation more likely. Clark *et al.* (1988) have described an internal focus of attention in most panic patients. Hypervigilance and repeated scanning of their bodies for any signs of danger lead to a greater probability of perceiving possible triggers for panic much in the way of a self-fulfilling prophecy. In addition, the more or less subtle forms of avoidance behaviour that many people develop may also serve to maintain their problems. For example, avoidance of physical exercise leads to poor physical fitness which in turn produces stronger cardiovascular responses to everyday physical challenges. Avoidance behaviour may also maintain the somatic preoccupation typical for may panic patients.

There are important differences between the schema presented here and a simple vicious circle model. Several components of our schema are lacking or not emphasized by simple vicious circle models. These include the explicit acknowledgement of situational factors and individual predispositions, the distinction between bodily events and their perception, and the identification of negative feedback processes. The positive feedback emphasized by the vicious circle metaphor cannot explain how panic attacks come to an end.

The main arguments for the PP models can be summarized as follows:

(a) *Internal cues as triggers for positive feedback loops*. Bodily sensations or specific cognitive events usually precede the onset of fear in panic attacks. Panic patients are more likely to experience physical symptoms and tend to respond to their perception with anxiety, somatic symptoms, and physiological arousal.
(b) *Association of internal cues with danger*. Panic patients tend to associate specific bodily and cognitive events with imminent danger via mechanisms ranging from interoceptive conditioning to conscious appraisal.
(c) *Situational factors and individual predispositions*. The occurrence of panic attacks depends strongly on situational factors.
(d) *Similarity of panic attacks and other types of anxiety*. Panic attacks and other types of anxiety are qualitatively similar, although a number of only quantitative differences exist.

In the following we will review the status of empirical support for these arguments. Similar but less comprehensive reviews have been presented by Margraf *et al.* (1986a, 1986b), Clark (1987), van den Hout (1987), and Ehlers *et al.* (1988c).

EMPIRICAL SUPPORT FOR PP MODELS

Internal cues as triggers for positive feedback loops

Bodily sensations usually precede the onset of fear in panic attacks. Panic patients are more likely to experience physical symptoms and tend to respond to their perception with anxiety, somatic symptoms, and physiological arousal.

Although the internal triggers for panic include cognitive changes such as the inability to concentrate or derealization, bodily symptoms are most prominent in panic attacks. Therefore most researchers have concentrated on body sensations as possible triggers for panic. Note, however, that for individual patients cognitive events such as derealization may be more important than bodily cues in the development of their panic attacks.

PP models predict that bodily symptoms usually precede the experience of panic. Studies using structured interviews support this hypothesis. Hibbert (1984) found in an interview study that the most frequently reported sequence of events in panic attacks was the perception of an unpleasant bodily sensation (e.g. dyspnea, palpitations, sweaty palms), followed by anxious-catastrophizing cognitions, and the experience of a full-blown panic attack. Similarly, Ley (1985) found that somatic symptoms preceded fear in the majority of patients interviewed. These results were replicated in a recent study by the Stanford group (Zucker *et al.* in press). The descriptions of typical panic attacks by 20 patients (interviewed by telephone without knowledge of their diagnostic status) were evaluated by blind raters who determined a bodily symptom as the first sign of panic in the great majority of all cases. Ottaviani and Beck (1987) could identify specific misattributions of physical sensations as panic triggers in each of 30 panic patients.

Ehlers *et al.* (1988b) demonstrated that panic patients tend to respond to perceived bodily changes with anxiety and physiological changes consistent with the positive feedback hypothesis. Panic patients and normal controls were given false feedback of an abrupt HR increase. Only the patients responded with increases in subjective anxiety and physiological arousal (skin conductance level, HR, systolic and diastolic blood pressure). Normal controls and patients who had not believed that the feedback was accurate did not show this response. Although it was not formally asked, one patient volunteered that she experienced a severe panic attack in response to the false feedback (Margraf *et al.*, 1987b). The positive feedback hypothesis is furthermore supported by the so-called panic induction studies reviewed above. As all pharmacologic panic provocation methods produce unpleasant physical sensations typical of panic attacks, they can be interpreted as a powerful way of triggering positive feedback.

This makes the assumption of an unknown direct biochemical effect on anxiety superfluous. The positive feedback hypothesis also explains the variety of panicogenic procedures some of which have opposite physiological effects. For example, hyperventilation and lactate infusion induce alkalosis, whereas inhalation of 5% CO_2 induces mild acidosis (Ehlers *et al.*, 1986a). In addition to being parsimonious, the hypothesis explains results that the MI models cannot explain. Examples are the 'blocking' of response to lactate after successful cognitive behavioural treatment or the effects of the subjects' expectations. Ehlers *et al.* (1988a) showed that the anticipation of CO_2-induced panic led to greater increases in anxiety and its physiological concomitants in panic disorder patients than in normal controls.

Many panic patients have characteristics that make them more likely to experience bodily sensations that may trigger positive feedback loops. Such attributes can be hyperventilation, 'weak' neurological signs, cardiovascular events and a number of other bodily precipitants. Numerous case reports have implicated such diverse conditions as cocaine abuse (Aronson and Craig, 1986), excessive aspartame ingestion (Drake, 1986), hyperthyroidism (Katherndahl and Vande Creek, 1983; Turner, 1985), vestibular disorders (Pratt and McKenzie, 1958), epileptiform disorder (Brodsky *et al.*, 1983), steroid medication (Raskin, 1984), sleep deprivation (Roy-Byrne *et al.*, 1986), and others. We will discuss only two examples here.

Best established is the relationship between panic and hyperventilation (Lum, 1981; Garssen *et al.*, 1983; Bonn *et al.*, 1984; Clark *et al.*, 1985; Ley, 1985, 1988; Margraf *et al.*, 1989; Rapee, 1987; Magarian, 1982). An excellent review of this topic is given by Bass *et al.* (1988). Standardized hyperventilation tasks produce symptoms similar or identical to panic attacks in 50–60% of panic patients (Bonn *et al.*, 1984; Clark *et al.*, 1985). Similar but less intense symptoms were observed in normal controls or other clinical groups (Lum, 1981; Clark and Hemsley, 1982; Thyer *et al.*, 1984). Salkovskis *et al.* (1986a) found lower pCO_2 values at rest in panic patients who rated their attacks as similar to the effects of hyperventilation than in matched normal controls. The perceived similarity of panic and hyperventilation correlated significantly with pCO_2 values and CO_2 normalized with successful treatment of panic. Rapee (1986) found significantly lower resting pCO_2 and greater distress associated with a hyperventilation test in patients with panic disorder than in those with generalized anxiety disorder. Gorman *et al.* (1986) reported lower pCO_2 in panic patients than in controls before lactate infusion. In addition, there are case reports showing hyperventilation in naturally occurring panic attacks using ambulatory monitoring of transcutaneous pCO_2 (Hibbert, 1986) or actual measures of $paCO_2$ during panic attacks in a hemodialysis patient (Salkovskis *et al.*, 1986b) or a physically healthy outpatient (Griez *et al.*, 1987). In keeping with the PP models, it is clear that hyperventilation is neither a necessary nor a sufficient condition for panic attacks.

A second group of factors leading to frequent bodily symptoms triggering panic may be related to 'weak' neurological signs. Vestibular dysfunctions could be important in those patients who mainly complain about dizziness and feelings of unsteadiness, two common panic attack symptoms. An early series of 12 cases where anxiety states directly followed vestibular disorders was reported by Pratt and McKenzie (1958). The most common psychological symptoms were panic attacks (7 patients) and fears of travelling (5 patients). Hood (1975) found a high prevalence of anxiety neurosis (41%) in patients referred with vestibular disorders and an abnormal response to caloric stimulation. A high prevalence of abnormal vestibular or auditory function in panic patients was reported by Jacob *et al.* (1985). In the absence of specific neurological disorders, 67% of their patients showed positional or spontaneous nystagmus, 56% had abnormal responses to caloric stimulation, 44% abnormal acoustic reflexes, 35% abnormal reponses to rotational tests, 32% abnormal responses to posturography, and 26% abnormal pure tone audiograms. Coyle and Sterman (1986) found that 19 (5%) of 350 referrals to an outpatient neurology service had panic attacks characterized by focal neurologic symptoms. With one exception, results from all neurologic examinations were normal. Eleven of the 19 patients (58%) had experienced at least one severe life event and in eight patients (42%) hyperventilation reproduced the specific focal symptoms. Unfortunately, the evidence from these studies is only tentative since none of them had a matched control group.

In conclusion, bodily symptoms have consistently been supported as possible triggers for panic attacks. A number of characteristics that make panic patients more likely to experience such symptoms have been identified. Panic patients tend to respond to certain perceived bodily sensations in a manner predicted by the positive feedback hypothesis.

Association of internal cues with danger

Panic patients tend to associate specific bodily and cognitive events with imminent danger via mechanisms ranging from interoceptive conditioning to conscious appraisal.

The prediction that panic patients are more likely than normal controls or other patients to associate body sensations with danger has been supported by a number of questionnaire studies (Chambless *et al.*, 1984; Reiss *et al.*, 1986; Foa 1987; van den Hout *et al.*, 1987). Foa (1987) showed that panic patients estimate the probability that physiological responses will cause harm much higher than normal controls or patients with other anxiety disorders. Ehlers *et al.* (1988c) also found that 59% of 54 panic patients but only 22% of 41 normal controls endorsed physical threat as their greatest worries, whereas worries about separation or social embarrassment did not differ between groups. In addition, all pertinent studies found that panic patients reported catastrophic ideation during panic attacks. These distortions centered around physical (e.g. death, heart attack) or mental (e.g. losing control, going crazy) catastrophes whereas patients with generalized anxiety disorder or normal controls reported less catastrophic ideation when being anxious (Beck *et al.*, 1974; Hibbert, 1984; Chambless *et al.*, 1984; Rapee, 1985a; McNally and Lorenz, 1987; Ottaviani and Beck, 1987; Rachman *et al.*, 1987; Zucker *et al.*, in press). Rachman *et al.* (1987) observed that the cluster of bodily sensations and cognitions that patients reported during panic attacks induced by exposure to feared situations was meaningfully linked. Thus, the interview and questionnaire data collected so far support the notion of specific cognitive distortions in panic patients. However, these studies depend on the patients' recollections of their panic attacks and they assess only conscious processes accessible by introspection.

To surmount these problems many recent studies have used the methods developed by psychophysiology and experimental cognitive psychology. In a series of studies Foa and her coworkers showed that agoraphobics with panic attacks show especially strong associations between interoceptive responses and threat (Foa, 1987; McNally and Foa, 1987). In two independent studies, panic patients were more likely than other anxiety patients or normal controls to select dangerous interpretations of ambiguous vignettes of external and internal situations (e.g. 'you feel discomfort in your chest area. Why?'). These differences disappeared with successful behavioural treatment (McNally and Foa, 1987). Clark *et al.* (1988) independently replicated these results and showed that only negative interpretations of bodily sensations are specific to panic patients. In a psychophysiological study of imagery (Foa, 1987) agoraphobics reported more fear and showed higher heart rates and more skin conductance fluctuations while imagining personalized external situations and interoceptive responses most associated with anxiety as well as their combinations than when imagining neutral material. In contrast, simple phobics were fearful while imagining material involving external stimuli but not when imagining the interoceptive cues alone. In the same vein, Clark *et al.* (1988) found that untreated panic patients show larger anxiety responses than normal controls or patients treated with cognitive behavioural therapy when reading word pairs of bodily symptoms and catastrophic consequences (e.g. breathlessness-suffocate).

Ehlers *et al.* (1988d) assessed reaction times in a modified Stroop color naming task using threat words and matched neutral words as stimulus material. In a first study panic patients showed a larger interference (significantly slower reaction times) when color naming physical threat words (e.g. cancer, stroke) than normal controls. In a second study the same result was obtained for nonclinical panickers. Clark *et al.* (1988) used a contextual priming task in which subjects were presented with a sentence which was complete except for the last word. Once they had read the sentence frame, subjects were shown the final word and asked to read it out loud as quickly as possible. The target words provided either a neutral or a negative interpretation of the bodily sensations usually specified in the sentence frame (e.g. 'If I had palpitations I could be dying/excited'). As would be predicted if panic patients were more likely to make negative interpretations, their reaction times were significantly faster in response to negative target words than to neutral words. There were no such differences in normal controls. Further control conditions ensured that the effect was due to sentence interpretation rather than simply to an overall tendency to respond faster to negative words.

The results of these studies are very consistent. They point to a high degree of interoceptive fear as a specific characteristic of panic patients compared to clinical and normal control groups. In addition, the effectiveness of experimental manipulation of appraisal in panic induction studies (reviewed in chapter 9) supports the notion that bodily sensations do not directly trigger panic but operate via an association with danger. Changing the appraisal or expectancy may make patients respond to panic induction like normals and normals respond like patients. An area for further specification of the PP models is the possible contribution of other associative mechanisms such as interoceptive conditioning. We will discuss this possibility below.

Situational factors and individual predispositions

The occurrence of panic attacks depends strongly on situational factors. Individual predispositions make people more 'vulnerable' to experience panic attacks although they are neither necessary nor sufficient conditions for panic.

Interindividual differences in the susceptibility to experience panic attacks, and to perceive internal cues and associate them with threat clearly demonstrate that there must be individual predispositions. However, the nature of these predispositions has not been convincingly established by empirical research. A number of potential physiological diatheses have been investigated. These include reduced efficiency of central alpha-2-adrenergic receptors (Charney and Heninger, 1986), low physical fitness (Taylor *et al.*, 1987), drug intolerance (e.g. caffeine, Boulenger *et al.*, 1984), and genetic factors (Marks, 1986). As discussed in the previous sections none of these diatheses has been shown to be present in all panic patients. However, there may be a common pathway by which different physiological factors increase the likelihood of panic attacks. Similar to the variety of substances used to induce panic in the laboratory, one common pathway may lie in the influence of physiological predispositions on the occurrence of bodily sensations feeding into the positive feedback loop. In addition, psychological predispositions such as anxious expectations (Lazarus and Averill, 1972; Epstein, 1976), selective attention to threat cues (Ehlers *et al.*, 1988c), attributional styles, lack of assertiveness (Goldstein and Chambless, 1978), learned associations (Breggin, 1964), and coping strategies (Lazarus and Averill, 1972; Epstein, 1976) also influence whether body sensations occur and whether they are perceived and associated with threat. Other psychological predispositions like the patients' learning history (reinforcement and modeling) with respect to reporting somatic symptoms and emotional experiences may influence whether a person reports panic attacks and seeks help for them (cf. cross-cultural studies on the report of pain, Sternbach and Tursky, 1965). The work of Pennebaker (1982) and others has clearly established the influence of psychological processes on physical symptoms.

Situational factors have an impact on whether body sensations occur and are perceived. Examples are body posture (Fiorica and Kem, 1985, cf. below the section on perception of body sensations) and complexity of concurrent external stimulation (Pennebaker, 1982). Situational variables further influence whether body sensations are associated with danger. A classical example is the presence of a spouse or therapist which often leads to immediate anxiety reduction. This clinical observation is corroborated by the results of Bonn *et al.* (1973) and Kelly *et al.* (1971) that patients do not panic in response to lactate because of the presence of doctors. The analysis of the places where panic attacks occur reveals a typical cluster of situations that share the characteristic that escape is difficult. Situations like driving on a freeway or standing in line in a crowded supermarket clearly increase the probability of having panic attacks (Mathews *et al.*, 1981; Thorpe and Burns, 1983; Marks, 1987b; also see chapter 2 by Waring). Thus, situational variables can in themselves be associated with danger and directly trigger a panic attack. Furthermore, diary studies show that many attacks labeled as 'spontaneous' by the patients occur in the same situations (Margraf *et al.*, 1987a). Other examples from clinical experience are the availability of explanations for body sensations like physical exercise and the availability of coping resources such as medication or relaxation. In addition, Bandura *et al.* (1985) have recently shown that perceived coping self-efficacy has strong effects on catecholamine secretion.

Clark (1987) has recently specified the cognitive processes involved in panic attacks that follow a period of heightened anxiety (e.g. upon entering a feared situation) or that are not preceded by such periods. In the first case the bodily sensations that trigger panic are consequences of the preceding anxiety. In the second case they are initially caused by other emotional states (e.g. anger, Freedman *et al.*, 1985) or innocuous events such as caffeine intake or changes in body posture. Clark (1987) notes the patients' perception of 'spontaneity' is caused by their failure to distinguish between the triggering bodily sensations and the subsequent panic.

Similarity of panic attacks and other types of anxiety

Panic attacks and other types of anxiety are qualitatively similar, although a number of quantitative differences exist.

There are several lines of evidence that are inconsistent with the notion of a qualitative difference between panic attacks and other forms of anxiety. Results from ambulatory monitoring (see below) as well as the panic induction studies reviewed above have failed to support this notion. As we argued earlier (Margraf *et al.*, 1986c), significant qualitative differences would exist if core symptoms or objective signs could be detected that occur exclusively in panic states or if clearly different patterns of symptoms and signs were observed. However, there are no symptoms or psychophysiological or biochemical changes that reliably and consistently differentiate panic attacks from nonattack periods, patients' attacks from normals' attacks, lactate-induced from placebo-induced attacks, or spontaneous from situational attacks (cf. Margraf *et al.*, 1986c, 1987a). Sheehan's observation of spontaneous panic attacks as a phenomenologically different kind of anxiety is not supported if one does not rely on patients' retrospective accounts but rather have them complete a panic diary after each attack. Figure 10.2 shows the pattern of symptoms in 87 situational and 88 spontaneous panic attacks recorded immediately after occurrence by 27 panic patients (Margraf *et al.*, 1987a). In the same vein, Barlow *et al.* (1985) found similar symptom severities for patients with situational (predictable, expected) and spontaneous (unpredictable, unexpected) attacks.

A number of questionnaire and interview studies compared symptom profiles of panic attacks and other types of anxiety, or of patients with panic and other anxiety disorders. Hughdahl and Öst (1985) reported similar subjective physiological and cognitive symptoms in agoraphobia and most other clinical phobias. With respect to our topic, the comparison of the anxiety of patients with panic disorder and generalized anxiety disorder is most important. On the whole, the results have shown similar symptom profiles for the two disorders (Hoehn-Saric, 1981, 1982; Anderson *et al.*, 1984; Barlow *et al.*, 1985; Cameron *et al.*, 1986; Turner *et al.*, 1986). The

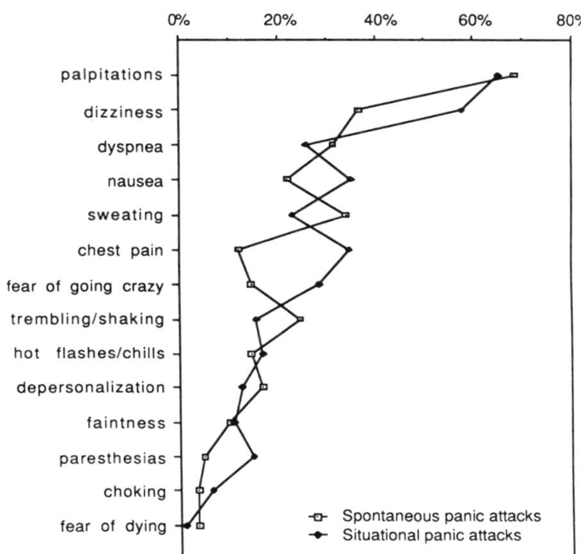

Figure 10.2 Symptom profiles of 88 'spontaneous' and 87 'situational' panic attacks assessed concurrently by diary. Differences between the two profiles were far from significant (Margraf *et al.*, 1987a).

occasional differences were not consistent across different studies and core symptoms or symptom patterns unique to panic patients have not been identified. However, Hibbert's (1984) and Argyle's (1988) studies indicate that cognitions are less catastrophic in panic disorder patients during gradual onset anxiety and in anxiety patients who have never had a panic attack. In this context it is interesting to note that already in 1978 Hallam pointed out the phenomenological similarity between agoraphobia and what was then still called 'anxiety neurosis.' This led Hallam (1978, 1983) to propose that these disorders should be classified together as anxiety states.

Finally, the phenomenon of panic is not specific to panic disorder or agoraphobia with panic attacks. Panic attacks have been found in substantial minorities of nonclinical subjects (Norton *et al.*, 1985, 1986; Margraf and Ehlers, 1988). However, some of the methods used in these studies are prone to yielding false positives and may therefore lead to an overestimation of panic attacks (cf. Margraf and Ehlers, 1988, and Chapter 3 by Von Korff and Eaton). Barlow *et al.* (1985) studied 108 patients with the DSM-III diagnoses of simple phobia, social phobia, generalized anxiety disorder, panic disorder, agoraphobia with panic attacks, obsessive-compulsive disorder, and major depressive episode. The great majority of patients in each of these categories (at least 83%) reported having experienced panic attacks. Although the frequency of attacks varied across diagnoses, there were only negligible differences in terms of symptom patterns.

FURTHER SPECIFICATIONS OF PP MODELS

The previous section has shown that the main arguments for the PP models are supported by a number of different lines of recent research. However, there are still many aspects of the PP models that require specification. In this section we will review some of the most important areas.

Perception of body sensations

PP models imply that the changes in body or cognitive functioning assumed to trigger panic attacks have to be perceived. Only few studies of this perceptual process in panic attacks have gone beyond the self-report measures reported above. Perceptual peculiarities may be related to the etiology or maintenance of panic disorder. In the following we will focus on interoception and more specifically on cardiac awareness since palpitations are the most commonly reported symptom of panic attacks (Barlow *et al.*, 1985; Margraf *et al.*, 1987a). Do panic patients differ from controls in their cardiac awareness? If we look at the patients' self-reports, the answer is yes. Panic patients report to be much more aware of sensations from their heart than non-anxious control subjects (King *et al.*, 1986). It is uncertain whether such self-reports would be corroborated by objective tests of cardiac perception. Untrained subjects generally show poor cardiac perception (Katkin, 1985). There is some, although inconsistent, evidence that persons with high state anxiety show better heart beat perception (Schandry, 1981) and that good cardiac perceivers are emotionally more responsive than poor perceivers (Schandry, 1983; Katkin, 1985). However, correlations between self-reported awareness of bodily function and objectively measured visceral sensitivity are very small (e.g. McFarland, 1975; Whitehead *et al.*, 1977). It is unclear whether these results in non-clinical populations can be generalized to panic patients.

There are only a few studies of cardiac awareness in patients with panic-related disorders. Tyrer *et al.* (1980) showed different short films to anxiety neurotics, phobics (including agoraphobia), and hypochondriacs and computed intraindividual correlations of self-rated and actual heart rate. Patients whose primary somatic symptoms were cardiac sensations showed the highest correlations. Closer to the phenomenon of panic is a recent study by Strian, Harbauer-Raum and associates (Harbauer-Raum, 1987; Stalmann *et al.*, 1987). These authors studied 27 cardiac neurotics, a diagnosis that probably represents a subgroup of panic disorder (Buller *et al.*, 1987), in a laboratory cardiac perception task. Patients were significantly more accurate in counting their heart beats without taking their pulse than 16 normal controls. They were also better than patients with mitral valve prolapse ($N=27$), hyperthyreosis ($N=5$), autonomic neuropathy ($N=12$) or normal controls in detecting cardiac arrhythmias occurring during 24-hour EKG-monitoring. In addition, the anxiety patients responded with significantly greater anxiety to the perception of arrhythmias. Ehlers *et al.* (1988c) compared panic disorder patients, infrequent panickers, and normal controls using Schandry's (1981) 'heart rate tracking' task that Harbauer-Raum (1987) had also used. They found a higher percentage of panic patients classified as good cardiac perceivers compared to either control group. There was no indication of better cardiac perception in infrequent panickers.

While these results are clearly in agreement with the PP models it is uncertain whether they can be generalized to the entire population of panic patients. The diagnosis of cardiac neurosis is much more homogeneous and not all panic patients are primarily concerned about their cardiac function. Ambulatory monitoring studies show that only a subgroup of all panic attacks with palpitations are accompanied by measurable changes in heart rate (Taylor *et al.*, 1983, 1986; Margraf *et al.*, 1987a). Panic patients also show a tendency to report somatic symptoms indiscriminately (Ehlers *et al.*, 1986b). The relationship between hyperventilation and many panic attacks also casts doubt on a greater interoceptive accuracy of panic patients. In this literature it is usually assumed that panic patients are unaware of their hyperventilation, i.e. show poor interoception in this respect. Thus, while panic patients insist that they are very aware of cardiac sensations it is unclear whether these sensations reflect objectively measurable changes in cardiac function. The evidence collected so far suggests that accurate cardiac perception is only found in a subgroup of panic patients. In these patients the 'supernormal' accuracy of cardiac awareness may be one factor contributing to the maintenance of the disorder.

The nature of bodily sensations likely to trigger panic attacks

Another area requiring specification is the nature of the bodily sensations that are likely to trigger panic attacks. It is important to note that not all sensations are equally likely to be associated with immediate bodily or mental catastrophes. In general the PP models would assume that cardiovascular and respiratory symptoms that could be indicative of acute disease such as myocardial infarct or suffocation are more likely to trigger panic than symptoms that are interpreted as signs of a cancer that will lead to death over a longer course of time. This notion is supported by the typical spectrum of panic symptoms reported in diary studies. In addition there may be idiosyncratic sensations in some persons. A second important characteristic is the time course of the sensations. Sudden abrupt changes are more likely than chronic, slow changes to lead to panic. Together these points may explain the difference between hypochondriasis and panic. They can also explain why some kinds of unpleasant bodily sensations do not lead to panic attacks in panic patients (e.g. experimentally induced hypoglycemia, cf. Uhde *et al.*, 1984; Schweizer *et al.*, 1986).

In the same vein, the PP models have to be distinguished from a simple fear of fear hypothesis. Clark (1987) pointed out that a simple mechanistic connection between fear or fear and panic would lead to overprediction. However, perceived anxiety does not always trigger panic and panic is not always a consequence of perceived anxiety. Clark argues that implying a cognitive process in the association of internal cues with threat and anxiety resolves the problem. Panic is triggered only if anxiety yields cues that are associated with immediate threat of bodily or mental catastrophes. Similarly, bodily sensations caused by other emotional or physiological changes can be associated with this type of threat and will then lead to panic.

The nature of the associative processes

The definition of what appraisal means within the PP models requires further specification. We understand appraisal not just as a conscious, verbal process, where the person makes self-statements but in a broader sense that encompasses non-conscious and non-verbal processing as well. In this sense, animals evaluating whether an approaching object is predator or belongs to a harmless species are also capable of appraisal. Clark (1987) has recently argued that catastrophic misinterpretations may be so fast and automatic that panic patients may not be aware of their appraisal process. As modern experimental psychology has shown such non-conscious mechanisms are not immune to objective quantitative research. In fact, they form a major focus of cognitive science. The application of these methods to the study of panic attacks has been reviewed above in the section on the association of internal cues with danger.

In addition to cognitive processes, interoceptive conditioning could account for at least part of the association between internal cues and anxiety responses. This hypothesis has not been tested in panic patients.

However, basic research shows that interoceptive conditioning is especially interesting with respect to 'spontaneous' panic attacks. Research in a Pavlovian framework has established that interoceptive events that are frequently outside awareness can readily serve as conditioned stimuli to a variety of responses (Razran, 1961). In addition, interoceptive conditioning is usually very stable over time. Although interoceptive conditioning may be slow in formation when weak unconditioned stimuli are used, very few or even single applications of a strong ('traumatic') stimulus may be enough to produce long lasting conditioned responses as exemplified by studies in dogs showing traumatic avoidance learning (Solomon and Wynne, 1953), on experimental psychogenic tachycardia (Gantt and Dykman, 1957), and on one-trial cardiac conditioning (Newton and Gantt, 1966). One-trial traumatic conditioning is not limited to the dogs used in the previously cited studies. Campbell *et al.* (1964) showed that in human volunteers a single experience of pharmacologically induced respiratory paralysis produced a conditioned response (increased frequency of skin-conductance fluctuations) that was very resistant to extinction and even became stronger as time passed. While respiratory paralysis is not part of the usual spectrum of experiences of panic patients or anxiety-provoking situations, hyperventilation and the fear of choking are. Jansen *et al.* (1987) recently showed that hyperventilation can be classically conditioned. In two studies healthy volunteers inhaled CO_2/O_2 mixtures six times. When they subsequently inhaled normal air, they showed hyperventilation solely in response to the inhalation procedure. The possibility of interoceptive conditioning needs to be studied in panic patients.

Conclusion on PP models

In our earlier reviews we concluded that alternative approaches to the MI models were promising but less comprehensive and less developed (Margraf *et al.*, 1986a, 1986b). Recent evidence makes a more positive conclusion appropriate. PP models are consistent with the major features of panic attacks and have received converging evidence from questionnaire, interview, and experimental studies. However, there are a number of issues requiring specification. In addition, PP models are at present better in explaining the maintenance of the disorder than in predicting the occurrence of the first panic attack. As of today, it is not possible to decide which of the different versions of PP models is the best representation of the clinical phenomena and their underlying mechanisms. While the multitude of factors taken into account seems appropriate to the complexity of panic and agoraphobia it also compromises the possibility for experimental scrutiny.

DISCUSSION OF ETIOLOGICAL MODELS

The rediscovery of panic attacks has had major consequences for the theory and therapy of anxiety disorders. Research guided by theoretical models has yielded more relevant information than the unsystematic search for possible correlates. In studies following the latter approach, findings have usually been negative or inconsistent if methodological confounds were ruled out or the same variable was investigated more than once. In contrast, theory-guided research has led to more accurate descriptive data, has increased our ability to explain the empirical results, and has provided the basis for successful new treatments.

A comparison of the major etiological models of panic showed considerable differences in the degree to which they agree with the empirical results gathered over the past few years. Medical illness (MI) models have focused too exclusively on the influence of physiological on psychological states. In their original form the MI models are not capable of accounting for important recent findings. The treatment specificity argument that formed the starting point for these models has been falsified. MI models cannot account for recent results of experimental panic induction studies. The spontaneity of panic attacks, genetic specificity, and the separation anxiety arguments are also not convincingly supported. Moreover, MI models make the problematic assumption of 'identity' (Schachter, 1970), implying a one-to-one relationship between a pattern of physiologic or biochemical processes and specific behaviours or psychologic states. However, there is no indication of such relationships. No central or peripheral physiologic change studied to date is a sufficient or necessary condition for the existence of a panic attack. The extreme biological diversity of panic induction methods and of organic pathologies that may be associated with panic is not in agreement with the assumption of identity. Moreover, panic is an emotion (Lader, 1975; Spielberger, 1972; Tyrer, 1984; Margraf *et al.*, 1986c) and thus theories of panic may profit from an integration into the broader framework of research on emotions which has long rejected the assumption of identity (Izard, 1977; Strongman, 1978; Plutchik and Kellerman, 1980; Lader, 1982). Having failed to do this MI models are unable to address the problem of panic attacks in all its complexity. However, they have had great heuristic value in stimulating an enormous body of research over the past two decades.

The only empirically based attempt to specify a concrete neuroanatomic substrate for panic attacks is the locus coeruleus (LC) hypothesis. Its original undifferentiated form is not consistent with much of the data. The reformulated version that focuses on the alpha$_2$-adrenergic autoreceptor is more promising. Although a number of difficult issues remain to be addressed (methodological confounds, unpredicted drug effects, absence of signs of NE activity in many panic attacks, specificity to panic patients, lack of longitudinal studies), the LC hypothesis may well point to a biological vulnerability in a subgroup of patients.

Psychophysiological (PP) models focus on the interaction between physiological and psychological processes in explaining panic disorder. Evidence supporting this perspective is rapidly accumulating. Studies of bodily sensations as triggers for panic, the association of internal cues with specific types of threat, positive feedback loops, situational factors, and individual predispositions are consistent with the PP models and in many cases contradict the MI models. In addition, based on this approach powerful treatments have been devised. Cognitive-behavioural interventions have been tested in case (Griez and van den Hout, 1983; Rapee, 1985b; Waddell *et al.*, 1984) and group studies (Barlow *et al.*, 1984; Bonn *et al.*, 1984; Clark *et al.*, 1985; Gitlin *et al.*, 1985; Griez and van den Hout, 1986; Salkovskis *et al.*, 1986a; Shear *et al.*, 1986 and 1988; Öst, 1988; Klosko *et al.*, 1988; Sartory and Olajide, 1988). All studies found marked and stable improvement or complete remission with follow-ups ranging from three months to two years. Although most of the studies used small samples, the consistency of the results is impressive. However, treatment efficacy provides only indirect support for etiological models.

Finally, there are other problems common to all etiological models of panic. In spite of the considerable progress achieved they are at present not better than a skilled clinician in predicting the occurrence of individual panic attacks. While factors influencing the probability of panic have been specified, the exact time of occurrence can still only retrospectively be explained with certainty. In addition, it is often overlooked that the available data are to a large degree correlational. Let us consider the example of the reformulated LC hypothesis. At present we do not know whether the postulated abnormality of the alpha$_2$-adrenergic autoreceptor existed before the patients had developed the full-blown panic syndrome. Therefore, any observed abnormality of NE regulation could equally well be a cause or a consequence of panic disorder. The same is true for the association of bodily changes with danger that is central to the PP models and most other findings presented in this chapter. The preponderance of correlational data is partly due to ethical reasons that prohibit experimental manipulations such as the induction of a mental disorder in previously normal subjects. However, there are other ways of gaining insight into possible causal antecedents of panic. Prospective longitudinal studies are required for more satisfactory etiological models. It will be most practical to study high-risk groups. One readily available and highly interesting group are so-called infrequent panickers who have experienced a few attacks but not the full-blown syndrome. Several studies (Norton *et al.*, 1985, 1986; Margraf and Ehlers, 1988) have shown that up to one third of unselected college students are infrequent panickers. This group offers the possibility of investigating predictors of panic disorder as well as protective factors.

In conclusion, a pure medical illness approach to panic has been shown insufficient, possible biological vulnerabilities have been revealed only for subgroups, and the necessity of a psychophysiological perspective has been underlined. In our opinion the greatest progress in understanding the etiology of panic will result from studies focusing on the interaction of the various influences on panic. However, the specific models proposed to integrate physiological and psychological factors have not yet been sufficiently established. We have discussed a number of areas requiring further specification. Furthermore, while multifactorial models seem appropriate to account for the complexity of clinical phenomena they compromise the possibility for experimental examination. The integration of different levels of analysis is a basic problem of all modern neuroscience (Weiner, 1978; van Praag, 1985; Uttal, 1987). Rather than biological or cognitive reductionism a true psychobiological perspective is needed.

ACKNOWLEDGEMENTS

Preparation of this chapter was supported by German Research Foundation Grants Ma 1116/1-1 and Eh 97/1-3.

REFERENCES

Anderson, D.J., Noyes, R. and Crowe, R.R. (1984) A comparison of panic disorder and generalized anxiety disorder, *American Journal of Psychiatry*, **141**, 572–5.

Aronson, T.A. and Craig, T.J. (1986) Cocaine precipitation of panic disorder, *American Journal of Psychiatry*, **143**, 643–5.

Argyle, N. (1988) The nature of cognitions in panic disorder, *Behaviour Research and Therapy*, **26**, 261–4.

Bandura, A., Taylor, C.B., Williams, S.L., Mefford, I.N. and Barchas, J.D. (1985) Catecholamine secretion as a function of perceived coping self-efficacy, *Journal of Consulting and Clinical Psychology*, **53**, 406–14.

Barlow, D.H. (1986a) Behavioral conception and treatment of panic, *Psychopharmacology Bulletin*, **22**, 803–6.

Barlow, D.H. (1986b) A psychological model of panic. In B.F. Shaw, F. Cashman, Z.V. Segal and T.M. Vallis (eds), *Anxiety Disorders: Theory, Diagnosis, and Treatment*, Plenum Press, New York.

Barlow, D.H., Cohen, A.S., Waddell, M.T., Vermilyea, B.B., Klosko, J.S., Blanchard, E.B. and DiNardo, P.A. (1984) Panic and generalized anxiety disorders: nature and treatment, *Behavior Therapy*, **15**, 431–49.

Barlow, D.H., Vermilyea, J., Blanchard, E.B., Vermilyea, B.B., DiNardo, P.A. and Cerny, J.A. (1985) The phenomenon of panic, *Journal of Abnormal Psychology*, **94**, 320–8.

Bass, C., Kartsounis, L. and Lelliott, P. (1988) Hyperventilation and its relationship with anxiety and panic, *Integrative Psychiatry*, in press.

Beck, A.T., Laude, R. and Bohnert, M. (1974) Ideational components of anxiety neurosis. *Archives of General Psychiatry*, **31**, 319–35.

Beck, A.T., Emery, G. and Greenberg, R.L. (1985) *Anxiety Disorders and Phobias—A Cognitive Perspective*, Basic Books, New York.

Bonn, J.A., Harrison, J. and Rees, W. (1973) Lactate infusion in the treatment of "free-floating anxiety". *Canadian Psychiatric Association Journal*, **18**, 41–5.

Bonn, J.A., Readhead, C.P.A. and Timmons, B.A. (1984) Enhanced adaptive behavioral response in agoraphobic patients pretreated with breathing retraining, *Lancet*, 665–9.

Boulenger, J.-P., Uhde, T.W., Wolff, E.A. and Post, R.M. (1984) Increased sensitivity to caffeine in patients with panic disorders, *Archives of General Psychiatry*, **41**, 1067–71.

Breggin, P.R. (1964) The psychophysiology of anxiety, *Journal of Nervous and Mental Disease*, **139**, 558–68.

Brehony, K.A. and Geller, E.S. (1981) Appraisal of research and proposal for an integrative model. In M. Hersen, R. Eisler and P. Miller (eds), *Progress in Behavior Modification*, Vol. 12, Academic Press, New York.

Brodsky, L., Zuniga, J.S., Casenas, E.R., Ernstoff, R. and Sachdev, H.S. (1983) Refractory anxiety: a masked epileptiform disorder? *The Psychiatric Journal of the University of Ottawa*, **8**, 42–5.

Buller, R., Maier, W. and Benkert, O. (1987) Das Herzangst-Syndrom—ein Subtyp des Panik-Syndroms. In D.O. Nutzinger, D. Pfersman, T. Welan and H.-G. Zapotoczky (eds), *Herzphobie*, Enke, Stuttgart.

Cameron, O.G., Thyer, B.A., Nesse, R.M. and Curtis, G.C. (1986) Symptom profiles of patients with DSM-III anxiety disorders, *American Journal of Psychiatry*, **143**, 1132–7.

Campbell, D., Sanderson, R.E. and Laverty, S.G. (1964) Characteristics of a conditioned response in human subjects during extinction trials following a single traumatic conditioning trial, *Journal of Abnormal and Social Psychology*, **68**, 627–39.

Chambless, D.L., Caputo, G.C., Bright, P. and Gallagher, R. (1984) Assessment of fear of fear in agoraphobics: The Body Sensations Questionnaire and the Agoraphobic Cognitions Questionnaire. *Journal of Consulting and Clinical Psychology*, **52**, 1090–97.

Charney, D.S. and Heninger, G.R. (1986) Abnormal regulation of noradrenergic function in panic disorders, *Archives of General Psychiatry*, **43**, 1042–54.

Clark, D.M. (1986) A cognitive approach to panic. *Behaviour Research and Therapy*, **24**, 461–70.

Clark, D.M. (1987) A cognitive model of panic attacks. In S. Rachman and J.D. Maser (eds), *Panic: Psychological Perspectives*, Lawrence Erlbaum, Hillsdale, NJ.

Clark, D.M. Salkovskis, P.M. and Chalkley, A.J. (1985) Respiratory control as a treatment for panic attacks, *Journal of Experimental Psychiatry and Behavior Therapy*, **16**, 23–30.

Clark, D.M. and Hemsley, D.R. (1982) The effects of hyperventilation: Individual variability and its relation to personality. *Journal of Experimental Psychiatry and Behavior Therapy*, **13**, 41–7.

Clark, D.M., Salkovskis, P.M., Gelder, M., Koehler, K., Martin, M., Anastasiades, P., Hackmann, A., Middleton, H. and Jeavons, A. (1988) Tests of a cognitive theory of panic. In I. Hand and H.-U. Wittchen (eds), *Treatment of Panic and Phobias—Modes of Application and Variables Affecting Outcome*, Springer, Berlin.

Coyle, P.K. and Sterman, A.B. (1986) Focal neurological symptoms in panic attacks, *American Journal of Psychiatry*, **143**, 648–9.

Drake, M.E. (1986) Panic attacks and excessive aspartame ingestion. *Lancet*, 13 September 1986, 631.

Ehlers, A. and Margraf, J. The psychophysiological model of panic. In P.M.G. Emmelkamp, W. Everaerd, F. Kraaymaat and M. van Son (eds), *Anxiety Disorders*, Swets, Amsterdam, in press.

Ehlers, A., Margraf, J., and Roth, W.T. (1986a) Experimental induction of panic attacks. In I. Hand and H.-U. Wittchen (eds), *Panic and Phobias*, Springer, Berlin.

Ehlers, A., Margraf, J., Roth, W.T., Taylor, C.B., Maddock, R.J., Sheikh, J., Kopell, M.L., McClenahan, K.L., Gossard, D., Blowers, G.H., Agras, W.S. and Kopell, B.S. (1986b) Lactate infusions and panic attacks: do patients and controls respond differently? *Psychiatry Research*, **17**, 295–308.

Ehlers, A., Margraf, J. and Roth, W.T. (1988a) Interaction of expectancy and physiological stressors in a laboratory model of panic. In D. Hellhammer, I. Florin and H. Weiner (eds), *Neurobiological Approaches to Human Disease*, Huber, Toronto.

Ehlers, A., Margraf, J., Roth, W.T., Taylor, C.B. and Birbaumer, N. (1988b) Anxiety induced by false heart rate feedback in patients with panic disorder, *Behaviour Research and Therapy*, **26**, 2–11.

Ehlers, A., Margraf, J., and Roth, W.T. (1988c) Selective information processing, interoception, and panic attacks. In I. Hand and H.-U. Wittchen (eds), *Panic and Phobias*, Springer, Berlin.

Ehlers, A., Margraf, J., Davies, S. and Roth, W.T. (1988d) Selective processing of threat cues in subjects with panic attacks, *Cognition and Emotion*, **2**, 201–19.

Epstein, S. (1976) The nature of anxiety with emphasis upon its relationship to expectancy. In C.D. Spielberger (ed.), *Anxiety, Vol. II*, Academic Press, New York.

Fiorica, V. and Kem, D.C. (1985) Plasma norepinephrine, blood pressure, and heart rate response to graded change in body position, *Aviation, Space, and Environmental Medicine*, **56**, 1166–71.

Foa, E.B. (1987) Emotional processing of fear: Exposure to corrective information. Invited address at the Annual Meeting of the European Association for Behaviour Therapy, Amsterdam, August 1987.

Foa, E. and Kozak, M. (1986) Emotional processing of fear: exposure to corrective information, *Psychological Bulletin*, **99**, 20–35.

Foa, E.B., Steketee, G. and Young, M.C. (1984) Agoraphobia: phenomenological aspects, associated characteristics, and theoretical considerations, *Clinical Psychology Review*, **4**, 431–57.

Freedman, R.R., Ianni, P., Ettedgui, E. and Puthezhath, N. (1985) Ambulatory monitoring of panic disorder, *Archives of General Psychiatry*, **42**, 244–8.

Gantt, W.H. and Dykman, R.A. (1957) Experimental psychogenic tachycardia. In P.H. Hoch and J. Zubin (eds), *Experimental Psychopathology*, Grune and Stratton, New York.

Garssen, B., Van Veenendaal, W. and Bloemink, R. (1983) Agoraphobia and the hyperventilation syndrome, *Behaviour Research and Therapy*, **21**, 643–9.

Gitlin, B., Martin, J., Shear, M.K., Frances, A., Ball, G. and Josephson, S. (1985) Behavior therapy for panic disorder, *Journal of Nervous and Mental Disease*, **173**, 742–3.

Goldstein, A.J. and Chambless, D.L. (1978) A reanalysis of agoraphobia, *Behavior Therapy*, **9**, 47–59.
Gorman, J.M., Cohen, B.S., Liebowitz, M.R., Fyer, A.J., Ross, D., Davies, S.O. and Klein, D.F. (1986) Blood gas changes and hypophosphatemia in lactate-induced panic, *Archives of General Psychiatry*, **43**, 1067–71.
Griez, E. and van den Hout, M.A. (1983) Treatment of phobophobia by exposure to CO_2-induced anxiety symptoms, *Journal of Nervous and Mental Disease*, **171**, 506–8.
Griez, E. and van den Hout, M.A. (1986) CO_2 inhalation in the treatment of panic attacks, *Behaviour Research and Therapy*, **24**, 145–50.
Griez, E., Pols, H.J. and van den Hout, M.A. (1987) Acid-base balance in real life, *Journal of Affective Disorders*, **12**, 263–6.
Hallam, R.S. (1978) Agoraphobia: a critical review of the concept, *British Journal of Psychiatry*, **133**, 314–19.
Hallam, R.S. (1983) Agoraphobia: deconstructing a clinical syndrome, *Bulletin of the British Psychological Society*, **36**, 337–40.
Hallam, R.S. (1985) *Anxiety. Psychological Perspectives on Panic and Agoraphobia*, Academic Press, London.
Harbauer-Raum, U. (1987) Wahrnehmung von Herzschlag und Arrhythmien—Eine Labor-Feldstudie an Patienten mit Herzphobie. In D.O. Nutzinger, D. Pfersman, T. Welan and H.-G. Zapotoczky (eds) *Herzphobie*, Enke, Stuttgart.
Hibbert, G.A. (1984) Ideational components of anxiety, *British Journal of Psychiatry*, **144**, 618–24.
Hibbert, G.A. (1986) The diagnosis of hyperventilation using ambulatory carbon dioxide monitoring. In H. Lacey and J. Sturgeon (eds), *Proceedings of the 15th European Conference for Psychosomatic Research*, Libby, London.
Hoehn-Saric, R. (1981) Characteristics of chronic anxiety patients. In D.F. Klein and J.G. Rabkin (eds), *Anxiety: New Research and Changing Concepts*, Raven Press, New York.
Hoehn-Saric, R. (1982) Comparison of generalized anxiety disorder with panic disorder patients, *Psychopharmacology Bulletin*, **18**, 104–8.
Hood, D.J. (1975) The definition of vestibular habituation. In R.F. Nauton (ed.), *The Vestibular System*, Academic Press, New York.
Hughdahl, K. and Öst, L.-G. (1985) Subjective, physiological, and cognitive symptoms in six different clinical phobias, *Personality and Individual Differences*, **6**, 175–88.
Izard, C.E. (1977) *Human Emotions*. Plenum Press, New York.
Jacob, R.G., Moller, M.B., Turner, S.M., and Wall, C. (1985) Otoneurological examination in panic disorder and agoraphobia with panic attacks: A pilot study, *American Journal of Psychiatry*, **142**, 715–20.
Jansen, A., van der Molen, M. and van den Hout, M.A. (1987) Over-ademen. Hyperventilatie en klassieke conditionering, *De Psycholoog*, **22**, 221–6.
Katherndahl, D.A. and Vande Creek, L. (1983) Hyperthyroidism and panic attacks. *Psychosomatics*, **24**, 491–6.
Katkin, E.S. (1985) Blood, sweat, and tears: Individual differences in autonomic self-perception. *Psychophysiology*, **22**, 125–37.
Kelly, D., Mitchell-Heggs, N. and Sherman, D. (1971) Anxiety and the effects of sodium lactate assessed clinically and physiologically, *British Journal of Psychiatry*, **119**, 129.
King, R., Margraf, J., Ehlers, A. and Maddock, R.J. (1986) Panic disorder—overlap with symptoms of somatization disorder. In I. Hand and H.-U. Wittchen (eds) *Panic and Phobias*, Springer, Berlin.

Klosko, J.S., Barlow, D.H., Tassinari, R.B. and Cerny, J.A. (1988) Comparison of alprazolam and cognitive behavior therapy in the treatment of panic disorder: a preliminary report. In I. Hand and H.-U. Wittchen (eds), *Treatments of Panic and Phobias—Modes of Application and Variables Affecting Outcome*, Springer, Berlin.

Lader, M. (1975) *The Psychophysiology of Mental Illness*, Routledge & Kegan Paul, London.

Lader, M, (1982) Biological differentiation of anxiety, arousal, and stress. In R.J. Matthew (ed.), *The Biology of Anxiety*, Brunner/Mazel, New York.

Lazarus, R.S. and Averill, J.R. (1972) Emotion and cognition: with special reference to anxiety. In C.D. Spielberger (ed.), *Anxiety. Vol. II*, Academic Press, New York.

Ley, R.A. (1985) Agoraphobia, the panic attack, and the hyperventilation syndrome, *Behaviour Research and Therapy*, **23**, 79–81.

Ley, R.A. (1988) Hyperventilation and lactate infusion in the production of panic attacks, *Clinical Psychology Review*, **8**, 1–18.

Lum, C. (1981) Hyperventilation and anxiety state, *Journal of the Royal Society of Medicine*, **74**, 1–4.

Magarian, G.J. (1982) Hyperventilation syndrome: Infrequently recognized common expressions of anxiety and stress, *Medicine*, **61**, 219–36.

Margraf, J. and Ehlers, A. (1988) Panic attacks in nonclinical subjects. In I. Hand and H.-U. Wittchen (eds), *Panic and Phobias 2*, Springer, Berlin.

Margraf, J., Ehlers, A. and Roth, W.T. (1986a) Biological models of panic disorder and agoraphobia—A review, *Behaviour Research and Therapy*, **24**, 553–67.

Margraf, J., Ehlers, A. and Roth, W.T. (1986b) Panic attacks: theoretical models and empirical evidence. In I. Hand and H.-U. Wittchen (eds), *Panic and Phobias*, Springer, Berlin.

Margraf, J., Ehlers, A. and Roth, W.T. (1986c) Sodium lactate infusions and panic attacks: a review and critique, *Psychosomatic Medicine*, **48**, 23–51.

Margraf, J., Taylor, C.B., Ehlers, A., Roth, W.T. and Agras, W.S. (1987a) Panic attacks in the natural environment, *Journal of Nervous and Mental Disease*, **175**, 558–65.

Margraf, J., Ehlers, A. and Roth, W.T. (1987b) Panic attack associated with false heart rate feedback. *Behavior Therapy*, **18**, 84–9.

Margraf, J., Ehlers, A. and Roth, W.T. (1988) Mitral valve prolapse and panic disorder: a review of their relationship, *Psychosomatic Medicine*, **50**, 93–113.

Margraf, J., Ehlers, A. and Roth, W.T. (1989) Expectancy effects and hyperventilation as laboratory stressors. In H. Weiner, I. Florin, R. Murison and D. Hellhammer (eds), *Frontiers of Stress Research*, Huber, Toronto.

Marks, I. (1986) Genetics of fear and anxiety disorders, *British Journal of Psychiatry*, **149**, 406–18.

Marks, I. (1987) *Fears, Phobias, and Rituals. Panic, Anxiety, and their Disorders*, Oxford University Press, New York.

Mathews, A.M., Gelder, M.G. and Johnston, D.W. (1981) *Agoraphobia: Nature and Treatment*, Guilford Press, New York.

McFarland, R.A. (1975) Heart rate perception and heart rate control, *Psychophysiology*, **12**, 402–5.

McNally, R.J. and Foa, E.B. (1987) Cognition and agoraphobia: bias in the interpretation of threat, *Cognitive Therapy and Research*, **11**, 567–82.

McNally, R.J. and Lorenz, M. (1987) Anxiety sensitivity in agoraphobics, *Journal of Behavior Therapy and Experimental Psychiatry*, **18**, 3–11.

Newton, J.E.O. and Gantt, W.H. (1966) One-trial cardiac conditioning in dogs, *Conditional Reflex*, **1**, 251–65.

Norton, G.R., Harrison, B., Hauch, J. and Rhodes, L. (1985) Characteristics of people with infrequent panic attacks, *Journal of Abnormal Psychology*, **94**, 216–21.

Norton, G.R., Dorward, J. and Cox, B.J. (1986) Factors associated with panic attacks in nonclinical subjects, *Behavior Therapy*, **17**, 239–52.

Öst, L.-G. (1988) Applied relaxation vs. progressive relaxation in the treatment of panic disorder, *Behaviour Research and Therapy*, **26**, 13–22.

Ottaviani, R. and Beck, A.T. (1987) Cognitive aspects of panic disorder, *Journal of Anxiety Disorders*, **1**, 15–28.

Pennebaker, J.W. (1982) *The Psychology of Physical Symptoms*, Springer, New York.

Plutchik, R. and Kellerman, H. (eds) (1980) *Emotion, Theory, Research and Experience*. Vol. 1, Academic Press, New York.

Pratt, R.T.C. and McKenzie, W. (1958) Anxiety states following vestibular disorders, *Lancet*, 16 August 1958, 347–9.

Rachman, S., Levitt, K. and Lopatka, C. (1987) Panic: the links between cognitions and bodily symptoms—I. *Behaviour Research and Therapy*, **25**, 411–23.

Rapee, R.M. (1985a) Distinctions between panic disorder and generalized anxiety disorder: clinical presentation, *Australian and New Zealand Journal of Psychiatry*, **19**, 227–32.

Rapee, R.M. (1985b) A case of panic disorder treated with breathing retraining, *Journal of Behavior Therapy and Experimental Psychiatry*, **16**, 63–5.

Rapee, R. (1986) Differential response to hyperventilation in panic disorder and generalized anxiety disorder, *Journal of Abnormal Psychology*, **95**, 24–8.

Rapee, R. (1987) The psychological treatment of panic attacks: theoretical conceptualization and review of evidence, *Clinical Psychology Review*, **7**, 427–38.

Raskin, D.E. (1984) Steroid-induced panic disorder, *American Journal of Psychiatry*, **141**, 1647.

Razran, G. (1961) The observable unconscious and the inferable conscious in current soviet psychophysiology: interoceptive conditioning, semantic conditioning, and the orienting reflex, *Psychological Review*, **68**, 81–147.

Reiss, S., Peterson, R.A., Gursky, D.M. and McNally, R.J. (1986) Anxiety sensitivity, anxiety frequency, and the prediction of fearfulness, *Behaviour Research and Therapy*, **24**, 1–8.

Roth, M. (1984) Agoraphobia, panic disorder, and generalized anxiety disorder: some implications of recent advances, *Psychiatric Developments*, **2**, 31–52.

Roy-Byrne, P.P., Uhde, T.W. and Post, R.M. (1986) Effects of one night's sleep deprivation on mood and behavior in panic disorder, *Archives of General Psychiatry*, **43**, 895–9.

Salkovskis, P.M., Jones, D.R.O. and Clark, D.M. (1986a) Respiratory control in the treatment of panic attacks: replication and extension with concurrent measurement of behaviour and pCO_2, *British Journal of Psychiatry*, **148**, 526–32.

Salkovskis, P.M., Warwick, H.M.C., Clark, D.M. and Wessels, D.J. (1986b) A demonstration of acute hyperventilation during naturally occurring panic attacks, *Behaviour Research and Therapy*, **24**, 91–4.

Sartory, G. and Olajide, D. (1988) Vagal innervation techniques in the treatment of panic disorder, *Behaviour Research and Therapy*, **26**, 431–44.

Schachter, S. (1970) The assumption of identity and the peripheralist-centralist controversies in motivation and emotion. In M. Arnold (ed.) *Feelings and Emotions*, Academic Press, New York.

Schandry, R. (1981) Heart beat perception and emotional experience, *Psychophysiology*, **18**, 483–8.

Schandry, R. (1983) On the relation between the improvement of cardiac perception and the increase of emotional experience, *Psychophysiology*, **20**, 468.

Schweizer, E.E., Winokur, A. and Rickels, K. (1986) Insulin-induced hypoglycemia and panic attacks. *American Journal of Psychiatry*, **143**, 654–5.

Shear, M.K., Ball, G., Gitlin, B. and Frances, A. (1986) Behavioral therapy efficacy for panic. Paper presented at the Annual Meeting of the American Psychiatric Association, Washington, DC, May 1986.

Shear, M.K., Ball, G.G., Josephson, S.C. and Gitlin, B.C. (1988) Cognitive-Behavioral treatment of panic. In I. Hand and H.-U. Wittchen (eds), *Treatments of Panic and Phobias—Modes of Application and Variables Affecting Outcome*, Springer, Berlin.

Solomon, R.L. and Wynne, L.C. (1953) Traumatic avoidance learning: Acquisition in normal dogs. *Psychological Monographs*, **67**, whole No. 354.

Spielberger, C.D. (1972) Anxiety as an emotional state. In C.D. Spielberger (ed.), *Anxiety*, Academic Press, New York.

Stalmann, H., Hartl, L., Pauli, P. and Strian, F. (1987) Perception of pathological cardiac activity, *Psychophysiology*, **24**, 614.

Sternbach, R.A. and Tursky, B. (1965) Ethnic differences among housewives in psychophysical and skin potential response to electric shock. *Psychophysiology*, **1**, 241–6.

Strongman, K. (1978) *The Psychology of Emotion*. 2nd edition. Wiley, Chichester.

Taylor, C.B., Telch, M.J. and Havvik, D. (1983) Ambulatory heart rate changes during panic attacks, *Journal of Psychiatric Research*, **17**, 261–6.

Taylor, C.B., Sheikh, J., Agras, W.S., Roth, W.T., Margraf, J., Ehlers, A., Maddock, R.J. and Gossard, D. (1986) Ambulatory heart rate changes in patients with panic attacks, *American Journal of Psychiatry*, **143**, 478–82.

Taylor, C.B., King, R.J., Ehlers, A., Margraf, J., Clark, D., Roth, W.T. and Agras, W.S. (1987) Treadmill exercise test and ambulatory measures in patients with panic attacks, *American Journal of Cardiology*, **60**, 48J–52J.

Thorpe, G.L. and Burns, L.E. (1983) *The Agoraphobic Syndrome*, Wiley, Chichester.

Thyer, B.A., Papsdorf, J.D. and Wright, P. (1984) Physiological and psychological effects of acute intentional hyperventilation, *Behaviour Research and Therapy*, **22**, 587–90.

Turner, S.M., McCann, B.S., Beidel, D.C. and Mezzich, J.E. (1986) DSM-III classification of the anxiety disorders: a psychometric study, *Journal of Abnormal Psychology*, **95**, 168–72

Turner, T.H. (1985) Agoraphobia and hyperthyroidism, *British Journal of Psychiatry*, **145**, 215–16.

Tyrer, P. (1984) Classification of anxiety, *British Journal of Psychiatry*, **144**, 78–83.

Tyrer, P., Lee, I. and Alexander, J. (1980) Awareness of cardiac function in anxious, phobic and hypochondriacal patients, *Psychological Medicine*, **10**, 171–4.

Uhde, T.W., Vittone, B.J. and Post, R.M. (1984) Glucose tolerance testing in panic disorder, *American Journal of Psychiatry*, **141**, 1461–3.

Uttal, W.R. (1987) The Psychobiology of Mind. In G. Adelman (ed.), *Encyclopedia of Neuroscience. Vol. II*, Birkhäuser, Boston.

van den Hout, M.A. (1987) The explanation of experimental panic. In S. Rachman and J.D. Maser (eds), *Panic: Psychological Perspectives*, Lawrence Erlbaum, Hillsdale, NJ.

van den Hout, M.A., van der Molen, M., Griez, E. and Lousberg, H. (1987) Specificity of interoceptive fears to panic disorders, *Journal of Psychopathology and Behavioral Assessment*, **9**, 99–106.

van Praag, H.M. (1985) Psychiatrists, beware of dichotomies! *Biological Psychiatry*, **21**, 247–8.

Waddell, M.T., Barlow, D.H. and O'Brien, G.T. (1984) A preliminary investigation of cognitive and relaxation treatment of panic disorder: Effects on intense anxiety vs. 'background' anxiety, *Behaviour Research and Therapy*, **22**, 393–402.

Weiner, H. (1978) The illusion of simplicity: The medical model revisited, *American Journal of Psychiatry*, **135**, July Supplement, 27–33.

Whitehead, W.E., Drescher, V.M., Heriman, P. and Blackwell, B. (1977) Relation of heart rate, heart rate control, and heart rate perception, *Biofeedback and Self-Regulation*, **2**, 371–92.

Zucker, D., Taylor, C.B., Brouillard, M., Ehlers, A., Margraf, J., Roth, W.T. and Agras, W.S. Cognitive aspects of panic attacks: content, course, and relationship to laboratory stressors. *British Journal of Psychiatry*, in press.

Section 4

Treatment Models and Approaches

Introduction: Treatment Models and Approaches

This section presents a number of different treatment approaches to panic. Each author was asked to specify their model of panic and its implication for treatment, to provide a practical description of treatment procedures, and to illustrate their procedures with case examples.

Two previous chapters in Section 2 of this book, by Isaac Marks and Manuel Zane, also presented treatment approaches, but as these chapters were primarily concerned with issues of classification and conceptualization they have been placed in the earlier section of the book. They too should be considered as valid contributions to this section.

The different treatment approaches represented necessarily overlap one another—for instance the majority use a form of behavioural exposure—but each has a different rationale resulting in considerable variations in technique.

Isaac Marks is acclaimed as the originator of the behavioural exposure approach (Boulougouris and Marks, 1969; Marks *et al.*, 1971). This was somewhat heretical in its day as it recommended procedures quite at variance with the prevailing practices of systematic desensitization. Nowadays exposure is practised throughout the world for a variety of different clinical conditions, particularly phobias. The approach was empirically driven, rather than theory driven; exposure to the feared stimulus was simply found to be effective. Habituation was used as a *post hoc* explanation for this effect. In his chapter Isaac Marks discusses key aspects of exposure including a self-help exposure package.

In the mid 1970s behaviourally oriented clinicians began to show a greater interest in the role of cognition, following the writings of Meichenbaum (1974) and Bandura (1977), and a new position combining elements of cognitive and behavioural therapy emerged under the hybrid term 'cognitive-behavioural' therapy (Kendall and Hollon, 1979). In the second chapter Ronald Rapee and David Barlow from the Center for Stress and Anxiety Disorders at Albany, New York, describe a set of treatment procedures which could be said to fall broadly within this cognitive-behavioural tradition. Their therapeutic approach consists of a new application of established behavioural or cognitive approaches to treat unexpected panic attacks. Their approach is at the forefront of cognitive behavioural approaches and has only recently been formally presented (Barlow and Cerny, 1988).

Robert Durham's chapter presents Beck's Cognitive Therapy approach to panic disorder. It is written from the viewpoint of a busy practitioner working in an ordinary National Health Service Clinical Psychology department in the UK, typically overstretched and taking a range of different clinical referrals. Durham explains how he chose Beck's Cognitive Therapy as an approach which was practical enough and broad enough to be of use in an ordinary clinical department. He discusses the treatment of mixed conditions involving panic, and how to treat the non-responding patient. It acts as an interesting counterpoint to the chapter written by Rapee and Barlow, who write from the 'purer' base of a specialized anxiety disorders clinic. It is not too surprising that Durham recommends an organizational solution to the provision of therapy which is economical on therapists' time.

Two innovative therapies, both involving exposure and both emerging in the late 1970s, have been included in this book. Neither is a mainstream therapy but the degree of detailed information they provide on panic contributes an additional dimension to a consideration of therapy. Manuel Zane first reported his 'contextual therapy' in 1978. He describes how this may be applied to panic disorder in Chapter 8 of this book. In 1976 Malcolm McFadyen developed a cognitive model for understanding and treating anxiety which applied aspects of Kelly's Personal Construct Theory, and Lazaurus and Spielberger's Cognitive theories to exposure therapy, first reporting this in 1981 (McFadyen and Baker, 1981; Baker and McFadyen, 1982). This represents a different approach to that of traditional behavioural, cognitive-behavioural, or cognitive positions in that he proposes that behavioural exposure is the most effective way of conducting *cognitive* therapy. While both M. Zane's and M. McFadyen's contributions can be seen as variations of Marks's exposure therapy, their advantage is that they provide a theoretical cognitive rationale which enables the therapist to structure the content of exposure sessions with considerable precision.

It is not unexpected given the volume and influence of Klein's research on panic disorder that antidepressant medication has in many places become the treatment of choice for panic. Dr Leslie Walker and Professor George Ashcroft, from the Department of Mental Health, Aberdeen University, have been involved in the research and treatment of panic disorder patients for a number of years, recently collaborating in a major research project with Howard Waring (1988). In their chapter on 'Pharmacological Approaches to the Treatment of Panic' they provide a useful practical review of the area, considering questions such as how best to select patients, select the drug of choice, decide on appropriate dosage and when to discontinue. They also consider the role of combined drug and behaviour therapy for complicated or severe cases and present their own model of panic, not dissimilar to Klein's, but employing concepts more congruent with those of modern physiological psychology.

The last chapter presents probably the best known self-help therapy for panic anxiety, that of Claire Weekes. Her contribution to the treatment of sufferers is considered in an introduction by myself, followed by a paper by Claire Weekes which deals with the issue of how to ensure that our treatments are effective on a long-term basis.

REFERENCES

Baker, R. and McFadyen, M. (1982) A cognitive invalidation approach to phobic anxiety, Paper presented at Symposium 'Approach to Anxiety-based Problems', at the Annual Merseyside Course in Clinical Psychology, Liverpool, 18th September.

Bandura, A. (1977) Self efficacy: toward a unifying theory of behavioral change, *Psychological Review*, **84**, 191–215.

Barlow, D.H. and Cerny, J. (1988) *The Psychological Treatment of Panic*, Guilford, New York.

Boulougouris, J. and Marks, I.M. (1969) Implosion (flooding): a new treatment for phobias, *British Medical Journal*, **2**, 721.

Kendall, P.C. and Hollon, S.D. (1979) *Cognitive-Behavioral Interventions: Theory, Research and Procedures*, Academic Press, New York.

McFadyen, M. and Baker, R. (1981) An invalidation model of anxiety reduction. Paper presented at the Annual Conference of the British Psychological Society, Scottish Branch, Bute.

Marks, I.M., Boulougouris, J. and Marset, P. (1971) Flooding versus desensitization in the treatment of phobic patients: a cross-over study, *British Journal of Psychiatry*, **119**, 353–75.

Meichenbaum, D.H. (1974) *Cognitive Behavior Modification*, General Learning Press, Morristown, New Jersey.

Waring, H.L. (1988) An investigation into the nature and response to treatment of panic attack symptoms in general practice attenders, MD Thesis, University of Aberdeen.

Zane, M.D. (1978) Contextual analysis and treatment of phobic behavior as it changes, *American Journal of Psychotherapy*, **32**, 338–58.

Chapter 11

Psychological Treatment of Unexpected Panic Attacks: Cognitive/Behavioural Components

RONALD M. RAPEE AND DAVID H. BARLOW

INTRODUCTION

Over a number of years there has been growing evidence that panic attacks are a form of anxiety seemingly distinct from chronic, generalized anxiety or agoraphobic avoidance (Barlow, 1988; Klein, 1964; Rapee, 1985b). If this notion is accepted, then it would follow that panic attacks may require unique treatment techniques for their effective alleviation.

Traditionally, the treatment of choice for panic attacks has been considered to be medication. Indeed, many valuable drug treatments for panic attacks have been investigated, as outlined in G. Ashcroft and L. Walker's chapter. Perhaps because of the tremendous interest in the drug treatment of panic attacks and perhaps, too, because of the widely-held belief that panic attacks represent some type of spontaneous, central, physiological discharge, psychological treatments of panic have been largely overlooked. While this situation is beginning to change, there currently still exists a dearth of well-controlled treatment outcome studies on the psychological alleviation of panic disorder.

In the present chapter, we give a brief overview of the psychological treatment of unexpected panic attacks. Because of the limited evidence available, we base our writing as much on clinical intuition and theoretical bases as empirical evidence. Hopefully, this situation will change in the near future. Certainly, there does exist enough evidence to draw some conclusions, most simply, that psychological treatments are effective in the reduction of panic attacks.

Panic Disorder: Theory, Research and Therapy. Edited by Roger Baker

THEORY

Later in the chapter we will be discussing each of the treatment techniques commonly used in the alleviation of panic attacks. At this point, we will examine the theoretical basis for each. However, it will be useful before we do this to describe some of the recent theories of panic attacks. In this way, it is easier to conceptualize the method and value of the treatment techniques and to design more effective treatment packages.

There have been a number of psychological theories of panic attacks described in recent years (e.g. Barlow, 1986, 1988; Beck and Emery, 1985; Clark, 1986; Ehlers and Margraf, in press; Ley, 1985; Rapee, 1987; van den Hout and Griez, 1983). These theories are perhaps better described as interactionist or psychophysiological since they emphasize an interaction between peripheral physiological sensations and psychological factors. According to these theories, panic attacks are seen as discrete fear reactions to a specific set of somatic sensations. In this way, unexpected panic attacks are seen as essentially the same as phobic reactions except that the trigger and stimuli are internal rather than external. As with any phobia, anxiety over possible recurrence of the phobic situation develops. In support of such a position, it has recently been demonstrated that patients with panic disorder who are given false feedback of heart-rate accelerations and who believe this feedback, report greater anxiety than non-anxious controls (Ehlers *et al.*, 1988). Similarly, a variety of laboratory procedures (including lactate infusions, carbon dioxide inhalations, and hyperventilation) which produce similar somatic sensations all elicit greater fear and/or anxiety in panic disorder patients than in non-anxious controls and even patients with other anxiety disorders (Barlow, 1988).

In naturally occurring panic attacks, the physiological sensations are believed to result from any of a number of mechanisms. For example, Ley (1985) stresses hyperventilation as the physiological trigger which results in the somatic sensations associated with most panic attacks. On the other hand, Barlow (1988) suggests somatic sensations can be elicited through a variety of mechanisms including chronic sympathetic nervous system arousal, physical exercise, and attentional factors.

Once these somatic sensations are perceived, the individual responds with anxiety. This anxiety is mediated by an association between the somatic sensations and information structures relating to immediate danger (such as death, insanity, and loss of control). The emotional reaction, in turn, is likely to lead to further physiological sensations thereby continuing the panic cycle. How the panic attack actually ends has not been a point for much research or theorizing to date. Presumably, there are a variety of factors which terminate the attack. The underlying alarm response that is fear is most likely self-limiting.

Anxiety which intensifies and spirals the attack is reduced by activities designed to ease the sensations such as taking medication, resting, or lessening of sensations through decreased bodily attention. This may be achieved through distraction techniques such as talking to someone or flicking oneself with a rubber band. Finally, some attacks may end when some degree of informational change occurs such as realizing that, at least this time, the individual will not die or lose control.

This cycle—somatic sensations eliciting fear and associations of immediate danger leading to anxiety and more sensations—constitutes the actual isolated, unexpected, panic attack. Of course, the attack is going to occur within a context of particular personality characteristics and is itself likely to result in chronic sequelae. It is these factors which will determine the impact which the panic attack has on an individual's life. A summary model is presented in Figure 11.1. (It can be seen how closely our model approximates to that of Margraf and Ehler's psychophysiological model of panic attacks presented in Chapter 10).

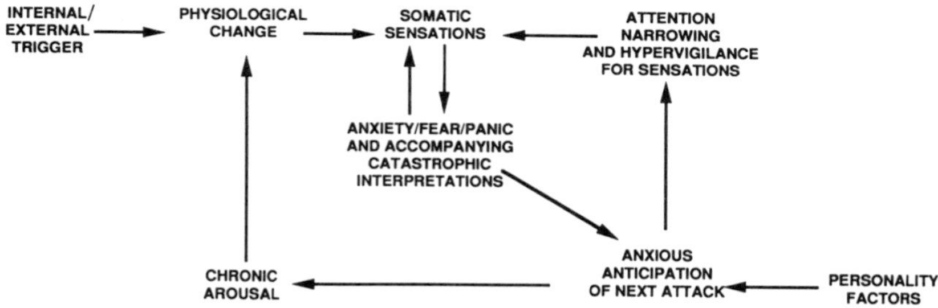

Figure 11.1 The maintenance of panic disorder. Reprinted from R.M. Rapee and D.H. Barlow (in press). The psychological treatment of panic attacks and agoraphobic avoidance. In John Walker, Colin Ross and Ron Norton(eds), *Panic Disorder Agoraphobia: A Guide for the Practitioner*, to be published by The Dorsey Press, Chicago, Illinois, © 1989. Reprinted with permission of the publisher.

Finally, one of the most debilitating aspects of panic attacks is the marked avoidance behavior which results in some sufferers. Why some patients should develop considerable avoidance and others virtually none is still an area requiring much investigation. Some recent work has begun to address this issue and has isolated factors such as specific attributions, social anxiety, unassertiveness, and introversion as differentiating between panic disorder patients with minimal and marked avoidance (Rapee and Barlow, in press).

TREATMENT

The use of psychological techniques in the treatment of panic attacks is only just beginning to be generally accepted. Until a few years ago, virtually no research had been conducted on the use of psychological techniques in the specific alleviation of panic attacks. This was probably due to a widely held belief that panic attacks are spontaneous, central, physiological events and as such require pharmacological treatment. Of course, this is an erroneous belief since a physical etiology does not necessarily imply a chemical treatment. Nevertheless, this view has been and continues to be held by many clinicians and researchers. In recent years, however, a number of studies have emerged demonstrating that psychological techniques can be successful in reducing the frequency and intensity of panic attacks.

Three groups have reported on the use of broad-based psychological treatment packages without medication in the treatment of panic disorder with agoraphobia patients with mild avoidance (Barlow *et al*., 1984; Sokol and Beck, cited in Beck, 1988; Gitlin *et al*., 1985).

In an uncontrolled trial, Gitlin *et al*. (1985) treated 11 subjects with panic disorder using a package which included education, abdominal breathing and exposure. The results indicated that 10 of 11 patients were panic free at post-treatment and at an average of five months follow-up. Interestingly, when asked during a post-treatment interview, most patients felt that education and reassurance about panic attacks which altered catastrophic cognitions had been the most beneficial factors in the treatment package followed by abdominal breathing.

Sokol and Beck (cited in Beck, 1988) reported on a series of 28 panic disorder patients treated at that centre using a comprehensive treatment package. The package focused on cognitive restructuring and interoceptive exposure. Twenty-six patients who completed treatment were panic free at post-test. These results were maintained at three-month follow-up for 20 patients assessed at that time.

The results reported by Barlow *et al*. (1984) were preliminary findings from a far larger treatment study being carried out at our clinic. In the earlier report, five subjects suffering panic disorder were treated with a combination of muscle relaxation, EMG biofeedback, the teaching of coping self-statements and the altering of anxiety provoking thoughts. They were compared with six panic disorder patients assigned to a wait list control group. The results indicated a significantly greater reduction of panic attacks in the treatment group over the control group. The larger study is currently nearing completion. It involves the comparison of four conditions: (1) waiting list control; (2) relaxation; (3) cognitive restructuring and interoceptive exposure; and (4) combined treatment. All treatments involve 15 weekly sessions with an individual therapist. The waiting list group are simply told that they are waiting for treatment and undergo all of the assessments of the other groups but never meet with a therapist. In the relaxation condition, subjects are taught progressive deep muscle relaxation and are encouraged to apply these techniques to threatening situations (e.g. imminent panic). In the cognitive restructuring condition, subjects are taught formal cognitive restructuring skills based largely on the work of Beck and Emery (1985). They are also encouraged to 'hypothesis test' which involves testing their belief about specific situations by confronting those situations. The hypothesis testing is especially applied to beliefs surrounding interoceptive stimuli. Finally, the combined treatment involves a combination of the relaxation and cognitive restructuring conditions.

Preliminary results from 62 patients have recently been presented (Craske and Barlow, 1987) and include 10 patients in the relaxation condition, 16 in the cognitive restructuring condition, 19 in the combined condition, and 17 wait list subjects. Essentially, no significant differences have so far been found between the three active conditions. All three conditions are superior to wait list on global ratings of clinical effectiveness, general anxiety, and reduction in number of panic attacks.

The results from these three studies point to the fact that psychological techniques can be highly effective in the alleviation of panic attacks. But, it does not speak to specific mechanisms of action since all three treatments contained elements now thought to be important in the treatment of panic disorder as described below. The remainder of this chapter will look in more detail at the individual treatment components.

Relaxation and breathing control techniques

Evidence

According to the model presented earlier (Figure 11.1), somatic sensations provide the feared stimuli in panic attacks. Therefore, learning to reduce or control these sensations should reduce panic attacks. The somatic sensations which trigger panic attacks have been suggested to be a result of either general autonomic arousal or more specific increases in respiration. The latter mechanism has probably received the most extensive investigation but the data are chiefly correlational in nature and direct causal studies are still awaited.

Three lines of evidence have been used to support a role for hyperventilation in panic attacks. First, it has been found that patients with panic disorder are more likely to report hyperventilatory symptoms such as dizziness, breathlessness, faintness, choking, and paresthesias than patients with other anxiety disorders (Rapee, 1985b; Sanderson *et al.*, 1987). Of course, this does not necessarily imply that panic disorder patients hyperventilate and may simply reflect an attentional bias in these patients (Sanderson *et al.*, 1987).

Second, some studies have demonstrated that panic disorder patients have abnormally low levels of carbon dioxide and bicarbonate at rest (Lum, 1976; Gorman *et al.*, 1986; Rapee, 1986; Salkovskis *et al.*, 1986). At least one of these studies has found a significantly lower resting pCO_2 in panic disorder patients than in patients with generalized anxiety disorder who had never experienced a panic attack (Rapee, 1986).

Finally, some evidence has suggested that patients with panic disorder respond with considerable distress to a brief period of voluntary hyperventilation and rate this experience as similar to their naturally occurring attacks (Garssen *et al.*, 1983; Rapee, 1986). It is this latter evidence which, while providing some support for the hyperventilation theory of panic attacks, has most strongly indicated its limitations. Rapee (1986) found that panic disorder patients reported more distress to 90 seconds of voluntary hyperventilation than did patients with generalized anxiety disorder. However, not one of the panic disorder patients reported that they actually had a 'panic attack'. Rather, they reported that while the experience was somatically very similar, they did not actually panic. Thus, it appears that hyperventilation alone cannot explain panic attacks and other (presumably psychological) factors must be involved. Nevertheless, these data do suggest that hyperventilation may be involved in the somatic sensations of at least some panic attacks.

A number of studies have demonstrated the value of breathing retraining in the treatment of panic attacks (e.g. Bonn *et al.*, 1984; Clark *et al.*, 1985; Rapee, 1985a; Salkovskis *et al.*, 1986). Unfortunately, some of the studies have included an educational component in their packages thereby not allowing results to be necessarily attributed to breathing control (Clark *et al.*, 1985; Rapee, 1985a; Salkovskis *et al.*, 1986). In addition, only one of these studies has involved a controlled comparison (Bonn *et al.*, 1984). In this study, 12 panic disorder with agoraphobia individuals were randomly allocated to treatment with either respiratory control training plus *in vivo* exposure or *in vivo* exposure alone. The success of the manipulation was demonstrated at follow-up by finding a significantly lower respiratory rate in the respiratory control group compared with the *in vivo* exposure only group. There was a non-significant trend for the group taught respiratory control to report fewer panic attacks compared to the other group at post-treatment. At six month follow-up, this difference between groups had become significant.

Similarly, some studies have begun to demonstrate the value of more general relaxation techniques in the alleviation of panic attacks (e.g. Ost, 1988). At this stage, questions remain as to whether these techniques share common mechanisms and, if so, whether these mechanisms refer to general arousal reduction, control of respiration, or some other factor.

Application

Since general relaxation techniques have been described for many years and are commonly employed by clinicians, we will not discuss their application here. Rather, we will focus on the practice of a breathing retraining technique as currently used at our clinic. On a general clinical note we should point out that patients are given a careful physical screening prior to treatment to ensure that those with major cardiovascular or respiratory disease are excluded from the hyperventilation provocation phase, or at least closely supervised during treatment.

Before discussing the role of overbreathing in panic attacks or even mentioning the term hyperventilation, the patient is asked to stand and breathe faster and deeper ('as if blowing up a balloon') for up to 90 seconds. The therapist generally demonstrates three or four breaths at approximately twice resting rate and depth. Once 90 seconds have elapsed (or the patient has shown some distress) the patient should be instructed to sit and breathe slowly and smoothly at a rate counted out by the therapist. After about a minute, most sensations should have abated and the experience can be discussed. The episode will generally have resulted in a number of somatic sensations commonly associated with the patient's panic attacks and thus serves as an excellent launching point for discussion of the role of hyperventilation in panic attacks.

The patient should be asked to describe the sensations they experienced and discuss the similarity to their usual panic symptoms. It should be pointed out that there would have been less anxiety associated with the symptoms since the patient had an explanation for the feelings, was in control of the manipulation, and was in a safe environment. Nevertheless, the importance of overbreathing in producing at least some of the physical symptoms associated with panic attacks can be demonstrated by this exercise.

At this point, the therapist should begin a didactic session on the physiology of hyperventilation. While the educational level of the patient will determine the detail into which this discussion can proceed, some understanding of what hyperventilation does and how it works will greatly aid acceptance and compliance with the breathing control technique. In addition, understanding of hyperventilation will help to allay many fears, a point to which we will return in the next section. Most importantly, the patient should learn:

1. that overbreathing through various physical changes, can cause many of the somatic sensations associated with panic attacks;
2. that this overbreathing can often be very subtle so that individuals may not realize that they are hyperventilating;
3. that the physical changes associated with hyperventilation are reversible and totally harmless.

A more detailed description of useful information for patients can be found in Rapee and Barlow (in press).

Once the patient fully understands the importance of hyperventilation in producing or at least perpetuating their physical sensations, they can be taught to control these sensations through control of respiration. The fundamental purpose is simply to reduce the amount of respiration in order to produce an increase in pCO_2 levels and decreased pH. To this end, the patient should be taught to breathe slowly and smoothly. So-called 'deep breathing' will be detrimental if minute volume is increased. Rather, 'slow breathing' is probably a better descriptor.

The patient should be instructed to sit in a comfortable chair and place one hand on their stomach (diaphragm) and one on their chest. In order to eliminate 'chest breathing' which is associated with chest pain and increased respiration, the patient needs to practice breathing so that most movement comes from the abdominal hand and little or none from the thoracic hand. They should be instructed to count the number '1' on the inspirations and mentally repeat the word 'relax' on expirations. If they wish, they can count '2' on the next breath and so on.

At first, most patients will encounter difficulty with two aspects of the technique. Forcing voluntary control over a normally automatic behavior such as respiration often interferes with that behavior. Thus, respiration at first, may become labored and erratic, often resulting in symptoms. If this occurs, the patient should be told to stop the exercise for a while and return to it when symptoms have abated. With practice, this will become easier. Once they can think about their breathing without causing a change in its pattern, they can begin to slow their counting and match their respiration to it. A rate of 10 to 12 moderately deep breaths per minute at rest should be sufficient to eliminate most symptoms.

The second difficult component relates to attention. Most patients will find that, early in practice, they will have great difficulty maintaining attention to the counting for more than a brief period. They should simply be encouraged to keep practicing and not become discouraged since they will improve with time. Good attentional capabilities are important both for general relaxation and in order to be able to apply the breathing retraining technique during a panic attack.

We generally suggest two, 10-minute practices per day. Practice should not stop as soon as the first positive results are experienced but will need to continue for some time. In addition to the formal practices, patients should be encouraged to engage in smaller practices whenever and wherever possible. When patients have established some degree of competence with the technique they should practice turning the symptoms 'on and off' by alternately hyperventilating and slowing the breathing to establish a sense of control over symptoms.

Cognitive modification

Evidence

Another active ingredient in the psychological treatment of panic attacks is likely to involve provision of accurate information and verbal alteration of abberant beliefs (cognitive restructuring). In the behavioral treatment package utilized by Gitlin *et al*. (1985), the patients reported that they found the corrective information which reduced catastrophic beliefs about panic attacks to be the most helpful component.

According to the model presented in Figure 11.1, catastrophic beliefs are fundamentally associated with panic attacks. Whether conscious beliefs are causally involved in the genesis of panic attacks has still not been satisfactorily demonstrated. However, there is growing evidence identifying at least a modifying role to specific beliefs in panic disorder patients.

A number of descriptive studies have found that panic disorder patients report more dramatic and catastrophic cognitions than patients with other anxiety disorders (Beck *et al*., 1974; Hibbert, 1984; Rapee, 1985b; Sanderson *et al*., 1987). For example, Sanderson *et al*. (1987) found that panic disorder with agoraphobia patients were significantly more likely to report a fear of dying or going crazy/losing control during panic attacks than patients with social phobia, obsessive-compulsive disorder and simple phobia during their episodes of fear. Similarly, panic patients have been found to report a greater belief that they are undergoing physical or psychological catastrophe (for example, heart attack, death, insanity) while experiencing their symptoms than patients with generalized anxiety disorder (Hibbert, 1984; Rapee, 1985b).

Thus, it seems that a tendency to activate dramatic beliefs regarding death, insanity and loss of control in response to somatic symptoms is a fundamental characteristic of patients with panic disorder. Whether such beliefs play a causal role in panic attacks is difficult to demonstrate. However, two recent studies have demonstrated that certain information can influence the intensity of laboratory induced panic attacks in panic disorder patients lending further support to the importance of psychological factors in panic attacks.

In the first study (Rapee *et al.*, 1986) 16 patients with panic disorder received single breath inhalations of a 50 per cent CO_2/50 per cent O_2 gas mixture. They were randomly allocated to two groups: an explanation group which was given full information as to the expected subjective and physiological effects of the inhalation and a no explanation group which was given minimal information as to what the inhalation should do. The no explanation group reported more subjective panic, a greater similarity of the experience to a natural panic attack, and a greater proportion of catastrophic cognitions than the explanation group. These results demonstrated in a panic disorder patient population that the provision of accurate information as to the source of somatic sensations could attenuate the emotional response to these sensations.

In a second study, Sanderson *et al.* (in press) administered continuous 15-minute inhalations of 5 per cent CO_2 in air to 20 patients diagnosed as having panic disorder with agoraphobia. All patients were given identical instructions as to what to expect from the inhalations. They were further told that a light in the room may or may not be illuminated. If the light was illuminated, they were informed that they would be able to control the amount of gas they received by use of a dial, but only to use it if absolutely necessary, whereas if the light were not illuminated, they would have no control over the gas. For 10 subjects the light was illuminated during the CO_2 administration. Thus, this group had an 'illusion of control'. For the remaining 10 subjects, the light was not illuminated (no control group). In fact, both groups received the same amount of CO_2 since the dial was actually inoperative. In addition, no subject actually used the dial. The illusion of control group reported significantly fewer panic attacks, fewer and less intense symptoms, less anxiety, less similarity to a naturally occurring panic attack, and less catastrophic cognitions than the no control group. Thus, these results suggest that a sense of control over somatic sensations can also attenuate the emotional response to these sensations in panic disorder patients.

Evidence appears to be accumulating that cognitive factors may have a role to play in some aspects of panic attacks, suggesting that cognitive restructuring may be of value in the treatment of panic attacks. Certainly, the study by Rapee *et al.* (1986) indicates that providing accurate information about the physiological sensations associated with panic attacks may relieve some of the resultant fear, perhaps by inducing a sense of control or correcting faulty attributions. While a number of clinicians believe that cognitive alterations are of value in the treatment of panic attacks, controlled trials are presently non-existent. As mentioned earlier, some studies have combined education with breathing retraining in the successful treatment of panic attacks (Clark *et al.*, 1985; Rapee, 1985a; Salkovskis *et al.*, 1986). Of course, we cannot tell which of these components is the active one. Controlled trials assessing the value of provision of information and cognitive restructuring alone are still awaited.

Application

General application of so called 'cognitive restructuring techniques' has been extensively discussed in a number of excellent texts and is covered in more detail from Beck's cognitive therapy position by R. Durham in Chapter 12. Therefore, we will not discuss the general procedures here but will focus on the specific aspects of cognitive restructuring which are likely to be especially relevant to panic attacks.

The fundamental principle of cognitive restructuring for panic attacks involves convincing the patient that his symptoms do not signify danger or loss of control. As mentioned earlier, panic disorder patients appear to believe that their somatic sensations indicate imminent catastrophe such as death, insanity, or loss of control (Rapee, 1985b). In some cases, these schema are maintained by inaccurate information. For example, one patient recently seen at our clinic believed that his continuing anxiety symptoms would eventually culminate in a much more severe mental disorder such as schizophrenia. Another patient believed, even while she was not actually panicking, that the palpitations she experienced could do long-term damage to her heart and maybe, if particularly severe, cause her heart to stop beating. Obviously, in these cases, provision of accurate information is a necessary first step. Occasionally, it may even be enough to remove most or all anxiety over sensations.

More commonly, panic disorder patients will present in a similar fashion to conventional phobics and perceive their fears as totally irrational. For example, it is quite common for a patient, while sitting calmly in the therapist's office, to report 'I *know* that I am not going to have a heart attack but at the time I am having a panic attack, I just don't believe that any more'. In these cases, more conventional cognitive restructuring procedures are likely to be necessary. Above all, repeated practice is the key issue. As in most phobic disorders, direct experience (exposure *in vivo*) is probably a more effective way of altering such automatic information structures but verbal cognitive techniques may help to speed the process.

Provision of accurate information involves two basic components. First, the patient must be taught enough about the basic physiological processes that they can understand what is involved at a peripheral level in panic attacks and realize that no actual physical harm will occur. Second, any specific misconceptions which the patient holds should be identified and cleared up.

At our clinic we currently provide patients with a written summary of the physiology of anxiety. During our treatment programs, approximately two sessions are spent going through this handout and making certain that the patient understands all aspects. The handout describes, in simple terms, the more important physiological changes which occur during the experience of fear or anxiety. Anxiety is described in terms of the 'fight/flight' response and it is continually stressed that the function of anxiety is to protect the body, not to harm it. Wherever possible, it is pointed out that the various urges, thoughts and sensations accompanying anxiety are natural and necessary. A model of a panic attack is then presented. In the simplified model, the panic attack is described as a set of natural and harmless somatic sensations which may occur for a variety of reasons and to which the individual responds with fear due to any of a number of incorrect beliefs.

The final part of the handout lists a number of common misconceptions together with correct information relating to these beliefs. Some of the misconceptions listed are as follows:

1. A belief that the individual will 'go crazy', usually implying some severe mental disorder such as schizophrenia for which the person may need to be 'locked away forever'.
2. A belief that the individual will in some sense totally lose control and perhaps 'run amok'.
3. A belief that the individual's nerves can in some way break or somehow become worn out so as to experience permanent damage.
4. A belief that the individual is currently undergoing a heart attack or some form of serious cardiovascular disease.

Copies of this handout, as well as an up-to-date version of our complete treatment program, are available from our Center.

In addition to teaching correct information relating to somatic sensations and panic attacks, more formal cognitive restructuring is often a valuable component. At our clinic we currently teach individuals that the logical errors that they make fall broadly into two types: overestimations of the probability of an aversive event and catastrophic estimations of its consequence. Anxious individuals generally tend to overestimate the likelihood that an aversive event will occur, particularly to themselves (Butler and Mathews, 1983). In addition, having decided that the aversive event will most likely occur, the anxious individual tends to overdramatize the effect that the event will have. We have found that breaking the general types of thinking into these two broad categories facilitates training in cognitive restructuring.

Patients are first taught to identify their overestimations of probability. At all points, patients are encouraged to describe real events in their lives in order to make the teaching and practice more salient. Throughout treatment, continuous monitoring of anxiety producing events and their associated beliefs is a vital aspect both in order to prompt practice and to provide material for treatment sessions (see Rapee and Barlow, in press for a sample monitoring form).

Probably the most difficult aspect of cognitive restructuring for the majority of patients will simply be to identify their abberant beliefs. This may be both because people are not generally accustomed to making what are normally automatic processes into conscious ones and because many people do not want to admit to themselves that they are thinking in this way.

Once patients can identify the thoughts accompanying their emotions, they should be taught to identify the implicit probabilities in those thoughts. For example, 'I will *never* survive' implies a zero per cent probability while 'I *will* have a heart attack' implies a 100 per cent probability. Patients should more realistically decide on the probabilities and record them. Even when patients are no longer thinking in absolute terms, they may still overestimate. In these cases, patients may have to be taught the meaning of their estimates. For example, one patient at our clinic was recently adamant that he had a 10 per cent chance of passing out during a panic attack. When it was pointed out to him that this meant that he would actually pass out during one out of every ten panic attacks, he changed his estimate to less than 1 per cent. Beck's notion of looking for evidence is a very important skill to introduce here (Beck and Emery, 1985). For example, the above patient was encouraged to think about how many panic attacks he had experienced in his life and how often he had actually fainted (never).

Once patients can more accurately identify the probability of the aversive event, they should be taught to realistically appraise its consequence. This can be introduced to patients by asking them what it would mean for them if the event were to occur. This is equivalent to the notion of 'decatastrophizing' proposed by Beck and Emery (1985). The terms 'what if' and 'so what' are useful to help identify realistic consequences. Once a possible consequence (no matter how bizarre) has been identified, it, too, should be subjected to appraisal of its likelihood.

Once patients have been taught these two components of irrational thinking, the two factors, realistic estimation of probability and realistic estimation of consequence, can then become combined and applied to any anxiety inducing event, in this case, the experience of somatic sensations. An example from one of our sessions is provided below.

Therapist: Tell me a little about the attack. How did it begin?

Patient: I'm not sure. I was just sitting there and listening to the sermon, when all of a sudden I couldn't catch my breath, my heart began to pound, and I just had to get out.

Therapist: Why did you *have* to get out? What would have happened if you had stayed?

Patient: I don't know; I probably would have suffocated.

Therapist: That's a pretty strong word, suffocated. How likely do you really think it was that you would have suffocated—have you ever suffocated before?

Patient: Of course not. I guess I wouldn't actually have suffocated, it was just so frightening to not be able to catch my breath.

Therapist: Again, look at the probability of what you are saying. Do you mean that you weren't breathing?

Patient: No . . . I don't know . . . I suppose I was just puffing a lot.

Therapist: And even if you were puffing a lot, what's the worst that could happen?

Patient: Well, I know I wouldn't suffocate and I have never passed out before . . . I guess it just felt uncomfortable.

Finally, a particularly important technique for patients with panic disorder is what Beck and Emery (1985) term 'generating alternative beliefs'. As discussed earlier, panic disorder patients have a tendency to catastrophically interpret their sensations. In many cases, there is a perfectly logical and obvious explanation for the sensations experienced. However, patients with panic disorder are particularly poor at entertaining these alternative hypotheses. For example, a patient recently treated at our clinic reported at one of her treatment sessions that she had experienced headaches, tension, and breathlessness for the whole of the preceding week, causing her a week of terror. Later in the conversation, it emerged that she had just stopped smoking, a habit in which she had engaged for 20 years. However, she found it extremely difficult to make a connection between this major life change and her physical sensations. If patients with panic disorder can be taught to identify alternative explanations for their sensations rather than the catastrophic ones in which they usually engage, their fear can often be quickly reduced. A good illustration of this effect can be found in a patient treated by the first author a few years ago. This patient experienced a particularly severe panic attack while visiting a boat show with her husband. She reported feeling as if the 'world were moving up and down' and thought she was about to faint. When she urgently related this fear to her husband, he burst out laughing and pointed out that they were standing on a pontoon and the world was indeed moving up and down. The patient reported an immediate drop in her anxiety and enjoyed the rest of the day.

Interoceptive exposure

Evidence

Exposure-based techniques have formed the basis of the armamentarium of behavior therapists in the treatment of phobic disorders for many years. Little controversy is raised by suggesting that exposure techniques are the most effective forms of treatment for phobic avoidance behavior. Indeed, numerous studies have demonstrated the value of *in vivo* exposure in the alleviation of agoraphobic avoidance (see Rapee and Barlow, in press for a review). Thus, if panic disorder is seen as sharing a number of features of phobic disorders (Figure 11.1), then it should follow that exposure-based techniques may also be valuable in the alleviation of panic attacks.

This point raises the question, exposure to what? Since patients suffering panic disorder without agoraphobia do not obviously avoid, arranging *in vivo* exposure exercises for them appears superficially to be impossible. However, if we look at the model presented earlier, the answer becomes obvious. Phobics are treated by exposing them to the stimuli which they specifically fear. In the case of patients with panic disorder, the stimuli which they fear are their own bodily sensations. Thus, exposure in the treatment of a panic attack should be to interoceptive cues.

The idea of using exposure to internal cues in the treatment of panic attacks is not new. Some authors have reported cases in which paradoxical intention has been successfully used in the alleviation of panic attacks (Goldstein, 1978). Paradoxical intention involves having the patient attempt not to avoid (and, in fact, to increase) symptoms and in this way probably acts as an exposure-based technique. The main problem clinically with this technique is that it relies on the natural occurrence of panic attacks which may be infrequent and variable in some patients.

In order to conduct more systematic exposure to somatic sensations, therapists have attempted to discover means by which such symptoms could be artificially produced. Over the years, many chemical means have been found by which feared sensations could be produced in patients suffering panic disorder including infusions of adrenalin, sodium lactate, and yohimbine, ingestion of caffeine and inhalation of CO_2 mixed with air or oxygen in various amounts (see Barlow, 1988 for a review). Two of these methods, infusion of sodium lactate and inhalation of CO_2/O_2, have been used in the treatment of panic disorder.

Bonn *et al.* (1973) reported on the successful treatment of 33 patients with panic attacks using repeated infusions of sodium lactate. Unfortunately, the trial was uncontrolled and did not utilize a direct measure of panic attacks. Rather, successful treatment was inferred from measures of overall anxiety levels.

Wolpe (1958) reported on the successful use of repeated CO_2/O_2 inhalations in the treatment of severely anxious individuals, presumably with panic attacks. More recently, Griez and van den Hout (1983) reported a case study in which an individual suffering panic disorder with agoraphobia was given repeated inhalations of a 35 per cent CO_2/65 per cent O_2 gas mixture as well as being asked to intentionally and repeatedly hyperventilate and exercise. This case study was extended by a controlled crossover comparison of the effects of CO_2/O_2 inhalations against propranolol (Griez and van den Hout, 1986). Fourteen patients suffering panic disorder with agoraphobia received two weeks treatment with each of the techniques in counterbalanced order. Gas inhalations produced a significant (50 per cent) reduction in the frequency of panic attacks while propranolol produced an insignificant (38 per cent) reduction.

While these data indicate that interoceptive exposure may be a valuable treatment technique in the alleviation of panic attacks, controlled evaluations of this specific component are still awaited. As a more viable technique for the private clinician, some authors have pointed to other methods of producing feared sensations (e.g. Barlow, 1988). These techniques will be discussed in more detail below. In brief, they can include such activities as climbing flights of stairs, head shaking, taking a hot bath, spinning in a chair, and voluntary hyperventilation.

Application

The principles and practice of interoceptive exposure are essentially the same as those for external exposure; only the cues are different. It is vital that patients understand the purpose of the exposure exercises and thus recapping the model of panic attacks is generally a good way to begin. In addition, it is important that patients understand how exposure is to proceed and theoretically how it works. A brief time spent at the beginning of the session discussing the theoretical principles and parameters of *in vivo* exposure can be very valuable. Because there are so many ways that exposure practices can be 'sabotaged', it is important that patients understand the mechanisms of exposure to maximize compliance and motivation. Preempting questions is often a good way to achieve this aim. For example, it is important to warn clients that there will be both good and bad days and also of the possibility of minor setbacks. In addition, the therapist may wish to discuss the importance of regular, systematic practice, the influence of general mood states such as depression, and the difference between doing exposure because it is necessary and doing exposure because it is a desired part of treatment. This latter point is important since many patients will report that they have often experienced symptoms of panic attacks and yet are still just as frightened of these sensations. It must be pointed out that doing graduated, systematic exposure which is under the patient's control is very different to unexpected and uncontrollable exposure.

The first step in interoceptive exposure is to establish a hierarchy of feared sensations just as one would for external exposure. Since most patients will not have thought very much in interoceptive terms, they will not simply be able to write down a hierarchy. For this reason, it is probably a good idea to practice a number of different sensation-producing techniques in order to rate their anxiety potential. In our clinic, we have a set list of sensation-producing techniques which we proceed through one at a time. For each technique, the patient rates the degree of fear which that technique produced on a 0–8 scale. Those techniques can then be arranged in increasing order of difficulty thereby forming the basis for the forthcoming treatment.

Some of the common techniques which we use in our clinic are as follows:

1. Head shaking—this is done by having the patient sit in a chair and shake their head from side to side with eyes open at a moderate rate of speed. The sensations generally produced include dizziness, blurred vision and unsteadiness.
2. Head lifting—this is done by having the patient place their head between their knees for a period of up to 30 seconds and then reasonably quickly sit up straight. The sensations produced are similar to the above technique although there are some subtle differences.
3. Running on the spot—the patient is asked to run in place moving both arms and legs reasonably vigorously. Both the duration and the vigor of the exercise can be gradually increased throughout treatment. This technique results in the usual symptoms of any aerobic exercise including breathlessness, hot flashes, pounding heart, sweating and even dizziness.
4. Breath holding—the patient is instructed to hold their breath for as long as possible. This technique results in sensations of chest tightness and suffocating/breathlessness.
5. Spinning on the spot—the patient is asked to stand in the center of a room and spin at a moderate rate. If a rotating chair is available, this is also a good way to conduct this exercise. The sensations produced include dizziness, blurred vision, and nausea.

6. Body tensing—The patient is instructed to lie, face down, on the floor and raise themselves into a push-up position so that only their toes and palms are touching the floor, then hold. This exercise is useful for a small subgroup of patients who are frightened of muscle tension.
7. Voluntary hyperventilation—The patient is instructed to breathe faster and deeper as if inflating a balloon. The initial period is generally up to 90 seconds but with practice, periods of 5 to 7 minutes are often reached. Generally, doubling the rate and depth of the patient's normal breathing results in strong sensations. These sensations include blurred vision, dizziness, breathlessness, hot flashes, and palpitations.

It is often a good idea for the therapist to demonstrate each of the above techniques before they are conducted. This insures that they are done correctly the first time and the maximum anxiety-inducing effect is experienced. Each should be done at first for a minimum amount of time, say 30 to 90 seconds, in order to produce the original hierarchy. Thereafter, both during treatment sessions and during homework exercises, the duration and intensity of the techniques can be gradually increased.

In addition to the techniques for producing somatic sensations described above, many common activities can result in strong symptoms and are likely to be avoided by panic disorder 'without' avoidance patients. Thus these activities can be included in the hierarchies of these patients. Some activities which are frightening to many patients with panic disorder and which a therapist should inquire about include the following: fast fairground rides, drinking a strong cup of coffee, hot saunas or showers, exercise classes or aerobic sports, and frightening movies.

COMBINING TECHNIQUES

The three techniques described independently in the preceding sections (breathing retraining, cognitive modification and interoceptive exposure) each have theoretical and empirical support for their putative value in the treatment of panic disorder. At present there have been no studies comparing these techniques in the alleviation of panic attacks and there is no empirical evidence examining which are necessary inclusions in treatment. Thus, the present state of the art would suggest that clinicians searching to maximize improvement should combine these three components into a single treatment package.

At our clinic we currently begin with information and cognitive restructuring, proceed to teaching of breathing control and finally introduce interoceptive exposure exercises. At many points the three components complement each other. For example, while teaching information about panic attacks, hyperventilation can be presented as one way in which symptoms are produced, thus setting the stage for teaching breathing retraining. Similarly, when breathing retraining is taught, cognitive restructuring can be reinforced as a technique to use at those times when patients are unable to control their symptoms with slowed breathing. The interoceptive exposure exercises, in addition to their direct value, can provide a setting for practice of the other techniques.

By combining these treatment components, an effective package for the reduction of panic attacks can be produced. As mentioned above, this combined treatment program, suitable for distribution to patients, is now available from our clinic. Research there suggests that such a combined treatment package can result in total elimination of panic attacks in 80 – 100 per cent of individuals. Research over the coming years will focus on such vital issues as long-term maintenance of treatment gains and predictors of response.

CONCLUSION

In this chapter, we have discussed the evidence suggesting that psychological treatments are effective in the alleviation of panic attacks and have reviewed some of the theoretical and empirical evidence highlighting the valuable components of such treatment. While data bearing on the necessary components of psychological treatment for panic attacks is scarce and inconclusive, there appears to be strong evidence suggesting that psychological treatments are highly effective in the reduction of panic attacks. This evidence provides an exciting alternative to the widely held view that medication is the treatment of choice for panic attacks. In fact, at our clinic we have recently completed a trial comparing our combined psychological treatment package with one of the most widely prescribed drugs, alprazolam (Klosko *et al.*, 1987). At post-treatment, the percentage of patients reporting no panic attacks was 87 per cent in the psychological treatment group and 50 per cent in the alprazolam group. Although psychological treatment was not statistically superior to alprazolam, it was significantly better than a wait list control group. This data suggests that psychological treatments are effective in the alleviation of panic attacks. There is reason to believe that psychological treatment will emerge as even more favorable at long-term follow-up (Barlow, 1988).

REFERENCES

Barlow, D.H. (1986) Behavioral conception and treatment of panic, *Psychopharmacology Bulletin*, **22**, 802–6.

Barlow, D.H. (1988) *Anxiety and its Disorders*, Guilford Press, New York.

Barlow, D.H., Cohen, A.S., Waddell, M.T., Vermilyea, B.B., Klosko, J.S., Blanchard, E.B. and DiNardo, P.A. (1984) Panic and generalized anxiety disorders: nature and treatment, *Behavior Therapy*, **15**, 431–49.

Beck, A.T. (1988) Cognitive approaches to panic disorder: theory and therapy. In S. Rachman and J.D. Maser (eds.), *Panic: Psychological Perspectives*, Lawrence Erlbaum Associates, Hillsdale, New Jersey.

Beck, A.T. and Emery, G. (1985) *Anxiety Disorders and Phobias: A Cognitive Perspective*, Basic Books, New York.

Beck, A.T., Laude, R. and Bohnert, M. (1974) Ideational components of anxiety neurosis, *Archives of General Psychiatry*, **31**, 319–25.

Bonn, J.A., Harrison, J. and Rees, L. (1973) Lactate infusion in the treatment of 'free-floating' anxiety, *Canadian Psychiatric Association Journal*, **18**, 41–5.

Bonn, J.A., Readhead, C.P.A. and Timmons, B.H. (1984) Enhanced adaptive behavioural response in agoraphobic patients pretreated with breathing retraining, *Lancet*, **2**, 665–9.

Butler, G. and Mathews, A. (1983) Cognitive processes in anxiety, *Advances in Behavior, Research and Therapy*, **5**, 51—62.

Clark, D.M. (1986) A cognitive approach to panic, *Behaviour Research and Therapy*, **24**, 461–70.

Clark, D.M., Salkovskis, P.M. and Chalkley, A.J. (1985) Respiratory control as a treatment for panic attacks, *Journal of Behavior Therapy and Experimental Psychiatry*, **16**, 23–30.

Craske, M.G. and Barlow, D.H. (1987) Behavioral treatment of panic: a controlled study, Paper presented at the Association for the Advancement of Behavior Therapy annual meeting. Boston, MA.

Ehlers, A. and Margraf, J. (1989) The psychophysiological model of panic attacks. In P.M.G. Emmelkamp (ed.), *Anxiety Disorders: Annual Series of European Research in Behaviour Therapy*, Vol. 4, Swets, Amsterdam (in press).

Ehlers, A., Margraf, J., Roth, W.T., Taylor, C.B. and Birbaumer, N. (1988) Anxiety induced by false heart rate feedback in patients with panic disorder, *Behaviour Research and Therapy*, **26**, 1–12.

Garssen, B., van Veenendaal, W. and Bloemink, R. (1983) Agoraphobia and the hyperventilation syndrome, *Behaviour Research and Therapy*, **21**, 643–9.

Gitlin, B., Martin, J., Shear, M.K., Frances, A., Ball, G. and Josephson, S. (1985) Behavior therapy for panic disorder, *Journal of Nervous and Mental Disease*, **173**, 742–3.

Goldstein, A.J. (1978) Case conference: the treatment of a case of agoraphobia by a multifaceted treatment program, *Journal of Behavior Therapy and Experimental Psychiatry*, **9**, 45–51.

Gorman, J.M., Cohen, B.S., Liebowitz, M.R., Fyer, A.J., Ross, D., Davies, S.O. and Klein, D.F. (1986) Blood gas changes and hypophosphatemia in lactate induced panic, *Archives of General Psychiatry*, **43**, 1067–71.

Griez, E. and van den Hout, M.A. (1983) Treatment of phobophobia by exposure to CO_2 induced anxiety symptoms, *Journal of Nervous and Mental Disease*, **171**, 506–8.

Griez, E. and van den Hout, M.A. (1986) CO_2 inhalation in the treatment of panic attacks, *Behaviour Research and Therapy*, **24**, 145–50.

Hibbert, G.A. (1984) Ideational components of anxiety: their origin and content, *British Journal of Psychiatry*, **144**, 618–24.

Klein, D.F. (1964) Delineation of two drug responsive anxiety syndromes, *Psychopharmacologia*, **5**, 397–408.

Klosko, J.S., Barlow, D.H., Tassinari, R.B. and Cerny, J.A. (1987) Comparison of alprazolam and cognitive behavior therapy in the treatment of panic disorder: A preliminary report, Paper presented at the annual convention of the Association for the Advancement of Behavior Therapy. Boston, MA.

Ley, R. (1985) Blood, breath and fears: a hyperventilation theory of panic attacks and agoraphobia, *Clinical Psychology Review*, **5**, 271–85.

Lum, L.C. (1976) The syndrome of habitual chronic hyperventilation. In O.W. Hill (ed.), *Modern Trends in Psychosomatic Medicine*, Vol. 3, Butterworths, London.

Ost, L.G. (1988) Applied relaxation vs. progressive relaxation in the treatment of panic disorder, *Behaviour Research and Therapy*, **26**, 13–22.

Rapee, R. (1985a) A case of panic disorder treated with breathing retraining, *Journal of Behavior Therapy and Experimental Psychiatry*, **16**, 63–5.

Rapee, R. (1985b) Distinctions between panic disorder and generalized anxiety disorder: Clinical presentation, *Australian and New Zealand Journal of Psychiatry*, **19**, 227–32.

Rapee, R. (1986) Differential response to hyperventilation in panic disorder and generalized anxiety disorder, *Journal of Abnormal Psychology*, **95**, 24–8.

Rapee, R. (1987) The psychological treatment of panic attacks: theoretical conceptualization and review of evidence, *Clinical Psychology Review*, **7**, 427–38.

Rapee, R.M. and Barlow, D.H. (in press) The psychological treatment of panic attacks and agoraphobic avoidance. In J.R. Walker, G.R. Norton and C. Ross (eds), *Panic Disorder Agoraphobia: A Guide for the Practitioner*, Dorsey Press, Chicago.

Rapee, R., Mattick, R. and Murrell, E. (1986) Cognitive mediation in the affective component of spontaneous panic attacks, *Journal of Behavior Therapy and Experimental Psychiatry*, **17**, 245–53.

Salkovskis, P.M., Jones, D.R.O. and Clark, D.M. (1986) Respiratory control in the treatment of panic attacks: replication and extension with concurrent measurement of behavior and pCO_2, *British Journal of Psychiatry*, **148**, 526–32.

Sanderson, W.C., Rapee, R.M. and Barlow, D.H. (1987) Differences in panic symptoms experienced by the DSM-III-Revised anxiety disorder categories, Presented at the 21st annual AABT convention, Boston, MA.

Sanderson, W.C., Rapee, R.M. and Barlow, D.H. (1989) The influence of perceived control on panic attacks induced via inhalation of 5.5% CO_2 enriched air. *Archives of General Psychiatry* (in press).

van den Hout, M. and Griez, E. (1983) Some remarks on the nosology of anxiety states and panic disorders, *Acta Psychiatrica Belgica*, **83**, 33–42.

Wolpe, J. (1958) *Psychotherapy by Reciprocal Inhibition*, Stanford University Press, Stanford.

Chapter 12

Cognitive Therapy of Panic Disorder

ROBERT C. DURHAM

INTRODUCTION

In this chapter I argue the case for treating cases of panic disorder within the general therapeutic framework developed by Beck and his colleagues. My primary focus will be on therapeutic work with complex or chronic conditions in which panic disorder occurs against a background of general anxiety. In view of the wide range of therapeutic approaches that can be taken with this problem, let me begin on an autobiographical note by describing my own interest in cognitive therapy. My initial training was in behaviour therapy which appealed to my practical nature but seemed of limited scope as an approach to the anxieties and depressions that were so common in the clinic. The dynamic psychotherapies, to which I was introduced during a period of study in North America, seemed to me more plausible that the behavioural model as an explanation of psychopathology but less so as a method of treatment. On returning to work as a clinical psychologist, without a clear therapeutic orientation, I also found it hard to accommodate the two very contrasting worlds of the research literature and the often chaotic mixture of pressure, time constraints, and human distress that comprises everyday clinical experience. The initial attraction of Beck's writing on emotional disorder (Beck, 1976) was the promise it held of lessening this gulf between theory and practice, on the one hand, and behavioural and insight-oriented psychotherapies, on the other. Subsequent experience with applying cognitive therapy to depression (Beck *et al.*, 1979) and anxiety (Beck and Emery, 1985) has resulted in a growing conviction that this is a system of psychotherapy that is grounded in the clinical realities of daily practice, that has a considerable breadth of application, that makes sense at a personal and professional level, and that can be readily articulated with the research base of academic psychology.

Panic Disorder: Theory, Research and Therapy. Edited by Roger Baker

The chapter is divided into four sections. The introductory section begins with a broad outline of the theoretical framework in which anxiety and panic are viewed by Beck. This is followed by two case studies illustrating some of the ways in which the specific treatment of panic attacks may need to be combined with therapy for more general problems of personal adjustment. The next section analyses some of the key issues that commonly arise in the psychological treatment of panic disorder so as to delineate the characteristics required of a comprehensive therapeutic approach to this problem. Cognitive therapy is then described in terms of general therapeutic principles as well as specific steps for treating panic disorder. The final section considers some of the limitations of individual therapy. It is suggested that marked individual differences in the needs and abilities of patients presenting with panic disorder require a flexible use of self-help, individual therapy, and long-term group support.

Cognitive model of panic disorder

A detailed grasp of the myriad complexities of cognitive theory is not a realistic proposition for the average clinician. Theoretical perspectives are in a continuous state of evolution and at their deepest level touch upon some of the most profoundly perplexing issues in human psychology. What is important rather is a working knowledge of the basic model, a broad framework for understanding and decision-making during therapy.

The deceptively simple starting point is the notion that emotional distress is very largely a result of people's interpretation of events rather than of the events themselves. In contrast to the realistic appraisal of threat shown by most individuals on most occasions, the generally anxious person is prone to overestimate the probability and severity of danger in a situation, and to underestimate both his own and other people's ability to cope. This acute sensitivity to threat, and the symptoms of autonomic arousal that result, are thought to come about when events in people's lives impinge on underlying vulnerabilities in their characteristic ways of construing themselves and the world about them. Thus, general beliefs, expectations, and assumptions interact with specific triggering events to give rise to an anxious style of thinking in which exaggerated perceptions of personal danger predominate. Anxiety states are then maintained by characteristic patterns of reciprocal interaction between the biological symptoms of anxiety, the perceptual processes which focus on these symptoms and other signs of threat, and the cognitive appraisal of these events as dangerous. A detailed account of this formulation can be found in Beck and Emery (1985).

The cognitive formulation of panic disorder can be stated in the following series of propositions:

1. The initial episode of panic is precipitated in vulnerable individuals by either psycho-social or physical stresses of an acute or chronic kind. The vulnerabilities on which life stresses impinge may be of a cognitive nature in terms of dysfunctional beliefs, a biological nature such as a labile autonomic nervous system, or some combination of the two.
2. The essential vulnerability in people who are prone to panic attacks is an extreme sensitivity to internal sensations that do not appear to be normal.
3. When a pathological explanation for these abnormal sensations seems very plausible (for example, as a sign of impending death, insanity, or loss of control), and when a non-pathological explanation is unavailable, the focus of attention of such patients becomes fixated on these internal sensations.
4. This fixation of attention then enhances the patient's sense of imminent danger resulting in an increased activation of the autonomic nervous system.
5. A vicious cycle then develops between the patient's catastrophic interpretations and the consequent intensification of anxiety-related symptoms.
6. This increasing spiral of anxiety symptoms and extreme fear interferes with task-related activity, further increasing a sense of loss of control. At this point the crucial factor in the onset of a full-blown panic attack is the patient's loss of any capacity to appraise his experience realistically. A period of cognitive disorientation ensues in which higher level reflective processes become dissociated from lower level automatic processes. The patient is then in the grip of an automatic chain reaction in which he experiences intense symptoms of autonomic arousal coupled with extreme fear that vital signs of biological or psychological well-being indicate a real danger of collapse.
7. The degree to which the patient then experiences subsequent panic attacks will depend on an interaction between a number of different factors. These will include the degree to which he avoids situations believed to be responsible for triggering off attacks, the reaction of significant others, the level of general tension experienced from day to day, and his ability to develop adaptive coping strategies for reducing levels of arousal and appraising internal sensations in a more realistic manner.

Again, a much more detailed exposition of this model can be found in Beck and Emery (1985) and more recently in Beck (1987). Clearly there are a number of unanswered questions in this type of explanation and these are explored at some length in other chapters of this volume. Rachman (1986) gives a useful overview of the strengths and weaknesses of Beck's model.

Illustrative case studies

The following two cases are offered as examples of how the successful treatment of panic disorder may need to address general problems of personal adjustment as well as the presenting complaint. It is not clear whether these two cases are typical of the general population of people with panic disorder. Indeed, this would be a worthwhile area of investigation in its own right. They have been selected from recent referrals in order to illustrate a general point.

Susan X

Susan was a thirty-one-year-old married woman referred for cognitive therapy shortly after the birth of her first child. The presenting problem was frequent panic attacks against a background of fluctuating levels of mild to moderate general tension and a variety of physical symptoms such as headaches and dizziness. These symptoms had become progressively worse over a three-year period after she had left home to get married. She had also suffered from several episodes of depression in her early twenties which had been treated initially by anti-depressants and latterly by a year of dynamic psychotherapy. Initial assessment revealed that Susan had a very close, over-involved relationship with her mother and had had considerable difficulty in separating from her in order to get married. She presented as a pleasant woman of above average intelligence with a general awareness of various methods of coping with anxiety and some insight into the origins of her difficulties. She had worked as a laboratory technician since leaving college but had given up this job to have her baby. The prospect of motherhood filled her with considerable anxiety but also a good deal of pleasure and it was clear that the baby had been planned in the security of a committed marital relationship.

Treatment consisted of fifteen 45-minute sessions over a period of six months, and a further six sessions extended over the following year. It was apparent early on in therapy that 'standard' approaches to helping Susan overcome her frequent panic attacks were consistently undermined by pervasive dysfunctional attitudes to coping with problems in general. Two themes were identified as being critical in this respect. One was a low tolerance for all forms of physical and psychological discomfort which she attributed to her parents' overprotective attitude and their tendency to 'put things off or give up when confronted with difficulties'. The other related theme was a tendency to be constantly overdemanding and critical of herself. These themes had emerged from a variety of automatic thoughts that had been elicited during attempts to implement cognitive and behavioural approaches to anxiety management. Examples of such thoughts were: 'I can only push myself if I'm really forced to'; 'I shouldn't have to be doing this'; 'Once I'm better I'll always have to be better and won't have any excuses'; 'If I'm not feeling absolutely fit then I must be ill and I won't be able to cope'; 'If I manage to do this well then something else is bound to go badly'. One of the unpleasant consequences of these thoughts for Susan was an absence of any contrast in her life between work and relaxation. She constantly wanted to relax and let go but attempts to do this always triggered off strong feelings of guilt and the thought that she was avoiding doing things that she should be doing.

Once the influence of these attitudes had become apparent to both of us, progress in treatment was steady and undramatic. A specific focus on the panic attacks was combined with general cognitive therapy methods for modifying dysfunctional attitudes. Susan showed an increasing acceptance of stress as an inevitable part of living and her panic attacks became increasingly less frequent and severe as she allowed herself to experiment with methods of controlling anxiety without the burden of believing that she always had to succeed. By the end of therapy she was still experiencing occasional episodes of excessive tension but had not experienced any panic attacks for six months.

Mrs M

This case concerns a forty-year-old woman who was referred to the psychiatric clinic by her general practitioner following an unsuccessful attempt to treat her frequent panic attacks with a minor tranquilliser. Initial psychiatric assessment revealed no obvious precipitants for the onset of her panic attacks three years previously. Although Mrs M complained of tension, difficulties in getting off to sleep and periods of low mood, she denied any particular worries or stresses and described herself as always having been a rather easygoing person until the panic attacks started. She lived with her husband and sixteen-year-old daughter, her two sons having left home some four years before. She had married a man twelve years older than herself shortly after leaving school. He had worked all his life as a building labourer but was currently unemployed and the modest family income was provided by Mrs M's part-time job in a local supermarket. She described herself as having several close friends and a fairly active social life. However, she regretted having only infrequent contact with her mother and two brothers who lived some distance away. She had had no previous contact with the psychiatric services and there was no family history of psychiatric illness.

Mrs M was very reluctant to take further medication and it was decided to treat her with relaxation training on a largely self-help basis. She made little progress with this approach over a three-month period and was then referred for cognitive therapy. When first seen she was experiencing an average of two to three panic attacks a week. She presented as a very tense individual who was having a considerable struggle to keep up an appearance of normality in the face of unpredictable attacks of panic that she described as absolutely terrifying. She was obviously uncomfortable with any attempt to explore personal issues as if fearing that this might fatally undermine her self-control during the session. However, she did comment that her panic attacks had started not long after her two sons had left home, and wondered if she had too much time on her hands. Little progress was apparent over the first three sessions. Her anxiety level was too high to permit much concentrated work on treatment issues and she complained that the intensity of the panic attacks was getting worse. This apparent impasse then changed quite abruptly in the middle of the fourth session. In response to a general enquiry about her husband's understanding of her panic attacks she paused for a long time, then wept openly and disclosed intense feelings of unhappiness with her marriage over many years. From this point on the quality of therapy was quite different. She began to talk about herself more openly and accepted that the departure of her two sons from the family home had brought into much sharper focus a longstanding conflict about whether or not to leave her husband. Subsequent sessions were spent as much on helping her to resolve this conflict as on helping her to cope with the panic attacks. She was seen on a regular basis over a period of five months. Her anxiety level fluctuated considerably but the overall pattern was one of steady improvement. At a one-year follow-up she was living apart from her husband and had been free of panic attacks for about six months.

KEY CLINICAL ISSUES

Relationship of panic disorder to stress and general anxiety

Although impressive advances in therapeutic technology have been made by focusing on specific disorders such as panic, the broad diagnostic subdivisions of neurotic disorder may be of limited clinical relevance over the long term. Researchers in psychiatry such as Peter Tyrer have proposed that many cases of neurosis are best classified as a single disorder—the general neurotic syndrome—which runs a prolonged course with variations in the predominance of different patterns of symptoms over time (Tyrer, 1984; Tyrer *et al.*, 1987). Certainly the temporal reliability of neurotic disorder is fairly low and for a number of purposes neurotic patients can be treated as a relatively homogeneous group. Phobic and depressive patients, for example, may differ from anxious ones in having specific symptoms together with those of anxiety rather than in having qualitatively distinct disorders (Prusoff and Klerman, 1974). Similarly, although chronic levels of tension are by no means necessary conditions for the occurrence of panic attacks (Stampler, 1982), many such patients do also suffer from general anxiety and depression and present with problems of excessive dependence on alcohol and tranquillizers. R. Hallam's point in Chapter 6 that 'the investigation of a few separate anxiety disorders does not do justice to the complexity of anxiety complaints' is well taken.

The mechanisms underlying the relationship between general stress and anxiety and episodes of panic are no doubt variable and complex. Life stresses presumably interact with personal vulnerabilities of a cognitive and biological kind so as to increase resting levels of autonomic activity. Considerable degrees of fluctuation in autonomic arousal in intensity, duration, and frequency of symptoms would appear to be typical of many generally anxious people, and it makes intuitive sense to suppose that higher levels of general stress may increase the probability of these fluctuations passing a chemical threshold which then triggers an intense autonomic discharge. This fluctuating pattern of arousal, with periodic panic attacks, can be clearly seen in the anxiety diary kept by Mrs M. Figure 12.1 charts her average anxiety level and frequency of panic attacks during the main period of therapy. Following the intense catharsis of the fourth session she decided to leave her husband and experienced a sudden and dramatic drop in anxiety level over the next two weeks. She then had a change of mind after talking with him about the problems and decided that she could not leave him after all. Her anxiety level and frequency of panic rose again until she decided on a period of separation and went to live with a friend. This again resulted in a marked decline in anxiety level. Over the following two months her progress continued to fluctuate but the overall pattern was of steady improvement. (At a more molecular level M. Zane illustrates in Chapter 8, with the case of Tess, how fluctuation also occurs *within* a session.)

It is not of course just antecedent factors that a comprehensive treatment programme needs to address. The intensely frightening nature of panic attacks typically gives rise to a good deal of nervous apprehension about when another attack will strike. How disruptive will it be this time? Will

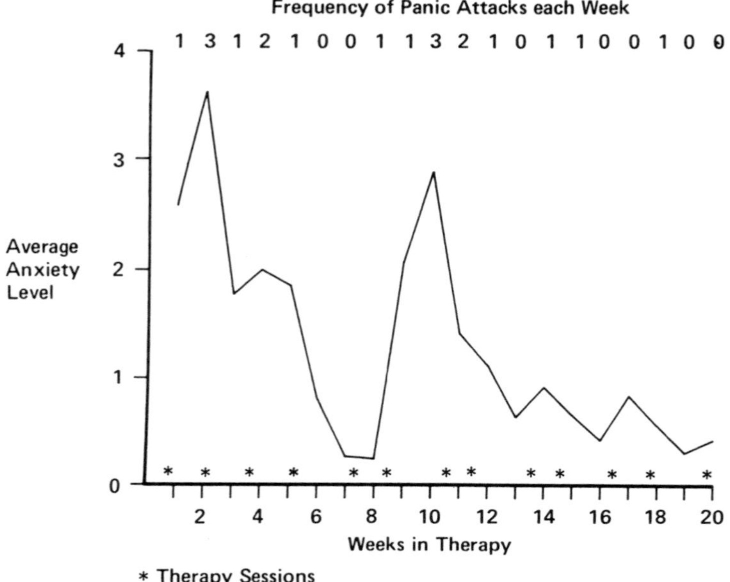

Figure 12.1 Anxiety level and number of panics during treatment of Mrs M.

this one be really bad? Again, it is not hard to see how such apprehension may increase the likelihood of further panic attacks by lowering an individual's ability to tolerate discomfort and by increasing general resting levels of anxiety. The adverse consequences of maladaptive ways of coping with the problem may have a ripple effect on many areas of family, work and social functioning. While symptomatic treatment that focuses solely on coping with panic attacks may also create a positive ripple effect that reverses these negative consequences, this is by no means always the case. Stable improvement will often require a broadly-based approach to therapy.

Identification of panic triggers

Beck (1987) has pointed out that only a small subset of those internal sensations that precede panic attacks are identifiable as typical symptoms of anxiety. A systematic study of specific triggers of catastrophic ideas by Ottaviani and Beck (1987) revealed a wide range of sensations including euphoria or excitement, fullness in the abdomen, sudden slowing of breathing, acute anger, feeling faint, and pains in the chest. It was also noted that there tended to be logical relationships between precipitating events and the specific triggering sensations for catastrophic ideas. For example, a person may run up a flight of stairs, experience very rapid heart beat, and interpret this as a sign of having a fatal heart attack. Thus, although certain patterns recur in a predictable manner, it is important to remember that patients may attach highly idiosyncratic meanings to their internal experiences. These meanings may also be relatively inaccessible in patients whose conceptualization of panic is dominated by global impressions of a spontaneous discharge of highly unpleasant emotion. The therapeutic task in such cases is by no means easy.

Role of medical treatment and investigation

The distressing and intense nature of panic symptoms naturally gives rise to the idea in some patients that they are suffering from a serious medical disorder. In a minority of cases this conviction can turn out to be well founded (McCue and McCue, 1984). Indeed, medical interest in panic disorder is underlined by the historical labels given to various manifestations of this condition over the years (e.g. irritable heart syndrome, effort syndrome, and cardiac neurosis). It is also clear that medication can be extremely effective in dampening down peripheral symptoms of autonomic arousal and thereby reducing the experience of tension and anxiety. However, if there are some important benefits of medical investigation and treatment there may also be adverse effects that can undermine psychological approaches to therapy. First, medical investigations may reinforce the idea that the essential cause of panic disorder is a biological malfunction when this is in fact not the case. Negative test results may not be believed. The tests may be thought insufficient or inadequate in some way. Negative findings may be communicated ambiguously or only indirectly. Psychological explanations may seem implausible and hard to understand.

Second, dependency on medication may undermine motivation to learn psychological methods of coping. Taking a pill is usually both swifter in its effects and less demanding than active attempts to cope. Prescribed medication fits in much better with the approach to health care adopted by Western societies that tends to discourage people from taking personal responsibility for their health. The psychological treatment of panic disorder will need to take account of these clinical realities. Effective therapists will require a framework that emphasizes the importance of socializing the patient into a psychological model and developing an active, collaborative therapeutic relationship that encourages persistence in the face of difficulties.

OVERVIEW OF TREATMENT

General principles of cognitive therapy

Cognitive therapy involves a variety of procedures for repeatedly exploring the connection between thinking and feeling. The central core of the enterprise consists of the elicitation of automatic thoughts, the identification of dysfunctional assumptions, the collaborative design of behavioural experiments, and the difficult art of Socratic questioning. Technical skill in these areas must, however, be combined with mastery of other much more general therapeutic processes. Thus, the tasks of assessment and orientation in the early sessions, the importance of warmth, empathy, and genuineness, the value of an accurate formulation, the development of a collaborative therapeutic relationship, the structuring of individual sessions, the choice of therapeutic techniques, and so on, should all be accorded as much weight by cognitive therapists as developing expertise in specific techniques. Indeed, the cognitive therapy manuals for depression and anxiety disorders (Beck *et al.*, 1979; Beck and Emery, 1985) are as much concerned with general therapeutic processes as with specific methods of treatment. There is no substitute for a detailed study of these manuals in parallel with guided supervision.

The general principles of cognitive therapy can be summarized as follows:

1. Time-limited: the typical duration of therapy is about 16 one-hour sessions.
2. Problem-oriented: the initial focus of therapy is on symptomatic relief and the resolution of specific problems, with increasing emphasis on changing maladaptive underlying assumptions as therapy progresses.
3. Educational: an important aspect of treatment is explicitly educational in character; by means of written handouts, homework assignments, and guided discovery the patient is taught general ways of coping with symptoms and personal problems.
4. Structured: throughout therapy, but particularly in the early stages, the therapist takes an active role in determining the nature and direction of treatment and the format of individual sessions.
5. Based on the cognitive-behavioural model of emotional disorder: the basic principles of this model provide the framework within which the patients' problems and symptoms are investigated.
6. Based on a collaborative patient–therapist relationship: investigation, hypothesis-testing, and decision-making are ideally a collaborative venture. Patient and therapist work together in an open partnership

in which the rationale and goals of treatment are explicit and in which hidden agendas are avoided.

Specific treatment of panic disorder

The main goal of treatment is that patients will learn that the sensations that typically trigger off panic attacks are unpleasant but not dangerous. The learning process is partly educational in character occurring at a conscious, symbolic level, and partly reflexive and automatic in character as a consequence of experiential trial and error. In both cases therapy is most successful when patients learn to view their catastrophic beliefs as ideas to be tested out in practice. The process of therapy can be usefully described as a series of steps as outlined below. However, I would find it hard to think of a single patient whose treatment has proceeded in the logical steps suggested.

Education/re-orientation

Most patients benefit considerably from a general course of instruction on the nature of anxiety and panic and a detailed review of the particular symptoms experienced during panic attacks as is also noted by Rapee and Barlow, McFadyen, and Weekes in their respective chapters on treatment. Diary keeping and self-help materials can encourage a more objective problem-solving perspective. The key to success in this early process of socialization is to use written material and modes of expresssion that are readily intelligible by the individual concerned. I struggled in vain to find self-help material that Mrs M could read with interest or understanding. Susan X on the other hand, was highly verbal and readily understood the cognitive model at an intellectual level. Her difficulty lay in applying the information to her own experience.

Reappraisal of automatic thoughts and images

The first step here is to explore with the patient the specific automatic thoughts and images that are experienced during the incipient and full-blown attack. This can be a relatively straightforward process as in Mrs M's case. Little prompting was needed to reveal that pains in her chest triggered off catastrophic thoughts that she was about to die of a heart attack. Her imagination was vivid and she almost relived the experience of panicking when asked to describe what was going through her mind at the time. In other cases the elicitation of automatic thoughts can be difficult. Their fleeting nature, sometimes bizarre content, and the tendency to avoid recalling emotionally painful thoughts (the phenomenon of cognitive avoidance), requires the therapist to exercise patience, sensitivity and persistence. The state-dependent nature of recall is also relevant here. Susan X, for example, although generally very tense, found it hard to recall with any immediacy or vividness the actual experience of panic attacks. Repeated questioning and probing of her experience of apparently 'spontaneous' panics was necessary. Thus, dizzy sensations while performing a yoga exercise triggered off the thought that she had a brain tumour, symptoms of a cold triggered off the idea that she was about to collapse. Susan was also more likely to experience panic walking along the street and accompanying her in this situation enabled a more direct assessment of automatic thoughts as they occurred. In general, the accessibility of catastrophic ideas is closely related to the vividness and immediacy of the panic experience.

The next step is to encourage a thorough-going reappraisal of the catastrophic thinking so that alternative non-pathological explanations can be brought to mind. Again, a variety of methods may need to be employed. Socratic questioning, direct instruction, and *in vivo* demonstration can all be important. In Mrs M's case Socratic questioning was of limited value. She simply had no idea of what alternative explanations there might be for her chest pains. Her knowledge of bodily functioning and basic biology was very limited and simple instruction was necessary first to plant the idea that her chest pains might be due to muscle tension in her chest. This explanation only became credible to her when she was then encouraged to test the idea by tensing up the muscles in her chest and observing the unpleasant sensations that resulted. The explanation was only useful therapeutically when she had written it down in her own words on a small index card and developed the habit of looking at it when feeling panicky. Self-talk procedures of this kind are of much greater help in the treatment of panic disorder than are the more elaborate dysfunctional thought records used with anxiety and depressive disorders. This latter method of record-keeping did, however, turn out to be useful with Susan X. She was able to learn not only some specific alternative explanations for her catastrophic ideas (for example, that her dizzy turns at yoga were probably due to adjustments in her blood pressure following changes in posture) but also more general coping strategies that involved identifying her typical thinking errors in a variety of situations.

Training in coping skills

A number of different approaches to the management of tension and anxiety symptoms may be useful either in forestalling imminent panic attacks or in terminating them once they have started. The therapeutic task here is to find a method that is helpful to the individual concerned.

Relaxation methods were of some benefit to Susan X in reducing general tension but were quite ineffective with Mrs M. She found simple breathing techniques to be much more valuable. Her sensitivity to bodily sensations was so great that she tended to perceive relaxation-induced changes as frightening.

In general, I have found distraction methods to be of most value. These involve learning to deliberately and systematically focus attention away from internal sensations and catastrophic thoughts. They can provide a very convincing demonstration of the cognitive model in action. Thus, marked reductions in anxiety level can often be achieved in a few minutes by concentrating attention on describing an object in sufficient detail to capture attention and inhibit anxious preoccupations. (This is also described by M. Zane as part of his contextual approach to therapy.) The best approach is first to model the method used and then to encourage *in vivo* practice in the consulting room. It is important to remember that although describing an object in the room is a simple activity, few people are able to do this in sufficient detail, and for long enough to inhibit anxiety, without a good deal of practice. Some people understand the task better if they are asked to imagine they are describing an object to a blind companion.

Induction of 'mini' panic attacks in the office

This is a central component in the cognitive therapy of panic disorder (Beck, (1988). It involves inducing the patient, in the relative security of the office, first to bring on some of the symptoms experienced in a panic and then to use cognitive or behavioural coping strategies to bring the symptoms under control. In doing so the therapist not only gains valuable information about the patient's cognitive processes during panic but is also able to provide him or her with 'on the spot' coaching in the effective use of coping strategies. Moreover, repeated demonstrations that panic attacks can be 'turned on' as well as 'turned off' provide a very powerful and direct test of the patient's catastrophic assumptions. If successful this can greatly increase the patient's sense of confidence and control, and may make all the difference between a temporary and more enduring improvement. However, getting to this point is seldom straightforward. There are wide individual differences in the triggers for panic attacks and hence in the type of experiences that are relevant to reproducing these triggers. It can also be understandably difficult to persuade some patients to take the risk of deliberately bringing on an experience that is not always easily controlled and may turn out to be highly unpleasant. In other cases the attempt to induce a 'mini' attack results in bodily sensation that, although unpleasant, are too dissimilar to the usual panicky sensations to be credible as the real experience. In short, this aspect of treatment takes trial and error, ingenuity and a willingness to take an active, adventurous approach to therapy.

Probably the best known way of inducing 'mini' panics is to ask the patient to hyperventilate or overbreathe for one or two minutes. This method has been advocated by Clark and Salkovskis (cf. Clark, 1986; Clark *et al.*, 1985) who have produced a detailed treatment manual and conducted a good deal of research in the area. They suggest that overbreathing may be implicated in up to 60 per cent of patients with panic disorder. The interested reader is strongly encouraged to read their work before using the approach. It is important to note here that medical contraindications for overbreathing include pregnancy and hypertension. My own experience with this method has been mixed. Some patients such as Mrs M are extremely susceptible to unpleasant sensations following even short periods of overbreathing, and can readily appreciate the similarity of these symptoms to those experienced during panic. Other patients, such as Susan X, either fail to experience unpleasant sensations or find the sensations that are produced to be a very implausible basis for understanding panic attacks. Alternative methods can then be explored. These include vigorous exercise, vivid imagery, and deliberately focusing on bodily sensations or anxious thoughts. It may also be necessary to leave the office if panic attacks are more likely to come on in certain situations, for example, when shopping or driving a car.

Graded exposure

Once the patient's beliefs and assumptions about panic attacks (their uncontrollability, catastrophic implications and so forth) have been tested, challenged and reappraised in the office, he or she can be encouraged to fully experience panics as they naturally occur but *without* using coping skills to control the attack. The rationale here is that such an experience will be a powerful demonstration that the panic attacks are not dangerous, just very unpleasant. In actual practice, or at least in my experience, relatively few patients manage to complete this stage exactly as described. If the previous stages have been successful the patient has acquired a new cognitive framework for interpreting symptoms that has begun to have the same reflexive, automatic quality as their initial catastrophic interpretation and this tends to prevent panic symptoms from developing into a full-blown attack. Moreover, the apparently paradoxical instruction to fully experience an attack often prevents it from occurring. Of course, when panic attacks are more probable in some situations than in others it is most important to encourage exposure in a planned manner.

THE LIMITATIONS OF STANDARD TREATMENT

Cognitive therapy has been developed largely in terms of individual treatment of about sixteen sessions. In my experience, however, with a routine and unselected series of such patients referred to a psychiatric outpatient clinic, a significant minority do not respond to this standard format. Therapy most often fails with people who have some combination of longstanding personality problems, chronically high levels of anxiety, social disadvantage and chronic medical conditions. It is not surprising, of course, that such factors interfere with the progress of treatment. The demands of cognitive therapy (for example, to focus attention repeatedly on one's thinking processes) are inevitably undermined by competing concerns that have a persistently distressing or disruptive influence on everyday functioning. In this final section of the chapter I suggest some modifications to standard practice that might better meet the needs of this important group of non-responders.

Individual differences in cognitive processing

For many years I paid lip-service to the importance of tailoring therapy to individual differences while blithely handing out standard copies of self-help material to everyone who came to see me. Only gradually did I come to realize that relatively few people were readily able to assimilate the contents of these handouts. A little research then revealed what is probably obvious to first year college students. It was either too simplistic, too complicated, boring to read, or not really relevant. Some people studied the material closely and carried it around with them, others hid it in a drawer. While I would not wish to minimize the degree to which therapists themselves can influence the manner in which self-help material is approached and assimilated, there are clearly individual differences in reading ability and customary modes of processing information that are also of considerable importance. It would be helpful if written material used in all phases of therapy was available at different levels of reading difficulty. Perhaps this same material would be more meaningful for some people if it was available on videotape or audiotape. I suspect that interactive computer systems could be very helpful in assessing progress. Indeed, the imaginative use of modern technology might remove some obstacles to progress that are linked to relatively stable differences in cognitive processing. This might be of particular help to socially disadvantaged patients whose mental health needs are often served very poorly by conventional therapeutic approaches (Lorion and Felner, 1986).

Assessing the acquisition of coping strategies

Another area of individual differences concerns the speed of learning. How many sessions are needed to teach someone to relax or to identify characteristic thinking errors? Are daily sessions over a week better than the same number of sessions spaced over two months? We can be reasonably certain that the answer to these questions will depend on the individual concerned. It is also likely that the criteria we use to assess learning in therapy are too imprecise at present to provide us with clear answers. We can assess the skills acquired by therapists with the use of measures such as the Cognitive Therapy Scale to rate audiotapes of therapy sessions (Shaw, 1983). We can also assess the presumed consequences of successful therapy with a variety of measures of symptomatic state and general level of functioning. Neither approach, however, is concerned with the more direct question of whether or not the patient in therapy has actually learned to challenge catastrophic thinking errors or to abort an incipient panic attack by some method of relaxation. Many measures of cognition have been developed in recent years but most of these focus on the frequency of negative self-statements (Clark, 1988). Of greater value would be measures of the degree to which patients have learnt those cognitively-based skills that are a direct result of being in cognitive therapy rather than any other type of therapy. An example of this might be a measure of individual ability to challenge automatic thoughts that was based on the dysfunctional thought record forms used in therapy.

The development of such measures would enable the therapist to obtain a much clearer idea of the speed of learning during treatment irrespective of current symptomatic state. This in turn would provide a guide for tailoring the frequency and duration of sessions to individual differences in learning and increase the prospects of obtaining a stable improvement in functioning. It might also lessen the influence of the therapist's own cognitive biases whereby successful outcomes in terms of short-term symptomatic improvement are erroneously attributed to specific therapeutic techniques rather than to the operation of more general therapeutic processes (Turk and Salovey, 1985).

A filter model of service delivery

The above considerations suggest the need to develop an approach to the delivery of treatment that is more flexible than time-limited individual therapy. Such an approach should attempt to meet the needs of individuals with widely differing capacities for learning and processing information. One possibility is outlined schematically in Figure 12.2 and might best be described as a 'filter' model of service delivery.

The first step would be a comprehensive interview to establish a primary diagnosis of panic disorder and to assess the presence of other complicating factors. The Anxiety Disorders Interview Schedule developed by Barlow and his colleagues (DiNardo *et al.*, 1983) would be an appropriate starting point. Relatively straightforward cases could then be assigned to the simplest level of intervention involving self-help material tailored to the reading ability and preferred mode of assimilating information of the individual concerned. There would be little professional input at this stage apart from orientating the individual to the material. More complex or chronic cases would be assigned to short-term, time-limited treatment groups which would use a 'packaged' structured learning approach. These groups would provide a basic foundation and framework for understanding and overcoming panic and anxiety disorders. There would be little emphasis on group dynamics but mutual support would be strongly encouraged. The next level of intervention would consist of intensive individual therapy as described in this chapter. It would be offered primarily to those patients who were able to make some progress with

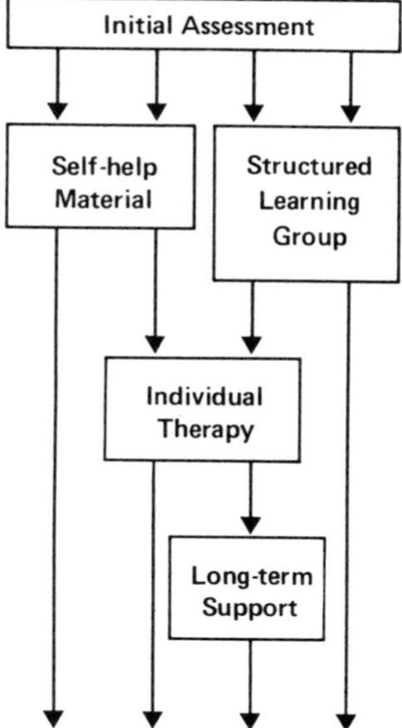

Figure 12.2 Filter model of service delivery.

either of the two initial stages but who required a more intensive learning environment or a more individual approach to specific difficulties. A final level of intervention involving relatively little professional input would consist of long-term support for chronic or severe problems that failed to respond to individual therapy. The emphasis at this stage would be on management and rehabilitation rather than on symptomatic relief and discharge (cf. Miller *et al.*, 1987). Intervention would be likely to involve significant others in the patient's environment and regular but infrequent contact. A minority of such patients might be better treated in a day hospital environment than an outpatient clinic. To summarize then I have suggested that individual treatment over a fixed period of time fails to meet the needs of a significant minority of patients. Rather than attempt to fit these varying needs into a standard format it may be more effective to adopt a flexible approach in which opportunities for individual therapy or long-term support would be made available if briefer interventions along self-help lines proved to be insufficient or inadequate.

CONCLUSION

There is as yet no adequate empirical basis for concluding that cognitive therapy is uniquely efficacious in the treatment of panic disorder. Although studies by Clark *et al.* (1985) and Sokol-Kessler and Beck (1986) are promising in this respect, large-scale outcome studies comparing cognitive therapy with medication and other psychological treatments have yet to be undertaken. There is, however, some evidence that cognitive-behavioural therapy may be effective in the treatment of general anxiety disorders (Butler *et al.*, 1987; Lindsay *et al.*, 1987). A study by Durham and Turvey (1987) compared Beck's cognitive therapy with behaviour therapy in the treatment of generally anxious patients some of whom also suffered from panic disorder. They found no differences between the two treatments at discharge. At six-month follow-up, however, there were significant differences on a number of measures. Cognitive therapy patients tended to show further improvement while behaviour therapy patients tended to revert to their pre-treatment state.

In the absence of adequate empirical evidence the value of cognitive therapy needs to be judged by other criteria. First, how well does it provide a coherent and plausible framework for modifying the various factors that are implicated in the onset and maintenance of the disorder? The clinical evidence I have presented in this chapter suggests that the successful treatment of panic disorder will often require a broadly-based approach that addresses underlying vulnerabilities and sources of stress in addition to the presenting problem. A similar point is made by Stampler (1982) at the end of his general review of panic disorder. It is a particular strength of cognitive therapy that cognitive and behavioural interventions of a very specific nature can be combined with methods of tackling much more general problems of adjustment. Second, is it a form of psychotherapy that enables therapists to address the clinical issues that commonly arise with this disorder? I would argue that it is in this area of engaging patients in therapy, structuring individual sessions and overcoming obstacles to progress that cognitive therapy is likely to be especially valuable.

Finally, it should be noted that cognitive therapy as described by Beck and his colleagues is a complex system of psychotherapy that is not easily acquired. As Rachman (1986) has emphasized, systematic instruction and supervised clinical experience are needed to learn the necessary skills. This may prove to be a limiting factor in the availability of this approach. There is also a great deal of work to be done in developing methods of delivering treatment that are sensitive to the varied abilities and needs of those who suffer from panic attacks.

REFERENCES

Beck, A.T. (1976) *Cognitive Therapy and the Emotional Disorders*, International Universities Press, New York.

Beck, A.T. (1987) Cognitive approaches to panic disorder: theory and therapy. In S. Rachman and J. Maser (eds), *Panic: Psychological Approaches*, Lawrence Erlbaum Associates, Hillside, New Jersey.

Beck, A.T. and Emery, G. (1985). *Anxiety Disorders and Phobias—A Cognitive Perspective*, Basic Books, New York.

Beck, A.T., Rush, A.J., Shaw, B.F. and Emery, G. (1979) *Cognitive Therapy of Depression*, Guilford, New York.

Butler, G., Cullington, A., Hibbert, G., Klimes, I. and Gelder, M. (1987) Anxiety management for persistent generalised anxiety, *British Journal of Psychiatry*, **151**, 535–42.

Clark, D.A. (1986) A cognitive approach to panic, *Behaviour Research and Therapy*, **24**, 461–70.

Clark, D.A. (1988) The validity of measures of cognition, *Cognitive Therapy and Research*, **12**, 1–20.

Clark, D.A., Salkovskis, P.M. and Chalkley, A.J. (1985) Respiratory control as a treatment for panic attacks, *Journal of Behaviour Therapy and Experimental Psychiatry*, **13**, 41–7.

DiNardo, P.A., O'Brien, G.J., Barlow, D.H., Waddell, M.T. and Blanchard, E.B. (1983) Reliability of DSM-III anxiety disorder categories using a new structured interview, *Archives of General Psychiatry*, **40**, 1070–78.

Durham, R.C. and Turvey, A.A. (1987) Cognitive therapy versus behaviour therapy in the treatment of chronic generalised anxiety, *Behaviour Research and Therapy*, **25**, 229–34.

Lindsay, W.R., Gamsu, C.V., McLaughlin, E., Hood, E. and Epsie, C.A. (1987) A controlled trial of treatments for generalised anxiety, *British Journal of Clinical Psychology*, **26**, 3–15.

Lorion, R.P. and Felner, R.D. (1986) Research on mental health interventions with the disadvantaged. In S.L. Garfield and A.E. Bergin (eds), *Handbook of Psychotherapy and Behaviour Change*, Wiley, New York.

McCue, E.C. and McCue, P.A. (1984) Organic and hyperventilatory causes of anxiety-type symptoms, *Behavioural Psychotherapy*, **12**, 308–17.

Miller, E., Morley, S. and Shepherd, G.W. (1987) Editorial: the trouble with treatment, *British Journal of Clinical Psychology*, **26**, 241–2.

Ottaviani, R. and Beck, A.T. (1987) Cognitive aspects of panic disorder, *Journal of Anxiety Disorders*, **1**, 15–28.

Prusoff, B. and Klerman, G.L. (1974) Differentiating depressed from anxious neurotic out-patients, *Archives of General Psychiatry*, **30**, 302–8.

Rachman, S. (1986) Special Review: A.T. Beck and G. Emery, with R.L. Greenberg. Anxiety disorders and phobias—a cognitive perspective, *Behaviour Research and Therapy*, **24**, 95–6.

Shaw, B.F. (1983) Specification of the training and evaluation of cognitive therapists for outcome studies. In J.B.W. Williams and R.L. Spitzer (eds), *Psychotherapy Research: Where are we and where should we go?* Guilford, New York.

Sokol-Kessler, L. and Beck, A.T. (1986) Cognitive therapy of panic disorders, Paper presented at the Annual Meeting of the Phobia Society of America, October, New York.

Stampler, F.M. (1982) Panic disorder: Description, conceptualisation and implications for treatment, *Clinical Psychology Review*, **2**, 469–86.

Turk, D.C. and Salovey, P. (1985) Cognitive structures, cognitive processes, and cognitive-behaviour modification: 11. Judgements and inferences of the clinician, *Cognitive Therapy and Research*, **9**, 19–33.

Tyrer, P. (1984) Classification of anxiety, *British Journal of Psychiatry*, **144**, 78–83.

Tyrer, P., Remington, M. and Alexander, J. (1987) The outcome of neurotic disorders after outpatient and day hospital care. *British Journal of Psychiatry*, **151**, 57–62.

Chapter 13

The Cognitive Invalidation Approach to Panic

MALCOLM MCFADYEN

INTRODUCTION

In seeking to understand and treat a disorder the clinician draws on two sets of related formulations. The first is about the nature of the disorder—what is 'wrong' with the person, and how the condition, state or syndrome has developed. The second is about the nature of the process, or processes, whereby one's therapeutic interventions are considered to have their effect—how does the treatment work?

These formulations are influenced by many factors—one's training, reading, clinical experience and assessment of research evidence. This is an ongoing process. No formulation can be claimed as proven. Aspects can be consistent or not consistent with research results, and when inconsistencies are established one has to modify the model accordingly. Likewise, new 'insights' based on clinical experience generate the need for further research to test validity. At any one time, the clinician operates on the basis of his 'best informed' formulation. This chapter presents a clinician's best informed formulation of panic disorder, and of its treatment by the behavioural technique of prolonged *in vivo* exposure.

It takes as a starting point the evidence of the effectiveness of behavioural exposure techniques (Marks, 1978a) in agoraphobia. Paradoxically, as the evidence for the effectiveness of these techniques grows, there has been increasing dissatisfaction with the conditioning models on which the techniques were based, both the model of the nature of agoraphobia and the model of how prolonged exposure works (Baker and McFadyen, 1985; Hallam, 1978; Marks, 1978b). It is not my purpose here to present a detailed examination of the inadequacies of these models, but the main points of complaint have been that the model of agoraphobia as a conditioned avoidance of public places is not consistent with known clinical features, and that

Panic Disorder: Theory, Research and Therapy. Edited by Roger Baker

while conditioning theory gave the initial impetus for the development of behavioural approaches, it has failed to continue to provide direction to research into, or development of, behavioural techniques.

The most significant change in thinking about the nature of agoraphobia has been a move away from considering it as being essentially like the common phobias such as of snakes or spiders, with the difference being only in the object of fear. There is now evidence that the differences between agoraphobia and the other more common phobias are more important than the apparent similarities. They have different clinical features (Klein, 1981; Snaith, 1968; Hallam, 1978, 1985) and a quite different etiology (Agras *et al.*, 1969, 1972). Hallam (1978) has convincingly argued that agoraphobia has more in common with other anxiety states of the kind usually now referred to as panic disorder.

We are thus left with an effective technique with a less than satisfactory rationale, applied to a disorder about which our thinking is undergoing radical change. It is against this background that many are seeking new formulations. The particular approach described here is one such attempt developed from the standpoint of a practising clinician. It is hoped that the ideas offered hold promise both of an increased theoretical understanding of the panic disorders, and of improving and extending the applicability of behavioural exposure.

A GENERAL MODEL OF ANXIETY

Before describing the formulation of panic disorder, it may be useful to briefly consider how normal anxiety is viewed. It has been pointed out by Epstein (1972) that the conditioning view of anxiety as simply an aversive state analogous to pain is a minority view. Many theorists on anxiety (Spielberger, R.S. Lazarus, Liddel, Goldstein, Rogers, Mandler, Kelly) emphasize the central role of cognition. The model represented schematically in Figure 13.1 is derived from the work of Spielberger (1966, 1972), Lazarus and Averill, (1972), Lazarus and Lannier (1978) and Kelly (1955, 1963). Spielberger and Lazarus present similar positions. The central postulate of both is that anxiety is generated and maintained by a person's 'appraisal' of threat. Both writers include physical and psychological harm (or potential harm) in their concept of threat. Lazarus distinguishes different aspects of appraisal: 'primary' appraisal referring to estimation of potential harm; 'secondary' appraisal referring to estimation of our capability to cope with the threatened harm, and 'reappraisal' based on feedback—this latter characterizing appraisal as a dynamic rather than static process—over time we continue to reassess the danger

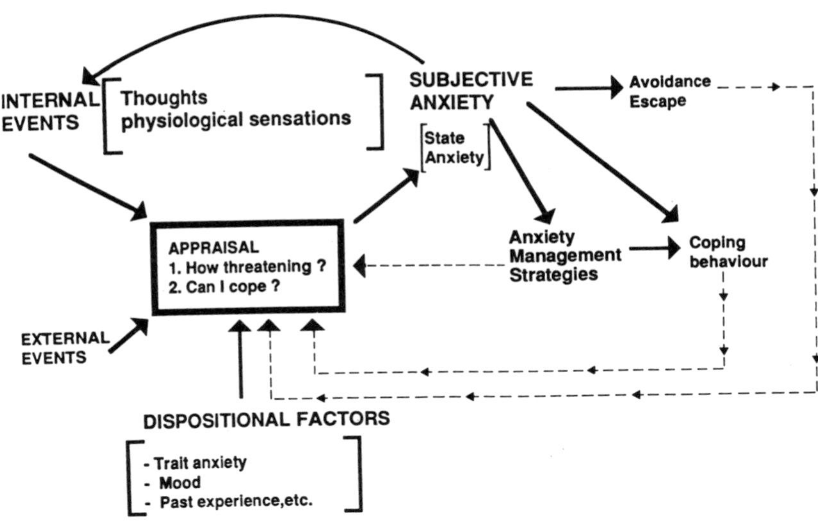

Figure 13.1 Schematic representation of anxiety model. (Dotted lines represent the process of validation/invalidation.)

and our ability to cope. Kelly's concept of validation/invalidation is added to provide the process through which our appraisal is continually modified by experience. Kelly states, 'Validation represents the compatibility (subjectively construed) between one's prediction and the outcome he observes. Invalidation represents incompatibility (subjectively construed) between one's predictions and the outcome he observes' (Kelly, 1963, p. 158).

The model states that threat may arise from external or internal events, or some combination of these—e.g. a job interview (external event); chest pain (internal event); an examination which we fear we will fail (combination of external and internal events). If I appraise the event as threatening and am uncertain of my ability to cope I experience subjective anxiety, which may consist of either, or both, of thoughts (say, fear of possible negative outcome) and of physiological sensations (nausea, tremulousness, etc.). The loop with internal events indicates that these add to the internal events being appraised. At this point I may opt to avoid or escape the situation, or I may opt to attempt to cope with the event, depending on my judgement of likely outcome. I may use anxiety management strategies to help me cope—deep breathing/relaxation, reasoning thoughts. At any of these stages my experience may confirm my appraisal or disconfirm it. Suppose I am in a difficult job interview and am feeling nauseous and tremulous. I think I can probably cope if I keep these under reasonable control through practising relaxation, or reassuring myself that anyway, there will be other, better jobs available. As the interview progresses the physical discomfort reduces and I reappraise the events as less threatening. Alternatively, as the interview progresses I become more uncomfortable, begin to notice my voice is breaking, and fear I will dry up altogether. I reappraise the event as more threatening and decide to escape as soon as possible by giving minimal answers to questions. In the first case my view that I would probably cope was validated, while in the second case it was invalidated.

This model may provide the framework within which we can understand not only normal anxiety, but also agoraphobia and other forms of panic disorder.

THE NATURE AND DEVELOPMENT OF AGORAPHOBIA AND PANIC DISORDER

Although there are differences in the way various panic-related disorders present at the time of request for treatment—agoraphobia, effort syndrome, illness 'phobias', panic disorder—there are considerable similarities in how they begin, and develop (e.g. Stampler, 1982).

Four features/stages can be identified:

1. The disorder typically begins with one or more sudden, unexpected full-blown panic attack.
2. These events are construed as highly dangerous.
3. Following the early spontaneous attacks the person becomes afraid of, and therefore oversensitive to internal physiological sensations.
4. The sufferer develops strategies to avoid, escape or minimize the feared effects of panic attacks.

The first panic attack

Agoraphobia and panic disorder typically begin with a sudden, unexpected, and full-blown panic attack.

These attacks are qualitatively different to high anxiety (Freedman *et al.*, 1985). The body responds as if one had a severe fright, but in the absence of any obvious precipitant. The symptoms consist of varying combinations of palpitations, tachycardia, shortness of breath, dizziness, nausea, tremulousness or weakness of limbs, and sweating. The event is experienced as highly physical and highly aversive.

Although we call it a panic attack, the person does not experience it as an attack of panic, but typically describes it as panicking because of what is happening to him*. In other words, he does not perceive anxiety as the cause of the physiological disturbance. He perceives the physiological discomfort as the cause of his panic.

How panic is construed

It is now becoming more generally appreciated that a panic attack is a self limiting response which does not lead to any psychological or physical harm (see later). However, the person experiencing the panic attack has no immediate understanding of what is happening to him. He construes the initial panic attack, or attacks, as not only uncomfortable but highly dangerous. In various studies of what sufferers think might happen to them (e.g. Burns and Thorpe, 1977; Waring, Chapter 2) some kind of serious physical harm is the most common fear. Others fear that the panic will build to an unbearable level, when they will suffer some kind of mental breakdown or lose control of themselves or run amok. Still others fear some sort of social harm—that they will make a fool of themselves in some way. Frequently fears are mixed—e.g. that the person will lose control of bladder or bowels, and thus suffer social humiliation.

In terms of the model of normal anxiety presented earlier we would suggest that the extreme fear reported in panic attacks is not simply due to the unpleasant nature of the physiological disturbance, but is mainly due to the interpretation of these as physically or psychologically dangerous. In other words, the extreme anxiety is understandable in terms of the person's appraisal of what is happening to him.

There is some evidence of the role of interpretation, or appraisal, in the responses of subjects in the study by Pitts and McLure (1967) who showed that subjects who had an anxiety disorder tended to report a panic attack when infused with sodium lactate, whereas 'normal' subjects did not. Pitts and McLure quote one 'normal' subject as saying 'If I didn't know you were doing this to me, and that you wouldn't let anything bad happen to me, I would be certain I was dying of a heart attack or something terrible'.

The catastrophic appraisals of panic attacks need not be regarded as irrational, or illogical or 'distorted', as suggested, for example, by Beck and his colleagues (1985). We do not know that panic attacks are not harmful through reason or logic, but through experience. It is suggested that such an interpretation is not distorted, but may be a common response to the experience of a panic attack.

*The Masculine will be used throughout as a grammatical convention.

The particular form of catastrophic thinking will vary from sufferer to sufferer. Some may focus on the particular physical symptoms and worry about having a heart attack, a brain tumour or stroke. Such variations are likely to be influenced by differences in past experiences. For example, sufferers with family experience of physical illness may interpret the threat physically, while those with family experience of mental illness may tend to interpret the threat as psychological.

Development of over-sensitivity to autonomic change

Following the early, unexpected, panic attacks the person usually, and perhaps not surprisingly, becomes afraid of sensations related to change in autonomic activity, with a consequent over-awareness, and over-monitoring, of internal physiological sensations. This development has the effect that later panic attacks are frequently self-induced. The person is alert for any sign of threat from within, leading him to be over-aware of normal symptoms of autonomic change which he now perceives as a potential threat—the start of another attack—thus setting off the body's natural fright response. Such a process is implied in the frequently used phrase to describe this stage of development as 'fear of fear'. From a different theoretical perspective this has been described as 'interoceptive conditioning' (Goldstein and Chambless, 1978).

Thus the early, unexpected, panic attacks can often be distinguished from the later ones which are set off through this fear of fear, or fear of having a panic. Perhaps we should restrict the term *panic attack* to the early, unexpected attacks, with a term such as *panic reaction* to describe the later self-generated responses.

The development of strategies to avoid, escape, or minimize the effects of panic attacks

After one or more panic attacks it is not surprising that the person develops various strategies to avoid, escape, or minimize the feared harm. This can mean avoiding certain activities—physical exertion, or avoiding certain situations—shops, public transport, crowds (the agoraphobic triad), or it may mean a more pervasive avoidance of potentially upsetting events.

Where avoidance is not always seen as possible or necessary, many sufferers take steps to have an escape route available. This could be literal in the sense of being near an exit, or metaphorical in having a prepared excuse for leaving a situation.

Finally where avoidance or escape are impossible or impractical, sufferers attempt to minimize the anticipated effect of a panic attack. The person who fears a heart attack may cease activity. The person who fears that he will be unable to sit still, or who fears that others will see him shaking or sweating, may engage in some activity to minimize this risk. A very common strategy is to attempt to distract oneself by engaging in activity.

These strategies will not only involve defining what the danger is, and what must be avoided, escaped or minimized, but will also involve identifying 'safety' factors (Burns and Thorpe, 1977)—conditions which the person thinks will act to reduce the perceived risk, such as being with a friend, taking alcohol, or tranquillizers.

All of these strategies are designed to prevent the outcome which the person fears will result if a panic attack were allowed to occur or to continue unchecked, and they therefore effectively prevent the person from discovering that the harm he fears does not happen.

THE SELF-MAINTAINING NATURE OF PANIC DISORDER

The features of agoraphobia and other panic disorders may be readily understood in terms of the general model of anxiety presented earlier.

Once the person misconstrues the nature and consequences of his panic attacks the other features are natural and normal developments. Over-sensitivity to autonomic symptoms results in the threat being continued beyond the original unanticipated panic attacks, and avoidance/escape/minimizing strategies effectively serve to prevent correction, or invalidation, of the interpretation of panic as dangerous. At this stage the disorder is effectively self-maintaining.

WHAT CAUSES THE FIRST PANIC?

Up to now we have been concerned with the development of panic disorder/agoraphobia after the early 'spontaneous' panic attacks. How are these first attacks accounted for?

It is suggested that there is no need to postulate a physiological (e.g. Klein *et al.*, 1985; Sheehan, 1982) or psychological (Goldstein and Chambless, 1978) abnormality as a necessary condition for these first panic attacks. It has already been suggested that the bodily reactions described by patients can be regarded as fright in the absence of any obvious external threat. It would seem reasonable to consider that there will be variations in the sensitivity of the trigger mechanism of the body's emergency response, and that at times of increased readiness to respond the system will occasionally trigger 'spontaneously'—a kind of false alarm.

Buglass *et al*. (1977) failed to find evidence that sufferers share common life events or life experiences.

When a person is under stress, e.g. conflict at home or work, illness, bereavement, there is considered to be such an increase in the readiness to respond of the body's emergency system—the so-called 'fight or flight' response. Other factors will also cause an increase in readiness to respond—e.g. endocrinological variation such as hypoglycaemia.

A critical factor in determining the person's reaction to such a false alarm would be whether he correctly construes the event. Evidence is lacking on the number of people who have such a reaction and correctly construe it. Misconstruing the event as unnatural and dangerous is certainly strikingly typical of patients, and perhaps of most people who experience this spontaneous triggering of the body's fright reaction.

The initial panic attack may be viewed as a normal, though not usual, stress reaction. There will obviously be many factors which affect a particular person's vulnerability. Some people are typically more threat sensitive than others—Spielberger's Trait Anxiety. However, such factors might better be seen as a predisposition to, rather than a prerequisite of, a panic attack.

DIFFERENCES IN HOW PANIC DISORDER PRESENTS

What determines that panic disorder in one person takes the form of agoraphobia, in another illness fears, and in yet another continuing unpredictable panic attacks? Some of this can simply be attributed to individual differences. Differences in interpretation of the symptoms will lead to differences in how the disorder develops. However, there is also the suggestion of change over time, with agoraphobia-type symptoms being more likely in later stages of development of panic disorder (Klein, 1964). There will, of course, be other changes over time as the person continues to try to make sense of what is happening to him in the light of experience and information. Some people accept the view of their general practitioner, or other medical practitioner, that they are not physically ill, but are suffering from 'anxiety', but then construe themselves to be at risk of psychological harm—'loss of control', 'mental breakdown', etc. For some people this change over time will mean a widening of what is regarded as potentially dangerous, for others it will mean a narrowing to only regarding certain specific conditions as threatening.

IMPLICATIONS FOR EXPOSURE TREATMENT

If the *cause* of the person's anxiety is the harm that he anticipates could result if a panic attack continued unchecked, then any conditions of exposure which invalidate his expectation of harm will help to reduce his anxiety. At the simplest level he might discover through exposure that the panic attack which he expected does not occur. If the therapist has stressed some kind of anxiety management training he may come to believe that he has learned to prevent the panic attack.

The formulation suggests, however, that exposure will be *most* effective when the person puts himself in the feared situation under conditions of perceived risk—in other words when the patient uses exposure to find out what does happen when he panics with no attempts at escape or control. If the person is panicking *because* he fears he will die, then finding that he does not must have a powerful anxiety reducing effect! This process is referred to as cognitive invalidation. The term 'invalidation', from George Kelly's Personal Construct Theory, refers to the process whereby when outcome is perceived to be contrary to what we expect then we tend to alter our expectations.

EXPOSURE AS COGNITIVE INVALIDATION

Exposure can thus be considered as an experiment conducted by the patient in which he can test out his hypothesis that panic is dangerous and will cause him harm if he allows it to continue unchecked. As with any other experiment the experimenter has to have an understandable rationale for undertaking the experiment. Some time is therefore spent providing information about anxiety, explaining how it arises; how the body responds; how it is self-limited, and how it has no serious adverse after-effects. In particular, information would be provided on those sensations which most frighten the patient. For many, explaining their panic attacks as a false alarm fright reaction is sufficient for them to be able to comprehend how this could account for their panic reactions. Others wish to check through particular symptoms to seek reassurance that these are understandable in terms of the body's emergency response.

Of course, by the time they present, many clients are experiencing over-sensitivity to physiological sensations and this also needs to be explained in order that they can make sense of their experiences. Many symptoms are better understood as *over-sensitivity* rather than the fright reaction—for example, the more pervasive feelings of physiological discomfort complained of by many patients.

Having provided this alternative explanation of their experiences, it is often unnecessary to have to propose exposure. Simply asking what the person needs to do to be convinced that they will not come to harm usually leads them to suggest the need for exposure. Further discussion may be needed to help the person tighten the design of his 'experiment'. This aims for an exposure session during which the person commits himself to having a panic attack without attempts at control, avoidance or escape.

At this stage the therapist's role is akin to that of research supervisor, an analogy previously suggested by Kelly (1970). However, it differs in one important respect—the research supervisor is rarely in the position of advising a student on an experiment on himself which the student regards as potentially dangerous. The design of the initial experiment will be less than perfect—it will be limited by the degree of risk the person is prepared to take. This usually results in a starting point for exposure which is not the worst situation the person fears, but is still one which carries significant risk—in effect, a steeply graded exposure programme. At this stage we cannot plan the complete series of experiments which will be necessary. As with any other research programme, later experiments will best be planned to take account of the results of earlier experiments.

Let us assume the person has gone off and completed the first 'experiment'. He has had a panic and has not attempted to escape or minimize its effect. The panic, although acutely uncomfortable, has indeed passed without him having come to whatever harm he feared. Should he now accept the alternative hypothesis—that his panic is a normal, non-harmful, self-limiting response? As with any researcher where the result is not as expected, he is sceptical—maybe the conditions were unusual, and the result atypical—after all one swallow does not make a summer! A number of 'replications' might be expected before the results are considered reliable.

Not only could one expect repetition, but it might be expected that the person will vary conditions, to be satisfied that the results are not limited to only certain circumstances. It might also be expected that the person will increase the level of 'risk'. With each exposure the person's prediction of a harmful outcome is invalidated until the prediction is no longer considered tenable—at which point 'treatment' is complete.

This account shows such exposure to be a more individual programme rather than a fixed 'package'. The patient is in control, and it is his reappraisals after each exposure ('reconstructions' in the language of Kelly's Personal Construct Theory) which guide the programme. Therapy is a joint venture with both the therapist and the patient having clear but different responsibilities. The therapist's responsibility is to help the patient understand what he is doing and why. The patient has final responsibility for the 'experiments' and the conclusions drawn. Some examples will help to illustrate the process.

COGNITIVE INVALIDATION WITH AN AGORAPHOBIC PATIENT

Mrs X was in her early thirties, married 13 years to a tradesman painter, with 3 children between 6 and 12 years. Her symptoms began about five years previously with a sudden attack of 'giddiness', palpitations and shortness of breath while she was waiting for a bus at a stop near her home. She initially interpreted the symptoms as having a physical origin. She had gone to a neighbour's house close to the bus stop—'I thought I would never make it'. Husband was summoned to take her home, where she went to bed. The family doctor was called and after a brief physical examination he pronounced her physically well and told her that her symptoms were 'anxiety'. Further panic attacks occurred over the next two months, one while queueing at the check-out of a supermarket, and one waiting to have her hair done. Over this time, Mrs X increasingly began to avoid situations involving shopping, travelling by public transport and other situations where she felt 'restricted'—restaurants, theatre, church. The latter particularly concerned her as both she and her husband were very much involved in church activities. After the first few panics she had begun to anticipate them and often abandoned planned outings. Further trips to her GP led her to understand that she had agoraphobia and she was prescribed a common benzodiazepine.

By the time of presentation she accepted that she was not physically ill, but feared that she would be overcome by the panic—that she would pass out or make a fool of herself. Life had been adjusted to fit with her disorder—she could go most places if accompanied by her husband, or her 12-year-old daughter, but she avoided completely church, theatre and restaurants. On 'good' days she could do some shopping on her own, as long as she avoided long queues. On 'bad' days she would stay at home. She avoided planning outings, or committing herself to outings in advance. She preferred to wait to see how she felt. Her confidence generally was poor—'I was never a particularly confident person, but not like this'. She used a benzodiazepine drug intermittently to help her cope with necessary outings, particularly on 'bad' days. Her understanding of her disorder was still rather vague, but was mainly construed as the psychological equivalent of having a 'weak heart'—she would be all right as long as she did not allow herself to get 'too upset'.

Over the first two appointments, one week apart, she was given the explanation that her panics could be seen as a kind of false alarm of the body's fright response. How panic attacks could relate to stress, and the subsequent development of over-sensitivity to physiological sensations was also explained.

These accounts 'made sense' to her, and she expressed relief that her symptoms might be understandable as a normal reaction. She was able to provide a number of possible 'causes' for her initial panic attacks—she had been worrying about her mother who had been seriously ill prior to the onset of her symptoms. She had been feeling fed-up being at home for some time, but the last child prevented her return to work. There was some guilt associated with these feelings and she felt unable to talk to anyone about this for fear of being considered a bad mother.

The 'over-sensitivity' made sense of her 'good' and 'bad' days. She was able to talk about how she tried to avoid potential upsets as this tended to result in 'bad' days.

Although she considered that the explanation made sense of her experience, and quickly appreciated how she could only confirm this by allowing herself to panic, she was very unsure as to whether she could take the necessary risks. After some discussion she proposed a trip to a supermarket as a first target, and we set a goal of at least two such trips without the help of drugs before the next appointment in two weeks time.

At the next session she reported having gone on three such trips, with her husband who waited outside in the car. She had briefed him on the nature of her 'experiment'. This had been 'hell'—she panicked almost continuously and had been on the point of leaving two or three times. However, she had waited and the panic did pass, after about 45 minutes, without her passing out or making a fool of herself. She admitted that she had not gone through the check-out until after the panic had subsided. She had felt exhausted but pleased with her first session.

The second trip was 'even better'—she had expected to panic, but it did not happen. The third was 'a disaster'—she had a major panic attack which did not stop until she left the shop. It left her feeling bad for days.

We discussed the interpretations of the 'outcomes' of her 'experiments'. She was asked in what way was the second trip 'better'? How did it affect her confidence that she would not pass out if she did panic in future? She was able to acknowledge that in fact she had really learnt nothing from this trip. She had been so pleased that no panic had occurred, that she re-set her objectives—i.e. she hoped she would not have another panic. This was why the third trip was 'a disaster'. In terms of her first objective to test what happened when she allowed a panic to occur unchecked, the third trip was very informative—she had not passed out—she had not made a fool of herself—and she had gone through the check-out! She had come in looking rather downcast, and left looking much brighter, with a commitment to adding a cinema trip to her two supermarket trips.

At the next session two weeks later, she reported having a panic attack only once in three trips to supermarkets (she went to two different ones). While she was pleased with the times she did not have a panic, she no longer regarded them as opportunities to 'experiment'. The time when she did panic again produced a negative outcome in terms of passing out, etc. She had gone to the cinema with her husband—could not say she enjoyed the film—indeed at times had hardly been able to concentrate because she was so scared by the panic attack she was having. However, again she was pleased. She had not passed out, nor made a fool of herself. Why she chose a cinema rather than theatre was because 'it is darker—no one can see you properly'. She admitted she had gone when it was relatively quiet and had occupied an aisle seat.

Two weeks later she was reporting having been to church. Again she had been very uncomfortable because of a panic attack, but she had not passed out, and had not felt foolish in spite of having considerable attention from people who were interested to see her back after such a time away. She had considered what she would say and was pleased that most people were highly supportive when she told them she was trying to overcome 'agoraphobia'. By this time, supermarkets only rarely produced panic—usually when she was stuck in a queue. She admitted that on one occasion it had taken her by surprise and she had left the shop, but returned after she had 'told' herself she should not miss the chance of another 'experiment'. By this time she had also been into town by bus. Again on one occasion she admitted that she got off when a panic attack came on suddenly. On other occasions she had continued her journey in spite of a panic attack. She spontaneously reported having looked at her reflection in shop windows, and mirrors, during one or two panic attacks and was surprised that 'you couldn't see anything much on the outside'. This boosted her confidence.

Over the next few sessions she continued to set more difficult experiments and some of the early experiments became routine. She could travel on her own by car and bus, and shopping was 'almost enjoyable'. She took the family to a pantomime—back of the stalls but not aisle seats—'I can't remember much of the first half, but I actually enjoyed the second part—once I survived the interval with the lights up I knew I could survive anything'.

She took the occasional tablet—not during exposure 'sessions'—during the early weeks, but voluntarily gave these up after six weeks.

In later sessions she was able to admit that her earliest exposure 'experiments' had been on 'good' days. She quickly realized this reduced their value, and thereafter deliberately went out to the supermarket on 'bad' days. She commented that she could not have begun with exposure on a bad day—it would have been considered 'too risky'.

We also discussed her loss of confidence more in later sessions using a non-directive counselling format. She was soon able to assert that she coped well with 'real' problems—listing family illness, all the usual crises of bringing up a family, etc. She decided she no longer needed to 'protect' herself. While she did not like being upset, she became able to accept that it was normal to have 'bad days', and no longer feared them. Indeed, the less afraid she was of them the less she experienced them, and her periods of upset or feeling 'down' passed more quickly. She was also later able to acknowledge that a desire to return to work at some stage did not make her a 'bad mother'.

Mrs X attended for 10 appointments, the first two at weekly intervals, then six at fortnightly intervals, one after a month and one after 3 months. At the final appointment she reported occasionally feeling 'as if' a panic attack was going to occur, but it did not develop. She had had one 'unexpected' attack during the meal at a dinner-dance.

> I almost ran, but I remembered you had warned that it could happen. The meal was hardly enjoyable, and afterwards I had all the old feelings—I was sure I was not going to make it across the room—my legs felt like jelly. However, I forced myself, and as usual I made it. It stopped quickly after that, and I really enjoyed the dance. I expect it will happen again sometime, but I think I'll be ready for it.

By this time she did not avoid situations, and was enjoying going into town shopping. She still had days when things went badly and she was upset or 'fed-up' but these were accepted as normal.

COGNITIVE INVALIDATION EXPOSURE WITH OTHER PANIC DISORDERS

Traditionally exposure has been seen as a treatment for agoraphobic disorders, with some form of habituation/extinction considered to be the process through which it worked (Marks, 1978b; Mathews *et al.*, 1981). This is continued in the panic disorder literature where there is often the suggestion that some form of combined treatment is necessary—drugs for the panic attacks and behavioural exposure for the phobic avoidance (Klein, 1981).

If exposure is operating through invalidation of fear of harm, then it is readily extended to other forms of panic disorder. The simplest extension is where the condition for panic occurring is *doing something* rather than *being somewhere*. Here the person would be encouraged to engage in the avoided behaviour, e.g. physical exertion in the case of so-called 'effort syndrome'.

A common variant of avoidance—either of places or activities—is an escape strategy. Here the person continues with life more normally, but is prepared to leave the situation or cease the activity at a particular level of perceived threat. For some, this will be onset of a panic attack. For others it will be at some level of discomfort which the person interprets as indicating likelihood of a panic attack. For these people, the necessary condition for invalidation is to be in the situation or engage in the activity without the usual escape.

What about the apparently more difficult situation, where the person reports his panics as entirely unpredictable, either in terms of place or behaviour? Here we can make use of two aspects of panic disorder.

One is the oversensitivity to normal fluctuations in autonomic activity. In the developed panic disorder the person is frequently hyper-alert to internal sensations as he construes these as potential signals of imminent panic. The person often reacts with the very panic response which he fears.

A colleague of the author had used a patient's particular sensitivity to sensations of dizziness to allow panics to be induced by spinning round. Another colleague (Dr Peter Slade—personal account) provided an account of using fairground rides, which produce quite normal and noticeable sensations, to induce panic attacks.

Alternatively one can use the fact that in the developed panic disorder the person usually develops some strategy for minimizing the construed threat of harm. Thus one person may stop whatever he is doing and sit down. Another, whose panics tend to occur when inactive, may engage in a distracting activity. Yet another may take a tranquillizer, or an alcoholic drink.

By encouraging the person not to engage in his usual strategy for minimizing the risk of whatever harm he anticipates, we can create the conditions necessary for him to invalidate his fear that panic will lead to harm. Often he can go beyond not engaging in a minimizing strategy, to maximize the risk by doing whatever he construes would be most dangerous.

For example, Mrs R. experienced most of her panics while at her place of work. She could not predict their onset, did not avoid attending work, but whenever she experienced a panic attack she would leave the factory building and go outside 'for some air'. For her the condition necessary for invalidating her fear was to remain at her work station when a panic attack occurred. She quickly learned that she did not collapse and her panic attacks gradually reduced in frequency and eventually ceased.

Mr B. adopted a very active strategy towards dealing with his panic attacks—he ran. He used this both as a strategy for prevention, and a strategy for controlling the effects of a panic. He worked long hours, under pressure of time, carrying out complicated repairs to electronic equipment, and during the day he would experience 'a build-up of tension'. He would often go for a run at lunchtime, and again in the evening to try to dispel this tension, and prevent it reaching 'danger level'. Most of his always unanticipated panics which were not frequent would occur when he was trying to relax—watching TV, reading, etc. When this happened he would engage in activity—the more active the better. If he could not go for a run he would find something in the house to do. Apart from a short period in the early stages of his difficulty when he had taken propranolol, he had refused to consider other drugs. Although he no longer took the drug he carried it with him—'just in case'. He feared that if he allowed his symptoms to continue without such controls he would 'crack up', 'have a mental breakdown'.

Mr B. was in his late twenties, and something of an adventurer. His leisure time had been divided between a number of dangerous sports at an international level which he wished to do again, should he ever 'recover'. He was particularly demoralized by his panic disorder, having always considered himself 'mentally very stable'—'the kind of person who did not have psychological problems'. The fact that he was experiencing these difficulties meant there was 'a flaw' in him. He now regarded himself as a potential 'liability'. At first he thought his panic attacks were due to a physical cause and described himself as being 'shattered' when all the tests proved negative and he was told he was suffering from 'anxiety'.

He was very relieved when his symptoms were explained as a false alarm of the body's emergency response and subsequent oversensitivity. He had some difficulty discussing potential sources of stress when his symptoms began about a year previously. He could comprehend physical threat, but admitted he had no concept of other kinds of stress. He indicated he would prefer to try to deal with his difficulties at the symptom level, and only if necessary would he wish to explore potential sources of stress.

He quickly grasped the concepts and implications of the cognitive invalidation approach, and threw himself into an exposure programme with his usual energy. This involved allowing the tension to build up without running or other activities aimed at dissipating the tension. When he had a panic attack he was to sit quietly without attempts at distraction until it passed. He voluntarily disposed of his last few propranolol tablets.

Most of the therapist input was directed to supporting him through the few times when he 'flunked' an 'experiment'—that is, when he engaged in activity before waiting to see if he 'cracked up'. Some time was spent allowing him to examine and challenge his view that 'real men don't flunk it'. He was able to do this quite successfully and with some humour at his 'a man's gotta do what a man's gotta do' approach to life, which he had not fully appreciated before.

After six sessions over 3 months he declared himself symptom free. He was still aware of tension at times, but no longer worried about it. Further panic attacks were seen as quite possible, but manageable. Interestingly he thought he would now be more understanding of people with psychological problems, whom he had previously considered 'just neurotic'. He hinted that he had 'a good idea' how the panic attacks had begun, but felt he did not need to discuss this. He had resumed his high risk sports activities and was pleased that he had not proved a 'liability'.

These examples give some indication of how the cognitive invalidation approach to panic disorder is put into practice. Both the longer examples are chosen to represent recurrent themes in therapy sessions which are seen as helping the person understand what is happening to him in such a way that he can use this understanding to deal with the problem actively and constructively. Part of this process may involve counselling towards helping the person appreciate and, if appropriate, resolve the source of the initial stress. The central focus, however, is on encouraging the person to test, through behavioural exposure, the (mistaken) beliefs which are considered to underlie and maintain his disorder.

CONCLUSION

Conceptually, this is an exciting time. Following their birth in the late 1950s behavioural techniques of anxiety reduction had their most rapid period of development during the 1960s and 1970s, by which time behavioural exposure had become the accepted treatment of choice for phobic anxiety disorders (Marks, 1978a, 1978b). While, in terms of technique development, the period since then may be regarded as one of relative stagnation, it may yet prove to be a significant time.

Progress in science normally comes through conceptual reformulations, or 'paradigm shifts'. The problem in clinical psychology has been that most changes in theoretical position have spawned a new set of therapy techniques, with a tendency simply to ignore the techniques associated with earlier theories. Thus it often appears as if each new formulation means beginning again—change with no clear sense of progress.

Perhaps with behavioural exposure treatment of panic disorder/agoraphobia we are at last seeing the possibility of conceptual change resulting not in the abandonment of a previous technique but in its improvement. The question is no longer about *whether* exposure works, but *how* it works (Bandura, 1977; Beck *et al.*, 1985; Clark, 1986), and how it can be improved. The Cognitive Invalidation Model is offered as one contribution to this enquiry.

REFERENCES

Agras, S., Sylvester, D. and Oliveau, D. (1969) The epidemiology of common fears and phobias, *Comprehensive Psychiatry*, **10**, 151.

Agras, W.S., Chapin, H.N. and Oliveau, D.C. (1972) The natural history of phobia: course and prognosis, *Archives of General Psychiatry*, **26**, 315.

Baker, R., and McFadyen, M. (1985) Cognitive Invalidation and the enigma of exposure. In E. Karas (ed.), *Current Issues in Clinical Psychology*, Vol. 2, Plenum, New York.

Bandura, A. (1977) Self-efficacy: towards a unifying theory of behaviour change, *Psychological Review*, **84**, 191.

Beck, A.T., Emery, G. and Greenberg, R.L. (1985) *Anxiety Disorders and Phobias: A Cognitive Perspective*, Basic Books, New York.

Buglass, D., Clarke, J., Henderson, A.S., Kreitman, N. and Presley, A.S. (1977) A study of agoraphobic housewives, *Psychological Medicine*, **7**, 73–86.

Burns, L.E. and Thorpe, G.L. (1977) Fears and clinical phobias: Epidemiological aspects and the national survey of agoraphobics, *Journal of International Medical Research*, **5** (Suppl. 1), 132–9.

Clark, D.M. (1986) A cognitive approach to panic, *Behaviour Research and Therapy*, **24**, 461–70.

Epstein, S. (1972) The nature of anxiety with emphasis upon its relationship to expectancy. In C.D. Speilberger (ed.), *Anxiety: Current Trends in Theory and Research*, Vol. 2, Academic Press, New York.

Freedman, R.R., Ianni, P., Ettedgui, E. and Puthezhath, N. (1985) Ambulatory monitoring of panic disorder, *Archives of General Psychiatry*, **42**, 244–8.

Goldstein, A.J. and Chambless, D.L. (1978) A reanalysis of agoraphobia, *Behaviour Therapy*, **9**, 47–59.

Hallam, R.S. (1978) Agoraphobia: a critical review of the concept, *British Journal of Psychiatry*, **133**, 314–19.

Hallam, R.S. (1985) *Anxiety. Psychological Perspectives on Panic and Agoraphobia.* Academic Press, London.

Kelly, G.A. (1955) *The Psychology of Personal Constructs*, Vols 1 and 2, Norton, New York.

Kelly, G.A. (1963) *A Theory of Personality*, Norton, New York.

Kelly, G.A, (1970) Behaviour is an experiment. In D. Bannister (ed.) *Perspectives in Personal Construct Theory*, Academic Press, London.

Klein, D.F. (1964) Delineation of two drug-responsive anxiety syndromes, *Psychopharmacologia*, **5**, 397–408.

Klein, D.F. (1981) Anxiety reconceptualised. In D.F. Klein and J.G. Rankin (eds) *Anxiety: New Research and Changing Concepts*, Raven Press, New York.

Klein, D.F., Rabkin, J.G. and Gorman, J.M. (1985) Etiological and pathophysiological inferences from the pharmacological treatment of anxiety. In A.H. Tuma and J.D. Maser (eds), *Anxiety and the Anxiety Disorders*, Lawrence Erlbaum, Hillsdale, New Jersey.

Lazarus, R.S. and Averill, J.R. (1972) Emotion and cognition: with special reference to anxiety. In C.D. Spielberger (ed.), *Anxiety: Current Trends in Theory and Research*, Vol. 2, Academic Press, New York.

Lazarus, R.S. and Launier, R. (1978) Stress-related transactions between person and environment. In L.A. Pervin and M. Lewin (eds), *Perspectives in International Psychology*, Plenum, New York.

Marks, I.M. (1978a) Exposure treatments: clinical applications. In W.S. Agras (ed.), *Behavior Modification: Principles and Clinical Applications*, 2nd Edn, Little, Brown and Co., Boston.

Marks, I.M. (1978b) Exposure treatment: conceptual issues. In W.S. Agras (ed.), *Behavior Modification: Principles and Clinical Applications*, 2nd Edn, Little, Brown and Co., Boston.

Mathews, A.M., Gelder, M.G. and Johnson, D.W. (1981) *Agoraphobia: Nature and Treatment*, Guilford Press, New York.

Pitts, F.N. and McClure, J. (1967) Lactate metabolism in anxiety neurosis, *New England Journal of Medicine*, **277**, 1329–36.

Sheehan, D.V. (1982) Panic attacks and phobias, *New England Journal of Medicine*, **307**, 156–8.

Snaith, R.P. (1968) A clinical investigation of phobias, *British Journal of Psychiatry*, **114**, 673.

Spielberger, C.D. (1966) Theory and research on anxiety. In C.D. Spielberger (ed.), *Anxiety and Behavior*, Academic Press, New York.

Spielberger, C.D. (1972) Anxiety as an emotional state. In C.D. Spielberger (ed.), *Anxiety: Current Trends in Theory and Research*, Vol. 1, Academic Press, New York.

Stampler, F.M. (1982) Panic disorder: description, conceptualisation, and implications for treatment, *Clinical Psychology Review*, Vol. 2, 469–86.

Chapter 14

Pharmacological Approaches to the Treatment of Panic

LESLIE WALKER AND GEORGE ASHCROFT

INTRODUCTION

In the last two decades, there has been a burgeoning interest in pharmacological approaches to the treatment of panic. More recently, a filip has been given to these approaches by the now widely held view, particularly in the USA, that there is a specific syndrome of panic disorder which has a strong genetic component (Torgersen, 1983), altered inter-ictal parahippocampal activity (Reiman, 1987), enhanced sensitivity to various substances such as caffeine, sodium lactate and carbon dioxide (Gorman *et al.*, 1984; Roy-Byrne and Uhde, 1988) and, perhaps most importantly, a differential response to drug treatment (Klein, 1964). Whilst controversy regarding the classification of panic phenomena is likely to continue for some time (Gelder, 1986), enough is already understood to enable effective pharmacological treatment to be offered on an empirical basis.

The aims of this chapter are to review the recent drug therapy literature, to provide practical guidelines for the use of pharmacological approaches to the treatment of panic, and to conceptualize these interventions within a broader framework.

REVIEW OF RECENT DRUG TRIALS

Table 14.1 shows the prescribed drugs currently in use for the treatment of panic together with a recent reference for each. The main groups are antidepressants, beta blockers and benzodiazepines. Many clinical trials

Panic Disorder: Theory, Research and Therapy. Edited by Roger Baker

have been carried out and have been systematically reviewed elsewhere (for example, Ballenger, 1986; Gorman *et al.*, 1984; Judd *et al.*, 1986; Marks, 1987; Modigh, 1987; Nagy, 1987; Sheehan and Soto, 1987).

Table 14.1 Drugs which have been used in the treatment of panic disorders.

Drug	Recent references
Tricyclic antidepressants	
Imipramine	Zitrin *et al.* (1983)
Clomipramine	Johnston *et al.* (1988)
Monoamine oxidase inhibitors	
Phenelzine	Solyom *et al.* (1981)
Other antidepressants	
Zimelidine	Evans *et al.* (1986)
Fluoxetine	Gorman *et al.* (1987)
Fluvoxamine	den Boer *et al.* (1987)
Tryptophan	Kahn *et al.* (1987)
Trazodone	Mavissakalian *et al.* (1987)
Benzodiazepines	
Alprazolam	Ballenger *et al.* (1988)
Diazepam	Dunner *et al.* (1986)
Clonazepam	Pollack *et al.* (1986)
Beta blockers	
Propanolol	Munjack *et al.* (1985)
Other drugs	
Buspirone	Napolliello and Domantoy (1988)
Clonidine	Liebowitz *et al.* (1981)

SELECTION OF PATIENTS

It has long been appreciated that depression and panic attacks commonly coexist and it has been argued, most forcibly by Marks, that tricyclic antidepressants and monoamine oxidase inhibitors exert their therapeutic effect on panic indirectly via alteration in mood. When patients are having panic attacks and are clinically depressed, there is wide agreement that they should be treated in the first instance using antidepressant medication. If they are not clinically depressed, our preference would still be to use an antidepressant, particularly clomipramine, imipramine, or doxepin; dose, however, would normally be well below that usually considered appropriate in depression (see below).

There has been controversy regarding the management of panic disorder accompanied by avoidance behaviour as in agoraphobia and in some cases of social phobia. On the one hand, researchers such as Marks (1987) claim that behaviour therapy based on the exposure principle is the treatment of first choice, whereas others such as Klein and Gorman (1987) believe that suppression of the panic using a tricyclic or monoamine oxidase inhibitor is usually sufficient to eliminate phobic avoidance without specific therapy for this. Furthermore, Klein argues that behaviour therapy without medication reduces phobic avoidance but does not necessarily abolish panic attacks. Some studies have found combined drug–behaviour therapy to be most effective (Telch *et al.*, 1985; Waring, 1988).

DRUG OF CHOICE

Most work has been carried out using imipramine. Reviewing these studies, Ballenger (1986) concluded that 'results from the four largest research trials report that 70%–90% of patients experience moderate or marked improvement in phobic symptoms and secondary disabilities'.

Clomipramine, whilst widely used clinically, has been evaluated less thoroughly than imipramine, perhaps because the former has not been routinely available in the United States of America. Modigh (1987) reviewed six double blind trials and five open trials and noted that 'many clinicians with experience of chlorimipramine treatment have the impression that the drug is highly effective and probably more effective than imipramine'.

At low dosage, clomipramine is a relatively specific 5-HT reuptake inhibitor. It is not surprising, therefore, that trials of very specific 5-HT reuptake inhibitors such as fluoxetine (Gorman *et al.*, 1987) and fluvoxamine (den Boer *et al.*, 1987) are beginning to appear.

It is likely also that we shall soon see the publication of trials in panic patients of the new generation of non-tricyclic anxiolytics which affect 5-HT systems, such as buspirone and ritanserin. Napolliello and Domantoy (1988) have indicated that Brystol-Myers Pharmaceutical Research and Development Division have data on file from a multicentre eight-week double-blind study comparing buspirone, imipramine and placebo. They reported that, in terms of anti-panic effect, buspirone was superior to placebo and inferior to imipramine.

Monoamine oxidase inhibitors, especially phenelzine, have been used in the treatment of panic since the early 1960s and may be at least as effective as tricyclic antidepressants (e.g. Sheehan *et al.*, 1980). Despite this, many clinicians are reluctant to use these drugs because of the dietary restrictions which are necessary. However, selective and reversible monoamine oxidase inhibitors have recently become available (e.g. moclobemide) and are said to carry less risk of a hypertensive crisis; it will be interesting to see if any are as effective as classical inhibitors such as phenelzine.

Until recently, it was believed that benzodiazepines were of little benefit in the treatment of panic (as opposed to anticipatory anxiety). However, several benzodiazepines and also a triazolobenzodiazepine, alprazolam, have been found to be effective (Ballenger *et al.*, 1988; Dunner *et al.*, 1986). Sheehan (1987) has provided practical guidelines for their use. Concern has been expressed that discontinuation may present a major problem for some patients. Fyer *et al.* (1987) found that of 17 patients, 15 had recurrent or increased panic attacks during withdrawal and only four patients completed withdrawal in a period of 4–5 weeks. On the basis of a multicentre trial Pecknold *et al.* (1988) recommended that alprazolam should be tapered over at least eight weeks, especially when high doses are involved. We avoid using benzodiazepines in panic patients except in a few cases to facilitate the introduction of an antidepressant.

Because somatic symptoms are an invariant accompaniment of panic, it has been suggested that beta-blocking agents such as propranolol may be especially helpful with this form of anxiety (Munjack *et al.*, 1985). Reports, however, are mixed and we agree with the verdict of Ballenger (1986) that further research is required.

DOSAGE

Reference has already been made to the appropriate dose range of tricyclic antidepressants for panic disorder patients. Almost all of the trials using imipramine have used doses which would normally be considered antidepressant. Zitrin *et al.* (1980), for example, built up to 150 mg daily increasing if necessary up to 300 mg daily. However, our experience is that 10–30 mg clomipramine daily—well below the recognized antidepressant range—can be very effective in blocking panic attacks. Gloger *et al.* (1981) found that 45 per cent of panic patients required less that 50 mg clomipramine daily. We have also had encouraging results with relatively low doses of the non-tricyclic fluoxetine (20–40 mg daily) (Lyle *et al.*, 1988).

Whatever the final dose used, there is wide agreement that with panic patients it is essential to commence tricyclic or MAOI therapy at a low dose. Even then, between 15 and 30 per cent of patients will experience a worsening of their symptoms which is so severe that they may discontinue taking medication.

ACCEPTABILITY

Zitrin *et al.* (1983) have pointed out that some patients are exquisitely sensitive to imipramine; even with doses as low as 10 mg daily, some patients develop insomnia, irritability, unusual energy and apprehension. Muskin and Fyer (1981) reported that this occurred in about 15 per cent of panic patients, although our experience with clomipramine suggests a higher frequency. Gorman *et al.* (1984) recommend that imipramine is commenced with a 10 mg dose at bed-time, increasing by 10 mg every other day to 50 mg per day and thereafter, if required, 25 mg increases every 3 days or 50 mg per week. They point out that, as panic patients tend to worry excessively about physical aspects of their problem, it is advisable to reassure them about these early side-effects.

It is our experience that some patients who cannot tolerate the side-effects of clomipramine are able to tolerate imipramine: the majority of those not tolerating imipramine manage with doxepin. Gorman *et al.* (1984) suggest switching from imipramine to desipramine when starting side-effects are too troublesome. In another study, Gorman *et al.* (1987) found that eight of 16 patients dropped out between two and six weeks after starting fluoxetine because of the side-effects, whereas in the Aberdeen trials using fluoxetine and clomipramine, while some patients had severe side-effects, none dropped out for this reason (Waring, 1988; Lyle *et al.*, 1988). Our impression is that fluoxetine is less likely than clomipramine to produce severe starting side-effects.

Interestingly, in a multicentre, double blind trial carried out in a general practice to compare the effectiveness and tolerability of clomipramine and diazepam in patients with agoraphobia or social phobia, tolerability of clomipramine was comparable to that of diazepam (Allsopp *et al.*, 1984). In contemporary Britain, the public are becoming increasingly unwilling to take benzodiazepines and increasingly willing to pursue litigation because of dependency.

Ballenger (1986) has suggested that the increase in heart rate which occurs with tricyclic antidepressants, often frightening to these patients, can be lowered using a beta blocker, and Modigh (1987) notes that initial aggravation of symptoms when starting antidepressant therapy can be compensated for, at least in part, by adding a benzodiazepine during the first weeks of treatment.

Unfortunately, even with reassurance and an early review appointment, up to one third of patients with panic attacks will experience severe side-effects and may discontinue tricyclic medication. For this reason, the search continues for pharmacological agents which have fewer side-effects and a rapid onset of anti-panic action.

DISCONTINUATION OF MEDICATION

Following cessation of panic attacks, it is unclear how long patients should be maintained on medication. Gorman *et al.* (1984) recommend six months as does Modigh (1987), although he also recommends that, after a symptom-free period of 3–4 months, the patient should be instructed to reduce the dose. He suggests that the maintenance dose for clomipramine will in most cases decrease to not more than 25 mg daily after 6–12 months of treatment. Pecknold *et al.* (1988) recommend that alprazolam should be continued for at least six months prior to gradual tapering.

Some patients will relapse on discontinuation, and there is a significant likelihood that panic attacks will resume after a period of drug-free remission. Zitrin *et al.* (1978, 1983) found that approximately 15–30 per cent of agoraphobic patients relapsed within two years of discontinuation of imipramine therapy. Relapse rates with MAOIs may be even higher (Solyom *et al.*, 1973; Kelly *et al.*, 1970). Fyer *et al.* (1987) found that during withdrawal from alprazolam of 17 patients, 15 patients had recurrent or increased panic attacks and nine had significant new withdrawal symptoms: only four completed withdrawal within 4–5 weeks.

Reviewing the literature, Pecknold (1987) concluded that 'studies of imipramine, clomipramine, monoamine oxidase inhibitors and alprazolam, have demonstrated an anti-panic effect. . .. However, when exposure is not made a part of the treatment, there is a much poorer resolution and a tendency for the patient to relapse'. As in the case of cognitive therapy for depression, psychological treatment for panic disorders may have prophylactic value. Sheehan and Soto (1987), Telch *et al.* (1985), Mavissakalian *et al.* (1983) and others have argued that a combined pharmacological and behavioural approach is superior.

It should be noted that a high drop-out rate is not specific to medication. Marks (1987) stated that 'the drop-out rate from exposure therapy is rather similar to that from imipramine or MAOIs—about a quarter of suitable patients either refuse to start or fail to complete an adequate trial'. This, however, is in marked contrast to our clinical experience using behavioural methods. Prior to *in vivo* self-exposure, we train patients in cue-controlled relaxation and, in some cases, combine this with anxiety management training with or without hypnosis. Using this approach, very few patients discontinue prior to an adequate trial of behaviour therapy.

ABERDEEN TRIALS

The overall integration of the evidence from the drug studies reviewed in the first part of this chapter is that selected tricyclic antidepressants and monoamine oxidase inhibitors are effective in the treatment of panic attacks. Many questions, however, remain to be answered regarding optimal treatment, for example, which drug is most effective, which dosage regime should be selected, how long should treatment continue, how many patients relapse after withdrawing the drug and what is the long-term prognosis. In addition, we require a satisfactory explanation of the mode of action of drugs in panic and an indication of the relative roles of behaviour therapy and drugs in the treatment of the disorder.

We and our colleagues have attempted to address some of these questions in a series of studies.

In Chapter 1 of this volume, Howard Waring describes the clinical features of a group of patients with panic attacks studied in general practice and hospital populations in Aberdeen. A double blind placebo controlled trial of low dose clomipramine (10–30 mg/day), behaviour therapy and combined clomipramine and behaviour therapy was carried out (Waring, 1988). Those patients with a primary depressive illness complicated by panic attacks were excluded from the study. Patients treated with clomipramine showed a rapid relief of panic symptoms with some 40 per cent being free of panic attacks by the end of four weeks treatment. An interesting phenomenon was noted; one third of the clomipramine patients experienced a marked exacerbation of symptoms often starting within an hour of the first dose of the drug and presenting for up to 48 hours. They were persuaded to continue with the drug (only 13 per cent of the clomipramine group withdrew in the first month) and the panic rapidly came under control.

In the behaviour therapy group 60 per cent had withdrawn from the trial by the time of the four-week assessment, probably because exposure was too steeply graded and more attention should have been given to relaxation training and anxiety management. Good control of symptoms was obtained in the remaining 40 per cent although disappearance of panic was slower than with clomipramine. Improvement was well maintained over a period of six-month follow-up.

Avoidance behaviour which was associated with panic in most patients was reduced by both drug treatment alone and by behaviour therapy but the most impressive results were obtained in the combined treatment group.

In an attempt to replicate the therapeutic efficacy of clomipramine while avoiding the patient's exacerbation of panic symptoms, we have carried out a preleminary study with fluoxetine, a selective 5-HT uptake inhibitor (Lyle *et al.*, 1988). The rationale behind this is that the early precipitation of symptoms may result from the potentiation of peripheral adrenergic activity while the subsequent therapeutic response may occur because of a reduction in peripheral adrenergic receptor sensitivity, a reduction in outflow from central noradrenergic systems originating in locus coeruleus neurones or an increase in central 5-HT activity.

If a selective 5-HT uptake inhibitor were to prove effective in panic attacks without first exacerbating symptoms then this would not only provide a significant therapeutic advance but would also add to our knowledge of the mechanisms involved in the control of panic.

Gorman *et al.* (1988) reported a small open trial of fluoxetine in which the drug appeared to be effective although exacerbation of symptoms was seen early in treatment. In a similar case study with fluoxetine in 12 patients we obtained rapid relief of panic symptoms without early increase in panic attacks although we did note an increase in tension and jitteriness in some patients in the first week of treatment.

A PSYCHOBIOLOGICAL MODEL OF PANIC AND ITS TREATMENT

In a previous publication (Ashcroft *et al.*, 1987) we have described a model for panic disorder. Panic is seen as mediated by a mechanism involved in the monitoring of secure exploration and the occurrence of panic indicates an assessment of the likely failure of this behaviour to provide safety. In reaching this assessment there will be an interaction between the severity of the perceived threat, the potential for escape and the perceived efficacy of environmental support.

Changes in social attachment may operate to reduce the threshold for the development of the panic response. Thus, many patients have experienced loss or separation in the months before the attacks start.

A model for the organization of the behavioural systems was developed (Ashcroft *et al.*, 1987) and is presented in modified form (Figure 14.1). Full details can be found in the original publication (Ashcroft *et al.*, 1987).

The comparators are a collection of systems involved in the assessment of response to novelty, threat and reward (Gray, 1982) with their location in hippocampal structures.

Mason and Iverson (1979) proposed that the dorsal noradrenergic bundle (DNAB) functions to direct selective attention to relevant stimuli in the environment. Input from the DNAB acting to alter the signal-to-noise ratio in the hippocampal comparator will change the sensitivity to social stimuli and hence the threshold for the panic response. Secure attachment appears to reduce the adverse response to novelty, and separation and loss seem to increase the response.

In rats Ellison (1975) examined the effect of selective lesions of 5-hydroxytryptamine (5-HT) and noradrenergic (NA) systems on exploratory behaviour in novel and familiar environments. In the novel environment low 5-HT rats showed evidence of fear and low levels of exploration while low NA rats 'fearlessly ambulated about the enclosure'. In the familiar colony environment, however, low 5-HT rats were fearless while low NA rats failed to explore.

It is as though the central NA system enhances and the 5-HT system suppresses the effects of unfamiliarity and novelty.

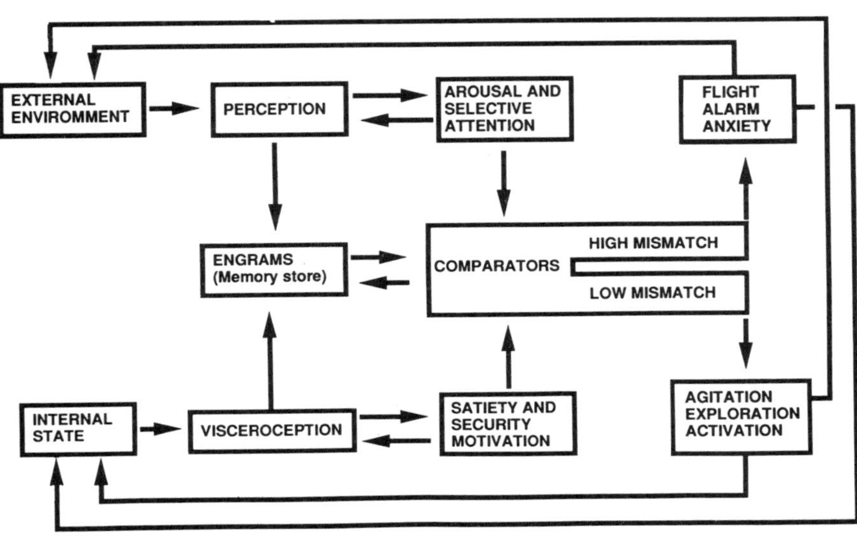

Figure 14.1 A model for panic.

The implications for therapy are that panic attacks may be managed by:

(a) Ensuring the existence of secure relationships.
(b) Reducing the perceived threat; this will include all the behaviour therapies and those therapies aiming to minimize the impact of internal cues, for example increased autonomic arousal.
(c) Drug treatments which diminish central noradrenergic tone and/or increase activity in central 5-HT systems.

A PRACTICAL TREATMENT REGIME

Following a full interview, physical examination with screening investigations if necessary to exclude endocrine, cardiac and neurological disease, a treatment plan is devised to suit each individual patient.

(a) Those with primary depressive disease complicated by panic attacks are treated for the depressive illness with full doses of antidepressants or ECT. We have noticed that in the presence of panic it is advisable to start with a small dose of antidepressant, say 25 mg clomipramine at night, to avoid the precipitation of more severe panic. This dose can then be increased progressively up to 150 mg or more in some cases over a period of 10 days. Diazepam 5 mg twice daily may be required for four or five days to facilitate introduction of the antidepressant in those rare patients with extreme generalized anxiety or agitation.

(b) Other symptomatic panic attacks, for example those complicating the withdrawal of alcohol or other drugs, usually respond to the usual 'drying out' regimes but, if not, they can be treated as below.

(c) In the absence of the conditions described above we commence treatment with 10 mg clomipramine at night. If panic has not subsided after 4–5 days the dose is increased to 20 mg and then, after a further 2–3 days, to 30 mg. Patients are told to expect improvement within one week of starting the drug. The possibility of an initial upsurge of symptoms is discussed with them and they are encouraged to persist with the drug with the expectation that improvement will follow. They are seen frequently during the early days of treatment. With this regime some 80 per cent of patients will achieve either complete remission of panic or marked relief within eight weeks.

(d) If patients fail to tolerate clomipramine then they are started on doxepin or imipramine. These drugs seem less potent than clomipramine but also less likely to precipitate severe panic symptoms. The dose regime is the same as clomipramine and if remission is not complete the patient can then be transferred to clomipramine without further problems.

(e) Occasionally, diazepam 5 mg twice daily is added to the regime to facilitate the introduction of clomipramine but the diazepam is always withdrawn after 5–7 days.

(f) With this drug regime most patients are able to overcome avoidance behaviour without further treatment. At first they may still complain of 'a fear of panic' which makes them apprehensive of undertaking new activities despite the absence of panic attacks. This symptom usually subsides once they are reassured and encouraged to overcome any recurring restrictions. Drug treatment should be continued for six months and follow-up continued for at least 12 months.

The above drug treatment regime allows general practitioners to treat successfully most patients with panic attacks and we now see only the more severe or complicated cases. In many of these we find that the best management is a combined drug–behaviour therapy approach. Currently, this always involves applied relaxation training (Hutchings *et al.*, 1980) which has two components: (1) training in cue controlled relaxation (with an audio-cassette recording for home practice) and (2) graded self-directed *in vivo* exposure. Usually, graded exposure in imagination during clinic sessions is also carried out. The patient is asked to imagine a feared situation. Then, when mild fear is experienced, the patient is asked to keep the image as clear as possible and, while experiencing the mild fear as fully as possible, to apply the cue-controlled relaxation skills. Sometimes a hypnotic induction is used to assist imagery and cue-controlled relaxation. (If panic attacks are continuing without significant avoidance behaviour, during hypnosis patients can usually be talked into producing mild feared bodily sensations, or alternatively these can sometimes be induced by hyperventilation (Clark *et al.*, 1985).) Exposure in imagination often increases the patient's confidence in coping with the feared situation, thereby reducing the perceived threat and facilitating *in vivo* exposure. Efforts are also directed at modifying anxiety provoking images and thoughts by providing the patient with basic information about the psychophysiology of anxiety and by using simple cognitive methods such as 'decatastrophization'.

We are now carrying out long-term follow-up studies of patients treated 4–5 years ago as there is little information regarding the long-term prognosis in this disorder.

REFERENCES

Allsopp, L.E., Cooper, G.L. and Poole, P.H. (1984) Clomipramine and diazepam in the treatment of agoraphobia and social phobia in general practice. *Current Medical Research Opinion*, **9**, 64–70.

Ashcroft, G.W., Palomo, T., Salzen, E.A. and Waring, H.L. (1987) Anxiety and depression. A psychobiological approach, *Psicopatologia* (Madrid), **7**, 2, 155–62.

Ballenger, J.C. (1986) Pharmacotherapy of the panic disorders, *Journal of Clinical Psychiatry*, **47**, 27–32 (Supplement).

Ballenger, J.C., Burrows, G.D., DuPont, R.L., Lesser, I.M., Noyes, R., Pecknold, J.C., Rifkin, A. and Swinson, R.P. (1988) Alprazolam in panic disorder and agoraphobia: results from a multicentre trial—1. Efficacy in short-term treatment, *Archives of General Psychiatry*, **45**, 413–22.

Clark, D.M., Salkovskis, P.M. and Chalkley, A.J. (1985) Respiratory control as a treatment for panic attacks, *Journal of Behaviour Therapy and Experimental Psychiatry*, **16**, 23–30.

Charney, D.S., Woods, S.W., Goodman, W.K., Rifkin, B., Kinch, M., Aiken, B., Quadrino, L.M. and Heninger, G.R. (1986) Drug treatment of panic disorder: The comparative efficacy of imipramine, alprazolam and trazodone, *Journal of Clinical Psychiatry*, **47**, 580–6.

den Boer, J.A., Westenberg, H.G.M., Kamerbeek, W.O.J., Verhoevan, W.M.A. and Kahn, R.S. (1987) Effect of serotonin uptake inhibitors in anxiety disorders. A double-blind comparison of clomipramine and fluvoxamine, *International Clinical Psychopharmacology*, **2**, 21–32.

Dunner, D.L., Ishiki, D., Avery, D.H., Wilson, L.G. and Hyde, T.S. (1986) Effect of alprazolam and diazepam on anxiety and panic attacks in panic disorder: a controlled study, *Journal of Clinical Psychiatry*, **47**, 458-60.

Ellison, G.D. (1975) Behaviour and the balance between norepinephrine and serotonin, *Neurobiologicae Experimentalis*, **35**, 499–575.

Evans, L., Kenardy, J., Schneider, P. and Hoey, H. (1986) Effect of a selective serotonin uptake inhibitor in agoraphobia with panic attacks. A double-blind comparison of zimelidine, imipramine and placebo, *Acta Psychiatrica Scandinavica*, **73**, 49–53.

Fyer, A.J., Liebowitz, M.R., Gorman, J.M., Campeas, R., Levin, A., Davies, S.O., Goetz, D. and Klein, D.A. (1987) Discontinuation of alprazolam treatment in panic patients, *American Journal of Psychiatry*, **144**, 323–8.

Gelder, M.G. (1986) Panic attacks: new approaches to an old problem, *British Journal of Psychiatry*, **149**, 346–352.

Gloger, S., Grunhaus, L., Birmacher, B. and Troudart, T. (1981) Treatment of spontaneous panic attacks with clomipramine, *American Journal of Psychiatry*, **138**, 1215–17.

Gorman, J.M., Liebowitz, M.R. and Klein, D. (1984) *Panic Disorder and Agoraphobia*, Upjohn Co., Kalamazoo.

Gorman, J.M., Liebowitz, M.R., Fyer, A.J., Goetz, D., Campeas, R.B., Fyer, M.R., Davies, S.O. and Klein, D.F. (1987) An open trial of fluoxetine, *Journal of Clinical Psychopharmacology*, **7**, 329–32.

Gray, J.A. (1982) An enquiry into the functions of the septohippocampal systems, *Behavioural and Brain Sciences*, **5**, 469–77.

Hutchings, D.F., Denney, D.R., Basgall, J. and Houston, B.K. (1980) Anxiety management and applied relaxation in reducing general anxiety, *Behaviour Research and Therapy*, **18**, 181–90.

Johnston, D.F., Troyer, I.E. and Whitsett, S.F. (1988) Clomipramine treatment of agoraphobic women, *Archives of General Psychiatry*, **45**, 453-9.

Judd, F.K., Norman, T.R. and Burrows, G.D. (1986) Pharmacological treatment of panic disorder, *International Clinical Psychopharmacology*, **1**, 3–16.

Kahn, R.S., Herman, G.M., Westenberg, M., Verhoeven, W.M.A., Gispen-deWied, C.C. and Hamerbeek, W.O.T. (1987) Effect of a serotonin precursor and uptake inhibitor in anxiety disorders: a double-blind comparison of

5-hydroxytryptophan, clomipramine and placebo, *International Clinical Psychopharmacology*, **2**, 33-45.

Kelly, D., Guirgfuis, W., Frammer, E., Mitchell-Hoggs, N. and Sargant, W. (1970) Treatment of phobic states with antidepressants: a retrospective study of 246 patients, *British Journal of Psychiatry*, **116**, 387–98.

Klein, D.F. (1964) Delineation of two drug-responsive anxiety syndromes, *Psychopharmacologia*, **5**, 397–408.

Klein, D.F. and Gorman, D.F. (1987) A model of panic and agoraphobic development. In S.J. Dencker and G. Wolmberg (eds), *Panic Disorders, Acta Psychiatrica Scandinavica* (Supplement No. 335), **76**, 87–96.

Liebowitz, M.R., Fyer, A.J., McGrath, P. and Klein, D.F. (1981) Clonidine treatment of panic disorder, *Psychopharmacology Bulletin*, **17**, 122–3.

Lyle, A., Walker, L.G. and Ashcroft, G.W. (1988) 'Fluoxetine in the treatment of panic attacks: an open trial', Paper in preparation.

Marks, I.M. (1987) *Fears, Phobias and Rituals*, Oxford University Press, New York.

Mason, T.S. and Iverson, S.D. (1979) Theories of dorsal bundle extinction effect, *Brain Research*, **80**, 107–37.

Mavissikalian, M., Michelson, L. and Dealy, R.S. (1983) Pharmacological treatment of agoraphobia: imipramine versus imipramine with programmed practice, *British Journal of Psychiatry*, **143**, 348–55.

Mavissikalian, M., Perel, J., Bowler, K. and Dealy, R. (1987) Trazodone in the treatment of panic disorder and agoraphobia with panic attacks, *Journal of Clinical Psychiatry*, **144**, 785–7.

Modigh, K. (1987) Antidepressant drugs in anxiety disorders. In S.J. Dencker and G. Wolmberg (eds), *Panic Disorder, Acta Psychiatrica Scandinavica* (Supplement No. 335), **76**, 57–72.

Munjack, D.J., Rebal, R., Shaner, R., Staples, F., Braun, R. and Leonard, M. (1985) Imipramine versus propranolol for the treatment of panic attacks: a pilot study, *Comprehensive Psychiatry*, **26**, 80–9.

Muskin, P.R. and Fyer, A.J. (1981) Treatment of panic disorder, *Journal of Clinical Psychopharmacology*, **1**, 81-90.

Nagy, A. (1987) Long-term treatment with benzodiazepines. In S.J. Dencker and G. Wolmberg (eds), *Panic Disorder, Acta Psychiatrica Scandinavica* (Supplement No. 335), **76**, 47–56.

Napolliello, M.J. and Domantoy, A.G. (1988) Newer clinical studies with buspirone. In M. Lader (ed.), *Buspirone: a New Introduction to the Treatment of Anxiety*, Royal Society of Medicine, London.

Pecknold, J.C. (1987) Behavioural and combined therapy in panic states, *Progress in Neuropsychopharmacology and Biological Psychiatry*, **11**, 97–104.

Pecknold, J.C., Swinson, R.P., Kutch, K. and Lewis, C.P. (1988) Alprazolam in panic disorder and agoraphobia: results from a multi-centre trial—111 Discontinuation effects, *Archives of General Psychiatry*, **45**, 429–36.

Pollack, M.N., Tesar, G.E. and Rosenbaum, J.F. (1986) Clonazepam in the treatment of panic disorder and agoraphobia: a one-year follow-up, *Journal of Clinical Psychopharmacology*, **6**, 302–4.

Reiman, E.M. (1987) The study of panic disorder using positron emission tomography, *Psychiatric Developments*, **1**, 63–78.

Roy-Byrne, P.R. and Uhde, T.W. (1988) Exogenous factors in panic disorder. Clinical and research implications, *Journal of Clinical Psychiatry*, **49**, 56–61.

Sheehan, D.V. (1987) Benzodiazepines in panic disorder and agoraphobia, *Journal of Affective Disorders*, **13**, 169–81.

Sheehan, D.V., Ballenger, J. and Jacobsen, G. (1980) Treatment of endogenous anxiety with phobic, hysterical and hypochondriacal symptoms, *Archives of General Psychiatry*, **37**, 51–9.

Sheehan, D.V. and Soto, S. (1987) Recent developments in the treatment of panic. In S.J. Dencker and G. Holmberg (eds), *Panic Disorder, Acta Psychiatrica Scandinavica* (Supplement No. 335), **76**, 75–84.

Solyom, L., Heseltine, G.F.D., McClure, D.J., Solyom, C., Ledwedge, B. and Steinberg, G. (1973) Behavior therapy versus drug therapy in the treatment of phobic neurosis, *Canadian Psychiatric Association Journal*, **18**, 25–32.

Solyom, D., Solyom, L., LaPierre, Y., Pecknold, J. and Mortor, L. (1981) Phenelzine and exposure in the treatment of phobias, *Biological Psychiatry*, **16**, 239–47.

Telch, M.J., Agras, W.S., Taylor, C.B., Roth, W.T. and Gallen, C.C. (1985) Combined pharmacological and behavioural treatment for agoraphobia, *Behaviour Research and Therapy*, **23**, 325–35.

Torgersen, S. (1983) Genetic factors in anxiety disorders, *Archives of General Psychiatry*, **40**, 1085–9.

Waring, H.L. (1988) 'An investigation into the nature and response to treatment of panic attack symptoms in general practice attenders'. MD Thesis, University of Aberdeen.

Zitrin, C.M., Klein, D.F. and Woerner, M.G. (1978) Behaviour therapy, supportive psychotherapy, imipramine and phobias, *Archives of General Psychiatry*, **35**, 307–16.

Zitrin, C.M., Klein, D.F. and Woerner, M.G. (1980) Treatment of agoraphobia with group exposure in vivo and imipramine, *Archives of General Psychiatry*, **37**, 63–72.

Zitrin, C.M., Klein, D.F., Woerner, M.G. and Ross, D.C. (1983) Treatment of phobias—1. Comparison of imipramine hydrochloride and placebo, *Archives of General Psychiatry*, **40**, 125–38.

Chapter 15

The Key to Resisting Relapse in Panic

CLAIRE WEEKES

INTRODUCTION TO CLAIRE WEEKES'S APPROACH (by Roger Baker)

In many ways Claire Weekes is a woman before her time. In 1962 when the terms 'behaviour therapy' and 'systematic desensitization' were new to the ears of therapists, Weekes was already explaining how panics were an important aspect of anxiety, and how fear of the physiological sensations induced spiralling levels of anxiety by the 'fear – adrenalin – fear cycle'. She recommended exposure to the feared sensations as the treatment of choice, but with clear instructions for patients on how to face exposure, though 'facing' or 'accepting' sensations were the terms she used rather than 'exposure'.

Self-help literature

Dr Weekes has written four books. *Self Help for Your Nerves* (1962), *Peace from Nervous Suffering* (1972) and *More Help for your Nerves* (1984) are all self-help books for sufferers with anxiety-related problems. *Peace from Nervous Suffering* concentrates especially on agoraphobia and panic and is probably her most succinct and effective text for sufferers. She has also produced a number of cassettes and LP records, providing self-help instructions and has made many appearances on TV and radio programmes throughout the world. Her books have sold by the thousand; *Self Help for your Nerves* is now in its 23rd edition, and has been translated into eight languages. In 1977 she was made an MBE for her contribution to medicine.

Simple Effective Treatment of Agoraphobia (1977) is her only book specifically directed towards clinicians, which with two articles in medical journals (1973, 1977) represents her main contribution on the topic of anxiety to the

Panic Disorder: Theory, Research and Therapy. Edited by Roger Baker

academic world. Her concepts are lay-medical ones, rather than framed in the prevailing theoretical constructs of psychology or psychiatry; perhaps this is one reason for her considerable popularity with the lay public and her relative lack of recognition amongst professionals.

Basic concepts

In her writings the focal concept is of physiological 'sensitization' of the nervous system 'by which I mean a state in which emotional and nervous responses are greatly intensified and come with unusual, sometimes alarming, swiftness'. Sensitization originates mainly from stimulation of the sympathetic nervous system. The symptoms of an intensely sensitized person may include 'a thumping heart', 'missed' heart beats, pain in the region of the heart, constantly quickly beating heart, attacks of palpitations, giddiness, sweating, agitation, tightness across the chest, a 'lump' in the throat, difficulty in swallowing solid food, a feeling of inability to take a deep breath, . . . and above all flashes of almost incapacitating panic (1977) (i.e. very similar to the DSM-III symptom list for classifying panic disorder). The initial part of the stress reaction is described by Dr Weekes as 'first fear'; it is seen as self-curative given time, rest, and in some cases tranquillization. Dr Weekes places enormous emphasis on what she calls 'second fear', that is the bewilderment and alarm created by the 'first fear' reaction. This secondary reaction produces more physiological sensations, which cause more alarm, etc., in an ever-increasing spiral of anxiety symptomatology. Both the somatic sensations of 'first fear' and the fearful appraisal involved in 'second fear' occur so quickly they seem like a single experience to the sufferer. Eliminating 'second fear' is the task of Weekes's therapy.

Therapy involves (1) an accurate understanding of the nature and cause of anxiety symptoms by the patient—indeed, 'if a technique needs a name, perhaps it could be called "coping through understanding"' (1973). In her books Dr Weekes gives a great deal of space to explaining individual anxiety symptoms and their causes. For example, regarding palpitations, she tells her readers in *Peace from Nervous Suffering*: 'If you could see how thick, and appreciate how powerful your heart muscle is, you would lose all fear of its bursting or being damaged by palpitations.' (2) Facing anxiety symptoms, not shrinking from upsetting feelings. Analysing, and describing them to oneself rather than pretending they do not exist. (3) Accepting feelings, not fighting them. Allowing feelings to occur with no attempt to stop them, and being prepared to live with them without any physical or cognitive avoidance. (4) 'Floating', letting go of a tense hold of oneself, and imagining oneself 'floating', 'gliding' or 'swimming' around physical objects, difficult situations or upsetting thoughts rather than retreating or fighting them head-on; (2), (3) and (4) virtually constitute physical and psychological exposure to situations and feelings. (5) Letting time pass. Understanding that recovery is a long process, and setbacks inevitable.

'Your illness is an illness in how you think', she says in 1972. 'It is very much an illness of your attitude to fear'.

Making contact with the reader

Dr Weekes is at her best when addressing sufferers. Her first book begins, 'If you are reading this book because you are having a nervous breakdown or because your nerves are "in a bad way", you are the very person for whom it is written, and I shall therefore talk directly to you as if you were sitting beside me.' She is very positive in her message with no 'grey areas' expressed—'the advice here will definitely cure you, if you follow it.' Again, the language of the layman, but usually distasteful to the academic. There is no doubt though that she has considerable skill in 'getting into the shoes' of the sufferer and making contact with her readers. As I read her books, what surprised me, even disturbed me, was the phenomenological accuracy of her descriptions of anxiety, derealization, loss of confidence, etc., and her ability to anticipate the sort of worries that patients express about these phenomena. I found myself repeatedly pondering, 'how did she acquire this knowledge?'—this epistemological question is somewhat resolved by examining her background.

After graduating in Science from Sydney University in 1922, Dr Weekes was subsequently elected a Fellow of the Linnean Society of New South Wales and went on to conduct zoological researches in Sydney until 1929, when she was awarded a DSc. Her zoological research, particularly with a Linnean orientation, would have stressed the art of meticulous observation and no doubt this emphasis was carried with her as she later graduated in medicine in 1945, worked as a general practitioner for five years, and subsequently specialized as a physician and later consultant physician, at the Rachel Forster Hospital in Sydney. Here her raw data were the accounts patients gave to her of their problems rather than zoological data, and she was especially interested in the effect of any accompanying nervous illness on physical disease. For the last twenty-five years, after retirement as a physician, she has almost exclusively specialized in the treatment of anxiety conditions, including agoraphobia, as well as treating some 2000 patients world wide by means of her 'Journals' (published later in *Peace from Nervous Suffering, Simple Effective Treatment of Agoraphobia* and *More Help for Your Nerves*). Her 1972 survey of 528 agoraphobic patients was taken from this sample. An additional point is that Dr Weekes had little formal psychiatric or psychological training. While one might see this as a handicap, it would mean that certain biases inherent in psychological or psychiatric theory are absent from her observations: it is not too surprising that a lay-medical approach with strong phenomenological underpinnings should emerge.

The paper presented in this chapter is based on a talk Dr Weekes gave as guest speaker at the Fourth National Phobia Conference sponsored by the Phobia Society of America, and Phobia Clinic, White Plains Hospital Medical Centre, New York on 7 May 1983. This talk was included as a chapter in *More Help for your Nerves* by Dr Weekes and the permission to reproduce it has been given by the author, the British publishers, Angus & Robertson (UK) and the American publishers, Bantam Books, Inc. The talk is not typical of her style when she talks directly to the patient 'as if you were sitting beside me'. It is somewhat more strident and assumes a working knowledge of her treatment approach. It concerns the important question of how to ensure that future recurrences of panic, which are almost inevitable, will not result in relapse.

THE KEY TO RESISTING RELAPSE IN PANIC by Claire Weekes

As we all know, there are many different ways of treating nervous illness. I am speaking now of anxiety states with, or without obsessions and phobias.

I recently read a book in which the author described most of the common methods of treatment of nervous illness used today. While they seemed different, they each claimed a good record of success. Whatever the treatment, in my opinion, success will depend on the sufferer's attitude to it.

If he is convinced that it will help him, the chances are it will: you know the saying, 'Nothing is but thinking makes it so.' However, in my opinion, a treatment based mainly on belief in it is in danger of working only temporarily. While ever the person treated continues to believe that it will work, he's probably safe; but let him begin to doubt and he's in for trouble. Let him begin to doubt any outside crutch on which he depends, and he's in danger.

For recovery, the sufferer must have, deep within himself, a special voice that says during any setback or dark moment. 'It's all right; you've been here before. You know the way out. You can do it again. It works, you know it works!' That voice speaks with authority and brings comfort only when it has been earned by the sufferer himself and it can be earned only by making the symptoms and experiences that torture *no longer matter*. *No longer mattering is the key*. It is not a question of some method of treatment spiriting misery away, anaesthetizing it. It is a question of the symptoms, the experiences, no longer mattering.

The necessity for the sufferer himself to earn the inner voice of assurance does not exclude outside help; for example, by giving understanding and direction and if possible by alleviating difficult, stressful circumstances.

The person alone all day with no programme of recovery to follow, no special interesting work to do, who has somehow to fill each hour (the exhausted housewife struggling to cope with the work, perhaps with a couple of children dragging at her skirt), the person who thinks himself too ill and weary to work, and who is ill and weary with adrenal glands partly depleted by too intense and too frequent stress—what a mountain such people have to climb to earn that inner voice, especially if panic and other symptoms come by merely thinking about them.

These people's minds are all geared ready to thwart; ready at every turn to put up a barricade. The mind will remember and remind, mock, tantalize, never leaving the body alone. It will twist, turn, spiral, cavort—always turning inward, inward, inward, clinging with tentacles of glue.

And yet all through this turmoil, the right comforting voice is there to be discovered. However, the sufferer needs to be shown how to make this discovery, how to make his torture no longer matter. It is not enough to simply have it subdued. Balance must be struck between the sufferer doing the work by himself and being helped. So the question is: What outside help should be given? First, let us consider tranquillization.

A while ago, I read in a London newspaper an article by a journalist who said she had been agoraphobic for many years, but could now go anywhere simply by taking a certain tablet three times a day. She gave the name of the pill; said she'd tried all the others and that none had worked as well as this one.

'And now,' she said, 'all I have to do is come off that little pill!' That's all she had to do—simply come off that pill. Only that! She had no idea that she was announcing that she had left her future in the hands of chance. She had left it to chance, because so much would depend on what she thought on the very day when she first went without her pills. I notice she wrote the article first.

If, on that special day, she thought, 'Well, all is well . . . I can go anywhere now. I don't need the pill. The pill's not important any longer; so I can forget about it!'—if she thought that way and did forget about the pill, all could be well—temporarily. I say temporarily, because if stress—similar to the stress that had originally brought her symptoms—returned, or if she simply thought of panic and panicked (particularly in some awkward situation) I wonder how long it would be before she reached for a pill? I don't really wonder: I know. It wouldn't be very long. And when she succumbed, how long before her inner voice said, 'You'll probably always need that pill, you know!' And that would be her master's voice speaking. The pill would be the master now.

And the voice could go on and say, 'And what will you do if it doesn't work this time! What will you do then?' I leave you to use your imagination about that one.

There is another kind of outside help: the kind used by quite a few self-help groups that teach members to go as far as they can without panicking and then if they feel panic, to come back and try again another day, until they can do that particular journey comfortably—without panicking.

But what will the inner voice say if, having got used to all those places, one day, when out, a member of that group—perhaps tired, perhaps sensitized by some worry, or perhaps simply remembering how he used to panic—what if he panics again! What does his little voice say then? It has a heyday.

One man in Canada belonged to a group of agoraphobic people who worked this way. He felt so far recovered that he was able to travel into the United States and managed very well. I believe he went as far as Las Vegas and did not panic.

The day after he returned home he went down to the bank to draw some money. The same old bank, the same teller with the thick-lensed glasses, even the same bankbook with the torn corner, and as he handed the bankbook to the teller he stood on the exact spot where he had so often panicked before. Of course, memory smote, and on came panic and *it was a smasher*! It beat all records, because with it came anguish and despair—above all, despair. From then on, he wasn't even back in square one; he was back in square minus-one. And his inner voice shouted, 'What are you going to do now? If, after all those months of getting-used-to, after all those weeks of successful travelling in the United States, if after all that, you can't even go to your bank without panicking, what *are* you going to do now?'

Then there is the person who gets help from a special doctor and who uses the doctor as a more or less permanent crutch. What happens if that doctor leaves the district? And the sufferer has to depend on himself? (He doesn't like the other doctors in the town much and they're not too keen on him.) What does his inner voice say? Well, it says the same old, 'What are you going to do now? You're really lost this time, brother!'

That doctor had been very kind and thoughtful but he had been no real help. He'd been a crutch for too long.

There is only one way to cure and that is for the therapist to help his patient develop an inner voice that says in a crisis. 'Go on, through. You've done it before. It works. You know it works. On, through!' An inner voice that is followed by a feeling of inner strength. *A real physical feeling*. Almost as if a piece of iron rod takes the place of quivering jelly.

Some of you are, I know, sceptical of my using the word cure, especially if I had said permanent cure. I am aware that many therapists believe there is no permanent cure for nervous illness. When I was on radio some years ago in New York with a physician and a psychiatrist, the psychiatrist corrected me when I used the word cure and said, 'You mean remission, don't you, Dr Weekes? We never speak of curing nervous illness!' I told her that I had cured far too many nervously ill people to be afraid to use the word.

I suppose were we to say that if a person saw a murder committed before his eyes, there would be no hope of his completely forgetting it, and we would be right. I think that perhaps that is what some therapists mean when they say nervous illness cannot be cured, only relieved. They believe that memory will always return and that the nerves of a once nervously ill person may respond to memory with such intensity because of their past experience, that the poor devil is doomed. I think maybe that's what they mean. Also I suspect that some therapists, who deny cure of nervous illness, may think, 'Once a weakling, always a weakling.' Maybe.

Of course, memory is always capable of recalling nervous symptoms and what a heyday an anxious inner voice has then. It says, 'It's all back again! Every lock, stock, and barrel. Every member of the family! We're all here. What are you going to do now? You'll never recover now, you know!' What power the wrong voice holds. But if the right earned voice is there it will come to the rescue and say, 'You've been here before, you know the way!' Then, in spite of being possibly shocked and temporarily thrown off balance, the owner of that inner voice does know what to do and gradually does it.

And that's what I mean by cure: having the right inner voice to support and lead through setbacks, through flash moments of despair, through bewilderment. That is cure. I don't mean that the once-nervously-ill person will always be at peace, will not have setbacks. Of course he may; surely he's entitled to be human. I mean that for a person to be cured, he must be able to take setbacks as they come (and they may come unexpectedly 30 years or more after the original illness); must take the setback directed by an inner voice that is the real tranquillizer. This is my meaning of cure.

And after each setback that inner voice is strengthened and what is more, each setback successfully navigated by that voice reinforces confidence, self-esteem. Can you see how important, almost essential, setbacks are when the right inner voice is being developed to be the guide?

I suppose it's a lucky person who goes through life without being nervously ill. But I wonder. A person who has been nervously ill has widened his understanding, his power to appreciate, to feel compassion, even to enjoy.

But of course he has to carry the scar of memory. You know the saying, 'Where ignorance is bliss, 'tis folly to be wise.' But if the sufferer has developed the strong, right inner voice, there is not so much folly for him in being wise.

But without the right voice, all is left to chance and that's very chancey. Also, the person, who has been 'cured' (and I put 'cured' in quotes) by chance, by luck, by some outside crutch on which he continues to depend, can know only the peace of ignorance and that's no peace at all. It is only a temporary quietness. As long as his luck holds, he's probably okay. But luck has a habit of changing. It's a fool who trusts his life to luck and we are talking about people's lives.

So I believe, in the work I have done, I have tried to show the patient how to develop the right inner voice. The person who recovers using the four concepts that I teach—facing, accepting, floating and letting time pass—has done so by *going through hell the right way* and so has developed that right inner voice.

But in doing so, he has to put his head on the block: has to put himself into stressful situations that he otherwise would have avoided. And that's where he often falters, even sometimes fails. However, I teach him to know that peace lies on the other side of panic, on the other side of failure, never on this side.

There is a clinic in Toronto, Canada, specializing in treating nervous illness and the superintendent wrote to me and asked permission to use phrases from one of my books. He said he had these printed on ballpoint pens which he gave to patients. One of the phrases chosen was: 'Recovery lies in the places and experiences you fear.' And that in my opinion is exactly right. I teach my patients never to be put off by the places and experiences they fear. These are their salvation.

The person who ventures into these places and experiences will of course sensitize himself more than if he avoided them; so I come again to the question of tranquillization.

For some people I prescribe temporary tranquillization but of course, I tailor the dose to the person. I always bear in mind that to earn the right kind of inner voice, the sufferer must go through his experiences acutely enough to learn that facing, accepting, and floating do the real work. He would never know this if he were continuously tranquillized. As I say, the question of tranquillization is a delicate one and must be tailored to the individual.

There are people who can, and prefer to, go through the greatest hell without tranquillizers; however, the majority want, and need, to be helped with tranquillizers during the most severe stages of their illness.

Nervous illness is so very tiring. There is not only muscular, emotional, and mental fatigue, there is also a kind of fatigue of the spirit, when the will to survive falters. I have found that when people reach this stage, to sedate and let them sleep even for a few hours can make all the difference.

It can refresh enough for them to find courage and strength to go on once more.

In my opinion, this is one of the main uses of tranquillizers—to relieve fatigue and also to take the sharp edge off suffering, when suffering becomes almost too great for a body to bear.

I say almost, because there are those who can and do bear it. However, we should never demand this unreasonably from our patients. As I say, tranquillization must be temporary and tailored to the individual.

So I leave you all with a suggestion: those of you treating nervous illness should find out what the inner voice of your patients is saying. In my opinion, when we think we have cured a patient but have not helped him earn the right inner voice, we have not cured at all, whatever method used.

If some of you suffer from nervous illness, find out what your inner voice is saying. Be honest about it. Face it. If it brings no reassurance, find a voice that does—by facing, accepting, floating and letting time pass. And remember, when we learn to walk and live *with* fear, we eventually walk and live *without* fear.

From *More Help for your Nerves* by Claire Weekes.

REFERENCES

Weekes, C. (1962) *Self Help for your Nerves*, Angus & Robertson, London.
Weekes, C. (1972) *Peace from Nervous Suffering*, Angus & Robertson, London.
Weekes, C. (1973) A practical treatment of agoraphobia, *British Medical Journal*, **2**, 469–71.
Weekes, C. (1977) *Simple Effective Treatment of Agoraphobia*, Angus & Robertson, London.
Weekes, C. (1978) Simple, effective treatment of agoraphobia, *American Journal of Psychotherapy*, **32**, 357–69.
Weekes, C. (1984) *More Help for Your Nerves*, Angus & Robertson, London.

Chapter 16

Synthesis

ROGER BAKER

INTRODUCTION

In this chapter an attempt will be made to draw together various major themes and emphases that have run through the book and if not to provide agreed solutions, at least to highlight areas of disagreement, and to suggest possibilities for future research.

DOES PANIC DISORDER EXIST?

It may seem rather unusual at this point in the book to be questioning the existence of panic disorder. However the existence of a unique biological entity of 'panic disorder' conceptualized in the manner of Klein or Sheehan is not unanimously accepted by the authors in this book. H. Waring, and L. Walker and G. Ashcroft argue that a specific biological disorder *is* valid, viewing panic as 'mediated by a mechanism involved in the monitoring of secure exploration' (Chapter 14). Other authors, such a M. Von Korff and W. Eaton, seem to accept the diagnosis as a convenient starting point on which to base research, but with no particular commitment to a biological concept of panic disorder. Yet others do not consider 'panic disorder' as a viable disorder at all. J. Margraf and A. Ehlers in their detailed review of medical and biological studies on panic reject the type of medical model put forward by Klein on the basis that the hypothesized treatment specificity, spontaneity of panic attacks and separation anxiety arguments cannot be sustained in the face of the empirical evidence. R. Hallam rejects the validity of an entity called 'panic disorder' on conceptual rather than empirical grounds: it is a disorder 'stipulated into existence as much as . . . hypothesised to exist'.

The relationship of panic disorder to other diagnoses is relevant to the question of whether it constitutes a separate biological disorder. I. Marks is a champion for retaining the diagnosis of agoraphobia 'which constitutes

Panic Disorder: Theory, Research and Therapy. Edited by Roger Baker

the lion's share of panic disorder' with the 'leftovers', i.e. non-situational panic, constituting 'panic disorder'. H. Waring's chapter on 'The Nature of Panic Attack Symptoms' demonstrates that when we select sufferers on the basis of panic attacks, agoraphobic sufferers and those with non-situational panic attacks can be found, with little to distinguish them apart from the situational context in which their panic attacks occur, except possibly the duration of symptoms and degree of mood disturbance. Many agoraphobic patients experience situational *and* spontaneous panic attacks. Other authors in this book (e.g. Hallam, Margraf and M. McFadyen) and other investigators (e.g. Mavissakalian, 1988; Turner *et al.*, 1986) confirm that there is little to distinguish agoraphobic and 'panic disorder' groups of patients other than the context in which panic attacks occur and duration of problem.

Following on from Klein's research, DSM III and DSM III-R recognize the separation of panic disorder from 'generalized anxiety disorder'. Margraf and Ehlers in Chapter 10 consider that the empirical evidence is not well established for distinguishing between the two disorders. While this may apply to somatic sensations, there is evidence (e.g. Hibbert, 1984; Barlow *et al.*, 1985; Holt and Andrews, 1989) that the cognitions of patients with panic disorder are danger-related whereas those of generalized anxiety disorder patients are not. Barlow *et al.* (1986) suggest that generalized anxiety is a residual category within the anxiety disorders and as such cannot be viewed as a separate condition although it is useful to separate a category of anticipatory anxiety about multiple life situations as opposed to anticipatory anxiety about panic attacks.

Panic attacks occur in depressive disorder, obsessional compulsive disorder and a range of different anxiety disorders as well as in schizophrenia. Grunhaus and Birmaher (1985) suggest that panic attacks could be viewed as a cross-syndromal condition rather than constituting a separate disorder, a position consistent with Hallam's contention that it would be more profitable to try to understand the structure and function of panic anxiety complaints in different clinical contexts rather than to try to create exclusive disorder categories. As far back as 1934, Diethelm was lamenting that 'studying the literature on panics, one is impressed by the desire of most authors to form new disease entities'!

DO PANIC ATTACKS EXIST?

Again this is an odd question for a book which has been describing and discussing panic attacks throughout. Generally those authors writing from a phenomenological viewpoint strongly support the idea that panic attacks are a qualitatively distinct phenomenon (e.g. Waring, Freedman,

Baker, McFadyen). M. Zane (Chapter 8), although retaining the overall term 'panic', criticizes the idea of a panic attack being a fixed entity in time. He indicates that the form a panic takes, like a stream of water, can change and vary according to the differing inputs of the environment, other people and sufferers themselves. A small input can dramatically change its course. 'Since in panicky situations, the nature of the dangers imagined may keep changing, even from moment to moment, it is reasonable to assume that the associated physiological responses also vary in kind and degree. Thus, this hypothesis predicts changing and varied physiological disturbances in states of panic.' The attempt to isolate a sort of 'pure' panic attack—a *tabula rasa*—would be, according to Zane, a vain endeavour.

Hallam views a panic attack as a fear-related term that some individuals apply to themselves, and he can easily conceive that it could 'be subsumed by and classified according to a different set of theoretical constructs'. Marks suggests that panic is at the moment a popular label for severe anxiety—'after all, mild and severe rheumatoid arthritis are not separate disorders'. Likewise Margraf and Ehlers argue from their review of a number of research investigations that panic attacks are not qualitatively distinct from other anxiety phenomena, just quantitatively so; 'there are no symptoms or psychophysiological or biochemical changes that reliably and consistently differentiate panic attacks from non-attack periods, patients' attacks from normals' attacks, lactate induced from placebo induced, or spontaneous from situational attacks'.

R. Freedman writing on 'Ambulatory Monitoring Findings on Panic' compares periods of high anxiety and periods of panic in the same sufferers. He records physiological differences between the two states, suggesting that a particular pattern of vasodilatation and vasoconstriction of blood vessels occurs during panic attacks, and that various physiological events are more pronounced during panic. He acknowledges the methodological difficulty of not measuring the effects of physical movement on increasing heart rate and temperature. Zane likewise reports heart-rate changes in a single patient (case no. 6, Rachael) in his chapter. Margraf *et al.* (1987) have also conducted ambulatory monitoring research in which the effects of physical movement are controlled; they are not able to conclude that panic is physiologically distinct from high levels of anxiety. Freedman argues that the particular Vitalog device that Margraf *et al.* used, gathers information on time samples of one minute at a time and may well miss the rather rapid changes in physiology which his own Medilog continuous recording device is able to detect. This is an empirical question which will no doubt be resolved.

There are two aspects of panic attacks which may place them in a distinct category from high anxiety. First patients themselves seem to be able to identify if they did or did not have a panic attack on a particular occasion. For example Zane's first case example, Sarah, states in answer to the question 'did you have a panic attack just now?'—'no, but if I wasn't here and hadn't focused on you that first wave would have built up—and then a second wave would have come up and I would have probably hit a full-fledged panic which I am terribly frightened of'. Secondly the phenomenology of panic described in Section 1 of this book suggests that sufferers develop catastrophic cognitions about somatic sensations after their first few panic attacks. Ninety-seven per cent of sufferers reported in retrospect that they were caught unawares by their first panic (Waring, Chapter 2) followed by a rapid and often devastating development of fear and avoidance in the lives of both those who became patients and 'hidden sufferers'. Chambless and Gracely's (1989) study indicates that the cognitions of panic attack sufferers are danger-oriented and Argyle's study (1988) that such cognitions occur during acute onset anxiety but extremely rarely in gradual onset anxiety. Also Hibbert (1984) indicates that danger-oriented cognitions were present in panic disorder patients during panic attacks but not in patients who experienced high levels of anxiety but had never had a panic attack. The nature of the cognition, then, may set panic attacks apart as a special clinical phenomenon.

Thus the existence of a unique phenomenon of a 'panic attack' is in question, though few would doubt that the experiences sufferers report, by whatever concepts we wish to describe them, are extremely harrowing. Zane presents what might be a most useful metaphor in this respect when he states that 'clinically fear and panic though qualitatively different seem linked quantitively as are water and steam passing from one phase to the other'.

WHAT IS A PANIC ATTACK?

Along what dimensions, then, should we define a panic attack? What are its characteristics? I would suggest that one important dimension is the *suddenness* of their onset. As just quoted, Argyle's data (1988) indicates that panic disorder patients perceived gradual attacks of anxiety differently to sudden attacks.

A second dimension might be the *number of somatic sensations* experienced. Again Argyle's (1988) research indicates significant differences in the number of symptoms experienced in panic attacks and gradual onset anxiety episodes (nine versus three symptoms from a list of 14 symptoms).

The DSM IIIR's cut-off of four or more symptoms for a panic attack would seem to accord well with this data.

Severity of sensations might be a third dimension, or possibly *increasing severity*. Hibbert (1984) concludes 'it would seem that the more severe and overwhelming the symptoms the more likely they are to be taken as evidence as a very real threat to the patient's sanity, health or competence'. DSM IIIR refers to increases in intensity. It might be that the increasing intensity of the sensations generates cognitions such as 'this experience will never end', 'this will reach such a pitch that I will have a nervous breakdown', 'I will soon be lost and not able to get back to reality'. One problem here is that the subject's report of severity or intensity of sensations may be confounded with the degree of *distress* experienced, which is basically cognitive. Borden and Turner (1989) have found greater distress about bodily sensations amongst panic disorder patients than general anxiety disorder patients.

Margraf and Ehlers in Chapter 10 hypothesize that the *type* of the somatic sensations may be essential to panic; 'cardiovascular and respiratory symptoms that could be indicative of acute disease such as myocardial infarct or suffocation are more likely to trigger panic than symptoms which are interpreted as signs of a cancer that will lead to death over a longer course of time'. Interestingly Argyle (1988) found cardiovascular and respiratory symptoms formed the first factor of a principal components analysis of panic attack symptoms. Rachman *et al*. (1987), Robinson and Birchwood (1988) and Street *et al*. (1989) have studied the interrelationship of various cognitions and somatic sensations during panic. More investigation is required into this potentially significant area.

The last dimension might well be the most crucial; that is the nature of the *catastrophic cognitions* the person has during panic. Beck *et al*. (1974) were among the first investigators to suggest that patients do have catastrophic cognitions (eg. dying, collapsing, insanity) which are firmly believed during high anxiety, a finding which has been subsequently confirmed (Hibbert, 1984; Chambless and Gracely, 1989; Franklin, 1987), and anyway is abundantly apparent in the case illustrations and data presented throughout this book. This dimension of the *catastrophic cognition* is perhaps the most difficult methodologically, as the cause and effect relationship between cognitions and *suddenness of onset, number of symptoms, severity of symptoms* and *type of symptoms* is not easily established. Does sudden onset of many symptoms of severe nature of a particular type induce a catastrophic cognition or vice versa? The picture is further complicated when one considers the avoidances and escape manoeuvres that develop around panic and the sensitization to somatic sensations; although initial panic attacks may have been sudden, severe and contained several symptoms of a particular type, later a single symptom may trigger an attack, and/or well practised avoidances may successfully abort a full attack leaving the patient with a truncated version of the original.

Rapee and Barlow's model (Chapter 11) suggests that physiological change precedes catastrophic appraisal in a panic attack. Margraf and Ehlers' model (Chapter 10) suggests bodily and/or cognitive changes can set off panic attacks. R. Durham in Chapter 12 presents a cognitive model after Beck in which dysfunctional beliefs, focus of attention and catastrophic interpretation are placed in a significant causal position. Margraf *et al.*'s (1987) study of false heart rate feedback demonstrated that an individual patient's cognitive appraisal can induce panic. C. Weekes (1977) points out that merely thinking about a panic attack can trigger off an attack.

Table 16.1 presents a possible schema for characterizing panic. The first scenario would be recognized fairly clearly as a panic attack and would appear to include all the dimensions sufficient for a panic though one or more categories might be redundant. The second scenario could not easily be recognized by a sufferer or clinician as a description of a panic attack. Which characteristics are relatively more important than others, what the direction of causality might be amongst the different dimensions, and how they interrelate is a matter for further analysis and research.

Table 16.1 Schema for characterizing panic attacks.

	Speed of onset	No. of symptoms	(Increasing) severity of symptoms	Type of symptoms	Cognition
1. A 'panic attack'	Sudden	Many	Severe	Sympathetic nervous system	Danger oriented
2. Anxiety, but not a 'panic attack'	Gradual	Few	Mild	Other bodily systems	Negative but not danger oriented

BUT WHAT *IS* A PANIC ATTACK?

In the last section we looked at what might constitute the defining characteristics of a panic attack but this does not tell us about its essential nature. Several hypotheses about the nature of panic attacks have been presented in this book. Both McFadyen, and Rapee and Barlow suggest that panic is basically the body's natural alarm system/emergency response that is triggered off. This is touched upon in Rapee and Barlow's chapter but is expanded in Barlow (1988). 'It would seem reasonable to consider that there will be variations in the sensitivity of the trigger mechanism of the body's emergency response', states McFadyen, 'and that at times of increased readiness to respond the system will occasionally trigger "spontaneously", a kind of false alarm'. In both Rapee and Barlow's and McFadyen's treatment approaches a full explanation about the body's flight/fight response and how the person has misconstrued this quite natural and normal response is given to patients at the beginning of treatment and regarded as an essential part of treatment.

Waring, Walker and Ashcroft provide a different explanation: a panic attack is a loss of control experience underpinned by a psychobiological mechanism concerned with basic attachment and security. The mechanism fails and the person experiences a breakdown of safety/security and a failure in their ability to cope with the world, in short a loss of control. This bears similarities to Laing's 'ontological insecurity' (1966) except Walker and colleagues see it not so much as a failure of self-identity as a failure of security mechanisms. Unlike McFadyen, and Rapee and Barlow, this explanation of panic is not given to patients as part of the treatment regime.

Weekes suggests that all anxiety disorder, including panic, results from a physiological oversensitivity of the nervous system, described as 'sensitization'. 'Emotional and nervous responses are greatly intensified and come with unusual, sometimes alarming, swiftness.' Thus there is a raised nervous system threshold so that normal stimuli result in abnormally intense responses, one such set of responses being panic. This appears similar to McFadyen's 'increased readiness to respond'. However, he is referring to a heightened awareness and fear of normal sensations rather than a physiological overactivity, and applies his explanation specifically to panic not all anxiety responses. Others (e.g. Scrignar, 1983) consider that 'autonomic hyperactivity is a precondition for the development of a panic attack' and that the feeling state associated with attacks is due to a widespread neural discharge in the limbic system of the brain. The existence of panic attacks in medical conditions such as temporal lobe epilepsy or hypoglycaemia, or in drug administration or withdrawal (Goldberg, 1988) suggests that a straightforward 'neural discharge' (i.e. non-psychological) panic attack can occur, but how far this purely biological explanation can be generalized to all panic attacks is debatable.

Although the type of 'cognitive' explanation given by Beck and McFadyen appear very similar, there is a crucial underlying difference which is brought out very clearly in Durham's explanation of panic in Chapter 12. Durham conceptualizes panic as the exaggerated perception of personal danger in a person with an anxious style of thinking. This anxious style of thinking develops in those individuals with a basic predisposition consisting of dysfunctional beliefs and attitudes, or a labile autonomic system, or a combination of the two. Like McFadyen, a panic attack is basically a misperception of somatic sensations as indicating real danger, but in Durham's case the misperception is based on personal vulnerability and in McFadyen's it is based on a genuine mistake in a normal person.

Zane presents yet another view of the nature of panic, regarding it as 'the psychophysiologic product of a disorganizing "phobogenic process" made up of automatic, bodily reactions to exponentially increasing and accelerating numbers of mainly privately imagined dangers that conflict with each other and with the person's realistically integrated responses'. This is something like information overload with disorganization of thinking and behaviour being the end result. In case 4, Harold, Zane illustrates his position very clearly; Figure 8.2 shows the rapidly accelerating number of danger cognitions and somatic sensations that can create disorganization. In stressing the endpoint of panic as disorganizing Zane is quite close to the original meanings of the word panic as discussed in Chapter 1. McFadyen, and Rapee and Barlow's 'emergency response system' sounds altogether a safer proposition—an adrenalin response is designed to help us in times of danger and is unlikely to cause us damage whereas a 'disorganizing' process sounds more ominous (though Zane does not in any way imply a sense of danger to patients).

The question of the degree to which behaviour actually becomes disorganized in panic states is fully discussed in Schultz (1964a) in the context of natural disasters, war situations, etc. While some observers regard panic as a regression to primitive irrational behaviour—as in the case of the man caught in a fire who runs towards a sheet of flames—Quarantelli (1964) argues that panic is asocial and non-rational, motivated and defined by the extent to which the person feels entrapped in the danger situation. Flight is always oriented towards escaping from the perceived threat—for instance the man running into flames believes the only escape door lies beyond the flames. Behaviour is not 'primitive'—people run around objects and can engage in higher level learned behaviour such as driving a car, to escape. These observations do have their limits—for instance occasionally soldiers under prolonged combat suddenly dash towards enemy fire (Deithelm, 1934); (if they survive) they are found in agitated, stuporose or paranoid states, often with other symptoms of acute psychosis and with high degrees of tension and anxiety. These states disappear in a few days to a few weeks when the person is removed from the war zone (Diethelm, 1934; Brosin, 1943). Hibbert's (1984) finding that the form of thought changes during panic (i.e. cognitions become more intrusive and credible) perhaps points the way to further research on changes in cognitive organization during panic rather than only changes in content of thought.

There are a few other possible explanations for panic attacks not covered in this volume. Schultz (1964b) suggested a hypothesis bearing similarities to Zane's account, based on Bindra (1959) and others, that there exists an optimal level of arousal for the organism at which behaviour is most efficient. Over a certain threshold of arousal, behaviour becomes less efficient and at maximal states, disorganized and non-rational. Panic would represent the point at which the person passes the threshold for organized behaviour.

Another hypothesis which has been quite popular is that put forward by Ley (1985) in which panic attacks are explained as the result of hyperventilation. Wolpe (1988) thinks that 'something more than linear anxiety is apparently implicated' in panic attacks, firmly aligning himself to the position that this 'something' is hyperventilation. Margraf and Ehlers discuss this in full in Chapter 10, concluding that 'hyperventilation is neither a necessary nor a sufficient condition for panic attacks'. Many investigators now agree with Rapee and Barlow that hyperventilation has some place in the explanation and treatment of panic for a subgroup of patients, but 'alone cannot explain panic attacks'.

Marks (1987) reviews possible conditioning theories of generalized anxiety and spontaneous panic, including uncontrollable aversive events as in experimental neurosis of animals, interoceptive CS's and/or US's outside awareness, instrumental interoceptive conditioning, incubated delay of traumatic events, a discharge from the locus coeruleus or some other neural system, but ultimately concludes that there is no adequate account and that 'conditioning terms describe events in laboratory animals where initial and subsequent events are known from the start; the labels are hard to apply to patients. Clinicians need a better terminology to make sense of what their patients describe.'

One other explanation of the nature of panic is described in rudimentary form by Harry Stack Sullivan (1953). He gives the example of a bridge over which we cross every day suddenly yielding a few inches beneath our feet; he notes the unpleasant visceral sensations, the loss of organized activity and paralysis of thought that can occur.

> Panic is in fact disorganisation of the personality. It arises from the utterly unforeseen failure of something completely trusted and vital for one's safety. Some essential aspect of the universe which one had long taken for granted, suddenly collapses; the disorganisation that follows is probably the most appalling state that man can undergo.

There have been many advances in self-psychology since Sullivan wrote this and current concepts related to the self have been considerably refined

(McReynolds, 1987; Cheshire and Thomae, 1987; Goldberg, 1980; Yardley and Honess, 1987; Guidano, 1987). It would be possible to construe panic in the tems of self-psychology as a disruption or disintegration of self structures/identity. In a recent survey carried out on panic attack patients by myself using Chambless's agoraphobic cognitions questionnaire and a number of added items it was noticeable that certain items were repeatedly endorsed, such as 'I will disintegrate personally and emotionally', 'I am having a nervous breakdown', 'I will be lost and not able to get back to reality'. One wonders how much the panic experience relates to some type of breakdown of the self or whether panic attacks merely 'feel that way'. The existence of depersonalization and derealization experiences during panic attacks would give support to this contention, though like hyperventilation only occur in a minority of sufferers (Chapter 2 indicates 20 per cent of panic patients), and also occur in the normal population (Marks, 1987).

CAUSES OF PANIC

The explanation of the nature of panic attacks is often related to its etiology. For instance, Walker and colleagues who suggest that panic is the failure of security mechanisms propose that loss events or separations commonly precede the onset of the first panic attack, and may play an important etiological role. Weekes (1972) proposes that sensitization can develop in two different ways; sudden sensitization 'may follow the stress of physical shock to the nerves such as an accident, an exhausting surgical operation, a difficult confinement, a severe haemorrhage, and so on'. Gradual sensitization follows 'continuous domestic stress, too strenuous dieting, any debilitating illness; anaemia—anything which puts nerves under stress for a considerable time'.

Margraf and Ehlers give a detailed review of both biological and psychological theories of etiology. The clearest positive conclusion to emerge (see Chapter 10) is that the 'psychophysiological model', commonly called the 'fear of fear' model, is strongly supported by empirical research. However, this model is primarily a maintenance model—it explains very adequately how panic attacks are maintained once they begin, but does not explain how they begin. McFadyen suggests the use of two different terms for the first and subsequent panic attacks—'panic attack' and 'panic reaction'. Whether or not terminology changes, it could clarify our understanding of panic if the initial and subsequent panic attacks were conceptually separated in research investigations.

A number of studies demonstrate that in the months preceding the appearance of the first panic attack the person has experienced a period of psychological crisis or conflict, drug administration or withdrawal or rebound, organic illness, or psychological or physical trauma (Faravelli, 1985; Goldberg, 1988; Kleiner and Marshall, 1987; Last *et al.*, 1984; McCue and McCue, 1984; Roy-Byrne *et al.*, 1986). Waring in Chapter 2 points out how difficult it is to make causal links between panic attacks and preceding events, a point well established in the life events literature (Paykel, 1983). Assuming that future research does validate the various links between major life events or organic conditions and panic attacks, the question must follow—'why do some people respond to crisis, loss or trauma with panic attacks and others do not?' To say that some people have a personal vulnerability to panic in either a psychological or biological sphere is too general to be of much practical use. We need to know what sort of vulnerability the person has and how it developed. Answers to these questions would probably benefit both prevention and treatment of panic, but have yet hardly been addressed.

Freud's 1894 paper on anxiety neurosis has had an enormous impact on thought about the etiology of panic attacks and may be implicitly adopted by clinicians or researchers who may themselves have no adherence to psychoanalytical theory. Although Freud's coitus interruptus views are disproved (see Chapter 9) the notion of anxiety attacks developing out of a state of accumulating excitation or anxiousness is still widely held. (This is not to say that other theoretical influences have played no part in the development of this view of panic.) Wolpe and Rowan (1988), for instance, have recently restated this general belief in asserting that 'the (panic) attack is a climactic consequence of anxiety that is unusually high or prolonged', further implicating hyperventilation in the explanation. Marks (1987) likewise regards general anxiety as forming a pervasive backdrop of tension in agoraphobia which 'merges into the more acute, abrupt phasic disturbance of spontaneous panics'. The view of panic as an almost inevitable consequence of high levels of tension and anxiety is given a certain credence if panic can be shown to be a commonly occurring phenomenon, as is tension and anxiety. Norton *et al.*'s study (1986) has been influential in suggesting that panic attacks *are* extremely frequent in the general population (prevalence of 360 per 1000 for panic attacks in the last year). Norton *et al.*'s sample was unrepresentative of the general population consisting of students from four university extension classes, 67 per cent being female, and their criteria for 'panic attacks' not described in the paper. Waring (1988) found that such questionnaire data produced many 'false positives' for panic attacks, as later revealed by interview. Von Korff and Eaton's prevalence finding of 30 per 1000 for simple panic attacks, severe and recurrent panic attacks, or panic disorder in Chapter 3 should be regarded as more reliable, and more in keeping with other studies (e.g. the Munich follow-up study, Wittchen, 1986). This being the case, if panic attacks were the result of periods of high or prolonged stress, why should only 3 per cent of the population experience panic? Should not we all experience panic attacks, since, after all, high levels of stress are the lot of most people at some time or other in their lives?

PANIC ONSET

The previous section concentrated on factors relating to the underlying causes of the first panic attacks. In this section I would like to turn our attention to those sufferers for whom panic attacks are unfortunately now a regular feature, and consider the immediate precipitants of panic attacks. I will be proposing that the so-called 'spontaneous' onset and the situational onset of panic can be viewed as essentially the same process rather than representing different conditions or disorders.

A number of interesting ideas about the 'spontaneity' of panic attacks have been proposed throughout this book. Margraf and Ehlers in Chapter 9 consider issues of spontaneity pointing out how Klein has changed the research goalposts by redefining 'spontaneity'. Marks summarizes the general position when he states that 'insofar as everything has a cause there must be some hidden trigger of spontaneous panic, but that trigger is not a particular external situation or thought about such a situation'. Several of the authors propose that panics are not 'spontaneous'—i.e. unelicited, without cues—it is just that they have different cues to situational/agoraphobic panic. McFadyen proposes that spontaneous panics are sometimes related to 'doing something' rather than 'being somewhere'. Waring suggests the fascinating idea that in effect 'doing nothing' is a cue, or more accurately 'the spontaneous form was not related to specific visual percepts but was more closely related to general perceptual vigilance. Thus states of relaxation or concentration on non-security-oriented cognitions may lead to sudden attacks which catch the victim unawares'. R. Freedman's case histories illustrate the sort of psychological factors that can be related to apparently 'spontaneous' attacks, i.e. an argument with a lover, a mother hearing the news that another child had threatened to kill her daughter at school. Previous work by Barlow *et al.* (1985) does demonstrate that unpredictable or unexpected attacks do occur but they contend that this is not because there are no cues but that they are out of the patient's awareness, a point made by Margraf and Ehlers in Chapter 9. Barlow suggests that mild exercise, sexual relations, sudden temperature changes, stress or other cues altering physiological functioning set off 'spontaneous' panic attacks, and indeed the therapy for unexpected panic attacks presented ı Chapter 11 by Rapee and Barlow is based on the contention that panic attacks are essentially the same as phobic reactions except that he trigger and stimuli are internal rather than external'. In some cases n which no stimulus was found for a panic attack, such as Lesser *et l.*'s (1985) study using EEG measurement of a night-time panic attack, ater studies have found an associated stimulus event (e.g. Roy-Byrne *et l.*, 1988—night-time panic attacks were associated with transition from tate 2 to 3 of non-REM sleep).

From the point of view of the panic attack sufferer and the clinician like external situations such as supermarkets or queues are relatively learly perceived and may give the impression of a unique type of onset nd a unique disorder. This may be an *impression* based on the fact that such ituations are visual and obvious. The more covert range of other elicitors nay just go unnoticed. Whether there are other factors which predispose atients to select external situations for their fears is a possibility with a long edigree, ranging from the Freudian notion that phobic patients reduce heir distress by projecting it onto external situations, to the preparedness view that human beings are predisposed to select certain situations such as crowds as Marks suggests in chapter 7. A more parsimonious view is that spontaneous and situationally specific panic onset are aspects of the same phenomenon.

AVOIDANCE OR ESCAPE FROM PANIC ATTACKS

The notion of non-avoidance in panic disorder, as suggested in DSM III, is also related to the situational versus spontaneous onset issue. The most clear cues are situational—crowds, transport, shops—and hence the avoidances or escape manoeuvres are fairly obvious. H. Waring's chapter indicates how avoidance or escape is a very common reaction to panic attacks, reported to occur in 66 per cent of sufferers in the week after their first panic attack, with undoubtedly further avoidances subsequently developing too. The interesting point is that the avoidances were of varying types apart from the avoidance of situations, including positive self-talk, focusing the mind on something else, worrying about another problem, use of alcohol or tranquillizers. Hibbert's (1984) study likewise lists similar types of avoidances found in his sample of panic disorder patients, distraction and reassurance of oneself featuring significantly. It would appear that no avoidance or 'it gets better on its own' does also occur though. Waring (1988) reports three patients (3.5 per cent of his sample) who did not seem to avoid panic. From a general knowledge of experimental psychology the existence of people who do nothing in the presence of extremely aversive stimuli (people genuinely believe they are about to die, collapse, go insane, etc.) is curious. Even 'freezing' as in rabbits faced with a predator could be viewed as a more positive response than 'doing nothing'. In summary, research might be clarified by considering situational and spontaneous panic attacks as conceptually the same in terms of both onset cues and avoidance/escape.

TREATMENT CONSIDERATIONS

Treatment investigations can be graded into various levels or stages; the first stage would be to establish whether a treatment regime, lock, stock and barrel, is effective. Assuming it is, we might go on to investigate whether it is more effective than a no treatment control, or an existing therapy, and in what ways. The most sophisticated level of enquiry would be to understand the process by which treatment works, which may involve unravelling its effective and ineffective components.

Much of the content of the treatment chapters revolves around the third and most sophisticated level of enquiry. Authors provide a model of panic, a rationale for treatment, and detail about how this can apply in practice to patients. The extensive research literature on the behavioural and cognitive treatment of agoraphobia and anxiety-related problems developed over the last two decades is assumed as a foundation for most of the therapies described. Although the various therapies have different rationales, emphases and practices, one element they all share in common is the use of exposure *in vivo*. For several approaches (e.g. Marks, McFadyen, Zane and Weekes) it is regarded as the primary treatment *method*, but with widely differing conceptions about the *process* involved.

In this section I will compare the various different concepts that authors have presented about the process of therapy, in particular the process of exposure therapy. The differences are surprising given the essential simplicity of exposure *in vivo*.

Marks regards habituation as the effective element of exposure, so that as long as the patient stays in the presence of the appropriate stimuli for long enough, treatment will be successful. Getting the person to stay is the key. 'Whether the phobias or rituals were originally conditioned or not is irrelevant for treatment; therapists need simply to delineate the evoking stimuli (the ES) and promote contact with them while discouraging avoidance (part of the ER)' (Marks, 1987). Weekes who also recommends exposure (but not calling it as such) regards this with dismay. In *Agoraphobia: Simple, Effective Treatment* (1977) she describes hearing a nurse therapist explain her treatment of an agoraphobic patient using exposure, with the simple rationale that 'it'll do you good'. She explains that it is not carrying out the exposure that is the effective element but *how* it is carried out; she levotes a great deal of attention to explaining how to accept frightening ensations, and not use the clever subterfuges of cognitive avoidance that are so common. She does not perceive habituation as the effective process but 'coping through understanding'.

Rapee and Barlow in their chapter describe an ingenious series of exercises designed to expose patients to the cues for 'unexpected' panic attacks. Their package also includes the two other elements of breathing control/relaxation and cognitive modification. They refer to 'interoceptive exposure' presumably accepting a habituation type model similar to Marks. Durham likewise describes the use of exposure for 'inducing "mini" panic attacks in the office' as one part of a wider range of treatments with cognitive therapy predominating. Both Rapee and Barlow, and Durham carefully explain panic attacks and the nature of exposure to clients and both also perceive it as a vehicle for teaching the client to gain control over panic symptoms. Rapee and Barlow talk of 'graduated systematic exposure which is under the patient's control' and use techniques such as breathing control and relaxation which interact with exposure in helping the patient to 'control their symptoms'. Durham states that 'a number of different approaches to the management of tension and anxiety symptoms may be useful either in forestalling imminent panic attacks or terminating them once they have started', quoting that he finds the teaching of the technique of distraction to patients extremely useful. Walker and Ashcroft likewise describe a range of mainly office-based psychological techniques aimed at reducing anxiety and helping the person to control their symptoms. Gaining control over anxiety symptoms is a widely applied principle in clinical practice—it can aid the development of a feeling of self-control, confidence and self-efficacy (Bandura, 1977). Williams (Williams and Zane, 1988) describes an approach to panic disorder in which teaching self-efficacy is the central aim.

The practice of exposure as explained by McFadyen would appear almost identical to that just described, but with a fundamentally different rationale guiding treatment. Like Weekes he recommends exposure in which the patient is encouraged to abandon all attempts at control or avoidance. He believes that this is the only way the person can discover that they do not need to control panic symptoms—panic symptoms subside by themselves without any active intervention from the sufferer. He regards attempts at teaching control by relaxation, distraction, controlled breathing, etc., as merely burdening patients with new avoidance strategies, albeit psychologically more sophisticated. The drawbacks of this position might be the unacceptability of the regime to some patients, and consequently high drop-out rate; also this may deny patients the sense of self-mastery over their symptoms though in practice patients seem to be pleased with their performance. It should be interesting to experimentally contrast these two differing versions of exposure.

McFadyen and Weekes are similar in encouraging patients to accept feelings, although it might be said that Weekes's instructions to 'float' through feared situations is a type of coping procedure. The main point at which the two approaches differ is in their understanding of the exposure process. Weekes's approach is aimed at reducing the patient's fear of somatic sensations, which she calls 'second fear' whereas McFadyen is using exposure to invalidate core cognitions such as 'I will pass out'. The practical outworkings of the two treatments however may be similar.

Zane likewise uses exposure but as part of a teaching process in which the patient is learning to respond to manageable tasks in the real world rather than the multiple fears in their imagination. 'All effective therapies,' he maintains 'cognitive, psychoanalytic, behavioural, exposure, inspirational or pharmacologic, albeit by different routes, probably are able to control panic when they enable the person to shift from responding to expanding numbers of imagined unmanageable dangers, which is disorganising, to relatively fixed, manageable involvements, which is organising.'

Obviously the use of medication, or medication combined with behavioural techniques as described by Walker and Ashcroft, employs different rationales, though it could be said that the use of drugs is more aligned to the concept of gaining control over symptoms, though the control is via an external agency, not as developed by the patient. There may be little opportunity for a sense of self-mastery to develop in the former case, though doubtless it could be argued that antidepressant medication relieves panic symptoms so as to enable the patient to enter feared situations more easily, thereby setting the scene for a possible enhancement of self-efficacy.

One aspect of treatment stressed by several authors is the crucial role of explanation about panic attacks to the patient. Personal accounts data (Chapter 5) from treated patients also indicates how important it is to give patients a satisfactory understanding of exposure. In most of the therapies described, the clinician spends time helping patients to understand panic and why exposure is necessary. How important is this aspect of treatment? What part of the treatment effect can be ascribed to explanation, and what part to exposure? Is any rationale as effective, or are some rationales more acceptable and effective than others? Research effort has started in this direction, and may prove of value.

Psychotherapy does not have a particularly high profile in the approaches described in this book, though it is interesting to note that one of the implications of Walker and Ashcroft's model of panic is that the therapist should 'ensure the existence of secure relationships'. This point is not developed in their chapter but could be important. R. Durham points out that one of the advantages of cognitive therapy is that it allows the therapist to utilize a very broad range of counselling skills, illustrating this in particular with the case of Mrs M, whose interpersonal difficulties with her husband were gradually unravelled during therapy, and appeared to be the major successful element in her therapy. Baker and McFadyen (1985) have suggested that although exposure may be the treatment of choice for reducing the 'secondary' fear of fear, for those cases in which emotional conflict was responsible for the onset of the initial panic attacks *and is still operative in the person's life,* counselling or psychotherapy directed at the conflict would be necessary for complete recovery.

IN TRANSITION?

The way in which scientists conceptualize their field periodically undergoes major change. Kuhn (1962) highlighted these 'paradigm shifts'. Faced with a new way of viewing phenomena, the scientist can respond in a number of ways. He or she can maintain the traditional view, 'shift' wholeheartedly to the new position, or try to integrate the old and the new. A few different options, some less respectable than others, include embracing an entirely different position to either the old or the new, withholding our judgement, leaving the field, 'blocking', vacillating between the old and the new, or even pretending no change is required. In psychiatry and clinical psychology there have been a number of recent upheavals in thinking about clinical problems and treatment in the last two decades. The emergence of Beck's cognitive therapy is one such upheaval, challenging both the more traditional pharmacological approaches in psychiatry and the behavioural approaches in psychology.

In concentrating on the apparently new topic of panic disorder in this book we are looking at a picture in miniature of what is happening more generally in the field of mental health. The fact that there are so many differing views, particularly in approaches to treatment, suggests we may be at a junction between several, if not 'paradigm' shifts, at least, 'conceptual' shifts. But one thing is sure about paradigm shifts—you can only appreciate if there has been one, and how significant it was, *after* the event. The clinical community needs time, as it were, to consolidate its new position before looking back to 'write its own history'. We are at an exciting juncture in thinking and research about panic. There is still much to learn, research and develop. Already the emphasis on panic has enriched our approach to the whole wider topic of anxiety. Who knows what impact the study of panic will ultimately have?

REFERENCES

Argyle, N. (1988) The nature of cognitions in panic disorder, *Behaviour Research and Therapy*, **26**, 261–4.

Baker, R. and McFadyen, M. (1985) Cognitive invalidation and the enigma of exposure. In E. Karas (ed.), *Current Issues in Clinical Psychology*, Vol. 2, Plenum, New York.

Bandura, A. (1977) Self-efficacy: toward a unifying theory of behavioral change, *Psychological Review*, **84**, 191–215.

Barlow, D.H. (1988) *Anxiety and its Disorders: the Nature and Treatment of Anxiety and Panic*, Guilford, New York.

Barlow, D.H., Blanchard, E.B., Vermilyea, J.A., Vermilyea, B.B. and Di Nardo, P.A. (1986) Generalized anxiety and generalized anxiety disorder: description and reconceptualization, *American Journal of Psychiatry*, **143**, 40–4.

Barlow, D.H., Vermilyea, J., Blanchard, E.B., Vermilyea, B.B., Di Nardo, P.A. and Cerny, J.A. (1985) The phenomenon of panic, *Journal of Abnormal Psychology*, **94**, 320–8.

Beck, A.T., Laude, R. and Bohnert, M. (1974) Ideational components of anxiety neurosis, *Archives of General Psychiatry*, **31**, 319–25.

Bindra, D. (1959) *Motivation*, Ronald Press, New York.

Borden, J.W. and Turner, S.M. (1989) Is panic a unique emotional experience? *Behavior Research and Therapy*, **27**, 363–8.

Brosin, H.W. (1943) Panic states and their treatment, *American Journal of Psychiatry*, **100**, 54–61.

Chambless, D.L. and Gracely, E.J. (1989) Fear of fear and the Anxiety Disorders, *Cognitive Therapy and Research*, **13**, 9–20.

Cheshire, N. and Thomae, H. (1987) *Self Symptoms and Psychotherapy*, Wiley, Chichester.

Diethelm, O. (1934) The nosological position of panic reactions, *American Journal of Psychiatry*, **13**, 1295–1316.

Faravelli, C. (1985) Life events preceding the onset of panic disorder, *Journal of Affective Disorders*, **9**, 103–5.

Franklin, J.A. (1987) The changing nature of agoraphobic fears, *British Journal of Clinical Psychology*, **26**, 127–33.

Freud, S. (1894) On the grounds for detaching a particular syndrome from neurasthenia under the description 'anxiety neurosis'. In J. Strachey (ed.), *The Standard Edition of the Complete Works of Sigmund Freud*, Volume III, 1962, Hogarth, London.

Goldberg, A. (1980) *Advances in Self Psychology*, International Universities Press, New York.

Goldberg, R.J. (1988) Clinical presentations of panic-related disorders, *Journal of Anxiety Disorders*, **2**, 61–75.

Grunhaus, L. and Birmaher, B. (1985) The clinical spectrum of panic attacks, *Journal of Clinical Psychopharmacology*, **5**, 93–9.

Guidano, V.F. (1987) *Complexity of the Self: a Developmental Approach to Psychopathology and Therapy*, Guilford Press, New York.

Hibbert, G.A. (1984) Ideational components of anxiety: their origin and content, *British Journal of Psychiatry*, **144**, 618–24.

Holt, D.E. and Andrews, G. (1989) Provocation and Panic: Three elements of the panic reaction in four Anxiety Disorders, *Behaviour Research and Therapy*, **27**, 253–61.

leiner, L. and Marshall, W.L. (1987) The role of interpersonal problems in the development of agoraphobia with panic attacks, *Journal of Anxiety Disorders*, **1**, 313–23.

uhn, T.S. (1962) *The Structure of Scientific Revolution*, Chicago University Press, Chicago.

aing, R.D. (1966) *The Divided Self*, Pelican, Harmondsworth.

ast, C.G., Barlow, D.H. and O'Brien, G.T. (1984) Precipitants of agoraphobia: role of stressful life events, *Psychological Reports*, **54**, 567–70.

esser, I.M., Poland, R.E., Holcomb, C. and Rose, D.E. (1985) Electroencephalographic study of night-time panic attacks, *Journal of Nervous and Mental Disease*, **173**, 744–6.

ey, R. (1985) Agoraphobia, the panic attack and hyperventilation syndrome, *Behaviour Research and Therapy*, **23**, 79–81.

Margraf, J., Ehlers, A. and Roth, W.T. (1987) Panic attack associated with perceived heart rate acceleration: a case report, *Behavior Therapy*, **18**, 84–9.

Margraf, J., Taylor, B., Ehlers, A., Roth, W.T. and Agras, W.S. (1987) Panic attacks in the natural environment, *Journal of Nervous and Mental Disease*, **175**, 558–65.

Marks, I.M. (1987) *Fears, Phobias and Rituals*, Oxford University Press, New York.

Mavissakalian, M. (1988) The relationship between panic, phobic and anticipatory anxiety in agoraphobia, *Behaviour Research and Therapy*, **26**, 235–40.

McCue, E.C. and McCue, P.A. (1984) Organic and hyperventilatory causes of anxiety-type symptoms, *Behavioural Psychotherapy*, **12**, 308–17.

McReynolds, P. (1987) Self-theory, anxiety and intrapsychic conflicts. In N. Cheshire and H. Thomae (eds.), *Self, Symptoms and Psychotherapy*, Wiley, Chichester.

Norton, G.R., Dorward, J. and Cox, B.J. (1986) Factors associated with panic attacks in nonclinical subjects, *Behavior Therapy*, **17**, 239–52.

Paykel, E.S. (1983) Methodological aspects of life events research, *Journal of Psychosomatic Research*, **27**, 341–52.

Quarantelli, E.L. (1964) The nature and conditions of panic. In D.P. Schultz (ed.), *Panic Behavior*, Random House, New York.

Rachman, S., Levitt, K. and Lopatka, C. (1987) Panic: the link between cognitions and bodily symptoms—I, *Behavior Research and Therapy*, **5**, 411–23.

Robinson, S. and Birchwood, M. (1988) Catastrophic cognitions in panic disorder, Presented at the 3rd World Congress in Behaviour Therapy, Edinburgh, 6th September.

Roy-Byrne, P.P., Geraci, M. and Uhde, T.W. (1986) Life events and course of illness in patients with panic disorder, *American Journal of Psychiatry*, **143**, 1033–5.

Roy-Byrne, P.P., Mellman, T.A. and Uhde, T.W. (1988) Biologic findings in panic disorder: neuroendocrine and sleep-related abnormalities, *Journal of Anxiety Disorders*, **2**, 17–29.

Street, L.L., Craske, M.G. and Barlow, D.H. (1989) Sensations, cognitions and the perceptions of cues associated with expected and unexpected panic attacks, *Behaviour Research and Therapy*, **27**, 189–98.

Schultz, D.P. (1964a) *Panic Behavior: Discussion and Readings*, Random House, New York.

Schultz, D.P. (1964b) Overview: individual threshold for panic behavior. In D.P. Schultz (ed.), *Panic Behavior*, Random House, New York.

Scrignar, C.B. (1983) *Stress Strategies: the Treatment of Anxiety Disorders*, Karger, Basel.

Sullivan, H.S. (1953) *Conceptions of Modern Psychiatry*, 2nd Edn, Norton, New York.

Turner, S.M., Williams, S.L., Beidel, D.C. and Mezzich, J.E. (1986) Panic disorder and agoraphobia with panic attacks: covariation along the dimensions of panic and agoraphobic fear, *Journal of Abnormal Psychology*, **95**, 384–8.

Waring, H. (1988) An investigation into the nature and response to treatment of panic attack symptoms in general practice attenders, MD Thesis, University of Aberdeen.

Weekes, C. (1972) *Peace from Nervous Suffering*, Angus & Robertson, London.

Weekes, C. (1977) *Simple Effective Treatment of Agoraphobia*. Angus & Robertson, London.

Williams, S.L. and Zane, G. (1988) Guided mastery and exposure treatments for severe performance related anxiety in agoraphobics, Paper presented at the 3rd World Congress in Behaviour Therapy, Edinburgh, 5 September.

Wittchen, H-U. (1986) Epidemiology of Panic Attacks and Panic Disorders. In I. Hand and H-U. Wittchen (eds.), *Panic and Phobias*, Springer, Berlin.

Wolpe, J. and Rowan, V.C. (1988) Panic disorder: a product of classical conditioning, *Behaviour Research and Therapy*, **26**, 441–50.

Yardley, K. and Honess, T. (1987) *Self and Identity: Psychosocial Perspectives*, Wiley, Chichester.

Index